PATTERNS OF
EXPOSITION 9

PATTERNS OF EXPOSITION 9

RANDALL E. DECKER
with the assistance of
Robert A. Schwegler

LITTLE, BROWN AND COMPANY
Boston   Toronto

Library of Congress Cataloging in Publication Data
Main entry under title:

Patterns of exposition 9.

   Rev. ed. of: Patterns of exposition 8 / [edited by]
Randall E. Decker.   c1982.
   Bibliography: p.
   1. College readers.   2. Exposition (Rhetoric)
I. Decker, Randall E.   II. Schwegler, Robert A.
III. Patterns of exposition 8.
PE1417.P392   1984   808'.0427   83-19909
ISBN 0-316-17926-4

Library of Congress Catalog Card Number 83-19909

ISBN 0-316-17926-4

9 8 7 6 5 4

MV

Published simultaneously in Canada
by Little, Brown & Company (Canada) Limited

Printed in the United States of America

To the Instructor

Patterns of Exposition 9 retains the basic principles and the general format of the previous editions with the addition of a chapter illustrating the use of patterns in argument. Use of the book remains high (the publisher tells us that *Patterns of Exposition* is still the most widely adopted composition anthology in the country), and we continue to poll instructor-users for evaluations of the selections and about the need for basic changes in the framework. We also reviewed the responses of students who returned questionnaires like the one at the back of this book. Although obviously we are unable to comply with all requests, we have seriously considered and fully appreciated all of them, and we have incorporated many suggestions into this new edition.

One important change we made in response to evaluations of the text is the addition of a section of argumentative essays. Although the focus of the text as a whole remains on exposition and the rhetorical patterns it employs, we recognize that many instructors like to include a section on argument in their courses, and that argument often uses the same rhetorical patterns as exposition. The argument section can be used in two ways: it may be taught as a separate unit, or the essays within it can be added to those in the expository chapters as further illustrations of the usefulness of the patterns. The argument chapter is similar in arrangement and approach to the other sections of the text, and the Guide to Terms has been revised to include terms and concepts particularly important in argument.

The demonstration paragraph located at the end of each introductory section has proven to be a useful feature of the text, and the paragraphs have been retained in this edition. We also continue the policy of using the "Further Readings" section for a few classical or near-classical selections, all of which have some elements of argument or persuasion. Instructors will find that these essays can be used along with the other sections of the book or on their own. These essays are presented without suggestions or questions so that instructors can make use of them in varying ways. In the instructor's manual, however, we still include a brief discussion of the selections along with suggestions for using them in class.

But throughout *Patterns of Exposition 9* we have tried, as always, to make possible the convenient use of all materials in whatever ways instructors think best for their own classes. With two exceptions, only complete essays or freestanding units of larger works have been included. With their inevitable overlap of patterns, they are more complicated than excerpts illustrating single principles, but they are also more realistic examples of exposition and more useful for other classroom purposes. Versatility has been an important criterion in choosing materials.

The total number of selections has been increased by four. Thirty-four of those best liked in the previous edition have been retained, though some have been moved to the new argument section. Sixteen are entirely new, and several of these are anthologized here for the first time.

Their arrangement is but one of many workable orders; instructors can easily develop another if they so desire. To make such variations convenient, we have nearly always placed interessay questions at the end of sequences, where they can be quickly detected and, if not suitable, easily eliminated or modified.

We have tried to vary the study questions — and undoubtedly have included far more than any one teacher will want — from the purely objective to those calling for some serious self-examination by the students. (The instructor's manual places further materials at the instructor's disposal.)

Suggestions for writing assignments to be developed from ideas in the essays are located immediately after each selection. But for classes in which the instructor prefers writing to be done according to the expository pattern under study at the time, regardless of subject matter, topic suggestions are located at the end of each section.

"A Guide to Terms," where matters from *Abstract* to *Unity* are briefly discussed, refers whenever possible to the essays themselves for illustrations. To permit unity and easy access, it is located at the back of the book, but there are cross-references to it in the study questions.

In all respects — size, content, arrangement, format — we have tried to keep *Patterns of Exposition 9* uncluttered and easy to use.

PUBLISHER'S NOTE

We maintain an unusual revision policy on *Patterns of Exposition*. It is revised every two years to ensure that its popular framework is always well stocked with fresh selections. However, for those who do not like to change texts so frequently, the previous edition does *not* go out of print. Thus two editions of *Patterns of Exposition* are available at all times.

An instructor's manual for *Patterns of Exposition 9* is available from the publisher. Instructors wishing to obtain a complimentary copy of the manual may address their requests (on school letterhead) to College Marketing, Little, Brown and Company, 34 Beacon Street, Boston, Massachusetts 02106.

ACKNOWLEDGMENTS

For their helpful criticism and suggestions the editors would like to thank Richard Beal, Faun Bernbach Evans, William J. Kelly, and especially Nancy Schwegler. We would also like to thank the staff at Little, Brown and Company: Carolyn Potts for her wise and patient counsel, Virginia Pye, Donna McCormick, and Julia Winston.

The continued success of *Patterns of Exposition* is due to a great extent to the many students and instructors who respond to questionnaires and offer helpful suggestions, making the job of revision easier. For their invaluable assistance with the ninth edition we would especially like to thank Mary Allen, Irene A. Bania, Carolyn Boles, Judith Boschalt, Gail Bounds, Larry D. Bradfield, Ralph W. Bradshaw, Jon C. Burton, Margaret Byrer, Audrey Caldwell, Larry A. Carlson, Suzette Carona, Charles W. Carter, Kathleen Clark, Paul H. Cook, Steven T. Corneliussen, Ethel P. Cornwell, Dianne

M. Daily, Yvonne Daizedeh, Pamela B. Drumheller, Linda Mae Eanes, Mary Louise Ellena, Thomasin Faye, Mildred Fischer, Louise Flegel, Cindy Forrest, James S. Fuller, Elisabeth Funk, Yvonne L. Giem, Joe Glaser, Margaret Gonsalves, Nedra Grogan, Kenneth A. Haj, Jean R. Halladay, Judith Halpern, W. K. Harlan, Janet L. Harris, Catherine A. Hebert, Dorothy M. Heiny, Gerald E. Hicks, Sally L. Hicks, Eugene Hnatko, Shameen Hussian, Fredric B. Irvin, Gilbert Jordan, Lee E. Keebler, William P. Keen, Richard Keller, Jan H. Kemp, Muriel E. J. Klafehn, Karl Knight, Victor B. Kotulak, Joseph M. Kratville, Henry Lavin, Jo Lockhart, Herman H. Mares, Elizabeth Masoni, Stephen Matanle, Jerry D. McElveen, Charles John McGeever, Lisa K. Miller, Gail Milton, Russell H. Moore, Louis E. Murphy, Jack Musgrave, Julie A. Myers, Larry O'Hanlon, Robert M. Otten, Julie Periault, Beverly Peterson, Katherine R. Pluta, Charles Plymell, Yvonne R. Ponsor, Virginia Portmann, J. Karen Ray, John Reiss, Paul Rellinger, Roda S. Rocha, Pat Rosenthal, Marcela Salazar, B. Sandlin, Janine Sandro, Jim Schmidt, Patricia T. Shedd, Vivian Shipley, Sandy Smith, Henry R. Sparapani, Frank Steele, Melvin Storm, M. Strauss-Noll, Lela Stromenger, Joe Survant, Diane Taylor, Linda Thanukos, Yvonnne M. Turner, Teresa M. Tyree, Karisa Vortlieb, Catherine Ward, Gail Weems, Allison Weld, Lois J. Wheasler, Margaret White, Rosemarie Wilcox, Brenda Williams, Henrietta F. Wilson, and Robert Wurster.

Table of Contents

Thematic Table of Contents

Work

Politics and Leaders

Men and Women

Science and Technology

Introduction

Exposition is one of the basic aims of communication, more important in many situations than the other aims — entertainment, persuasion, or self-expression. Sometimes we may write to entertain, as do the novelist and to a certain extent the sports writer; or we may try to persuade in the manner of the lawyer, salesperson, or the preacher. We may even choose to express our beliefs and feelings in personal letters and conversation. Yet much of the writing and speaking everyday activities call for is expository in purpose, requiring us to share our knowledge of a subject. People in specialized professions are also frequent users of exposition.

Exposition means explanation, simply an *exposing* of information or ideas. Its primary function is not to tell a story or create vivid pictures for the reader, although exposition often *uses* narration and description among many other techniques. Its primary function is not to convey an author's feelings about a subject, though this perspective may at times be a valuable element in exposition. The primary function of exposition is not to convince or persuade, though argumentative and expository writing share many techniques and may each contain elements of the other. The primary function of exposition itself is merely *to explain*.

Beyond our need for informally written and spoken explanations, we use the processes of written exposition throughout college — in reports, term papers, essay examinations. Most of us use exposition throughout our working lives — in letters, in memoranda, in business and professional reports. Hence there are practical reasons why most college composition courses are devoted primarily to study and practice in exposition. For the same reasons this book concentrates on patterns of expository writing and other techniques commonly used. But because argument is closely related to exposition and shares many techniques with it, this book also contains a section on argument, arranged according to those expository patterns that appear frequently in argumentative writing. (The last part, "Further Readings," offers an even wider variety composition forms and subject matter.) There is nothing new about the ten basic patterns of exposition; we have been using most of them since we first tried to explain why birds fly south in the winter. But mature writing depends partly on the author's being able to use *deliberately* whichever techniques will do the job best, with the least chance of misunderstanding. We study these techniques to get a clearer view of their functions and possibilities, with the aim of being able to use them more effectively in our own writing.

We examine and practice these techniques separately, realizing that they are seldom used separately in practical writing. After all, when we observe and practice for hours a skill involved in tennis or golf, we are not assuming that an entire game will be made up of serving or putting. In writing, we know there is no reason why a process analysis should not be used to assist comparison in some explanations, why illustration might not be valuably aided in certain developments by narration. In good writing, if the patterns do not overlap, it is simply because one alone is sufficient for the purpose.

The patterns of exposition are useful techniques in other kinds of writing as well, particularly in argument. The editorial writer arguing against a proposed government project might compare it to other such projects in the past that have been expensive failures or might analyze cause-and-effect relationships and use a series of examples to show that the project will not meet the needs of those it is supposed to serve. In the argument section of this book, we see how the expository patterns work in a different kind of writing. One of the goals of this book is to create an awareness of the patterns and of the roles they can play in different kinds of expression.

But besides the study of writing techniques in a college anthology, we have a right to expect real benefit from the reading itself. Reading and thinking about new ideas or experiences are excellent ways to widen horizons, to broaden our interests — and this broadening is an important phase of becoming educated. In general, each set of essays in this book progresses in complexity and depth. Challenges help our understanding to reach an ever higher level.

The manner of approaching each reading, or the study of it, may be suggested by the instructor. If not, a worthwhile system for the student to give at least a fair trial is this:

1. For the first reading, relax. Read the selection casually, as you would some magazine article, for whatever enjoyment or new ideas you can get without straining. Do not stop to look up new words unless the sentences in which they are used are meaningless until you do. But have a pencil in hand and mark all words you are doubtful about, and they go on.

2. When you have finished the first reading, put the book down; for a few minutes think over what you have read.

3. Then use the dictionary to help you understand the words you have marked. Do not make the mistake of finding the first or the shortest definition of a word, and trying to memorize it. Instead, look at the various meanings, and for the word's uses as noun, verb, and modifier. *Think* about them. Pronounce the word. Use it in a few sentences. Identify it with similar words you already know. Then see how the author has used it.

4. After you understand all the words, read and think briefly about the assigned questions and remarks following the selection. (The paragraphs in each selection are numbered for easy reference.)

5. Then reread the essay, pausing at times to think and to *question*, underlining important ideas, marking sentences or phrases that seem to you especially interesting, misleading, amusing, or well expressed.

6. Then return to the questions at the end. You will probably find that you have already provided most of the answers. If not, give the questions further thought, referring again to the essay and to "A Guide to Terms" or earlier explanations wherever necessary for thorough understanding.

7. Next try to *evaluate* the selection. What was the author trying to explain? Was the author successful in explaining? Was the endeavor worthwhile?

Useful as these selections can be, they are not intended as models for imitation by students. Each was written, as all expository projects should be, to give a particular audience a particular explanation. (Or, in the case of argument essays, to persuade a particular audience.) The style of some selections is much too informal for most college writing. Other styles, perhaps from a slower and more sedate age than ours, would be too stately for today. Pure imitation is not the purpose of our study.

But each of the selections does demonstrate one or more of the *patterns* of exposition, which are as useful now as ever. Each can provide, too, some profitable study of other sound principles of writing — principles of effective sentences and paragraphs, mature diction, forceful introductions and closings. The consideration of all these principles, instead of being handled in separate sections, is a continuing study within the basic framework of the expository patterns. The book is designed so that instructors and students can use it in several ways.

1

Illustrating Ideas by Use of *Example*

The use of examples to illustrate an idea under discussion is the most common, and frequently the most efficient, pattern of exposition. It is a method we use almost instinctively; for instance, instead of talking in generalities about the qualities of a good city manager, we cite Harry Hibbons as an example. We may go further and illustrate Harry's virtues by a specific account of his handling of a crucial situation during the last power shortage or hurricane. In this way we put our abstract ideas into concrete form — a process that is always an aid to clarity. (As a matter of fact, with the "for instance" in this very paragraph, examples are employed to illustrate even the *use* of example.)

Lack of clear illustrations may leave readers with only a hazy conception of the points the writer has tried to make. Even worse, readers may try to supply examples from their own knowledge or experience, and these might do the job poorly or even lead them to an impression different from that intended by the author. Since writers are the ones trying to communicate, clarity is primarily their responsibility.

Not only do good examples put into clear form what otherwise might remain vague and abstract, but the writing also becomes more interesting, with a better chance of holding the reader's attention. With something specific to be visualized, a statement also becomes more convincing — but convincing within certain limitations. If we use the Volvo as an example of Swedish workmanship, the reader is probably aware that this car may not be entirely typical. Although isolated examples will not hold up well in logical argu-

1

ment, for ordinary purposes of explanation the Volvo example could make its point convincingly enough. In supporting an argument, however, we need either to choose an example that is clearly typical or to present several examples to show we have represented the situation fairly.

As in the selection and use of all materials for composition, of course, successful writers select and use examples cautiously, always keeping in mind the nature of their reader-audience and their own specific purpose for communicating. To be effective, each example must be pertinent, respecting the chief qualities of the generality it illustrates. Its function as an example must be either instantly obvious to the readers or fully enough developed so that they learn exactly what it illustrates, and how. Sometimes, however, illustration may be provided best by something other than a real-life example — a fictional anecdote, an analogy, or perhaps a parable that demonstrates the general idea. Here even greater care is needed to be sure these examples are both precise and clear.

Illustration is sometimes used alone as the basic means of development; but it also frequently assists other basic techniques, such as comparison and contrast. In either of its functions, authors may find their purpose best served by one well-developed example, possibly with full background information and descriptive details. But sometimes citing several shorter examples is best, particularly if the authors are attempting to show a trend or a prevalence. In more difficult explanations, of course, a careful combination of the two techniques — using both one well-developed example and several shorter examples — may be worth the extra time and effort required.

Whichever method is used, the writers are following at least one sound principle of writing: they are trying to make the general more specific, the abstract more concrete.

Sample Paragraph (Example)

The topic sentence, what paragraph is about. Also happens to be the *generality* in need of specific examples.

Many Ilona Valley people prefer to support local charitable organizations, rather than the big, impersonal agencies. One of the local favorites, Ilona Relief Service, is a model of efficiency and compassion and enjoys an unblemished reputation. Last year, for

Developed example.

Use of minor examples.

Several *undeveloped examples*, to show prevalence. (Author has used combination of illustrative techniques.)

instance, on May 18, a hurricane at noon devastated six blocks of a Casey residential area; but by nightfall well-trained volunteers had every one of the homeless provided with shelter and bed; an emergency kitchen was set up at the local fairground and was dispensing soup, cheese, bread and molasses, and apples. All children under age six had something tangible to hold on to: a rag doll, a toy truck, a fuzzy panda — all donated. And hardly a month goes by without a similar demonstration of compassion and efficiency: Ilona Relief promptly on the scene after a boating accident or chemical spill, a record freezing temperature, an apartment house fire in Waldoville, or the disastrous flood of 1979. It is no mystery why Ilona Relief is the favored charity of the Valley.

DAVID SCHOENBRUN

DAVID SCHOENBRUN, born in 1915, has performed a wide variety of tasks in the various news media, including foreign correspondence for newspapers and magazines, and radio and television broadcasting in this country and abroad. During World War II he served in Europe and Africa with the U.S. Office of War Information and the U.S. Army Intelligence. Since 1965 Schoenbrun has been news commentator and chief correspondent for Metromedia in New York and, since 1970, guest commentator at the New School for Social Research. Among his recent books are *The New Israelis* (1973), *Triumph in Paris* (1976), and *Soldiers of the Night: The Story of the French Resistance* (1980).

A Traffic Light Is a Brainless Machine

"A Traffic Light Is a Brainless Machine" (editors' title) briefly illustrates the use of a simple example by which to demonstrate a simple fact: in this case, the "intellectualism" of the French people. Using dialogue, a narrative method, the author is able to make his point more colorfully — and hence more memorably — than if he had simply told us that the French like to reason things out for themselves.

The "intellectualism" of the French is found at every level of society. 1 The café waiter, the taxicab driver, the restaurateur, the so-called "little people" of France are the most stimulating, if frequently exasperating, conversationalists in the world. Of them all, the most anarchistic and voluble is the taxicab driver. I deliberately provoke arguments with them — an easy thing to do — to see what they will say next. Of the hundreds of discussions in cabs one remains in my memory as uniquely, superbly French. It could not have occurred in any other country, except possibly in Brooklyn, where there exists a species of man akin in spirit if not in actual form to the French.

From *As France Goes*, © 1968 by David Schoenbrun. Reprinted by permission of the author and the author's agents, Scott Meredith Literary Agency, Inc., 845 Third Avenue, New York, New York 10022.

It was midnight in Paris and we were rolling along the Quai 2 d'Orsay toward the Avenue Bosquet, where I live, on the left bank of the river Seine. As we came to the Pont Alexandre III, the cab slowed down, for the traffic light was red against us, and then, without stopping, we sailed through the red light in a sudden burst of speed. The same performance was repeated at the Alma Bridge. As I paid the driver, I asked him why he had driven through two red lights.

"You ought to be ashamed of yourself, a veteran like you, 3 breaking the law and endangering your life that way," I protested.

He looked at me, astonished. "Ashamed of myself? Why, I'm 4 proud of myself. I am a law-abiding citizen and have no desire to get killed either." He cut me off before I could protest.

"No, just listen to me before you complain. What did I do? 5 Went through a red light. Well, did you ever stop to consider what a red light is, what it means?"

"Certainly," I replied. "It's a stop signal and means that traffic is 6 rolling in the opposite direction."

"Half-right," said the driver, "but incomplete. It is only an 7 automatic stop signal. And it does not mean that there is cross traffic. Did you see any cross traffic during our trip? Of course not. I slowed down at the light, looked carefully to the right and to the left. Not another car on the streets at this hour. Well, then! What would you have me do? Should I stop like a dumb animal because an automatic, brainless machine turns red every forty seconds? No, monsieur," he thundered, hitting the door jamb with a huge fist. "I am a man, not a machine. I have eyes and a brain and judgment, given me by God. It would be a sin against nature to surrender them to the dictates of a machine. Ashamed of myself, you say? I would only be ashamed of myself if I let those blinking lamps do my thinking for me. Good night, monsieur."

Is this bad, is this good? Frankly I no longer am sure. The 8 intellectual originality of the French is a corrupting influence if you are subjected to it for long. I never doubted that it was wrong to drive through a red light. After more than a decade of life in Paris, however, I find my old Anglo-Saxon standards somewhat shaken. I still think it is wrong to drive through a stop signal, except possibly very late at night, after having carefully checked to make sure there is no cross traffic. After all, I am a man, not a machine.

Meanings and Values

1a. Does it seem to you that Schoenbrun may be overgeneralizing when he says this episode could not have happened in any other country, "except possibly in Brooklyn" (par. 1)? On what do you base your answer?

 b. If so, does the statement damage the author's credibility?

2a. What do you think was the author's purpose in writing this selection? (See Guide to Terms: *Evaluation*.)

 b. How well did he achieve his purpose?

 c. Was the purpose worth achieving?

Expository Techniques

1a. In which paragraph do we find the generality that needs to be more specific?

 b. Is it abstract, or concrete? Why? (Guide: *Concrete/Abstract*.)

 c. In which paragraph, or paragraphs, is the example?

 d. Is it abstract, or concrete? Why?

2a. Does the example prove anything about the intellectualism of the French?

 b. Just what are the advantages in this method of explaining?

3a. Cite the use of qualification in paragraph 8 that helps to make one of the author's points. (Guide: *Qualification*.)

 b. How well does that paragraph perform the functions of a good closing? (Guide: *Closings*.)

Diction and Vocabulary

1a. In discussing the "intellectualism" of the French (par. 1), does the author imply that the French are more intelligent than other people?

 b. Explain clearly the difference, if any, between the two words.

2a. Does the author imply in paragraph 8 that Anglo-Saxons are more law-abiding than other people? If so, how could this opinion be justified?

 b. If not, what are the "Anglo-Saxon standards"?

Suggestions for Writing and Discussion

1a.   How do you feel about running red lights when no one is coming?

b.   What about breaking other laws when no one would be hurt?

2a.   What do you think would happen if we all interpreted such things for ourselves and used our own judgment as a yardstick?

(NOTE: Suggestions for topics requiring development by use of EXAMPLE are on page 32, at the end of this section.)

ANDY ROONEY

Andrew A. Rooney was born in 1920, in Albany, New York. He was drafted into the army while still a student at Colgate University; he served in the European theatre of operations as a *Stars and Stripes* reporter. After the war Rooney began what has been a prolific and illustrious career as a writer-producer for various television networks — chiefly for CBS — and has won numerous awards, including the Writers Guild Award for Best Script of the Year (six times — more than any other writer in the history of the medium) and three National Academy Emmy awards. In 1965 Rooney wrote the script for the first Telstar transatlantic satellite broadcast, which was carried by all three networks and translated into eleven other languages. As well as being the author of six books, Rooney has contributed to *Esquire, Harper's, Playboy, Saturday Review,* and several other magazines. Rooney also writes a syndicated column, which appears in more than 250 newspapers, and has lectured on documentary writing at various universities. His most recent books are *A few Minutes with Andy Rooney* (1981) and *And More by Andy Rooney* (1982). He now lives in Rowayton, Connecticut.

In and of Ourselves We Trust

"In and of Ourselves We Trust" was one of Rooney's syndicated columns. Strikingly similar in theme to the Schoenbrun selection, Rooney's piece also uses one simple example to illustrate a generality. But unlike Schoenbrun, he draws from it a more far-reaching set of conclusions: that we have a "contract" with each other to stop for red lights — and further, that our whole system of trust depends on everyone doing the right thing.

Last night I was driving from Harrisburg to Lewisburg, Pa., a distance of about 80 miles. It was late, I was late, and if anyone asked me how fast I was driving, I'd have to plead the Fifth Amendment to avoid self-incrimination.

Reprinted by permission: Chicago Tribune–New York News Syndicate, Inc.

At one point along an open highway, I came to a crossroads   2
with a traffic light. I was alone on the road by now, but as I
approached the light, it turned red, and I braked to a halt. I looked
left, right, and behind me. Nothing. Not a car, no suggestion of
headlights, but there I sat, waiting for the light to change, the only
human being for at least a mile in any direction.

I started wondering why I refused to run the light. I was not   3
afraid of being arrested, because there was obviously no cop anywhere around and there certainly would have been no danger in
going through it.

Much later that night, after I'd met with a group in Lewisburg   4
and had climbed into bed near midnight, the question of why I'd
stopped for that light came back to me. I think I stopped because it's
part of a contract we all have with each other. It's not only the law,
but it's an agreement we have, and we trust each other to honor it:
We don't go through red lights. Like most of us, I'm more apt to be
restrained from doing something bad by the social convention that
disapproves of it than by any law against it.

It's amazing that we ever trust each other to do the right thing,   5
isn't it? And we do, too. Trust is our first inclination. We have to
make a deliberate decision to mistrust someone or to be suspicious
or skeptical.

It's a darn good thing, too, because the whole structure of our   6
society depends on mutual trust, not distrust. This whole thing we
have going for us would fall apart if we didn't trust each other most
of the time. In Italy they have an awful time getting any money for
the government because many people just plain don't pay their
income tax. Here, the Internal Revenue Service makes some gestures toward enforcing the law, but mostly they just have to trust
that we'll pay what we owe. There has often been talk of a tax revolt
in this country, most recently among unemployed auto workers in
Michigan, and our government pretty much admits that if there
were a widespread tax revolt here, they wouldn't be able to do
anything about it.

We do what we say we'll do. We show up when we say we'll   7
show up.

I was so proud of myself for stopping for that red light. And   8
inasmuch as no one would ever have known what a good person I
was on the road from Harrisburg to Lewisburg, I had to tell
someone.

Meanings and Values

1a. Explain the concept of a "contract we all have with each other" (par. 4).

  b. How is the "agreement" achieved (par. 4)?

2 . Why do you suppose exceeding the speed limit (par. 1) would not also be included in the "contract"? Or is there some other reason for Rooney's apparent inconsistency?

3a. If you have read the Schoenbrun selection, does the Rooney piece clarify in any way the so-called Anglo-Saxon standards? If so, how?

  b. In this respect, might we find any significance in the facts that the cab driver was French and the tax evaders Italian? Explain carefully.

Expository Techniques

1a. What generality is exemplified by the solution to Rooney's red-light enigma?

  b. In this instance, what does the generality have to do with the central theme? (See Guide to Terms: *Unity.*)

  c. Is there any disadvantage in this generality's location? Explain.

  d. Does the example prove anything?

  e. Do you think it is a good example of what it illustrates? Is it typical?

2. What other uses of example do you find in the selection?

3. How effective do you consider Rooney's closing? Why? (Guide: *Closings.*)

4. If you have read both the Schoenbrun piece and this one, is there any way either theme could have been developed other than by use of example? Explain the alternatives.

Diction and Vocabulary

1. Does it seem to you that the diction and vocabulary levels of this selection are appropriate for the purpose intended? Why, or why not? (Guide: *Diction.*)

2. Could this be classified as a formal essay? Why? (Guide: *Essay.*)

Suggestions for Writing and Discussion

Choose one of the following passages from this selection to develop for further discussion. You may agree or disagree, or both, but organize your ideas for most effective presentation:

1.   "[Most of us are] more apt to be restrained from doing something bad by the social convention that disapproves of it than by any law against it."

2.   "Trust is our first inclination."

3.   " . . . the whole social structure of our society depends on mutual trust, not distrust."

(NOTE: Suggestions for topics requiring development by use of EXAMPLE are on page 32, at the end of this section.)

JAMES THURBER

JAMES THURBER (1894–1961) was a writer and cartoonist whose essays, short stories, and line drawings have helped enliven and illuminate American life for half a century. He joined the staff of *The New Yorker* in 1925, and most of his writings were first published in that magazine. Some of his collections are *Is Sex Necessary?* (1929, with E. B. White), *The Owl in the Attic* (1931), *Let Your Mind Alone!* (1937), *The Thurber Carnival* (1945), *The Thurber Album* (1952), and *Thurber Country* (1953). His more recent books are *Alarms and Diversions* (1957), *The Years with Ross* (1959), and *Lanterns and Lances* (1961).

Courtship Through the Ages

"Courtship Through the Ages" was first published in 1939 by *The New Yorker*, and was included the same year in Thurber's book *My World — and Welcome to It*. Although it would be misleading to call any one selection "typical" of writing as varied as Thurber's, this one is at least representative of the kind of humor that made him famous. It also serves, for us, to illustrate example usage to show a "prevalence."

Surely nothing in the astonishing scheme of life can have non- 1
plussed Nature so much as the fact that none of the females of any of the species she created really cared very much for the male, as such. For the past ten million years Nature has been busily inventing ways to make the male attractive to the female, but the whole business of courtship, from the marine annelids up to man, still lumbers heavily along, like a complicated musical comedy. I have been reading the sad and absorbing story in Volume 6 (Cole to Dama) of the *Encyclopaedia Britannica*. In this volume you can learn all about cricket, cotton, costume designing, crocodiles, crown jewels, and Coleridge, but none of these subjects is so interesting as the Courtship

of Animals, which recounts the sorrowful lengths to which all males must go to arouse the interest of a lady.

We all know, I think, that Nature gave man whiskers and a 2 mustache with the quaint idea in mind that these would prove attractive to the female. We all know that, far from attracting her, whiskers and mustaches only made her nervous and gloomy, so that man had to go in for somersaults, tilting with lances, and performing feats of parlor magic to win her attention; he also had to bring her candy, flowers, and the furs of animals. It is common knowledge that in spite of all these "love displays" the male is constantly being turned down, insulted, or thrown out of the house. It is rather comforting, then, to discover that the peacock, for all his gorgeous plumage, does not have a particularly easy time in courtship; none of the males in the world do. The first peahen, it turned out, was only faintly stirred by her suitor's beautiful train. She would often go quietly to sleep while he was whisking it around. The *Britannica* tells us that the peacock actually had to learn a certain little trick to wake her up and revive her interest: he had to learn to vibrate his quills so as to make a rustling sound. In ancient times man himself, observing the ways of the peacock, probably tried vibrating his whiskers to make a rustling sound; if so, it didn't get him anywhere. He had to go in for something else; so, among other things, he went in for gifts. It is not unlikely that he got this idea from certain flies and birds who were making no headway at all with rustling sounds.

One of the flies of the family Empidae, who had tried every- 3 thing, finally hit on something pretty special. He contrived to make a glistening transparent balloon which was even larger than himself. Into this he would put sweetmeats and tidbits and he would carry the whole elaborate envelope through the air to the lady of his choice. This amused her for a time, but she finally got bored with it. She demanded silly little colorful presents, something that you couldn't eat but that would look nice around the house. So the male Empis had to go around gathering flower petals and pieces of bright paper to put into his balloon. On a courtship flight a male Empis cuts quite a figure now, but he can hardly be said to be happy. He never knows how soon the female will demand heavier presents, such as Roman coins and gold collar buttons. It seems probable that one day the courtship of the Empidae will fall down, as man's occasionally does, of its own weight.

The bowerbird is another creature that spends so much time   4
courting the female that he never gets any work done. If all the male
bowerbirds became nervous wrecks within the next ten or fifteen
years, it would not surprise me. The female bowerbird insists that a
playground be built for her with a specially constructed bower at the
entrance. This bower is much more elaborate than an ordinary nest
and is harder to build; it costs a lot more, too. The female will not
come to the playground until the male has filled it up with a great
many gifts: silvery leaves, red leaves, rose petals, shells, beads,
berries, bones, dice, buttons, cigar bands, Christmas seals, and the
Lord knows what else. When the female finally condescends to visit
the playground, she is in a coy and silly mood and has to be chased
in and out of the bower and up and down the playground before she
will quit giggling and stand still long enough even to shake hands.
The male bird is, of course, pretty well done in before the chase
starts, because he has worn himself out hunting for eyeglass lenses
and begonia blossoms. I imagine that many a bowerbird, after
chasing a female for two or three hours, says the hell with it and
goes home to bed. Next day, of course, he telephones someone else
and the same trying ritual is gone through with again. A male
bowerbird is as exhausted as a night-club habitué before he is out of
his twenties.

The male fiddler crab has a somewhat easier time, but it can   5
hardly be said that he is sitting pretty. He has one enormously large
and powerful claw, usually brilliantly colored, and you might suppose that all he had to do was reach out and grab some passing cutie.
The very earliest fiddler crabs may have tried this, but, if so, they got
slapped for their pains. A female fiddler crab will not tolerate any
caveman stuff; she never has and she doesn't intend to start now. To
attract a female, a fiddler crab has to stand on tiptoe and brandish
his claw in the air. If any female in the neighborhood is interested —
and you'd be surprised how many are not — she comes over and
engages him in light badinage, for which he is not in the mood. As
many as a hundred females may pass the time of day with him and
go on about their business. By nightfall of an average courting day, a
fiddler crab who has been standing on tiptoe for eight or ten hours
waving a heavy claw in the air is in pretty sad shape. As in the case
of the male of all species, however, he gets out of bed next morning,
dashes some water on his face, and tries again.

The next time you encounter a male web-spinning spider, stop   6 and reflect that he is too busy worrying about his love life to have any desire to bite you. Male web-spinning spiders have a tougher life than any other males in the animal kingdom. This is because the female web-spinning spiders have very poor eyesight. If a male lands on a female's web, she kills him before he has time to lay down his cane and gloves, mistaking him for a fly or a bumblebee who has tumbled into her trap. Before the species figured out what to do about this, millions of males were murdered by ladies they called on. It is the nature of spiders to perform a little dance in front of the female, but before a male spinner could get near enough for the female to see who he was and what he was up to, she would lash out at him with a flat-iron or a pair of garden shears. One night, nobody knows when, a very bright male spinner lay awake worrying about calling on a lady who had been killing suitors right and left. It came to him that this business of dancing as a love display wasn't getting anybody anywhere except the grave. He decided to go in for web-twitching, or strand-vibrating. The next day he tried it on one of the nearsighted girls. Instead of dropping in on her suddenly, he stayed outside the web and began monkeying with one of its strands. He twitched it up and down and in and out with such a lilting rhythm that the female was charmed. The serenade worked beautifully; the female let him live. The *Britannica's* spider-watchers, however, report that this system is not always successful. Once in a while, even now, a female will fire three bullets into a suitor or run him through with a kitchen knife. She keeps threatening him from the moment he strikes the first low notes on the outside strings, but usually by the time he has got up to the high notes played around the center of the web, he is going to town and she spares his life.

Even the butterfly, as handsome a fellow as he is, can't always win a mate merely by fluttering around and showing off. Many butterflies have to have scent scales on their wings. Hepialus carries a powder puff in a perfumed pouch. He throws perfume at the ladies when they pass. The male tree cricket, Oecanthus, goes Hepialus one better by carrying a tiny bottle of wine with him and giving drinks to such doxies as he has designs on. One of the male snails throws darts to entertain the girls. So it goes, through the long list of animals, from the bristle worm and his rudimentary dance steps to man and his gift of diamonds and sapphires. The golden-eye drake raises a jet of water with his feet as he flies over a lake; Hepialus has his powder puff, Oecanthus his wine bottle, man his

etchings. It is a bright and melancholy story, the age-old desire of
the male for the female, the age-old desire of the female to be
amused and entertained. Of all the creatures on earth, the only
males who could be figured as putting any irony into their courtship
are the grebes and certain other diving birds. Every now and then a
courting grebe slips quietly down to the bottom of a lake and then,
with a mighty "Whoosh!" pops out suddenly a few feet from his girl
friend, splashing water all over her. She seems to be persuaded that
this is a purely loving display, but I like to think that the grebe
always has a faint hope of drowning her or scaring her to death.

I will close this investigation into the mournful burdens of the   8
male with *Britannica's* story about a certain Argus pheasant. It
appears that the Argus displays himself in front of a female who
stands perfectly still without moving a feather. . . . The male Argus
the *Britannica* tells about was confined in a cage with a female of
another species, a female who kept moving around, emptying
ashtrays and fussing with lampshades all the time the male was
showing off his talents. Finally, in disgust, he stalked away and
began displaying in front of his water trough. He reminds me of a
certain male (*Homo sapiens*) of my acquaintance who one night after
dinner asked his wife to put down her detective magazine so that he
could read a poem of which he was very fond. She sat quietly
enough until he was well into the middle of the thing, intoning with
great ardor and intensity. Then suddenly there came a sharp, disconcerting *slap!* It turned out that all during the male's display, the
female had been intent on a circling mosquito and had finally
trapped it between the palms of her hands. The male in this case did
not stalk away and display in front of a water trough; he went over
to Tim's and had a flock of drinks and recited the poem to the fellas. I
am sure they all told bitter stories of their own about how their
displays had been interrupted by females. I am also sure that they all
ended up singing "Honey, Honey, Bless Your Heart."

Meanings and Values

1a.   Clarify the meaning of "irony of situation" by using at least one
      example from this essay. (See Guide to Terms: *Irony*.)
 b.   Use at least three examples to illustrate the meaning of "verbal
      irony."

2. Thurber's writing is sometimes said to have nearly universal appeal — not only because of the humor, but also because of his subjects and his attitude toward them. What appeals would this subject have to various types of people you know?

3a. The author's themes are usually deeper than they may at first appear to be, and they are sometimes quite serious. How seriously is he concerned about the mating foolishness of human males? How can you tell?

b. Explain the relation of this matter of attitude to that of tone in writing. (Guide: *Style/Tone.*)

c. Describe Thurber's tone in this essay, using no more than two or three descriptive words.

4. How much literal truth, if any, is in the allegation that "none of the females . . . really cared very much for the male, as such" (par. 1)?

5. Do you think we are really laughing at the animals themselves when we go to the zoo? If not, what do we laugh at? Explain carefully.

Expository Techniques

1. How does the author remind us with each new example, without making an issue of it, that he is describing people as well as (perhaps even more than) wildlife?

2. List the general ways in which humor is achieved in this selection and illustrate each with a specific example.

3. Briefly explain why some people would classify these examples as personification, whereas others would not. (Guide: *Figures of Speech.*)

4a. Which of the common transitional devices is (or are) used as a bridge between paragraphs 2 and 3? (Guide: *Transition.*)

b. Between 3 and 4?

c. Between 4 and 5?

d. How do such matters relate to coherence? (Guide: *Coherence.*)

Diction and Vocabulary

1. Which, if any, of the ways listed in answering question 2 of "Expository Techniques" are matters of diction? Why? (Guide: *Diction.*)

2. If you are not already familiar with the following words as used in this essay, study their meanings as given in the dictionary: nonplussed, lumbers (par. 1); condescends, habitué (4); brandish, badinage (5); doxies (7); intoning, disconcerting (8).

Suggestions for Writing and Discussion

1. Explain fully, using specific examples, the real reasons for amusement at a zoo (or, for some people, a barnyard).

2. How do young men today try to impress the young women they are interested in?

3. Examine the possibility that women are interested in male "displays" because such reactions have been "programmed" into them from their earliest childhood.

4. If you are familiar with the aims and methods of the women's liberation movement, how do you think its more radical members would react to Thurber's impressions of courtship?

(NOTE: Suggestions for topics requiring development by use of EXAMPLE are on page 32, at the end of this section.)

WILLIAM F. BUCKLEY, JR.

WILLIAM F. BUCKLEY, JR., was born in 1925, in New York, where he now lives with his wife and son. He graduated from Yale University and holds honorary degrees from a number of universities, including Seton Hall, Syracuse University, Notre Dame, and Lafayette College. He has been editor-in-chief of *National Review* since 1955, a syndicated columnist since 1962, and a host of public televisons's "Firing Line" since 1966. Generally considered one of the most articulate conservative writers, Buckley has published in various general circulation magazines and has received numerous honors and awards. He lectures widely and is the author of several novels and nonfiction books, among them *God and Man at Yale: The Superstitions of "Academic Freedom"* (1951), *Saving the Queen* (1976), *Stained Glass* (1978), *Who's on First* (1980), *Marco Polo, If You Can* (1982), and *Atlantic High* (1982).

Why Don't We Complain?

First published in *Esquire*, "Why Don't We Complain?" is a good illustration of the grace and wit that characterize most of Buckley's writing. For students of composition, it can also provide another demonstration of the use of varied examples — some well developed, others scarcely at all — to make a single generality more specific. And the generality itself, as we can see toward the end, is of considerably broader significance than it appears at first.

It was the very last coach and the only empty seat on the entire train, so there was no turning back. The problem was to breathe. Outside, the temperature was below freezing. Inside the railroad car the temperature must have been about 85 degrees. I took off my overcoat, and a few minutes later my jacket, and noticed that the car was flecked with the white shirts of the passengers. I soon found my hand moving to loosen my tie. From one end of the car to the other,

Reprinted by permission of Wallace & Sheil Agency, Inc. First published in *Esquire*. Copyright © 1961 by William F. Buckley, Jr.

as we rattled through Westchester County, we sweated; but we did not moan.

I watched the train conductor appear at the head of the car. 2 "Tickets, all tickets, please!" In a more virile age, I thought, the passengers would seize the conductor and strap him down on a seat over the radiator to share the fate of his patrons. He shuffled down the aisle, picking up tickets, punching commutation cards. *No one addressed a word to him.* He approached my seat, and I drew a deep breath of resolution. "Conductor," I began with a considerable edge to my voice. . . . Instantly the doleful eyes of my seatmate turned tiredly from his newspaper to fix me with a resentful stare: what question could be so important as to justify my sibilant intrusion into his stupor? I was shaken by those eyes. I am incapable of making a discreet fuss, so I mumbled a question about what time were we due in Stamford (I didn't even ask whether it would be before or after dehydration could be expected to set in), got my reply, and went back to my newspaper and to wiping my brow.

The conductor had nonchalantly walked down the gauntlet of 3 eighty sweating American freemen, and not one of them had asked him to explain why the passengers in that car had been consigned to suffer. There is nothing to be done when the temperature *outdoors* is 85 degrees, and indoors the air conditioner has broken down; obviously when that happens there is nothing to do, except perhaps curse the day that one was born. But when the temperature outdoors is below freezing, it takes a positive act of will on somebody's part to set the temperature *indoors* at 85. Somewhere a valve was turned too far, a furnace overstocked, a thermostat maladjusted: something that could easily be remedied by turning off the heat and allowing the great outdoors to come indoors. All this is so obvious. What is not obvious is what has happened to the American people.

It isn't just the commuters, whom we have come to visualize as 4 a supine breed who have got on to the trick of suspending their sensory faculties twice a day while they submit to the creeping dissolution of the railroad industry. It isn't just they who have given up trying to rectify irrational vexations. It is the American people everywhere.

A few weeks ago at a large movie theater I turned to my wife 5 and said, "The picture is out of focus." "Be quiet," she answered. I obeyed. But a few minutes later I raised the point again, with mounting impatience. "It will be all right in a minute," she said apprehensively. (She would rather lose her eyesight than be around when I make one of my infrequent scenes.) I waited. It was *just* out of focus — not glaringly out, but out. My vision is 20-20, and I assume that is the vision, adjusted, of most people in the movie house. So, after hectoring my wife throughout the first reel, I finally prevailed upon her to admit that it *was* off, and very annoying. We then settled down, coming to rest on the presumption that: (a) someone connected with the management of the theater must soon notice the blur and make the correction; or (b) that someone seated near the rear of the house would make the complaint in behalf of those of us up front; or (c) that — any minute now — the entire house would explode into catcalls and foot stamping, calling dramatic attention to the irksome distortion.

What happened was nothing. The movie ended, as it had   6
begun, *just* out of focus, and as we trooped out, we stretched our faces in a variety of contortions to accustom the eye to the shock of normal focus.

I think it is safe to say that everybody suffered on that occasion.   7
And I think it is safe to assume that everyone was expecting someone else to take the initiative in going back to speak to the manager. And it is probably true even that if we had supposed the movie would run right through the blurred image, someone surely would have summoned up the purposive indignation to get up out of his seat and file his complaint.

But notice that no one did. And the reason no one did is because   8
we are all increasingly anxious in America to be unobtrusive, we are reluctant to make our voices heard, hesitant about claiming our rights; we are afraid that our cause is unjust, or that if it is not unjust, that it is ambiguous; or if not even that, that it is too trivial to justify the horrors of a confrontation with Authority; we will sit in an oven or endure a racking headache before undertaking a head-on, I'm-here-to-tell-you complaint. That tendency to passive compliance, to a heedless endurance, is something to keep one's eyes on — in sharp focus.

I myself can occasionally summon the courage to complain, but   9
I cannot, as I have intimated, complain softly. My own instinct is so strong to let the thing ride, to forget about it — to expect that someone will take the matter up, when the grievance is collective, in my behalf — that it is only when the provocation is at a very special key, whose vibrations touch simultaneously a complexus of nerves,

allergies, and passions, that I catch fire and find the reserves of courage and assertiveness to speak up. When that happens, I get quite carried away. My blood gets hot, my brow wet, I become unbearably and unconscionably sarcastic and bellicose; I am girded for a total showdown.

Why should that be? Why could not I (or anyone else) on that   10
railroad coach have said simply to the conductor, "Sir" — I take that back: that sounds sarcastic — "Conductor, would you be good enough to turn down the heat? I am extremely hot. In fact, I tend to get hot every time the temperature reaches 85 degr — " Strike that last sentence. Just end it with the simple statement that you are extremely hot, and let the conductor infer the cause.

Every New Year's Eve I resolve to do something about the   11
Milquetoast in me and vow to speak up, calmly, for my rights, and for the betterment of our society, on every appropriate occasion. Entering last New Year's Eve, I was fortified in my resolve because that morning at breakfast I had had to ask the waitress three times for a glass of milk. She finally brought it — after I had finished my eggs, which is when I don't want it any more. I did not have the manliness to order her to take the milk back, but settled instead for a cowardly sulk, and ostentatiously refused to drink the milk — though I later paid for it — rather than state plainly to the hostess, as I should have, why I had not drunk it, and would not pay for it.

So by the time the New Year ushered out the Old, riding in on   12
my morning's indignation and stimulated by the gastric juices of resolution that flow so faithfully on New Year's Eve, I rendered my vow. Henceforward I would conquer my shyness, my despicable disposition to supineness. I would speak out like a man against the unnecessary annoyances of our time.

Forty-eight hours later, I was standing in line at the ski repair   13
store in Pico Peak, Vermont. All I needed, to get on with my skiing, was the loan, for one minute, of a small screwdriver, to tighten a loose binding. Behind the counter in the workshop were two men. One was industriously engaged in servicing the complicated requirements of a young lady at the head of the line, and obviously he would be tied up for quite a while. The other — "Jiggs," his workmate called him — was a middle-aged man, who sat in a chair puffing a pipe, exchanging small talk with his working partner. My pulse began its telltale acceleration. The minutes ticked on. I stared at the idle shopkeeper, hoping to shame him into action, but he was

impervious to my telepathic reproof and continued his small talk with his friend, brazenly insensitive to the nervous demands of six good men who were raring to ski.

Suddenly my New Year's Eve resolution struck me. It was now 14 or never. I broke from my place in line and marched to the counter. I was going to control myself. I dug my nails into my palms. My effort was only partially successful:

"If you are not too busy," I said icily, "would you mind handing 15 me a screwdriver?"

Work stopped and everyone turned his eyes on me, and I 16 experienced that mortification I always feel when I am the center of centripetal shafts of curiosity, resentment, perplexity.

But the worst was yet to come. "I am sorry, sir," said Jiggs 17 deferentially, moving the pipe from his mouth. "I am not supposed to move. I have just had a heart attack." That was the signal for a great whirring noise that descended from heaven. We looked, stricken, out the window, and it appeared as though a cyclone had suddenly focused on the snowy courtyard between the shop and the ski lift. Suddenly a gigantic army helicopter materialized, and hovered down to a landing. Two men jumped out of the plane carrying a stretcher, tore into the ski shop, and lifted the shopkeeper onto the stretcher. Jiggs bade his companion good-by, was whisked out the door, into the plane, up to the heavens, down — we learned — to a nearby army hospital. I looked up manfully — into a score of man-eating eyes. I put the experience down as a reversal.

As I write this, on an airplane, I have run out of paper and need 18 to reach into my briefcase under my legs for more. I cannot do this until my empty lunch tray is removed from my lap. I arrested the stewardess as she passed empty-handed down the aisle on the way to the kitchen to fetch the lunch trays for the passengers up forward who haven't been served yet. "Would you please take my tray?" "Just a *moment*, sir!" she said, and marched on sternly. Shall I tell her that since she is headed for the kitchen *anyway*, it could not delay the feeding of the other passengers by more than two seconds necessary to stash away my empty tray? Or remind her that not fifteen minutes ago she spoke unctuously into the loudspeaker the words undoubtedly devised by the airline's highly paid public relations counselor: "If there is anything I or Miss French can do for you to make your trip more enjoyable, *please* let us — " I have run out of paper.

I think the observable reluctance of the majority of Americans   19
to assert themselves in minor matters is related to our increased
sense of helplessness in an age of technology and centralized political and economic power. For generations, Americans who were too
hot, or too cold, got up and did something about it. Now we call the
plumber, or the electrician, or the furnace man. The habit of looking
after our own needs obviously had something to do with the assertiveness that characterized the American family familiar to readers of
American literature. With the technification of life goes our direct
responsibility for our material environment, and we are conditioned
to adopt a position of helplessness not only as regards the broken air
conditioner, but as regards the overheated train. It takes an expert to
fix the former, but not the latter; yet these distinctions, as we
withdraw into helplessness, tend to fade away.

Our notorious political apathy is a related phenomenon. Every   20
year, whether the Republican or the Democratic Party is in office,
more and more power drains away from the individual to feed vast
reservoirs in far-off places; and we have less and less say about the
shape of events which shape our future. From this alienation of
personal power comes the sense of resignation with which we
accept the political dispensations of a powerful government whose
hold upon us continues to increase.

An editor of a national weekly news magazine told me a few   21
years ago that as few as a dozen letters of protest against an editorial
stance of his magazine was enough to convene a plenipotentiary
meeting of the board of editors to review policy. "So few people
complain, or make their voices heard," he explained to me, "that we
assume a dozen letters represent the inarticulated views of
thousands of readers." In the past ten years, he said, the volume of
mail has noticeably decreased, even though the circulation of his
magazine has risen.

When our voices are finally mute, when we have finally sup-   22
pressed the natural instinct to complain, whether the vexation is
trivial or grave, we shall have become automatons, incapable of
feeling. When Premier Khrushchev first came to this country late in
1959, he was primed, we are informed, to experience the bitter
resentment of the American people against his tyranny, against his
persecutions, against the movement which is responsible for the
great number of American deaths in Korea, for billions in taxes

every year, and for life everlasting on the brink of disaster; but Khrushchev was pleasantly surprised, and reported back to the Russian people that he had been met with overwhelming cordiality (read: apathy), except, to be sure, for "a few fascists who followed me around with their wretched posters, and should be horse-whipped."

I may be crazy, but I say there would have been lots more   23
posters in a society where train temperatures in the dead of winter are not allowed to climb to 85 degrees without complaint.

Meanings and Values

1. By what means, if any, does Buckley's scolding of the American people avoid being disagreeable?

2. Restate completely what you believe to be the meaning of the last sentence of paragraph 8.

3. Why do you think the author said to "strike that last sentence" of the quoted matter in paragraph 10?

4. Explain the connection between anti-Khrushchev posters and complaining about the heat in a train (par. 23).

5a. State in your own words the central theme of this selection. (See Guide to Terms: *Unity.*)

  b. Does it seem to you that this is the best way to have developed the theme? If not, what might have been a better way?

6. On a specific-to-general continuum, where would you place "Why Don't We Complain?" Why? (Guide: *Specific/General.*)

Expository Techniques

1a. Which of the standard methods of introduction does the first paragraph demonstrate? (Guide: *Introductions.*)

  b. How successful is its use?

2a. What generality do Buckley's examples illustrate? (You may use his words or your own.)

  b. In what way, if at all, does this statement differ from his central theme?

  c. In this respect, how does the writing differ from most?

3. Why do you think the Khrushchev example is kept until last? (Guide: *Emphasis.*)

4.   What seems to be the purpose, or purposes, of paragraphs 4 and 12?

5.   Assuming that this piece is typical of Buckley's writing, what aspects of his style or tone will probably make his writing identifiable when you next encounter it? (Guide: *Style/Tone*.)

Diction and Vocabulary

1.   Explain the meaning (in par. 22) of Khrushchev's being "met with overwhelming cordiality (read: apathy)"?

2.   Explain the allusion to Milquetoast in paragraph 11. (Guide: *Figures of Speech*.)

3a.   Were you annoyed by Buckley's liberal use of "dictionary-type" words? To what extent? Why were you annoyed?"

 b.   Cite any of these that were used without good reason.

 c.   To what extent is this use a matter of style?

4.   Use the dictionary as needed to understand the meanings of the following words: virile, doleful, sibilant, discreet (par. 2); gauntlet, consigned (3); supine, faculties, dissolution, rectify (4); hectoring (5); purposive (7); unobtrusive, ambiguous (8); provocation, complexus, unconscionably, bellicose, girded (9); infer (10); ostentatiously (11); impervious, reproof (13); centripetal (16); deferentially (17); unctuously (18); technification (19); apathy, phenomenon, dispensations (20); stance, plenipotentiary, inarticulated (21); automatons (22).

Suggestions for Writing and Discussion

1.   Discuss, if you can, the idea that readers of American literature are familiar with the "assertiveness that characterized the American family" (par. 19).

2.   An apathy such as Buckley describes, if permitted to develop to its extreme, could have disastrous results. Explore what some of these might be.

3.   Buckley is generally thought to be one of the most effective spokespeople for the conservative right. Explain how you could have guessed his political views by what he says in this largely nonpolitical essay. Be specific.

(NOTE: Suggestions for topics requiring development by use of EXAMPLE are on page 32, at the end of this section.)

MATTHEW DOUGLAS

MATTHEW DOUGLAS was born in East Grand Rapids, Michigan in 1949. He received a B.A. from the University of Michigan, where he majored in English and anthropology; an M.S. in aquatic biology from Eastern Michigan University; and a Ph.D. in entomology and ecology from the University of Kansas. He has written a book on the ecology of butterflies, several college science textbooks, and articles in scholarly and popular magazines including *Science, Evolution,* and *Natural History.* In addition, he writes a biweekly column for the *Boston Herald* and is a nationally syndicated columnist.

The Butterfly Connection

"The Butterfly Connection," first published in *Science Digest,* uses a well-developed example to illustrate a generality. The long example itself consists of a series of shorter, closely related examples. The essay's appeal lies not only in the surprising information presented in the example but also in the important point it makes about the unseen relationships in the natural world.

Just how interconnected *is* the animal world? Is it true that if we   1
change any part of that world we risk unduly damaging life in other, larger parts of it?

Once we thought scientists knew the answers to these ques-   2
tions. But the more we tug and tear at nature's web, the more we stumble onto crucial interrelationships that were until recently completely undreamed of.

Consider what happened in Britain a few years ago when   3
urbanization detroyed the habitats of two species of tiny ants and caused their extinction. The loss of the ants was bad enough, but the

Reprinted by permission of Dr. Matthew M. Douglas, *The Science Argus.* First appeared in *Science Digest,* © 1983 by the Hearst Corporation.

27

nature-loving public was appalled when it learned that the ants' death also meant the extinction in Britain of the beautiful European blue butterfly, with which these ants had a close, if little recognized, symbiotic relationship.

We will, of course, never know the true extent of the loss. Who   4
knows what other organisms — microscopic or otherwise — may have met their doom along with the ant-butterfly odd couple? So the nature of the long unsuspected ties between ant and blue butterfly is worth grasping, if only for its cautionary value against similar ecological missteps.

The adult blue, or lycaenid, butterfly is tiny — about big   5
enough to cover a 20 cent stamp. In their sluglike caterpillar stage, many lycaenids have several types of glands on their abdomens that either give off an odor attractive to ants or produce a sugary solution, known as honeydew, which the ant symbionts eat. The honeydew oozes out of Newcomer's gland, a complex structure made up of four glandular bags, minute muscles and, occasionally, bizarre tentacles that whirl about when the caterpillars move.

Sensing a honeydew feast, the ants swarm across the lycaenid   6
caterpillar, probing for the Newcomer's gland. The ants are drawn not by the smell of the honeydew but by the odor of volatile substances given off by tiny glands called perforated cupolas that surround the Newcomer's gland. . . .

Ordinary butterfly caterpillars have no use for these ants; they   7
twist and sway to dislodge them from their abdomens. But lycaenid larvae possessing the "honey" glands passively welcome the invaders. Surprisingly, the larvae's secretions seem both to attract ants and to prevent these ants from attacking them. Substances seeping from the cupolas apparently pacify the ants the way catnip does a cat.

The ants, for their part, protect the caterpillars from parasites   8
and predators. They may even gang together and carry caterpillars from old, chewed-up leaves onto fresh food sources, much in the way that humans herd sheep and cows to greener pastures.

Obviously, there has been a long history of coevolutionary   9
adaptation between ants and butterflies. For example, some adult lycaenids will not lay eggs on a plant unless stimulated to do so by just the right species of ant. Moreover, the protective cuticle, or skin, of some lycaenids is up to 60 times thicker than that of similar

caterpillars; this adaptation prevents puncturing of the skin by the ants' sharp mandibles — their pincerlike jaws.

In some species, a fully grown caterpillar is carried into the ant 10
nest. There, while the butterfly slowly develops within the caterpillar, the ants *feed their own larvae* to the guest. Over the winter, the growing, delicate butterfly-to-be is protected in a cozy chamber, complete with temperature and humidity controls.

But when spring comes, the idyll ends. Now the butterflies may 11
be *attacked* as they emerge from the cocoon; the solicitous ants become feared predators. Fortunately, the newborn butterflies are covered with a coating of tiny scales that easily flakes off as the ants' jaws clamp down on it. With scales coating their feet, antennae and mandibles like talcum powder, the ants are left floundering and clutching at empty air. The butterflies meanwhile slip free and emerge intact.

Clearly, these ant-lycaenid relationships are highly susceptible 12
to ecological disruption. How many more now unknown affinities will come to light only after the bulldozers have passed by?

Meanings and Values

1.   Where would this writing be placed on an objective–subjective continuum? Why? (See Guide to Terms: *Objective/Subjective*.)

2a.   How can the tone of this selection best be described? (Guide: *Style/Tone*.)

  b.   What, if anything, does this indicate about the author's attitude toward his subject? Toward his audience?

3.   In what ways can the ants' treatment of the butterflies be seen as examples of "irony of situation"? (Guide: *Irony*.)

4.   Douglas claims that "we stumble onto crucial interrelationships that were until recently completely undreamed of" (par. 2). Does he suggest ways we could avoid disrupting these relationships, or is he simply trying to make us think about how we can avoid future problems like the one he describes in the essay?

Expository Techniques

1a.   At what points in the essay does the author state his central theme?

  b.   Do you think the essay would be more effective if the central theme were stated less directly or in different places?

2a. The long example that takes up the body of this essay actually consists of a series of shorter examples. What transitional devices does the author use to move from one short example to the next? (Guide: *Transition.*)

b. Are the short examples arranged in a way that makes them relatively easy to understand? Would some other arrangement be more effective?

c. The author illustrates a generality by presenting an example of the relationship between two insects. Would the essay have been more effective if he had chosen to use more examples involving a wider variety of animals?

d. Are the examples concrete enough to be effective? Are they too concrete? (Guide: *Concrete.*)

3a. What standard techniques are used here for closing? (Guide: *Closings.*)

b. How effectively are they used?

4. One of Douglas's aims as an author is to reach as many people as possible with science that is easy to read. Does the example in this essay succeed in making a complex scientific subject understandable for a general audience? Explain.

Diction and Vocabulary

1a. What technical or scientific terms does the author use in this essay?

b. Is their use necessary? (Guide: *Diction.*)

c. Does the author explain the terms or leave it up to the reader to discover what they mean?

2a. What figures of speech does the author use in paragraphs 7 and 8 to help explain the relationship between the ants and the butterflies? (Guide: *Figures of Speech.*)

b. What do these figures of speech contribute to the tone of the essay or reveal about the author's attitude toward the subject?

3. Why does the author refer to the time the caterpillars spend with the ants as an "idyll" (par. 11)?

4. Use the dictionary as needed to understand the meanings of the following words: unduly (par. 1); urbanization, habitats, symbiotic (3); ecological (4); symbionts, glandular (5); volatile, perforated, cupolas (6); pacify (7); parasites, predators (8); coevolutionary, adaptation, cuticle, mandibles (9); larvae (10); floundering (11); affinities (12).

Suggestions for Writing and Discussion

1. Explain in detail at least one other set of interrelationships between animals, plants, or plants and animals.

2. What value is there, if any, in knowing about such things as the relationship of ants and the European blue butterfly?

3. Is it important to preserve animals and plants from extinction even if they are somewhat rare already? Give examples.

4. Can you think of any instances where construction or urban development has had positive effects on plant and animal life? Negative effects? Unintended effects?

(NOTE: Suggestions for topics requiring development by use of EXAMPLE follow.)

Writing Suggestions for Section 1
Example

Use one of the following statements or another suggested by them as your central theme. Develop it into a unified composition, using examples from history, current events, or personal experience to illustrate your ideas. Be sure to have your reader-audience clearly in mind, as well as your specific purpose for the communication.

1. Successful businesses keep employees at their highest level of competence.
2. Not all women want to be "liberated."
3. Women's liberation achievements present dilemmas for both males and females.
4. Laws holding parents responsible for their children's crimes would (or would not) result in serious injustices.
5. Letting people decide for themselves which laws to obey and which to ignore would result in anarchy.
6. You can't always tell a nonconformist by the way he looks.
7. Good sportsmanship is far more than shaking hands with the winner.
8. Religion in the United States is not dying.
9. Democracy is not always the best form of government.
10. Colonialism was not entirely bad.
11. Nearly anyone can have a creative hobby.
12. The general quality of television commercials may be improving (or deteriorating).
13. Major corporations have begun taking steps to preserve the environment (or have resisted steps to preserve the environment).
14. "Some books are to be tasted; others swallowed; and some few to be chewed and digested." (*Francis Bacon,* English scientist-author, 1561–1626.)
15. Good teachers are hard to find.

2

Analyzing a Subject by *Classification*

People naturally like to sort and classify things. The untidiest urchin, moving into a new dresser of his own, will put his handkerchiefs together, socks and underwear in separate stacks, and perhaps his toads and snails (temporarily) into a drawer of their own. He may classify animals as those with legs, those with wings, and those with neither. As he gets older, he finds that schoolteachers have ways of classifying *him*, not only into a reading group but, periodically, into an "A" or "F" category, or somewhere in between. On errands to the grocery store, he discovers the macaroni in the same department as the spaghetti, the pork chops somewhere near the ham. In reading the local newspaper, he observes that its staff has done some classifying for him, putting most of the comics together and seldom mixing sports stories with the news of bridal showers. Eventually he finds courses neatly classified in the college catalogue, and he knows enough not to look for biology courses under "Social Science." (Examples again — used to illustrate a "prevalence.")

Our main interest in classification here is its use as a structural pattern for explanatory writing. Many subjects about which either students or graduates may need to write will remain a hodgepodge of facts and opinions unless they can find some system of analyzing the material, dividing the subject into categories, and classifying individual elements into those categories. Here we have the distinction usually made between the rhetorical terms *division* and *classification* — for example, dividing "meat" into pork, beef, mutton, and fowl, then classifying ham and pork chops into the category of "pork." But this distinction is one we need scarcely pause for here; once the need for analysis is recognized, the dividing and classifying become inevitable companions and result in the single scheme of "classification" itself, as we have been discussing it. The original division into parts merely sets up the system that, if well chosen, best serves our purpose.

Obviously, no single system of classification is best for all purposes. Our untidy urchin may at some point classify girls according to athletic prowess, then later by size or shape or hair color. (At the same time, of course, the girls may be placing him into one or more categories.) Other people may need entirely different systems of classification: the music instructor classifies girls as sopranos, altos, contraltos; the psychologist, according to their behavior patterns; the sociologist, according to their ethnic origins.

Whatever the purpose, for the more formal uses of classification ("formal," that is, to the extent of most academic and on-the-job writing), we should be careful to use a logical system that is complete and that follows a consistent principle throughout. It would not be logical to divide Protestantism into the categories of Methodist, Baptist, and Lutheran, because the system would be incomplete and misleading. But in classifying Protestants attending some special conference — a different matter entirely — such a limited system might be both complete and logical. In any case, the writer must be careful that classes do not overlap: to classify the persons at the conference as Methodists, Baptists, Lutherans, and clergy would be illogical, because some are undoubtedly both Lutheran, for instance, and clergy.

In dividing and classifying, we are really using the basic process of outlining. Moreover, if we are dealing with classifiable *ideas*, the resulting pattern *is* our outline, which has been our aim all along — a basic organizational plan.

This process of classification frequently does, in fact, organize much less tangible things than the examples mentioned. We might wish to find some orderly basis for discussing the South's post-Civil War problems. Division might give us three primary categories of information: economic, political, and social. But for a full-scale consideration of these, the major divisions themselves may be subdivided for still more orderly explanation: the economic information may be further divided into agriculture and industry. Now it is possible to isolate and clarify such strictly industrial matters as shortage of investment capital, disrupted transportation systems, and lack of power development.

Any plan like this seems almost absurdly obvious, of course —
after the planning is done. It appears less obvious, however, to
inexperienced writers who are dealing with a jumble of information
they must explain to someone else. This is when they should be
aware of the patterns at their disposal, and one of the most useful of
these, alone or combined with others, is classification.

Sample Paragraph (Classification)

(Topic sentence, the main stream to which everything else must serve as tributary.)

Division, into four basic categories.

("Throat" is a metaphor.)

Classification, into the general category of "commerce.")

For the most part Ilona Valley enjoys a well-balanced economy. Young people graduating from one of the two big high schools, if they prefer not to go to college, still have some choice as to the kind of work they will do. They might get a job on one of the Valley's numerous ranches, with the hope of becoming a foreman or even owner; they might work in the woods or in one of the eight sawmills; or they might, especially if they live near the lower end, the throat where the Valley constricts before entering the mountain passes, work on one of the many fishing boats based "outside" in Bayport. A fourth category of employment, of course, is commerce: the various retail stores and service stations, restaurants, taverns, banks, and a big retail lumber yard that advertises as the only one in the country located in a river. (It's on an island, of course, connected by bridge to the rest of Waldoville.) Opportunities are not exactly unlimited in the Valley, to be sure, but many people have built happy and prosperous lives here for themselves and their families.

ERIC BERNE

ERIC BERNE (1910–1970) was a graduate of McGill University's School of Medicine. A psychiatrist, he wrote extensively in that field, lectured at various universities, and served on the psychiatric staff of Mount Sinai Hospital in New York City. He later engaged in private practice and research in California. His books include *Games People Play* (1964), *The Happy Valley* (1968), *Sex in Human Loving* (1970), and *What Do You Say After You Say Hello?* (1972).

Can People Be Judged by Their Appearance?

"Can People Be Judged by Their Appearance?" was originally published in Berne's *Mind in Action* (1947) and was later included in a revised edition of his book *A Layman's Guide to Psychiatry and Psychoanalysis* (1947). This explanation of one theory of basic human types is an example of a scientific subject made readable for nonscientists. Using division and classification as his primary pattern of development, Berne also relies to varying extents on most of the other expository patterns: illustration, comparison and contrast, process analysis, cause and effect, definition, and description.

Everyone knows that a human being, like a chicken, comes from an 1
egg. At a very early stage, the human embryo forms a three-layered tube, the inside layer of which grows into the stomach and lungs, the middle layer into bones, muscles, joints, and blood vessels, and the outside layer into the skin and nervous system.

Usually these three grow about equally, so that the average 2
human being is a fair mixture of brains, muscles, and inward organs. In some eggs, however, one layer grows more than the others, and when the angels have finished putting the child

together, he may have more gut than brain, or more brain than muscle. When this happens, the individual's activities will often be mostly with the overgrown layer.

We can thus say that while the average human being is a 3 mixture, some people are mainly "digestion-minded," some "muscle-minded," and some "brain-minded," and correspondingly digestion-bodied, muscle-bodied, or brain-bodied. The digestion-bodied people look thick; the muscle-bodied people look wide; and the brain-bodied people look long. This does not mean the taller a man is, the brainier he will be. It means that if a man, even a short man, looks long rather than wide or thick, he will often be more concerned about what goes on in his mind than about what he does or what he eats; but the key factor is slenderness and not height. On the other hand, a man who gives the impression of being thick rather than long or wide will usually be more interested in a good steak than in a good idea or a good long walk.

Medical men use Greek words to describe these types of body- 4 build. For the man whose body shape mostly depends on the inside layer of the egg, they use the word *endomorph.* If it depends mostly upon the middle layer, they call him a *mesomorph.* If it depends mostly upon the outside layer, they call him an *ectomorph.* We can see the same roots in our English words "enter," "medium," and "exit," which might just as easily have been spelled "ender," "mesium," and "ectit."

Since the inside skin of the human egg, or endoderm, forms the 5 inner organs of the belly, the viscera, the endomorph is usually belly-minded; since the middle skin forms the body tissues, or soma, the mesomorph is usually muscle-minded; and since the outside skin forms the brain, or cerebrum, the ectomorph is usually brain-minded. Translating this into Greek, we have the viscerotonic endomorph, the somatotonic mesomorph, and the cerebrotonic ectomorph.

Words are beautiful things to a cerebrotonic, but a viscerotonic 6 knows you cannot eat a menu no matter what language it is printed in, and a somatotonic knows you cannot increase your chest expansion by reading a dictionary. So it is advisable to leave these words and see what kinds of people they actually apply to, remembering again that most individuals are fairly equal mixtures and that what we have to say concerns only the extremes. Up to the present, these types have been thoroughly studied only in the male sex.

Viscerotonic Endomorph. If a man is definitely a thick type rather than 7 a broad or long type, he is likely to be round and soft, with a big chest but a bigger belly. He would rather eat than breathe comfortably. He is likely to have a wide face, short, thick neck, big thighs and upper arms, and small hands and feet. He has overdeveloped breasts and looks as though he were blown up a little like a balloon. His skin is soft and smooth, and when he gets bald, as he does usually quite early, he loses the hair in the middle of his head first.

The short, jolly, thickset, red-faced politician with a cigar in his 8 mouth, who always looks as though he were about to have a stroke, is the best example of this type. The reason he often makes a good politician is that he likes people, banquets, baths, and sleep; he is easygoing, soothing, and his feelings are easy to understand.

His abdomen is big because he has lots of intestines. He likes to 9 take in things. He likes to take in food, and affection and approval as well. Going to a banquet with people who like him is his idea of a fine time. It is important for a psychiatrist to understand the natures of such men when they come to him for advice.

Somatotonic Mesomorph. If a man is definitely a broad type rather 1(than a thick or long type, he is likely to be rugged and have lots of muscle. He is apt to have big forearms and legs, and his chest and belly are well formed and firm, with the chest bigger than the belly. He would rather breathe than eat. He has a bony head, big shoulders, and a square jaw. His skin is thick, coarse, and elastic, and tans easily. If he gets bald, it usually starts on the front of the head.

Dick Tracy, Li'l Abner, and other men of action belong to this 1) type. Such people make good lifeguards and construction workers. They like to put out energy. They have lots of muscles and they like to use them. They go in for adventure, exercise, fighting, and getting the upper hand. They are bold and unrestrained, and love to master the people and things around them. If the psychiatrist knows the things which give such people satisfaction, he is able to understand why they may be unhappy in certain situations.

Cerebrotonic Ectomorph. The man who is definitely a long type is 1: likely to have thin bones and muscles. His shoulders are apt to sag and he has a flat belly with a dropped stomach, and long, weak legs. His neck and fingers are long, and his face is shaped like a long egg.

His skin is thin, dry, and pale, and he rarely gets bald. He looks like an absent-minded professor and often is one.

Though such people are jumpy, they like to keep their energy and don't fancy moving around much. They would rather sit quietly by themselves and keep out of difficulties. Trouble upsets them, and they run away from it. Their friends don't understand them very well. They move jerkily and feel jerkily. The psychiatrist who understands how easily they become anxious is often able to help them get along better in the sociable and aggressive world of endomorphs and mesomorphs. 13

In the special cases where people definitely belong to one type or another, then, one can tell a good deal about their personalities from their appearance. When the human is engaged in one of its struggles with itself or with the world outside, the individual's way of handling the struggle will be partly determined by his type. If he is a viscerotonic, he will often want to go to a party where he can eat and drink and be in good company at a time when he might be better off attending to business; the somatotonic will want to go out and do something about it, master the situation, even if what he does is foolish and not properly figured out, while the cerebrotonic will go off by himself and think it over, when perhaps he would be better off doing something about it or seeking good company to try to forget it. 14

Since these personality characteristics depend on the growth of the layers of the little egg from which the person developed, they are very difficult to change. Nevertheless, it is important for the individual to know about these types, so that he can have at least an inkling of what to expect from those around him, and can make allowances for the different kinds of human nature, and so that he can become aware of and learn to control his own natural tendencies, which may sometimes guide him into making the same mistakes over and over again in handling his difficulties. 15

Meanings and Values

1. Consider men you have known who fit, or nearly fit, into one or another of the three categories of build.

a. Do they also have the traits described by Berne in paragraphs 8, 9, 11, and 13? Or do you know, perhaps, a "thick" man who hates banquets, a "wide" man who writes poetry, or a "long" man who bullies people?

b. If so, should we assume that these are learned characteristics? Explain.

2. Illustrate clearly how an understanding of basic types of people can be important to the layperson.

3. In view of the fact that so many of a person's characteristics are determined before birth, what room does the author leave for the possibility of altering or controlling these natural tendencies?

Expository Techniques

1a. Most people, according to the author, are not classifiable in the categories he discusses. Is the classification system then faulty, since it does not include everyone?

b. Explain the difference, if any, between this system and the faulty classification of Protestants mentioned in the introduction to this section.

2. Study the general organization of this essay.

a. Which paragraphs give an overall preview of Berne's classification system?

b. Which paragraphs are devoted to explanations of individual categories?

c. Where does the author bring the categories together again to show the importance of the whole analysis?

d. Can you work out another plan that would have presented his material as meaningfully?

3. The author ends each detailed account of type characteristics with a statement of why the psychiatrist needs to know these things (pars. 9, 11, 13). Why is this a valuable technique, even though the essay was not written for psychiatrists?

4. Show the value of the parallel structures in paragraphs 4 and 5. (See Guide to Terms: *Parallel Structure.*)

5. In your opinion, do Berne's occasional attempts at humor — e.g., "the angels" and "cannot eat a menu" — benefit or detract from his explanation? Why?

Diction and Vocabulary

1a. Are the numerous Greek words as bothersome as you expected them to be when you first glanced at the essay? Why, or why not?

    b.   Do you think the author expects us really to master them? If not, why did he use them?

    2.   Aside from the Greek words, you probably found no words with which you were not already familiar. Is this a result of the subject matter, the author's concern for his audience, or something else? Explain.

Suggestions for Writing and Discussion

    1.   At the time this essay was written, the types had been "thoroughly studied only in the male sex." Even if the same general traits were characteristic of women, might tradition and social pressures tend to modify the natural tendencies more in women than in men (e.g., women are "not supposed" to go around flexing their muscles or getting into fist fights)? Explain any differences that you would expect.

    2.   Using examples for illustration, show that basic nature can be changed — or, if you prefer, that such change is very difficult or impossible.

    3.   Show the practical importance — especially for success in your future career — of understanding people and why they act as they do.

    4.   Develop the thesis that people of opposite types can sometimes get along more congenially than those of the same type.

(NOTE: Suggestions for topics requiring development by use of CLASSIFICATION are on page 70, at the end of this section.)

JAMES DAVID BARBER

JAMES DAVID BARBER was born in Charleston, West Virginia, in
1930. He received his B.A. and M.A. from the University of
Chicago and holds a Ph.D. in political science from Yale University. Barber has served in various capacities on the faculties of
Stetson and Yale universities, and he is a frequent guest lecturer
at other universities throughout the country. At present he is
professor of political science at Duke University. Barber has contributed steadily to both scholarly and popular periodicals and
has written and edited several important political science books,
including *Race for the Presidency* (1978) and *The Pulse of Politics*
(1980).

Four Types of President

"Four Types of President" (editor's title) is selected from Barber's
most widely known book, *The Presidential Character: Predicting
Performance in the White House.* In this piece he attempts to explain,
by division and classification, a much more complex subject than
those of the other authors of this section; the resulting system,
however, is admirably simple. Also worth a beginning writer's
study are the distinctive elements of Barber's style.

Who the President is at a given time can make a profound difference   1
in the whole thrust and direction of national politics. Since we have
only one President at a time, we can never prove this by comparison, but even the most superficial speculation confirms the com-
monsense view that the man himself weighs heavily among other
historical factors. A Wilson re-elected in 1920, a Hoover in 1932, a
John F. Kennedy in 1964 would, it seems very likely, have guided
the body politic along rather different paths from those their actual
successors chose. Or try to imagine a Theodore Roosevelt en-

From the book *The Presidential Character* by James David Barber. © 1972, 1977 by James
David Barber. Published by Prentice-Hall, Inc., Englewood Cliffs, N.J. 07632.

sconced behind today's "bully pulpit" of a Presidency, or Lyndon Johnson as President in the age of McKinley. Only someone mesmerized by the lures of historical inevitability can suppose that it would have made little or no difference to government policy had Alf Landon replaced FDR in 1936, and Dewey beaten Truman in 1948, or Adlai Stevenson reigned through the 1950s. Not only would these alternative Presidents have advocated different policies — they would have approached the office from very different psychological angles. It stretches credibility to think that Eugene McCarthy would have run the institution the way Lyndon Johnson did.

The first baseline in defining Presidential types is *activity-passivity*. How much energy does the man invest in his Presidency? Lyndon Johnson went at his day like a human cyclone, coming to rest long after the sun went down. Calvin Coolidge often slept eleven hours a night and still needed a nap in the middle of the day. In between, the Presidents array themselves on the high or low side of the activity line.

The second baseline is *positive-negative affect* toward one's activity — that is, how he feels about what he does. Relatively speaking, does he seem to experience his political life as happy or sad, enjoyable or discouraging, positive or negative, in its main effect. The feeling I am after here is not grim satisfaction in a job well done, not some philosophical conclusion. The idea is this: is he someone who, on the surfaces we can see, gives forth the feeling that he has *fun* in political life? Franklin Roosevelt's Secretary of War, Henry L. Stimson, wrote that the Roosevelts "not only understood the *use* of power, they knew the *enjoyment* of power, too. . . . Whether a man is burdened by power or enjoys power; whether he is trapped by responsibility or made free by it; whether he is moved by other people and outer forces or moves them — that is the essence of leadership."

The positive-negative baseline, then, is a general symptom of the fit between the man and his experience, a kind of register of *felt* satisfaction.

Why might we expect these two simple dimensions to outline the main character types? Because they stand for two central features of anyone's orientation toward life. In nearly every study of personality, some form of the active-passive contrast is critical; the general tendency to act or be acted upon is evident in such concepts as dominance-submission, extraversion-introversion, aggression-timidity, attack-defense, fight-flight, engagement-withdrawal, approach-avoidance. In everyday life we sense quickly the general energy output of the people we deal with. Similarly we catch on fairly quickly to the affect dimension — whether the person seems to be optimistic or pessimistic, hopeful or skeptical, happy or sad. The two baselines are clear and they are also independent of one another: all of us know people who are very active but seem discouraged, others who are quite passive but seem happy, and so forth. The activity baseline refers to what one does, the affect baseline to how one feels about what he does.

Both are crude clues to character. They are leads into four basic character patterns long familiar in psychological research. In summary form, these are the main configurations:

Active-positive. There is a congruence, a consistency, between much activity and the enjoyment of it, indicating relatively high self-esteem and relative success in relating to the environment. The man shows an orientation toward productiveness as a value and an ability to use his styles flexibly, adaptively, suiting the dance to the music. He sees himself as developing over time toward relatively well-defined personal goals — growing toward his image of himself as he might yet be. There is an emphasis on rational mastery, on using the brain to move the feet. This may get him into trouble; he may fail to take account of the irrational in politics. Not everyone he deals with sees things his way and he may find it hard to understand why.

Active-negative. The contradiction here is between relatively intense effort and relatively low emotional reward for that effort. The activity has a compulsive quality, as if the man were trying to make up for something or to escape from anxiety into hard work. He seems ambitious, striving upward, power-seeking. His stance toward the environment is aggressive and he has a persistent problem in managing his aggressive feelings. His self-image is vague and discontinuous. Life is a hard struggle to achieve and hold power, hampered by the condemnations of a perfectionistic conscience. Active-negative types pour energy into the political system, but it is an energy distorted from within.

Passive-positive. This is the receptive, compliant, other-directed 9
character whose life is a search for affection as a reward for being
agreeable and cooperative rather than personally assertive. The
contradiction is between low self-esteem (on grounds of being un-
lovable, unattractive) and a superficial optimism. A hopeful attitude
helps dispel doubt and elicits encouragement from others. Passive-
positive types help soften the harsh edges of politics. But their
dependence and the fragility of their hopes and enjoyments make
disappointment in politics likely.

Passive-negative. The factors are consistent — but how are we to 10
account for the man's *political* role-taking? Why is someone who
does little in politics and enjoys it less there at all? The answer lies in
the passive-negative's character-rooted orientation toward doing
dutiful service; this compensates for low self-esteem based on a
sense of uselessness. Passive-negative types are in politics because
they think they ought to be. They may be well adapted to certain
nonpolitical roles, but they lack the experience and flexibility to
perform effectively as political leaders. Their tendency is to withdraw, to escape from the conflict and uncertainty of politics by
emphasizing vague principles (especially prohibitions) and pro-
cedural arrangements. They become guardians of the right and
proper way, above the sordid politicking of lesser men.

Active-positive Presidents want most to achieve results. Ac- 11
tive-negatives aim to get and keep power. Passive-positives are after
love. Passive-negatives emphasize their civic virtue. The relation of
activity to enjoyment in a President thus tends to outline a cluster of
characteristics, to set apart the adapted from the compulsive, compliant, and withdrawn types.

The first four Presidents of the United States, conveniently, ran 12
through this gamut of character types. (Remember, we are talking
about tendencies, broad directions; no individual man exactly fits a
category.) George Washington — clearly the most important President in the pantheon — established the fundamental legitimacy of
an American government at a time when this was a matter in
considerable question. Washington's dignity, judiciousness, his
aloof air of reserve and dedication to duty fit the passive-negative or
withdrawing type best. Washington did not seek innovation, he

sought stability. He longed to retire to Mount Vernon, but fortunately was persuaded to stay on through a second term, in which, by rising above the political conflict between Hamilton and Jefferson and inspiring confidence in his own integrity, he gave the nation time to develop the organized means for peaceful change.

John Adams followed, a dour New England Puritan, much   13
given to work and worry, an impatient and irascible man — an active-negative President, a compulsive type. Adams was far more partisan than Washington; the survival of the system through his Presidency demonstrated that the nation could tolerate, for a time, domination by one of its nascent political parties. As President, an angry Adams brought the United States to the brink of war with France, and presided over the new nation's first experiment in political repression: the Alien and Sedition Acts, forbidding, among other things, unlawful combinations "with intent to oppose any measure or measures of the government of the United States," or "any false, scandalous, and malicious writing or writings against the United States, or the President of the United States, with intent to defame . . . or to bring them or either of them, into contempt or disrepute."

Then came Jefferson. He too had his troubles and failures — in   14
the design of national defense, for example. As for his Presidential character (only one element in success or failure), Jefferson was clearly active-positive. A child of the Enlightenment, he applied his reason to organizing connections with Congress aimed at strengthening the more popular forces. A man of catholic interests and delightful humor, Jefferson combined a clear and open vision of what the country could be with a profound political sense, expressed in his famous phrase, "Every difference of opinion is not a difference of principle."

The fourth President was James Madison, "Little Jemmy," the   15
constitutional philosopher thrown into the White House at a time of great international turmoil. Madison comes closest to the passive-positive, or compliant, type; he suffered from irresolution, tried to compromise his way out, and gave in too readily to the "warhawks" urging combat with Britain. The nation drifted into war, and Madison wound up ineptly commanding his collection of amateur generals in the streets of Washington. General Jackson's victory at New Orleans saved the Madison administration's historical reputation;

but he left the Presidency with the United States close to bankruptcy and secession.

These four Presidents — like all Presidents — were persons 16
trying to cope with the roles they had won by using the equipment they had built over a lifetime. The President is not some shapeless organism in a flood of novelties, but a man with a memory in a system with a history. Like all of us, he draws on his past to shape his future. The pathetic hope that the White House will turn a Caligula into a Marcus Aurelius is as naive as the fear that ultimate power inevitably corrupts. The problem is to understand — and to state understandably — what in the personal past foreshadows the Presidential future.

Meanings and Values

1. Is this selection more nearly objective or subjective writing? Why? (See Guide to Terms: *Objective/Subjective*.)

2. What seems to be the author's opinion of "historical inevitability" (par. 1)? Justify your answer.

3. What have been some of the most important "historical factors" (par. 1) that have combined with the character of recent presidents to shape their conduct in office?

4a. How, if at all, could a person be "made free" by responsibility (par. 3)?

  b. Does Stimson's statement constitute a paradox? Why, or why not? (Guide: *Paradox*.)

5. Why was the "fundamental legitimacy of an American government" in question (par. 12), even after the Revolutionary War was won?

6a. In paragraph 5, Barber makes clear that his classification system applies to ordinary people, not just to presidents. If you have also read Berne's system of classifying types of people, do you find any parallels between the two?

  b. If you do, show the parallels. If not, are they then contradictory to each other? Why, or why not?

Expository Techniques

1a. If this seems to be a more complicated classification system than the others in this section, try to determine why.

b.   Devise, if you can, a simpler way to present the material. Is yours more, or less, effective? Why?

2.   In paragraph 12, Barber says that no individual man exactly fits a category. Must we therefore conclude that it is not a complete and logical system? Why, or why not?

3a.   Cite the paragraphs in which the author uses examples as an expository technique.

b.   Do the examples improve the effectiveness of the writing, or merely slow down the reading? Why?

4a.   Cite examples of parallel structure in at least two paragraphs. (Guide: *Parallel Structure.*)

b.   How is their use a matter of syntax and of style? (Guide: *Syntax* and *Style/Tone.*)

5.   What other qualities of Barber's writing are relevant to style? Use examples to illustrate.

6a.   What is the apparent purpose of paragraph 11 and the last sentence of paragraph 5?

b.   Would you use this technique if you were doing similar writing? Why, or why not?

Diction and Vocabulary

1a.   Which, if any, of your answers to question 5 of "Expository Techniques" are also matters of diction? (Guide: *Diction.*)

b.   If none of them are, why did you not consider diction a distinctive element of Barber's style? (Guide: *Style/Tone.*)

2a.   Why are the baselines "crude" clues to character (par. 6)?

b.   Are they therefore not valid? Why, or why not?

3a.   The author uses two qualifications in the final sentence of paragraph 7. What are they? (Guide: *Qualification.*)

b.   What is gained by their use?

4a.   How might the careless reader misunderstand the meaning of "His stance toward the environment is aggressive . . . " (par. 8)?

b.   In view of the author's apparent purpose and reader-audience, is there any reason to believe he would be concerned about this possible ambiguity? Explain.

c.   How, if at all, is this a matter of connotation? (Guide: *Connotation/ Denotation.*)

5a.   What are the meanings, both literal and figurative, of the allusions in paragraph 16? (Guide: *Figures of Speech.*)

b. Cite at least one example each of simile and metaphor in paragraph 2 or 7.

6. Consult the dictionary as needed for full understanding of the following words: ensconced, mesmerized (par. 1); array (2); essence (3); configurations (6); congruence (7); discontinuous (8); dispel, elicits (9); compliant (9, 15); gamut; pantheon, judiciousness (12); dour, irascible, nascent, defame (13); catholic (14); irresolution, ineptly (15).

Suggestions for Writing and Discussion

1. Analyze your own character patterns and determine which category they best fit. For what practical purposes might such analysis be used?

2. How can we reliably analyze and categorize a candidate's character during the fakery of a presidential campaign?

3. To what extent should we consider the national situation or "other historical factors" at the time of election in relation to the candidates' character types?

4. If Barber's meaning of "character" differs from your own — e.g., if it is more or less concerned with integrity — explain the differences.

5. Where do the three most recent presidents best fit into Barber's classification system? Justify your answer.

(NOTE: Suggestions for topics requiring development by use of CLASSIFICATION are on page 70, at the end of this section.)

ALISON LURIE

ALISON LURIE, born in 1926, in Chicago, Illinois, is professor of English at Cornell University. She is the author of two children's books and six novels, including *The War Between the Tates* (1974) and *Only Children* (1979). Her latest book, *The Language of Clothes* (1981), is a study of fashions in clothing and their meanings.

Hats

In "Hats" (editors' title), a selection from *The Language of Clothes*, Lurie uses division and classification to explore some of the many relationships among human beings and their hats. Though the organization of this piece is complex, it is nonetheless easy to follow because the author presents the categories in chronological order and makes frequent use of illustration and comparison to clarify her explanations.

Traditionally whatever is worn on the head, whether or not it grows there naturally, is a sign of the mind beneath it. The hat therefore, like the hair, expresses ideas and opinions. Since the head is one of the most vulnerable parts of the body, many hats also have a protective function, shielding their wearers from extremes of climate and from human aggression. The man's hat of the nineteenth and early twentieth century, which was derived ultimately from the medieval helmet, protected its wearer both physically and psychologically. The heavy crown deflected blows; the brim shaded the face from strong sunlight and close scrutiny; the conventional shape expressed the conventionality of the mind it covered. The stiffer the hat, in general, the higher the social class of its wearer and/or the more conventional his views: the aristocrat in his topper, the City man in his bowler, were literally hard-headed. The symbolically appropriate disadvantage of such hats was that they were easy to knock off if anyone dared to do so. Working men and boys, on the other hand, wore soft cloth caps, less formidable-looking but harder to remove; their prestige, such as it was, was less easily damaged by direct assault.

Women's hats, too, once had important symbolic meanings, 2 though here social role rather than social status was uppermost. Throughout most of the nineteenth century all respectable wives, widows and spinsters wore not one but two symbolic head coverings. Except for young unmarried girls, an indoor cap of muslin or silk, trimmed with lace and/or ribbon, was an essential part of the everyday costume. It was donned on arising, and could be dispensed with only for formal evening entertainments. Usually this cap was white, expressing the conventional purity and delicacy of the mind within; if the woman was in mourning it might be black (more suitable as a container of sad thoughts) or trimmed with a black ribbon.

When the middle-class woman left her house, even to walk in 3 the garden, she put on a hat or bonnet — over her cap if she wore one. She thus shielded her pure and private thoughts, covering them with an elaborate and conventional representation of contemporary public femininity. A well-dressed female who appeared out of doors without her hat, or indoors without a cap (if she was old enough to wear one), was assumed to be emotionally distracted, mentally disturbed or of loose morals.

By the 1890s caps had been given up by all but the elderly or 4 exceptionally prim; but men's and women's hats continued to flourish for the next half-century, offering a remarkable variety of expressive form. In America the hat was a status symbol of a special kind. These were the great years of European immigration, and as boatload after boatload of hatless peasants landed, those who wanted to make it plain that they were not themselves ignorant "greenhorns," or that they were of a higher class origin than most immigrants, took care to wear hats. . . .

After World War II, the symbolic hat began to disappear. 5 Women who a few years earlier would never have left home without a hat, even to go down to the corner store, were now tying a scarf over their hair or going bareheaded. In the 1950s the symbolic female hat was obligatory only for formal occasions: lunches in town, business meetings, church; by 1960 it was optional everywhere. Women's hats continued to be manufactured and sold, but now mainly as decorative accessories.

The symbolic man's hat also disappeared after World War II, 6 though more gradually. By 1970, though the British businessman may have owned a bowler, the lawyer or doctor a soft felt, the commercial traveler a porkpie and the working man a cap, more often than not he did not wear it. In America, the same thing happened; eventually, even in a large city, a man who was wearing a symbolic hat in good weather was assumed to be either (1) a conscious dandy or eccentric, (2) on his way to some ceremonial function or (3) over sixty.

Strictly utilitarian hats were still occasionally worn: knitted 7 wool caps for cold weather, plastic or waterproofed sou'westers for rain, floppy straws and cotton baseball caps (some with green celluloid visors) for glaring sun. The prestige of all such hats, however, was very low, and many people preferred to be cold, wet or blinded rather than wear them, especially on formal occasions. Sometimes, for protection from the elements, they wore an old symbolic hat, inefficient as this usually turned out to be. The standard man's fedora needed reblocking after every rainstorm, and the soft felt became a sodden pudding. Women's symbolic hats were even more vulnerable. The New Look cartwheel blew off in the slightest breeze, the ladylike straw of the fifties wilted and the Jackie Kennedy pillbox with its wisp of symbolic veil was of no use whatsoever.

The disappearance of the symbolic hat over the last thirty years 8 is one of the oddest chapters in the entire history of costume. After covering their heads ceremonially for centuries most people simply gave up doing so, and this in spite of frantic sobs and threats from the fashion industry. A tremendous advertising campaign was mounted: consumers were reminded that no real lady or gentleman was ever seen in public hatless; they were warned that their desertion of the hat would throw thousands of deserving persons out of work, and afflict millions with head colds and pneumonia. It was all to no avail; every year, more and more men and women went bareheaded.

During the late sixties and early seventies the only real enthu- 9 siasm for headgear was among members of the counterculture, who adopted eccentric varieties of symbolic hats in a spirit of play or satire. For a while every political demonstration or outdoor concert was a seething mass of coonskin caps, Mexican sombreros, calico sunbonnets, gypsy scarves, shiny black toppers, antique military helmets and garden-party straws trimmed with fading real or paper flowers. Those who did not wear hats often tied a leather thong or a beaded or embroidered band around their heads Indian fashion (occasionally with an upstanding feather), possibly to keep their rather scattered thoughts together, possibly to symbolize the fact that their mind was in the grip of some obsessive idea.

Interestingly enough, the disappearance of the conventional hat was accompanied and paralleled by a severe simplification of formal etiquette. On all but the most formal occasions, rules of precedence and seating were forgotten. Strangers were introduced by their first names alone, often without regard for rank, age and sex; bank tellers, waitresses and airline stewards presented themselves to the public as "Hi, I'm Billie." Instead of talking about the weather or the news of the day, people one had known for five minutes would begin to describe their current emotional state and reveal intimate details of their lives; this process, known as "letting it all hang out," was often literally echoed in the costume. What seemed to be taking place both in terms of dress and in terms of manners was the abandonment of the formal public self symbolized by the hat. Men or women who had once been willing or even eager to assume a standardized role in public now wanted to operate at all times as spontaneous individuals. A "gentleman" no longer tipped his symbolic hat to a "lady" to show the conventional respect due her sex; he no longer had a hat to tip. . . .

In the sixties and seventies the symbolic hat seemed almost as sure of extinction as the passenger pigeon. Currently, however, it seems to be making a limited comeback. This movement began some years ago in the American Wild West with the increasing popularity of cowboy hats among noncowboys. Today a majority of men in this part of the country, especially in Texas, wear some type of "Western" hat — and so do a number of the women.

The cowboy hat, originally part of the practical working garb of men who had to ride long distances in an extreme climate, has over the past century become heavy with symbolic meaning. Basically it suggests toughness and independence, but many subtle variations of this message are possible, depending among other things on the color and shape of the hat and on its trimmings. The Hollywood

convention White Hat=Good Guy, Black Hat=Bad Guy still operates: men who wish to appear as rebels or desperate characters
prefer the darker shades, and straight arrows the lighter ones.
Ambiguous, subtle or secretive types may favor grayed hues, while
the more common tans and browns that repeat the colors of the
Western landscape are worn (or thought to be worn) by natural,
down-to-earth men. Plain leather hatbands, no doubt on the principle of contagious magic, suggest the simple approach to life and
physical energy of the beef cattle to which the leather once be-
longed; expensive hand-tooled bands and decorations of silver and
feathers imply a high-flying life style and an extensive bank
account. The shape of the Western hat is also a form of communication. In general, the higher the crown, the higher the self-esteem of
the wearer; the wider the brim, the closer his connection to the
realities of outdoor life on the Western plains, where shelter from
sun, rain, dust and wind are of primary importance.

In the past few years Western hats have begun to multiply   13
outside the Wild West. Today they are on sale in both New York and
London — although those who can afford the prices (among them,
Bob Dylan and the King of Sweden) still order theirs from Texas
Hatters in Houston. Sometimes the message of these hats is merely
one of fashionable chic, but often, especially when they are part of a
complete or partial Western outfit, they may be read as a guide to
character and status.

The utilitarian hat, meanwhile, is gradually becoming more   14
acceptable, especially among men, whose relatively short hair and
susceptibility to baldness make them vulnerable to extremes of
climate. Knitted wool caps are still non-U[1] in town for anyone over
the age of eighteen; but there are now more respectable alternatives,
some of which have begun to take on symbolic meanings of their
own. The black fur hat that can be folded down to cover the ears on
very cold days is associated with men of middle age and northern
European origin or interests. There is also the floppy Irish tweed
hat; widely advertised as becoming to all ages and sexes, it is in fact
becoming to no one, but has the advantage that no type of precipita-
tion can make it look worse than it already does. In the true country
this hat is quite respectable; in town, however, its wearer appears to
belong to a rural aristocracy of the species that is hardly distinguishable from the rural peasantry.

---

[1]Not characteristic of the upper classes or the fashionable — EDS.

The flat wool cap which was in the past traditionally worn for golfing, shooting and many spectator sports is another possible utilitarian hat, and perhaps today the most popular one. In rural or suburban settings it may give a certain style and dash to the costume. The man who wears such a cap in the city, however, is automatically marked down one notch below the social status implied by the rest of his outfit; and he may even be suspected of owning a one-acre suburban estate that he has christened Tall Pines or The Snuggery.

Women who like to appear as tomboys or good sports may wear some type of male utilitarian hat, though not usually for purely utilitarian reasons. More often, when the weather is bad, they will shield their heads with scarves, and here they have a large vocabulary of expressive possibilities. The fabric of which the scarf is made can be related to outdoor temperatures, or it can be a class indicator — wool being considered aristocratic, chiffon *nouveau riche,* silk upper-middle class, cotton middle class or arty and synthetics working class. Another important consideration is the manner in which the scarf is tied, whether conventionally under the chin, exotically at the nape of the neck or on top of the head turban or charlady style. But most significant of all, probably, is the color and (if any) the pattern of the scarf, which, like color and pattern generally, convey a whole range of subtle and important personal messages.

Meanings and Values

1a. Lurie classifies hats according to their symbolic or utilitarian functions, according to the sex of the wearer, and according to historical period. Does one basis for classification seem more important than the others, or are they of equal importance?

b. The subject of hats may seem like a simple one, but the author has chosen a rather complicated system of classification for it. Is the system too complicated, or does the subject deserve such thorough treatment? (See Guide to Terms: *Evaluation.*)

2a. Explain the difference between symbolic hats and utilitarian hats, drawing examples from the selection or your experience.

b. Can any hat be classified as purely utilitarian? Purely symbolic? Give examples.

3. What does the author mean when she says that "the man's hat of the nineteenth and early twentieth century . . . protected its wearer . . . psychologically" (par. 1)?

4a.   What is the central theme of this piece? (Guide: *Unity*.)
 b.   Is the central theme clearly stated anywhere in the selection?
5a.   Can hats be considered symbols? (Guide: *Symbol*.)
 b.   If so, are they natural, personal, or conventional symbols?
6.   By abandoning symbolic hats in recent decades, what messages
      have women been conveying?
7.   The author claims that "the disappearance of the conventional hat
      was accompanied and paralleled by a severe simplification of formal
      etiquette" (par. 10). Does she appear to approve or disapprove of
      this phenomenon? (Guide: *Style/Tone*.)
8.   What does the author think about the kind of person who wears a
      "floppy Irish tweed hat" (par. 14)? Explain.
9.   Where would you place this selection on an objective-subjective
      continuum? Why? (Guide: *Objective/Subjective*.)
10.   If you have read the Berne piece at the beginning of this section,
      what kinds of hats do you think each category of men he describes
      would wear?

Expository Techniques

1a.   List, if you can, the categories of hats and their symbolic meanings
      as presented by Lurie.
 b.   Are the categories distinct, or do they overlap?
 c.   Would the essay be more effective if the categories were either given
      names or announced more clearly to the reader in some other way?
2.   What illustrations, if any, does the author provide to support her
      claim that "the disappearance of the symbolic hat over the last thirty
      years is one of the oddest chapters in the entire history of costume"
      (par. 8)?
3a.   The closing of this selection is rather abrupt. Do you think it is
      appropriate?
 b.   What other closing strategies might the author have used? (Guide:
      Closings.)
4.   This piece uses historical narrative along with classification as a
      means of organization. Do the transitions between paragraphs re-
      flect one of the patterns or both? (Guide: *Transition*.)

Diction and Vocabulary

1a.   A "City man" (par. 1) is a businessman who works in the London
      financial district. Why is it appropriate to refer to such a person as
      "hard-headed" (par. 1)?

b. Is "hard-headed," as the author uses it, a cliché? (Guide: *Clichés.*)

2. Because terms used to describe fashions change quickly and are often forgotten after a few years, you may not recognize some of the terms used in this selection. If you do not recognize the names of these hats, look them up in a dictionary or in an encyclopedia under "hats" or "clothing": topper, bowler (par. 1); porkpie (6); sou'wester, fedora, cartwheel, pillbox (7); coonskin cap; sombrero (9).

3. The words and phrases used in this selection range from the very formal, "donned on arising" (par. 2), to the quite informal, "straight arrow" (12). Is this wide range in vocabulary appropriate to the author's subject or her treatment of the subject? (Guide: *Diction.*)

4a. What does Lurie mean when she says, "he may even be suspected of owning a one-acre suburban estate that he has christened Tall Pines or The Snuggery" (par. 15)?

b. When she says "are worn (or thought to be worn)" (par. 12)?

5. Use the dictionary as necessary to understand how the author uses the following words: vulnerable, crown, formidable (par. 1); spinsters, muslin, donned (2); prim (4); obligatory (5); dandy (6); utilitarian, reblocking, wisp (7); precedence, intimate, standardized (10); contagious, self-esteem (12); chic (13); chiffon, *nouveau riche*, charlady (16).

Suggestions for Writing and Discussion

1. Discuss the differences, if any, between the way men and women communicate through their choices in clothing or through the other choices (food, friends, hobbies) they make in their daily lives.

2. The author believes that clothing (including hats) can be considered a "language." Do you agree with her? Explain.

3. Is it important for us to be able to "read" the messages people send us through their clothing, and it is important for us to be careful of what we "say" with our own clothing? Use examples to support your view.

4. Classify one or more articles of children's clothing or toys in order to show that they convey messages in a manner similar to that described by Lurie in her discussion of adult's clothing.

(NOTE: Suggestions for topics requiring development by use of CLASSIFICATION are on page 70, at the end of this section.)

DESMOND MORRIS

DESMOND MORRIS was born in 1928, in England, and educated at
Birmingham University (B.S.) and Oxford (Ph.D.). He was later
researcher in animal behavior at the Department of Zoology,
Oxford, and for several years served as curator of mammals at the
Zoological Society of London. Morris has increasingly specialized
in human behavior and now holds a Research Fellowship at
Oxford, where he spends much of his time writing. He is the
author of some fifty scientific papers and a dozen books. In 1967
he published *The Naked Ape,* which has sold over 8 million copies
and been translated into twenty-three languages. Other recent
books have been *The Human Zoo* (1970), *Intimate Behaviour* (1972),
Manwatching (1977), as co-author, *Gestures: Their Origins and Distribution* (1979), and *Animal Days* (1980).

Territorial Behaviour

"Territorial Behaviour" is a chapter from *Manwatching.* The selection is straightforward in purpose and execution: Morris's divisions of territorial behaviour, though simple and obvious, provide a firm and valid structure for the writing.

A territory is a defended space. In the broadest sense, there are   1
three kinds of human territory: tribal, family and personal.

It is rare for people to be driven to physical fighting in defence   2
of these "owned" spaces, but fight they will, if pushed to the limit.
The invading army encroaching on national territory, the gang
moving into a rival district, the trespasser climbing into an orchard,
the burglar breaking into a house, the bully pushing to the front of a
queue, the driver trying to steal a parking space, all of these intruders are liable to be met with resistance varying from the vigorous to
the savagely violent. Even if the law is on the side of the intruder,

the urge to protect a territory may be so strong that otherwise peaceful citizens abandon all their usual controls and inhibitions. Attempts to evict families from their homes, no matter how socially valid the reasons, can lead to siege conditions reminiscent of the defence of a medieval fortress.

The fact that these upheavals are so rare is a measure of the success of Territorial Signals as a system of dispute prevention. It is sometimes cynically stated that "all property is theft," but in reality it is the opposite. Property, as owned space which is *displayed* as owned space, is a special kind of sharing system which reduces fighting much more than it causes it. Man is a co-operative species, but he is also competitive, and his struggle for dominance has to be structured in some way if chaos is to be avoided. The establishment of territorial rights is one such structure. It limits dominance geographically. I am dominant in my territory and you are dominant in yours. In other words, dominance is shared out spatially, and we all have some. Even if I am weak and unintelligent and you can dominate me when we meet on neutral ground, I can still enjoy a thoroughly dominant role as soon as I retreat to my private base. Be it ever so humble, there is no place like a home territory.

Of course, I can still be intimidated by a particularly dominant individual who enters my home base, but his encroachment will be dangerous for him and he will think twice about it, because he will know that here my urge to resist will be dramatically magnified and my usual subservience banished. Insulted at the heart of my own territory, I may easily explode into battle — either symbolic or real — with a result that may be damaging to both of us.

In order for this to work, each territory has to be plainly advertised as such. Just as a dog cocks its leg to deposit its personal scent on the trees in its locality, so the human animal cocks its leg symbolically all over his home base. But because we are predominantly visual animals, we employ mostly visual signals, and it is worth asking how we do this at the three levels: tribal, family and personal.

First: the Tribal Territory. We evolved as tribal animals, living in comparatively small groups, probably of less than a hundred, and we existed like that for millions of years. It is our basic social unit, a group in which everyone knows everyone else. Essentially, the tribal territory consisted of a home base surrounded by extended hunting grounds. Any neighbouring tribe intruding on our social space would be repelled and driven away. As these early tribes swelled into agricultural super-tribes, and eventually into industrial nations, their territorial defence systems became increasingly elaborate. The tiny, ancient home base of the hunting tribe became the great capital city, the primitive war-paint became the flags, emblems, uniforms and regalia of the specialized military, and the war-chants became national anthems, marching songs and bugle calls. Territorial boundary-lines hardened into fixed borders, often conspicuously patrolled and punctuated with defensive structures — forts and look-out posts, checkpoints and great walls, and, today, customs barriers.

Today each nation flies its own flag, a symbolic embodiment of its territorial status. But patriotism is not enough. The ancient tribal hunter lurking inside each citizen finds himself unsatisfied by membership in such a vast conglomeration of individuals, most of whom are totally unknown to him personally. He does his best to feel that he shares a common territorial defence with them all, but the scale of the operation has become inhuman. It is hard to feel a sense of belonging with a tribe of fifty million or more. His answer is to form sub-groups, nearer to his ancient pattern, smaller and more personally known to him — the local club, the teenage gang, the union, the specialist society, the sports association, the political party, the college fraternity, the social clique, the protest group, and the rest. Rare indeed is the individual who does not belong to at least one of these splinter groups, and take from it a sense of tribal allegiance and brotherhood. Typical of all these groups is the development of Territorial Signals — badges, costumes, headquarters, banners, slogans, and all the other displays of group identity. This is where the action is, in terms of tribal territorialism, and only when a major war breaks out does the emphasis shift upwards to the higher group level of the nation.

Each of these modern pseudo-tribes sets up its own special kind of home base. In extreme cases non-members are totally excluded, in others they are allowed in as visitors with limited rights and under a control system of special rules. In many ways they are like miniature nations, with their own flags and emblems and their own border guards. The exclusive club has its own "customs barrier": the doorman who checks your "passport" (your membership card) and prevents strangers from passing in unchallenged. There is a government: the club committee; and often special displays of the tribal elders: the photographs or portraits of previous officials on the walls. At the heart of the specialized territories there is a powerful feeling of security and importance, a sense of shared defence against the outside world. Much of the club chatter, both serious and joking, directs itself against the rottenness of everything outside the club boundaries — in that "other world" beyond the protected portals.

In social organizations which embody a strong class system, such as military units and large business concerns, there are many territorial rules, often unspoken, which interfere with the official hierarchy. High-status individuals, such as officers or managers, could in theory enter any of the regions occupied by the lower levels in the pecking order, but they limit this power in a striking way. An officer seldom enters a sergeant's mess or a barrack room unless it is for a formal inspection. He respects those regions as alien territories even though he has the power to go there by virtue of his dominant role. And in businesses, part of the appeal of unions, over and above their obvious functions, is that with their officials, headquarters and meetings they add a sense of territorial power for the staff workers. It is almost as if each military organization and business concern consists of two warring tribes: the officers versus the other ranks, and the management versus the workers. Each has its special home base within the system, and the territorial defence pattern thrusts itself into what, on the surface, is a pure social hierarchy. Negotiations between managements and unions are tribal battles fought out over the neutral ground of a boardroom table, and are as much concerned with territorial display as they are with resolving problems of wages and conditions. Indeed, if one side gives in too quickly and accepts the other's demands, the victors feel strangely cheated and deeply suspicious that it may be a trick. What they are missing is the protracted sequence of ritual and counter-ritual that keeps alive their group territorial identity. 9

Likewise, many of the hostile displays of sports fans and teenage gangs are primarily concerned with displaying their group image to rival fan-clubs and gangs. Except in rare cases, they do not attack one another's headquarters, drive out the occupants, and reduce them to a submissive, subordinate condition. It is enough to have scuffles on the borderlands between the two rival territories. This is particularly clear at football matches, where the fan-club headquarters becomes temporarily shifted from the club-house to a 10 section of the stands, and where minor fighting breaks out at the unofficial boundary line between the massed groups of rival supporters. Newspaper reports play up the few accidents and injuries which do occur on such occasions, but when they are studied in relation to the total numbers of displaying fans involved, it is clear that the serious incidents represent only a tiny fraction of the overall group behaviour. For every actual punch or kick there are a thousand war-cries, war-dances, chants and gestures.

Second: the Family Territory. Essentially, the family is a breeding unit and the family territory is a breeding ground. At the centre of this space, there is the nest — the bedroom — where, tucked up in bed, we feel at our most territorially secure. In a typical house the bedroom is upstairs, where a safe nest should be. This puts it farther away from the entrance hall, the area where contact is made, intermittently, with the outside world. The less private reception rooms, where intruders are allowed access, are the next line of defence. Beyond them, outside the walls of the building, there is often a symbolic remnant of the ancient feeding grounds — a garden. Its symbolism often extends to the plants and animals it contains, which cease to be nutritional and become merely decorative — flowers and pets. But like a true territorial space it has a conspicuously displayed boundary-line, the garden fence, wall, or railings. Often no more than a token barrier, this is the outer territorial demarcation, separating the private world of the family from the public world beyond. To cross it puts any visitor or intruder at an immediate disadvantage. As he crosses the threshold, his dominance wanes, slightly but unmistakably. He is entering an area where he senses that he must ask permission to do simple things that he would consider a right elsewhere. Without lifting a finger, the territorial owners exert their dominance. This is done by all the hundreds of small ownership "markers" they have deposited on their family territory: the ornaments, the "possessed" objects positioned in the rooms and on the walls; the furnishings, the furniture, the colours, the patterns, all owner-chosen and all making this particular home base unique to them.

It is one of the tragedies of modern architecture that there has been a standardization of these vital territorial living units. One of the most important aspects of a home is that it should be similar to other homes only in a general way, and that in detail it should have many differences, making it a *particular* home. Unfortunately, it is cheaper to build a row of houses, or a block of flats, so that all the family living-units are identical, but the territorial urge rebels against this trend and house-owners struggle as best they can to make their mark on their mass-produced properties. They do this with garden-design, with front-door colours, with curtain patterns, with wallpaper and all the other decorative elements that together create a unique and different family environment. Only when they have completed this nest-building do they feel truly "at home" and secure.

When they venture forth as a family unit, they repeat the   13
process in a minor way. On a day-trip to the seaside, they load the car with personal belongings and it becomes their temporary, port-able territory. Arriving at the beach, they stake out a small territorial claim, marking it with rugs, towels, baskets and other belongings to which they can return from their seaboard wanderings. Even if they all leave it at once to bathe, it retains a characteristic territorial quality and other family groups arriving will recognize this by setting up their own "home" bases at a respectful distance. Only when the whole beach has filled up with these marked spaces will newcomers start to position themselves in such a way that the inter-base distance becomes reduced. Forced to pitch between several existing beach territories, they will feel a momentary sensa-tion of intrusion, and the established "owners" will feel a similar sensation of invasion, even though they are not being directly inconvenienced.

The same territorial scene is being played out in parks and fields   14
and on riverbanks, wherever family groups gather in their clustered units. But if rivalry for spaces creates mild feelings of hostility, it is true to say that without the territorial system of sharing and space-limited dominance, there would be chaotic disorder.

Third: the Personal Space. If a man enters a waiting-room and   15
sits at one end of a long row of empty chairs, it is possible to predict where the next man to enter will seat himself. He will not sit next to the first man, nor will he sit at the far end, right away from him. He will choose a position about halfway between these two points. The next man to enter will take the largest gap left, and sit roughly in the middle of that, and so on, until eventually the latest newcomer will be forced to select a seat that places him right next to one of the already seated men. Similar patterns can be observed in cinemas, public urinals, airplanes, trains and buses. This is a reflection of the

fact that we all carry with us, everywhere we go, a portable territory called a Personal Space. If people move inside this space, we feel threatened. If they keep too far outside it, we feel rejected. The result is a subtle series of spatial adjustments, usually operating quite unconsciously and producing ideal compromises as far as this is possible. If a situation becomes too crowded, then we adjust our reactions accordingly and allow our personal space to shrink. Jammed into an elevator, a rush-hour compartment, or a packed room, we give up altogether and allow body-to-body contact, but when we relinquish our Personal Space in this way, we adopt certain special techniques. In essence, what we do is to convert these other bodies into "nonpersons." We studiously ignore them, and they us. We try not to face them if we can possibly avoid it. We wipe all expressiveness from our faces, letting them go blank. We may look up at the ceiling or down at the floor, and we reduce body movements to a minimum. Packed together like sardines in a tin, we stand dumbly still, sending out as few social signals as possible.

Even if the crowding is less severe, we still tend to cut down our social interactions in the presence of large numbers. Careful observations of children in play groups revealed that if they are high-density groupings there is less social interaction between the individual children, even though there is theoretically more opportunity for such contacts. At the same time, the high-density groups show a higher frequency of aggressive and destructive behaviour patterns in their play. Personal Space — "elbow room" — is a vital commodity for the human animal, and one that cannot be ignored without risking serious trouble.

Of course, we all enjoy the excitement of being in a crowd, and this reaction cannot be ignored. But there are crowds and crowds. It is pleasant enough to be in a "spectator crowd," but not also appealing to find yourself in the middle of a rush-hour crush. The difference between the two is that the spectator crowd is all facing in the same direction and concentrating on a distant point of interest. Attending a theatre, there are twinges of rising hostility towards the stranger who sits down immediately in front of you or the one who squeezes into the seat next to you. The shared armrest can become a polite, but distinct, territorial boundary-dispute region. However, as soon as the show begins, these invasions of Personal Space are forgotten and the attention is focused beyond the small space where the crowding is taking place. Now, each member of the audience feels himself spatially related, not to his cramped neighbours, but to the actor on the stage, and this distance is, if anything, too great. In the rush-hour crowd, by contrast, each member of the pushing throng is competing with his neighbours all the time. There is no escape to a spatial relation with a distant actor, only the pushing, shoving bodies all around.

Those of us who have to spend a great deal of time in crowded conditions become gradually better able to adjust, but no one can ever become completely immune to invasions of Personal Space. This is because they remain forever associated with either powerful hostile or equally powerful loving feelings. All through our childhood we will have been held to be loved and held to be hurt, and anyone who invades our Personal Space when we are adults is, in effect, threatening to extend his behavior into one of these two highly charged areas of human interaction. Even if his motives are clearly neither hostile nor sexual, we still find it hard to suppress our reactions to his close approach. Unfortunately, different countries have different ideas about exactly how close is close. It is easy enough to test your own "space reaction": when you are talking to someone in the street or in any open space, reach out with your arm and see where the nearest point on his body comes. If you hail from western Europe, you will find that he is at roughly fingertip distance from you. In other words, as you reach out, your fingertips will just about make contact with his shoulder. If you come from eastern Europe, you will find you are standing at "wrist distance." If you come from the Mediterranean region, you will find that you are much closer to your companion, at little more than "elbow distance."

Trouble begins when a member of one of these cultures meets and talks to one from another. Say a British diplomat meets an Italian or an Arab diplomat at an embassy function. They start talking in a friendly way, but soon the fingertips man begins to feel uneasy. Without knowing quite why, he starts to back away gently from his companion. The companion edges forward again. Each tries in this way to set up a Personal Space relationship that suits his own background. But it is impossible to do. Every time the Mediterranean diplomat advances to a distance that feels comfortable for him, the British diplomat feels threatened. Every time the Briton moves back, the other feels rejected. Attempts to adjust this situation often lead to a talking pair shifting slowly across a room,

18

19

and many an embassy reception is dotted with western-European fingertip-distance men pinned against the walls by eager elbow-distance men. Until such differences are fully understood and allowances made, these minor differences in "body territories" will continue to act as an alienation factor which may interfere in a subtle way with diplomatic harmony and other forms of international transaction.

If there are distance problems when engaged in conversation, then there are clearly going to be even bigger difficulties where people must work privately in a shared space. Close proximity of others, pressing against the invisible boundaries of our personal body-territory, makes it difficult to concentrate on non-social matters. Flat-mates, students sharing a study, sailors in the cramped quarters of a ship, and office staff in crowded work-places, all have to face this problem. They solve it by "cocooning." They use a variety of devices to shut themselves off from the others present. The best possible cocoon, of course, is a small private room — a den, a private office, a study or a studio — which physically obscures the presence of other nearby territory-owners. This is the ideal situation for non-social work, but the space-sharers cannot enjoy this luxury. Their cocooning must be symbolic. They may, in certain cases, be able to erect small physical barriers, such as screens and partitions, which give substance to their invisible Personal Space boundaries, but when this cannot be done, other means must be sought. One of these is the "favoured object." Each space-sharer develops a preference, repeatedly expressed until it becomes a fixed pattern, for a particular chair, or table, or alcove. Others come to respect this, and friction is reduced. This system is often formally arranged (this is my desk, that is yours), but even where it is not, favoured places soon develop. Professor Smith has a favourite chair in the library. It is not formally his, but he always uses it and others avoid it. Seats around a messroom table, or a boardroom table, become almost personal property for specific individuals. Even in the home, father has his favourite chair for reading the newspaper or watching television. Another device is the blinkers-posture. Just as a horse that over-reacts to other horses and the distractions of the noisy race-course is given a pair of blinkers to shield its eyes, so people studying privately in a public place put on pseudo-blinkers in the form of shielding hands. Resting their elbows on the table, they sit with their hands screening their eyes from the scene on either side.

A third method of reinforcing the body-territory is to use per- 21 sonal markers. Books, papers and other personal belongings are scattered around the favoured site to render it more privately owned in the eyes of companions. Spreading out one's belongings is a well-known trick in public-transport situations, where a traveller tries to give the impression that seats next to him are taken. In many contexts carefully arranged personal markers can act as an effective territorial display, even in the absence of the territory owner. Experiments in a library revealed that placing a pile of magazines on the table in one seating position successfully reserved that place for an average of 77 minutes. If a sports-jacket was added, draped over the chair, then the "reservation effect" lasted for over two hours.

In these ways, we strengthen the defences of our Personal 22 Spaces, keeping out intruders with the minimum of open hostility. As with all territorial behaviour, the object is to defend space with signals rather than with fists and at all three levels — the tribal, the family and the personal — it is a remarkably efficient system of space-sharing. It does not always seem so, because newspapers and newscasts inevitably magnify the exceptions and dwell on those cases where the signals have failed and wars have broken out, gangs have fought, neighbouring families have feuded, or colleagues have clashed, but for every territorial signal that has failed, there are millions of others that have not. They do not rate a mention in the news, but they nevertheless constitute a dominant feature of human society — the society of a remarkably territorial animal.

Meanings and Values

1. What are the characteristics that enable you to classify this selection as formal, informal, or familiar? (See Guide to Terms: *Essay.*)

2a. What are some of the "socially valid" reasons that justify evicting a family from its home (par. 3)?

b. If you think there are no such valid reasons, justify your stand.

3a. List other subgroups that give members a "powerful feeling of security and importance" (par. 8).

b. What are the territorial signals of each group?

4a.   In one sentence, state the central theme of this selection. (Guide: *Unity*.)

b.   Does the writing have unity? Why, or why not?

5a.   What was the author's apparent purpose?

b.   How successfully does he accomplish this purpose?

c.   How worthwhile was it? Why?

Expository Techniques

1a.   Is this classification system logical, complete, and consistent in all respects? Cite any exceptions and state what is wrong.

b.   What other basis can you suggest for organizing the dicussion of the territorial behavior of humans? Which do you prefer? Why?

2a.   Into how many categories does the author divide the solutions of people sharing cramped living or working quarters?

b.   Cite two of the solutions in each division.

3a.   Demonstrate the value of using examples by eliminating them entirely from any one portion of this selection, leaving only the generalities.

b.   What would be the effect on the reader?

4a.   It is possible (but not very rewarding) to argue about whether this selection has a one-paragraph or a five-paragraph introduction. Assuming the latter to be the author's intention, which of the standard introductory techniques does he use? (Guide: *Introductions*.)

b.   How successfully does he perform the four potential functions of an introduction? Be specific.

Diction and Vocabulary

1.   How can you account for the unusual spelling of some of the words, such as "behaviour" (title), "defence" (par. 2), and "colours" (par. 11)?

2.   Why do you think the author considered the word "*displayed*" important enough to be italicized (par. 3)?

3a.   Of what might a "symbolic" exploding into battle consist (par. 4)?

b.   What makes some of the barriers listed in paragraph 20 "symbolic"?

c.   Explain how the uses of "symbolic" and "symbolically" in these paragraphs and in paragraphs 5, 7, and 11 are, or are not, consistent with the discussion of "symbol" in this book. (Guide: *Symbol*.)

4a.   What, if anything, is noteworthy about the diction or syntax of this selection? (Guide: *Diction and Syntax.*)

b.   To what extent, if at all, is Morris's writing characterized by his style? (Guide: *Style/Tone.*) You may want to compare his style, or lack of it, with that of an author previously read.

Suggestions for Writing and Discussion

1.   Select one of the subgroups listed in answering question 3 of "Meanings and Values" and discuss it more fully — explaining, perhaps, just what the members get out of belonging.

2.   The owners of a home also assert their dominance through subtle and unconscious actions as well as objects. Discuss these actions and explain why such asserted dominance is not resented by the average visitor.

3.   Most of Morris's discussion of family territory seems to refer to family-owned homes. What are the limitations on renters, especially of apartments, in displaying their territorial signals? To what extent do you suppose a desire for greater territorial display contributes to most people's dream of one day owning their own home?

(NOTE: Suggestions for topics requiring development by use of CLASSIFICATION follow.)

Writing Suggestions for Section 2
Classification

Use division and classification (into at least three categories) as your basic method of analyzing one of the following subjects from one interesting point of view. (Your instructor may have good reason to place limitations on your choice of subject.) Narrow the topic as necessary to enable you to do a thorough job.

1. College students.
2. College teachers.
3. Athletes.
4. Coaches.
5. Salespeople.
6. Hunters (or fishermen).
7. Parents.
8. Marijuana users.
9. Police officers.
10. Summer (or part-time) jobs.
11. Sailing vessels.
12. Horses (or other animals).
13. Television programs.
14. Motivations for study.
15. Methods of studying for exams.
16. Lies.
17. Selling techniques.
18. Tastes in clothes.
19. Contemporary music.
20. Love.
21. Immorality.
22. Attitudes toward life.

3

Explaining by Means of
Comparison and *Contrast*

One of the first expository methods we used as children was *comparison*, noticing similarities of objects, qualities, and actions, or *contrast*, noticing their differences. We compared the color of the new puppies with that of their mother, contrasted our father's height with our own. Then the process became more complicated. Now we employ it frequently in college essay examinations or term papers when we compare or contrast forms of government, reproductive systems of animals, or ethical philosophies of humans. Later, in the business or professional world, we may prepare important reports based on comparison and contrast — between kinds of equipment for purchase, the personnel policies of different departments, or precedents in legal matters. Nearly all people use the process, though they may not be aware of this, many times a day — in choosing a head of lettuce, in deciding what to wear to school, in selecting a house or a friend or a religion.

In the more formal scholastic and professional uses of comparison and contrast, however, an ordered plan is needed to avoid having a mere list of characteristics or a frustrating jumble of similarities and differences. If authors want to avoid communication blocks that will prevent their "getting through" to their readers, they will observe a few basic principles of selection and development. These principles apply mostly to comparisons between two subjects only; if three or more are to be considered, the usual method is to compare or contrast them in pairs.

A *logical* comparison or contrast can be made only between

subjects of the same general type. (Analogy, a special form of comparison used for another purpose, is discussed in the next section.) For example, contrasting a pine and a maple could be useful or meaningful, but little would be gained, except exercise in sentence construction, by contrasting the pine and the pansy.

Of course, logical but informal comparisons that are merely incidental to the basic structure, and hence follow no special pattern, may be made in any writing. Several of the preceding selections make limited use of comparison and contrast; Barber does some contrasting of presidential types, Lurie compares hats from different historical periods, and Morris uses some comparison between tribal territorial behavior now and in prehistoric times. But once committed to a formal, full-scale analysis by comparison and contrast, the careful writer ordinarily gives the subjects similar treatment. Points used for one should also be used for the other, and usually in the same order. All pertinent points should be explored — pertinent, that is, to the purpose of the comparison.

The purpose and the complexity of materials will usually indicate their arrangement and use. Sometimes the purpose is merely to point out *what* the likenesses and differences are, sometimes it is to show the *superiority* of one thing over another — or possibly to convince the reader of the superiority, as this is also a technique of argumentation. The purpose may be to explain the *unfamiliar* (wedding customs in Ethiopia) by comparing it to the *familiar* (wedding customs in Kansas). Or it may be to explain or emphasize some other type of *central idea*, as in most of the essays in this section.

One of the two basic methods of comparison is to present all the information on the two subjects, one at a time, and to summarize by combining their most important similarities and differences. This method may be desirable if there are few points to compare, or if the individual points are less important than the overall picture they present. Therefore, this procedure might be a satisfactory means of showing the relative difficulty of two college courses or of comparing two viewpoints concerning an automobile accident. (Of course, as in all other matters of expository arrangement, the last subject discussed is in the most emphatic position.)

However, if there are several points of comparison to be considered, or if the points are of individual importance, alternation of the material would be a better arrangement. Hence, in a detailed comparison of Oak Valley and Elm Hill hospitals, we might compare their sizes, locations, surgical facilities, staffs, and so on, always in the same order. To tell all about Oak Valley and then all about Elm Hill would create a serious communication block, requiring readers constantly to call on their memory of what was cited earlier or to turn back to the first group of facts again and again in order to make the meaningful comparisons that the author should have made for them.

Often the subject matter or the purpose itself will suggest a more casual treatment, or some combination or variation of the two basic methods. We might present the complete information on the first subject, then summarize it point by point within the complete information on the second. In other circumstances (as in "The Spider and the Wasp" in Section 5), it may be desirable simply to set up the thesis of likeness or difference, and then to explain a *process* that demonstrates this thesis. And although expository comparisons and contrasts are frequently handled together, it is sometimes best to present all similarities first, then all differences — or vice versa, depending on the emphasis desired. In argument, the arrangment we choose is that which best demonstrates the superiority of one thing (or plan of action) over another. This may mean a point-by-point contrast or the presentation of a weaker alternative before a stronger one.

In any basic use of comparison (conveniently, the term is most often used in a general sense to cover both comparison and contrast), the important thing is to have a plan that suits the purpose and material thoughtfully worked out in advance.

Sample Paragraph (Comparison/Contrast)

(Topic sentence of paragraph. Also a very vague generality, to be made more specific by examples.)

Comparison, noting likenesses, using the point-by-point method.

("Apple pie . . . art": metaphor.)

Who can tell what a town is really like by looking at it! Riverton is a prosperous place of 3,127 people, three miles from the river; ten miles further up, on the other side, is equally prosperous Eden, population, 3,120 people. Both places are good to look at, could easily be models for some apple-pie calendar art. And they are alike in another respect: nobody in either place knows what makes their people so different. Riverton's six churches

74

("Booze": colloquial usage, consistent only with an informal style.)

Transitional, to other side of contrast.
Contrast, noting differences. Discusses several aspects of one town, then turns to the other.

("Shady ladies": colloquial.)

Simple, direct use of *contrast*.

are full on Sundays and Wednesday nights. The sale of booze was banned in 1960; there are no dance halls, card games, or shady ladies. But anyone who wants a wilder time than the square dance sponsored monthly by the Town Board can always go up to Eden, where there's only one church, poorly attended and in need of paint, but five thriving taverns. Most of these feature shady ladies, dark dance floors, and wicked-looking card rooms in back. Several broad-minded couples even formed a "free-trade society" called the Swinging Dingles. But last year in Riverton when a new dentist tried to start a similar diversion, they promptly arrested him for disturbing the peace and took him to the county jail over on the coast.

MARK TWAIN

MARK TWAIN was the pen name of Samuel Clemens (1835–1910). He was born in Missouri and became the first author of importance to emerge from "beyond the Mississippi." Although best known for bringing humor, realism, and Western local color to American fiction, Mark Twain wanted to be remembered as a philosopher and social critic. Still widely read, in most languages and in all parts of the world, are his numerous short stories (his "tall tales," in particular), autobiographical accounts, and novels, especially *Adventures of Huckleberry Finn* (1884). Ernest Hemingway called the last "the best book we've had," an appraisal with which many critics agree.

Two Ways of Seeing a River

"Two Ways of Seeing a River" (editor's title) is from Mark Twain's "Old Times on the Mississippi," which was later expanded and published in book form as *Life on the Mississippi* (1883). It is autobiographical. The prose of this selection is vivid, as in all of Mark Twain's writing, but considerably more reflective in tone than most.

Now when I had mastered the language of this water and had come to know every trifling feature that bordered the great river as familiarly as I knew the letters of the alphabet, I had made a valuable acquisition. But I had lost something, too. I had lost something which could never be restored to me while I lived. All the grace, the beauty, the poetry, had gone out of the majestic river! I still kept in mind a certain wonderful sunset which I witnessed when steamboating was new to me. A broad expanse of the river was turned to blood; in the middle distance the red hue brightened into gold, through which a solitary log came floating, black and conspicuous; in one place a long, slanting mark lay sparkling upon the water; in another the surface was broken by boiling, tumbling rings that were as many-tinted as an opal; where the ruddy flush was faintest was a

1

smooth spot that was covered with graceful circles and radiating lines, ever so delicately traced; the shore on our left was densely wooded, and the somber shadow that fell from this forest was broken in one place by a long, ruffled trail that shone like silver; and high above the forest wall a clean-stemmed dead tree waved a single leafy bough that glowed like a flame in the unobstructed splendor that was flowing from the sun. There were graceful curves, reflected images, woody heights, soft distances, and over the whole scene, far and near, the dissolving lights drifted steadily, enriching it every passing moment with new marvels of coloring.

I stood like one bewitched. I drank it in, in a speechless rapture. 2 The world was new to me and I had never seen anything like this at home. But as I have said, a day came when I began to cease from noting the glories and the charms which the moon and the sun and the twilight wrought upon the river's face; another day came when I ceased altogether to note them. Then, if that sunset scene had been repeated, I should have looked upon it without rapture and should have commented upon it inwardly after this fashion: "This sun means that we are going to have wind to-morrow; that floating log means that the river is rising, small thanks to it; that slanting mark on the water refers to a bluff reef which is going to kill somebody's steamboat one of these nights, if it keeps on stretching out like that; those tumbling 'boils' show a dissolving bar and a changing channel there; the lines and circles in the slick water over yonder are a warning that that troublesome place is shoaling up dangerously; that silver streak in the shadow of the forest is the 'break' from a new snag and he has located himself in the very best place he could have found to fish for steamboats; that tall dead tree, with a single living branch, is not going to last long, and then how is a body ever going to get through this blind place at night without the friendly old landmark?"

No, the romance and beauty were all gone from the river. All 3 the value any feature of it had for me now was the amount of usefulness it could furnish toward compassing the safe piloting of a steamboat. Since those days, I have pitied doctors from my heart. What does the lovely flush in a beauty's cheek mean to a doctor but a "break" that ripples above some deadly disease? Are not all her visible charms sown thick with what are to him the signs and symbols of hidden decay? Does he ever see her beauty at all, or doesn't he simply view her professionally and comment upon her unwholesome condition all to himself? And doesn't he sometimes wonder whether he has gained most or lost most by learning his trade?

Meanings and Values

1. No selection could better illustrate the intimate relationship of several skills with which students of writing should be familiar, especially the potentials in "point of view" (and attitude), "style," and "tone."

a. What is the point of view in paragraph 1? (See Guide to Terms: *Point of View*.)

b. Where, and how, does it change in paragraph 2?

c. Why is the shift important to the author's contrast?

d. Show how the noticeable change of tone is related to this change in point of view. (Guide: *Style/Tone*.)

e. Specifically, what changes in style accompany the shift in tone and attitude?

f. How effectively do they all relate to the central theme itself? (Remember that such effects seldom just "happen"; the writer *makes* them happen.)

2a. Is the first paragraph primarily objective or subjective? (Guide: *Objective/Subjective*.)

b. How about the latter part of paragraph 2?

c. Are your answers to 2a and 2b related to point of view? If so, how?

3a. Does the author permit himself to engage in sentimentality? (Guide: *Sentimentality*.) If so, how could it have been avoided without damage to his theme's development?

b. If not, what restraints does the author use?

4. Do you think the last sentence refers only to doctors? Why, or why not?

5. List other vocations in which you assume (or perhaps know) that the beauty and romance eventually give way to practical realities; state briefly, for each, why this hardening should be expected.

Expository Techniques

1a. Where do you find a second comparison or contrast? Which is it?

b. Is the comparison/contrast made within itself, with something external, or both? Explain.

c.   Is this part of the writing closely enough related to the major con-
     trast to justify its use? Why or why not?

2a. In developing the numerous points of the major contrast, would an
     alternating, point-to-point system have been better? Why, or why
     not?

b.   Show how the author uses organization within the groups to assist
     in the overall contrast.

3a. What is the most noteworthy feature of syntax in paragraphs 1 and
     2? (Guide: *Syntax.*)

b.   How effectively does it perform the function intended?

4.   What is gained by the apparently deliberate decision to use rhetori-
     cal questions only toward the end? (Guide: *Rhetorical Questions.*)

Diction and Vocabulary

1.   Why would the colloquialism in the last sentence of paragraph 2
     have been inappropriate in the first paragraph? (Guide: *Colloquial
     Expressions.*)

2a. Compare the quality of metaphors in the quotation of paragraph 2
     with the quality of those preceding it. (Guide: *Figures of Speech.*)

b.   Is the difference justified: Why, or why not?

Suggestions for Writing and Discussion

1.   Select for further development one of the vocations in your answer
     to question 5 of "Meanings and Values." How would one's attitude
     be apt to change from the beginning romantic appeal?

2.   Show how, if at all, Mark Twain's contrast might be used to show
     parallels to life itself — e.g., differences in the idealism and atti-
     tudes of youth and maturity.

3.   Explore the possibility, citing examples if possible, of being able to
     retain *both* the "rapture" and the "usefulness."

(NOTE: Suggestions for topics requiring development by use of COMPARI-
         SON and CONTRAST are on page 109, at the end of this section.)

BRUCE CATTON

Bruce Catton (1899–1978) was a Civil War specialist whose early career included reporting for various newspapers. In 1954 he received both the Pulitzer Prize for historical work and the National Book Award. He served as director of information for the United States Department of Commerce and wrote many books, including *Mr. Lincoln's Army* (1951), *Glory Road* (1952), *A Stillness at Appomattox* (1953), *The Hallowed Ground* (1956), *America Goes to War* (1958), *The Coming Fury* (1961), *Terrible Swift Sword* (1963), *Never Call Retreat* (1966), *Waiting for the Morning Train: An American Boyhood* (1972), and *Gettysburg: The Final Fury* (1974). For five years, Catton edited *American Heritage*.

Grant and Lee: A Study in Contrasts

"Grant and Lee: A Study in Contrasts" was written as a chapter of *The American Story*, a collection of essays by noted historians. In this study, as in most of his other writing, Catton does more than recount the facts of history: he shows the significance within them. It is a carefully constructed essay, using contrast and comparison as the entire framework for his explanation.

When Ulysses S. Grant and Robert E. Lee met in the parlor of a   1
modest house at Appomattox Court House, Virginia, on April 9, 1865, to work out the terms for the surrender of Lee's Army of Northern Virginia, a great chapter in American life came to a close, and a great new chapter began.

These men were bringing the Civil War to its virtual finish. To   2
be sure, other armies had yet to surrender, and for a few days the fugitive Confederate government would struggle desperately and vainly, trying to find some way to go on living now that its chief support was gone. But in effect it was all over when Grant and Lee

signed the papers. And the little room where they wrote out the terms was the scene of one of the poignant, dramatic contrasts in American History.

They were two strong men these oddly different generals, and they represented the strengths of two conflicting currents that, through them, had come into final collision.

Back of Robert E. Lee was the notion that the old aristocratic concept might somehow survive and be dominant in American life.

Lee was tidewater Virginia, and in his background were family, culture, and tradition . . . the age of chivalry transplanted to a New World which was making its own legends and its own myths. He embodied a way of life that had come down through the age of knighthood and the English country squire. America was a land that was beginning all over again, dedicated to nothing much more complicated than the rather hazy belief that all men had equal rights and should have an equal chance in the world. In such a land Lee stood for the feeling that it was somehow of advantage to human society to have a pronounced inequality in the social structure. There should be a leisure class, backed by ownership of land; in turn, society itself should be keyed to the land as the chief source of wealth and influence. It would bring forth (according to this ideal) a class of men with a strong sense of obligation to the community; men who lived not to gain advantage for themselves, but to meet the solemn obligations which had been laid on them by the very fact that they were privileged. From them the country would get its leadership; to them it could look for the higher values — of thought, of conduct, or personal deportment — to give it strength and virtue.

Lee embodied the noblest elements of this aristocratic ideal. Through him, the landed nobility justified itself. For four years, the Southern states had fought a desperate war to uphold the ideals for which Lee stood. In the end, it almost seemed as if the Confederacy fought for Lee; as if he himself was the Confederacy . . . the best thing that the way of life for which the Confederacy stood could ever have to offer. He had passed into legend before Appomattox. Thousands of tired, underfed, poorly clothed Confederate soldiers, long since past the simple enthusiasm of the early days of the struggle, somehow considered Lee the symbol of everything for which they had been willing to die. But they could not quite put this feeling into words. If the Lost Cause, sanctified by so much heroism and so many deaths, had a living justification, its justification was General Lee.

Grant, the son of a tanner on the Western frontier, was everything Lee was not. He had come up the hard way and embodied nothing in particular except the eternal toughness and sinewy fiber of the men who grew up beyond the mountains. He was one of a body of men who owed reverence and obeisance to no one, who were self-reliant to a fault, who cared hardly anything for the past but who had a sharp eye for the future.

These frontier men were the precise opposites of the tidewater aristocrats. Back of them, in the great surge that had taken people over the Alleghenies and into the opening Western country, there was a deep, implicit dissatisfaction with a past that had settled into grooves. They stood for democracy, not from any reasoned conclusion about the proper ordering of human society, but simply because they had grown up in the middle of democracy and knew how it worked. Their society might have privileges, but they would be privileges each man had won for himself. Forms and patterns meant nothing. No man was born to anything, except perhaps to a chance to show how far he could rise. Life was competition.

Yet along with this feeling had come a deep sense of belonging to a national community. The Westerner who developed a farm, opened a shop, or set up in business as a trader could hope to prosper only as his own community prospered — and his community ran from the Atlantic to the Pacific and from Canada down to Mexico. If the land was settled, with towns and highways and accessible markets, he could better himself. He saw his fate in terms of the nation's own destiny. As its horizons expanded, so did his. He had, in other words, an acute dollars-and-cents stake in the continued growth and development of his country.

And that, perhaps, is where the contrast between Grant and Lee becomes most striking. The Virginia aristocrat, inevitably, saw himself in relation to his own region. He lived in a static society which could endure almost anything except change. Instinctively, his first loyalty would go to the locality in which that society existed. He would fight to the limit of endurance to defend it, because in defending it he was defending everything that gave his own life its deepest meaning.

The Westerner, on the other hand, would fight with an equal tenacity for the broader concept of society. He fought so because everything he lived by was tied to growth, expansion, and a constantly widening horizon. What he lived by would survive or fall with the nation itself. He could not possibly stand by unmoved in the face of an attempt to destroy the Union. He would combat it with everything he had, because he could only see it as an effort to cut the ground out from under his feet.

So Grant and Lee were in complete contrast, representing two 12 diametrically opposed elements in American life. Grant was the modern man emerging; beyond him, ready to come on the stage, was the great age of steel and machinery, of crowded cities and a restless burgeoning vitality. Lee might have ridden down from the old age of chivalry, lance in hand, silken banner fluttering over his head. Each man was the perfect champion of his cause, drawing both his strengths and his weaknesses from the people he led.

Yet it was not all contrast, after all. Different as they were — in 13 background, in personality, in underlying aspiration — these two great soldiers had much in common. Under everything else, they were marvelous fighters. Furthermore, their fighting qualities were really very much alike.

Each man had, to begin with, the great virtue of utter tenacity 14 and fidelity. Grant fought his way down the Mississippi Valley in spite of acute personal discouragement and profound military handicaps. Lee hung on in the trenches at Petersburg after hope itself had died. In each man there was an indomitable quality . . . the born fighter's refusal to give up as long as he can still remain on his feet and lift his two fists.

Daring and resourcefulness they had, too: the ability to think 15 faster and move faster than the enemy. These were the qualities which gave Lee the dazzling campaigns of Second Manassas and Chancellorsville and won Vicksburg for Grant.

Lastly, and perhaps greatest of all, there was the ability, at the 16 end, to turn quickly from war to peace once the fighting was over. Out of the way these two men behaved at Appomattox came the possibility of a peace of reconciliation. It was a possibility not wholly realized, in the years to come, but which did, in the end, help the two sections to become one nation again . . . after a war whose bitterness might have seemed to make such a reunion wholly impossible. No part of either man's life became him more than the part he played in their brief meeting in the McLean house at Appomattox. Their behavior there put all succeeding generations of Americans in their debt. Two great Americans, Grant and Lee — very different, yet under everything very much alike. Their encounter at Appomattox was one of the great moments of American history.

Meanings and Values

1a. Clarify the assertions that through Lee "the landed nobility justified itself" and that "if the Lost Cause . . . had a living justification," it was General Lee (par. 6).

b. Why are these assertions pertinent to the central theme?

2a. Does it seem reasonable that "thousands of tired, underfed, poorly clothed Confederate soldiers" (par. 6) had been willing to fight for the aristocratic system in whch they would never have had even a chance to be aristocrats? Why, or why not?

b. Can you think of more likely reasons why they were willing to fight?

3. Under any circumstances today might such a social structure as the South's be best for a country? Explain.

4a. What countries of the world have recently been so torn by internal war and bitterness that reunion has seemed, or still seems, impossible?

b. Do you see any basic differences between the trouble in those countries and that in America at the time of the Civil War?

5a. The author calls Lee a symbol (par. 6). Was Grant also a symbol? If so, of what? (See Guide to Terms: *Symbol*.)

b. How would you classify this kind of symbolism?

Expository Techniques

1. Make an informal list of paragraph numbers from 3 to 16, and note by each number whether the paragraph is devoted primarily to Lee, to Grant, or to direct comparison or contrast of the two. This chart will show you Catton's basic pattern of development. (Notice, for instance, how the broad information of paragraphs 4–6 and 7–9 seems almost to "funnel" down through the narrower summaries in paragraphs 10 and 11 and into paragraph 12, where the converging elements meet and the contrast is made specific.)

2. What new technique of development is started in paragraph 13?

3a. What is gained, or lost, by using one sentence for paragraph 3?

b. For paragraph 4?

4a. How many paragraphs does the introduction comprise?

b. How successfully does it fulfill the three basic requirements of a good introduction? (Guide: *Introductions.*)

5. Show how Catton has constructed the beginning of each paragraph so that there is a smooth transition from the one preceding it. (Guide: *Transition.*)

6. The author's conclusion is really only the explanation of one of his integral points — and this method, if not carefully planned, runs the risk of ending too abruptly and leaving the reader unsatisfied. How has Catton avoided this hazard? (Guide: *Closings.*)

7a. What seems to be the author's attitude toward Grant and Lee?

b. Show how his tone reflects this attitude. (Guide: *Style/Tone.*)

Diction and Vocabulary

1. Why would a use of colloquialisms have been inconsistent with the tone of this writing?

2a. List or mark all metaphors in paragraphs 1, 3, 5, 7–11, 16. (Guide: *Figures of Speech.*)

b. Comment on their general effectiveness.

3. If you are not already familiar with the following words, study their meanings as given in the dictionary and as used in this essay: virtual, poignant (par. 2); concept (4); sinewy, obeisance (7); implicit (8); tenacity (11); diametrically, burgeoning (12); aspiration (13); fidelity, profound, indomitable (14); succeeding (16).

4. Explain how the word "poignant" aptly describes this contrast of two men (par. 2).

Suggestions for Writing and Discussion

1. Find, by minor research, an incident in the life of Grant or Lee that will, in suitable essay form, illustrate one of Catton's points.

2. Select some other dramatic moment in history and show its long-range significance.

3. Select some important moment in your life and show its long-range significance.

4. Explain how someone you know symbolizes a philosophy or way of life.

(NOTE: Suggestions for topics requiring development by use of COMPARI-SON and CONTRAST are on page 109, at the end of this section.)

ANNE ROIPHE

ANNE RICHARDSON ROIPHE (born 1935) is a native New Yorker.
After graduating from Sarah Lawrence, she pursued further stud-
ies in Munich, Germany. Upon her return to the United States,
Roiphe worked for a public relations firm and did research for
Forbes. Her first novel, *Digging Out*, published in 1968, was met
with great enthusiasm. She has since published *Up the Sandbox*
(1971), which was made into a movie, *Long Division* (1973), and
Torch Song (1977). Her articles appear frequently in *Vogue* and *The
New York Times Magazine*.

Confessions of a Female Chauvinist Sow

"Confessions of a Female Chauvinist Sow" first appeared in *New
York* magazine. This is an informal essay (which some would
classify as "familiar"), and the author uses personal examples
liberally to illustrate her central theme. It is a theme, however,
that depends directly on comparison and contrast for its primary
development.

I once married a man I thought was totally unlike my father and I   1
imagined a whole new world of freedom emerging. Five years later
it was clear even to me — floating face down in a wash of despair —
that I had simply chosen a replica of my handsome daddy-true. The
updated version spoke English like an angel but — good God! —
underneath he was my father exactly: wonderful, but not the right
man for me.

Most people I know have at one time or another been fouled up   2
by their childhood experiences. Patterns tend to sink into the unconscious only to reappear, disguised, unseen, like marionette
strings, pulling us this way or that. Whatever ails people — keeps
them up at night, tossing and turning — also ails movements no
matter how historically huge or politically important. The women's

movement cannot remake consciousness, or reshape the future, without acknowledging and shedding all the unnecessary and ugly baggage of the past. It's easy enough now to see where men have kept us out of clubs, baseball games, graduate schools; it's easy enough to recognize the hidden directions that limit Sis to cake-baking and Junior to bridge-building; it's now possible for even Miss America herself to identify what *they* have done to us, and, of course, *they* have and *they* did and *they* are. . . . But along the way we also developed our own hidden prejudices, class assumptions and an anti-male humor and collection of expectations that gave us, like all oppressed groups, a secret sense of superiority (co-existing with a poor self-image — it's not news that people can believe two contradictory things at once).

Listen to any group that suffers materially and socially. They   3
have a lexicon with which they tease the enemy: ofay, goy, honky, gringo. "Poor pale devils," said Malcolm X loud enough for us to hear, although blacks had joked about that to each other for years. Behind some of the women's liberation thinking lurk the rumors, the prejudices, the defense systems of generations of oppressed women whispering in the kitchen together, presenting one face to their menfolk and another to their card clubs, their mothers and sisters. All this is natural enough but potentially dangerous in a revolutionary situation in which you hope to create a future that does not mirror the past. The hidden anti-male feelings, a result of the old system, will foul us up if they are allowed to persist.

During my teen years I never left the house on my Saturday   4
night dates without my mother slipping me a few extra dollars — mad money, it was called. I'll explain what it was for the benefit of the new generation in which people just sleep with each other: the fellow was supposed to bring me home, lead me safely through the asphalt jungle, protect me from slithering snakes, rapists and the like. But my mother and I knew young men were apt to drink too much, to slosh down so many rye-and-gingers that some hero might well lead me in front of an oncoming bus, smash his daddy's car into Tiffany's window, or, less gallantly, throw up on my new dress. Mad money was for getting home on your own, no matter what form of insanity your date happened to evidence. Mad money was also a wallflower's rope ladder; if the guy you came with suddenly fancied someone else, well, you didn't have to stay there and suffer, you could go home. Boys were fickle and likely to be

unkind; my mother and I knew that, as surely as we knew they tried to make you do things in the dark they wouldn't respect you for afterwards, and in fact would spread the word and spoil your rep. Boys liked to be flattered; if you made them feel important, they would eat out of your hand. So talk to them about their interests, don't alarm them with displays of intelligence — we all knew that, we groups of girls talking into the wee hours of the night in a kind of easy companionship we thought impossible with boys. Boys were prone to have a good time, get you pregnant, and then pretend they didn't know your name when you came knocking on their door for finances or comfort. In short, we believed boys were less moral than we were. They appeared to be hypocritical, self-seeking, exploitative, untrustworthy and very likely to be showing off their precious masculinity. I never had a girl friend I thought would be unkind or embarrass me in public. I never expected a girl to lie to me about her marks or sports skill or how good she was in bed. Altogether — without anyone's directly coming out and saying so — I gathered that men were sexy, powerful, very interesting, but not very nice, not very moral, humane and tender, like us. Girls played fairly while men, unfortunately, reserved their honor for the battlefield.

Why are there laws insisting on alimony and child support?   5
Well, everyone knows that men don't have an instinct to protect their young and, given half a chance, with the moon in the right phase, they will run off and disappear. Everyone assumes a mother will not let her child starve, yet it is necessary to legislate that a father must not do so. We are taught to accept the idea that men are less than decent; their charms may be manifold but their characters are riddled with faults. To this day I never blink if I hear that a man has gone to find his fortune in South America, having left his pregnant wife, his blind mother and taken the family car. I still gasp in horror when I hear of a woman leaving her asthmatic infant for a rock group in Taos because I can't seem to avoid the assumption that men are naturally heels and women the ordained carriers of what little is moral in our dubious civilization.

My mother never gave me mad money thinking I would ditch a   6
fellow for some other guy or that I would pass out drunk on the floor. She knew I would be considerate of my companion because, after all, I was more mature than the boys that gathered about. Why was I more mature? Women just are people-oriented; they learn to

be empathetic at an early age. Most English students (students interested in humanity, not artifacts) are women. Men and boys — so the myth goes — conceal their feelings and lose interest in anybody else's. Everyone knows that even little boys can tell the difference between one kind of a car and another — proof that their souls are mechanical, their attention directed to the non-human.

I remember shivering in the cold vestibule of a famous men's athletic club. Women and girls are not permitted inside the club's door. What are they doing in there, I asked? They're naked, said my mother, they're sweating, jumping up and down a lot, telling each other dirty jokes and bragging about their stock market exploits. Why can't we go in? I asked. Well, my mother told me, they're afraid we'd laugh at them.

The prejudices of childhood are hard to outgrow. I confess that every time my business takes me past that club, I shudder. Images of large bellies resting on massage tables and flaccid penises rising and falling with the Dow Jones average flash through my head. There it is, chauvinism waving its cancerous tentacles from the depths of my psyche.

Minorities automatically feel superior to the oppressor because, after all, they are not hurting anybody. In fact, they feel morally better. The old canard that women need love, men need sex — believed for too long by both sexes — attributes moral and spiritual superiority to women and makes of men beasts whose urges send them prowling into the night. This false division of good and bad, placing deforming pressures on everyone, doesn't have to contaminate the future. We know that the assumptions we make about each other become a part of the cultural air we breathe and, in fact, become social truths. Women who want equality must be prepared to give it and to believe in it, and in order to do that, it is not enough to state that you are as good as any man, but also it must be stated that he is as good as you and both will be humans together. If we want men to share in the care of the family in a new way, we must assume them as capable of consistent loving tenderness as we.

I rummage about and find in my thinking all kinds of anti-male prejudices. Some are just jokes and others I will have a hard time abandoning. First, I share an emotional conviction with many sisters that women given power would not create wars. Intellectually I know that's ridiculous; great queens have waged war before; the likes of Lurleen Wallace, Pat Nixon and Mrs. General Lavelle can be depended upon in the future to guiltlessly condemn to death other people's children in the name of some ideal of their own. Little girls, of course, don't take toy guns out of their hip pockets and say "Pow, pow" to all their neighbors and friends like the average well-adjusted little boy. However, if we gave little girls the six-shooters, we would soon have double the pretend body count.

Aggression is not, as I secretly think, a male-sex-linked characteristic: brutality is masculine only by virtue of opportunity. True, there are 1,000 Jack the Rippers for every Lizzie Borden, but that surely is the result of social forms. Women as a group are indeed more masochistic than men. The practical result of this division is that women seem nicer and kinder, but when the world changes, women will have a fuller opportunity to be just as rotten as men and there will be fewer claims of female moral superiority.   11

Now that I am entering early middle age, I hear many women complaining of husbands and ex-husbands who are attracted to younger females. This strikes the older woman as unfair, of course. But I remember a time when I thought all boys around my age and grade were creeps and bores. I wanted to go out with an older man: a senior or, miraculously, a college man. I had a certain contempt for my coevals, not realizing that the freshman in college I thought so desirable, was some older girl's creep. Some women never lose that contempt for men of their own age. That isn't fair either and may be one reason why some sensible men of middle years find solace in young women.   12

I remember coming home from school one day to find my mother's card game dissolved in hysterical laughter. The cards were floating in black rivers of running mascara. What was so funny? A woman named Helen was lying on a couch pretending to be her husband with a cold. She was issuing demands for orange juice, aspirin, suggesting a call to a specialist, complaining of neglect, of fate's cruel finger, of heat, of cold, of sharp pains on the bridge of the nose that might indicate brain involvement. What was so funny? The ladies explained to me that all men behave just like that with colds, they are reduced to temper tantrums by simple nasal congestion, men cannot stand any little physical discomfort — on and on the laughter went.   13

The point of this vignette is the nature of the laughter — us laughing at them, us feeling superior to them, us ridiculing them behind their backs. If they were doing it to us, we'd call it male   14 chauvinist pigness; if we do it to them, it is inescapably female chauvinist sowness and, whatever its roots, it leads to the same isolation. Boys are messy, boys are mean, boys are rough, boys are stupid and have sloppy handwriting. A cacophony of childhood memories rushes through my head, balanced, of course, by all the well-documented feelings of inferiority and envy. But the important thing, the hard thing, is to wipe the slate clean, to start again without the meanness of the past. That's why it's so important that the women's movement not become anti-male and allow its most prejudiced spokesmen total leadership. The much-chewed-over abortion issue illustrates this. The women's-liberation position, insisting on a woman's right to determine her own body's destiny, leads in fanatical extreme to a kind of emotional immaculate conception in which the father is not judged even half-responsible — he has no rights, and no consideration is to be given to his concern for either the woman or the fetus.

Woman, who once was abandoned and disgraced by an unwanted pregnancy, has recently arrived at a new pride of ownership or disposal. She has traveled in a straight line that still excludes her sexual partner from an equal share in the wanted or unwanted pregnancy. A better style of life may develop from an assumption that men are as human as we. Why not ask the child's father if he would like to bring up the child? Why not share decisions, when possible, with the male? If we cut them out, assuming an old-style indifference on their part, we perpetrate the ugly divisiveness that has characterized relations between the sexes so far.

Hard as it is for many of us to believe, women are not really superior to men in intelligence or humanity — they are only equal.

Meanings and Values

1a. How would you describe the author's point of view in this selection? (See Guide to Terms: *Point of View*.)

b. How did the tone help determine your answer? (Guide: *Style/Tone*.)

2. In the last sentence of paragraph 2 there is an example of irony. (Guide: *Irony*.)

a. What kind is it?

b. Could it also be used to illustrate the meaning of "paradox"? (Guide: *Paradox*.) Why, or why not?

3a. Exactly what is the "myth" with which Roiphe is primarily concerned?

b. Is it explained more by comparison or by contrast?

c. Which aspects of it, if any, do young women of your acquaintance still seem to believe? Explain.

4. Show the special significance, in relation to the theme, of the author's mother's last answer in paragraph 7.

5. How is it possible, if at all, to "guiltlessly" condemn to death other people's children (par. 10)?

Expository Techniques

1. The central theme of this essay becomes clear more slowly than in most expository writings. (Guide: *Unity.*)

a. At what point did you first become aware of it?

b. Where is it first clearly stated?

c. Is this statement specific or general? (Guide: *Specific/General.*)

d. What is the primary function of the rest of the essay?

2a. Is the further development accomplished more by comparison or by contrast? Explain.

b. Cite paragraphs by which your answer to question 2a can best be illustrated.

c. Which pattern of exposition previously studied does the author use more freely in her comparison/contrast? How effectively?

3. Which of the standard means of introducing an exposition are used in this essay? (Guide: *Introduction.*)

4a. Examples of both rhetorical and nonrhetorical questions can be found in paragraphs 6 and 7. (Guide: *Rhetorical Questions.*) Identify one of each and show the difference.

b. Cite one further question used as a rhetorical device.

5a. Cite two examples of parallel structure in paragraph 14. (Guide: *Parallel Structure.*)

b. What advantage, if any, is gained by use of this technique?

6. How effective is the brief closing paragraph? (Guide: *Closings.*) Why?

Diction and Vocabulary

1a. What is the significance of the word "sow," as used in the title?

b. How, if at all, is this significance a matter of connotation? (Guide: *Connotation/Denotation.*)

2a.   Cite five figures of speech that you consider particularly effective. (Guide: *Figures of Speech.*)

b.   Indicate the kind of each.

3a.   Which, if any, of the author's figures of speech could also be classed as a cliché? (Guide: *Clichés.*)

b.   If there are any clichés, is their use justified here? Why, or why not?

4.   Would you consider any of the author's expressions colloquial? (Guide: *Colloquial Expressions.*) If so, which?

5.   Explain briefly how your answers to questions 2–4 are related to matters of style. (Guide: *Style/Tone.*)

6.   Use the dictionary as necessary to understand the meanings of the following words: lexicon (par. 3); empathetic, artifacts (6); flaccid (8); chauvinism (8, 14); canard (9); masochistic (11); coevals, solace (12); vignette, cacophony (14).

Suggestions for Writing and Discussion

1.   Show by use of examples that it is also possible in other matters to "believe two contradictory things at once" (par. 2).

2.   Has it been your observation that girls are less likely than boys to embarrass one in public or lie about such things as grades or sexual prowess (par. 4)? Explain the difference, if any.

3.   What justification is there for laws forcing men to pay alimony and/or child support (par. 5)?

4.   Is there any *natural* reason that mothers are less apt to desert their children than fathers? In your estimation, is one desertion more reprehensible than the other? Explain.

5.   Explore the author's assertion (par. 11) that women are more masochistic than men.

6.   If applicable, select any one aspect of Roiphe's "myth" about men-women differences and show why you still consider the difference more fact than myth.

(NOTE: Suggestions for topics requiring development by use of COMPARISON and CONTRAST are on page 109, at the end of this section.)

ROBERT JASTROW

Robert Jastrow was born in 1925, in New York City. He received his B.A., M.A., and Ph.D. from Columbia University. He is currently professor of astronomy and geology at Columbia and professor of earth science at Dartmouth College. He was formerly director of the Goddard Institute for Space Studies. As an author, he is best known for his textbook (with Malcolm H. Thompson) *Astronomy: Fundamentals and Frontiers* (1972) and for a trilogy of books tracing the development of the universe and the evolution of intelligence: *Red Giants and White Dwarfs* (1967), *Until the Sun Dies* (1977), and *The Enchanted Loom* (1981).

Brains and Computers

In this chapter from *The Enchanted Loom*, Jastrow uses a comparison and contrast pattern to present a surprisingly clear explanation of a subject that is quite complicated but that is nonetheless of interest to most readers. By making careful use of examples and definitions within the overall comparison framework, Jastrow manages to keep even the most technical parts of the selection readable and interesting.

Circuits, wires and computing are strange terms to use for a biological organ like the brain, made largely of water, and without electronic parts. Nonetheless, they are accurate terms because brains work in very much the same way as computers. Brains think; computers add and subtract; but both devices seem to work on the basis of the same fundamental steps in logical reasoning.

All arithmetic and mathematics can be broken down into these fundamental steps. Most kinds of thinking can also be broken down into such steps. Only the highest realms of creative activity seem to defy this analysis, but it is possible that even creative thinking could be broken down in this way, if the subconscious mind could be penetrated to examine the processes that appear at the conscious level as the flash of insight, or the stroke of genius.

The basic logical steps that underlie all mathematics and all   3
reasoning are surprisingly simple. The most important ones are called AND and OR. AND is a code name for the reasoning that says, "If 'a' is true *and* 'b' is true, then 'c' is true." OR is a code name for the reasoning that says, "IF 'a' is true *or* 'b' is true, then 'c' is true." These lines of reasoning are converted into electrical circuits by means of devices called "gates." In a computer the gates are made out of electronic parts — diodes or transistors. In the brain of an animal or a human, the gates are neurons or nerve cells. A gate — in a computer or in a brain — is an electrical pathway that opens up and allows electricity to pass through when certain conditions are satisfied. Normally, two wires go into one side of the gate, and another wire emerges from the other side of the gate. The two wires coming into the gate on one side represent the two ideas "a" *and* "b". The wire going out the other side of the gate represents the conclusion "c" based on these ideas. When a gate is wired up to be an AND gate, it works in such a way that if electrical signals flow into it from both the "a" and "b" wires, an electrical signal then flows out the other side through the "c" wire. From an electrical point of view, this is the same as saying, "If 'a' *and* 'b' are true, then 'c' is true."

When the gate is wired as an OR gate, on the other hand, it   4
permits electricity to pass through the outgoing, or "c", wire if an electrical signal comes into the other side through either the "a" wire *or* the "b" wire. Electrically, this is the same as saying, "If 'a' *or* 'b' is true, then 'c' is true."

How do these two kinds of gates do arithmetic? How do they   5
carry on a line of reasoning? Suppose a computer is about to add "1" and "1" to make "2"; this means that inside the computer a gate has two wires coming into it on one side, representing "1" and "1", and a wire coming out on the other side, representing "2". If the gate is wired as an AND gate, then, when electrical signals come into it through both of the "1" wires, it sends a signal out the other side through the "2" wire. This gate has added "1" and "1" electrically to make "2".

Slightly different kinds of gates, but based on the same idea,   6 can subtract, multiply and divide. Thousands of such gates, wired together in different combinations, can do income tax returns, algebra problems and higher mathematics. They can also be connected together to do the kinds of thinking and reasoning that enter into everyday life. Suppose, for example, that a company distributes several different lines of goods, and its management assigns a computer the task of keeping a continuous check on the inventories in these various product lines. Inside that computer, certain gates will be wired as AND gates to work in the following way: two wires coming into one side of the gate carry signals that indicate "stock depleted" and "sales volume heavy." If the stock is depleted *and* the sales are brisk, the gate opens, and a decision comes through: Order more goods!

OR gates are just as important in reasoning. Suppose that the same company also relies on its computer for guidance in setting prices. That means that a certain gate inside the computer is wired as an OR gate; coming into one side of this gate is a wire that idicates cash flow, another wire that indicates prices charged by a competitor for similar products, and a third wire that indicates the inventory in this particular product. If the company needs cash, *or* it is being undersold by its competitors, *or* it has an excess inventory, then the decision gate opens and a command comes through: Cut prices!

In a simple computer, the gates are wired together permanently, so that the computer can only do the same tasks over and over again. This kind of computer comes into the world wired to do one set of things, and can never depart from its fixed repertoire. A computer that solves the same problems in the same way, over and over again, is like a frog that can only snap at dark, moving spots; if either kind of brain is presented with a novel situation, it will react stupidly, or not react at all, because it lacks the wiring necessary for a new response to a new challenge. Such brains are unintelligent.

Larger, more complex computers have greater flexibility. In these computers, the connections between the gates can be changed, and they can be wired up to do different kinds of things at different times; their repertoire is variable. The instructions for connecting the gates to do each particular kind of problem are stored in the computer's memory banks. These instructions are called the computer's "program." When a computer expert wants his machine to stop one kind of task and start another, he inserts a new program into the computer's memory. The new program automatically erases the old one, takes command of the machine, and sets about doing its appointed task.

However, this computer is still not intelligent; it has no innate flexibility. The flexibility and intelligence reside in its programmer. But if the memory banks of the computer are extremely large a great advance in computer design becomes possible, that marks a highlight in the evolution of computers comparable to the first appearance of the mammals on the earth. A computer with a very large memory can store a set of instructions lengthy enough to permit it to learn by experience, just like an intelligent animal. Learning by experience requires a large memory and a very long set of instructions, i.e., a complicated program, because it is a much more elaborate way of solving problems than a stereotyped response would be. When a brain — electronic or animal — learns by experience, it goes through the following steps: first, it tries an approach; then it compares its result with the desired result, i.e., the goal; then, if it succeeds in achieving its goal, it sends an instruction to its memory to use the same approach next time; in the case of failure, it searches through its reasoning or computations to pinpoint the main source of error; finally, the brain adjusts the faulty part of its program to bring the result into line with its desires. Every time the same problem arises, the brain repeats the sequence and makes new adjustments to its program. A large computer has programs that work in just that fashion. Like a brain, it modifies its reasoning as its experience develops. In this way, the computer gradually improves its performance. It is learning.

A brain that can learn possesses the beginnings of intelligence. The requirements for this invaluable trait are, first, a good-sized memory, and, second, a wiring inside the brain that permits the circuits connecting the gates to be changed by the experience of life. In fact, in the best brains — judging brain quality entirely by intelligence — many circuits are unwired initially; that is, the animal is born with a large number of the gates in its brain more or less unconnected with one another. The gates become connected gradually, as the animal learns the best strategies for its survival. In man, the part of the brain filled with blank circuits at birth is greater than in any other animal; that is what is meant by the plasticity of human behavior.

Large computers have some essential attributes of an intelligent   12
brain: they have large memories, and they have gates whose connections can be modified by experience. However, the thinking of
these computers tends to be narrow. The richness of human
thought depends to a considerable degree on the enormous number
of wires, or nerve fibers coming into each gate in the human brain. A
gate in a computer has two, or three, or at most four wires entering
on one side, and one wire coming out the other side. In the brain of
an animal, the gates may have thousands of wires entering one side,
instead of two or three. In the human brain, a gate may have as
many as 100,000 wires entering it. Each wire comes from another
gate or nerve cell. This means that every gate in the human brain is
connected to as many as 100,000 other gates in other parts of the
brain. During the process of thinking innumerable gates open and
close throughout the brain. When one of these gates "decides" to
open, the decision is the result of a complicated assessment involving inputs from thousands of other gates. This circumstance explains much of the difference between human thinking and computer thinking.

Furthermore, the gates in the brains of an animal or a human do   13
not work on an "all-or-nothing" basis. The AND gate in a computer,
for example, will only open if *all* the wires coming into it carry
electrical signals. If one wire entering a computer gate fails to carry a
signal, the gate remains shut. If every one of the 100,000 pathways
into a gate in a human brain had to transmit an electrical signal
before that gate could open, the brain would be paralyzed. Instead,
most gates in the brain work on the principle of ALMOST, rather
than AND or OR. The ALMOST gate makes human thought so
imprecise, but so powerful. Suppose that 50,000 wires enter one
side of a gate in a human brain; if this were an AND gate in a
computer, all 50,000 things would have to be true simultaneously
before that gate opened and let a signal through. In real life, 50,000
things are rarely true at the same time, and any brain that waited for
such a high degree of assurance before it acted would be an exceedingly slow brain. It would hardly ever reach a decision, and the
possessor of a brain like that would not be likely to pass its genes on
to the next generation.

Real brains work very differently. Wired largely out of   14
ALMOST gates, they only require that, say, 10,000 or 15,000 things

out of 50,000 shall be true about a situation before they act, or perhaps an even smaller number than that. As a consequence, they are inaccurate; they make mistakes sometimes; but they are very fast. In the struggle for survival, the value to the individual of the speed of such a brain more than offsets the disadvantages in its imprecision.

Meanings and Values

1a.   Is the purpose of this essay to explain something about computers, or about brains, or about both? (See Guide to Terms: *Purpose*.)

 b.   State in one sentence the central theme of this selection. (Guide: *Unity*.)

2a.   Is this essay addressed to people who already know a good deal about the topic or to people who know relatively little? How do you know?

3a.   List the similarities between computers and brains discussed in this essay.

 b.   List the differences.

 c.   List any important similarities or differences you can think of that the author does not mention.

 d.   If you find that the author chose to ignore some similarities and differences, why do you think he did so? Would mentioning these elements have affected the unity of the essay, or are there some good reasons for leaving them out?

4a.   Does the author believe that human brains are superior to computers? Explain.

 b.   If so, does he believe they are likely to remain this way in the future?

5.   Many people claim that a computer is only as smart as the person who programs it. According to Jastrow, is this true?

6.   What does the author mean when he says that a human or animal brain that acted only on an 'all-or-nothing' basis "would hardly ever reach a decision, and the possessor of a brain like that would not be likely to pass its genes on to the next generation" (par. 13)? (Hint: He is referring to a widely accepted theory of evolution.)

7a.   State in your own words the definitions of an AND gate, and OR gate, and an ALMOST gate.

 b.   Are Jastrow's definitions of these phenomena clear and informative or confusing and needlessly complex? (Guide: *Evaluation*.)

 c.   Did your opinion of Jastrow's definitions change after you tried writing your own? In what ways?

Expository Techniques

1a. How many paragraphs make up the introduction in this essay?

b. Which of the standard introductory techniques does the author use? (Guide: *Introductions.*)

c. Does the author make any special attempt in the introduction to interest readers in his topic? If so, is the attempt successful?

d. Write another introduction for this essay using one of the standard introductory techniques that the author has not used.

2a. Writers often use parallel structures to highlight comparisons and contrasts. Identify places in this essay where Jastrow uses parallel paragraphs or parts of paragraphs and indicate the specific reasons he uses them. (Guide: *Parallel Structure.*)

b. Identify parallel sentences and discuss their use in the essay.

c. Identify parallel sentence parts and discuss their use in the essay.

3a. Does this essay follow an alternating, point-by-point pattern, or does it cover all points on one of its subjects and then all points on the other?

b. Make a list of the paragraphs in the essay, indicating which are devoted primarily to comparison, which to contrast, and which to both.

c. Is this essay organized in the most effective manner? Consider both the essay's topic and the author's purpose. (Guide: *Evaluation.*)

4a. Are there any places in the essay where you found the explanations hard to follow?

b. What other expository patterns that you have studied could the author have used to help make the explanations clearer?

c. In which paragraphs does the author use examples or definitions to aid the explanation?

5. Is this essay formal or informal? Why? (Guide: *Essay.*)

6a. At what point in the essay does the author move from explaining the basic principles of brains and computers to evaluating their strengths and weaknesses? (Note: "To evaluate" is "to show the superiority of one thing over another.")

b. If the author intended to make evaluation an important part of this essay, why did he wait until well into the essay to introduce it?

c. Does the presence of an evaluation make this essay into an argument, or is its overall aim expository? (Guide: *Argument.*)

Diction and Vocabulary

1a. Identify the figure of speech used in the following sentence and tell why you think the author chose to use it: "When one of these gates 'decides' to open, the decision is the result of a complicated assessment involving inputs from thousands of other gates" (par. 12). (Guide: *Figures of Speech.*)

b.   What other figures of speech are used in the essay? Why?

2a. This essay contains a number of technical terms or words used in special senses. The author often defines such words right after he uses them for the first time, calling the reader's attention to the definition either by special sentence structures or by some of the many other ways a writer can emphasize a particular point. Look through the essay to find terms that the author defines for the reader and try to identify the ways he calls attention to the terms and their definitions. (Note: "I.e." is an abbreviation for the Latin phrase *id est*, meaning "that is.")

3.   The author uses the words "intelligent" and "intelligence" frequently in the essay. In your own words define what they mean in terms of this essay.

4a. The subject of this essay is complicated and scientific. Did the essay use as many dictionary-type words or technical terms as you might expect given the topic?

b.   If so, do you think the author could have avoided using some of them? How?

c.   If not, why do you think the author avoided using them?

5.   If you are not familiar with any of the following words, consult your dictionary as necessary: circuits (par. 1); diodes, transistors, neurons (3); inventories, depleted (6); cash flow, excess (7); repertoire, novel (8); variable (9); innate, computations (10); plasticity (11); attributes, assessment (12); imprecise (13).

Suggestions for Writing and Discussion

1.   If you have any experience working with computers (or computerized games), list and explain the ways they are both smarter and dumber than human beings. Give specific examples.

2.   One computer expert believes that eventually computers will be able to teach themselves and will become so intelligent that we will be lucky if they decide to keep us as pets. On the basis of what you have learned from this essay and from your other reading and experience, do you believe this to be true? Discuss.

3.   Assuming that computers will play increasingly important roles in our lives in the future, explore what may be the immediate and ultimate effects of the computer revolution on your own life — or, if you prefer, on your children's lives.

(NOTE: Suggestions for topics requiring development by use of COMPARISON and CONTRAST are on page 109, at the end of this section.)

LAURENCE SHAMES

LAURENCE SHAMES grew up in Newark, New Jersey. He has published articles in a wide variety of magazines, including *American Photographer* and *Playboy,* and he has been an announcer for a classical music station in New York. He is an avid squash player.

Champs

"Champs," first published in the "Ethics" section of *Esquire* magazine, illustrates how comparison can be an effective tool for understanding and describing human behavior. In the course of the essay Shames uses several comparisons, each slightly different in form and each contributing in a different way to the essay's central theme. Despite its complexity, the essay is both easy to follow and easy to understand, because the author follows a clear plan in each of the comparisons.

On an old squash team of mine, there were two guys — we'll call them Mutt and Jeff — who, while they were not dissimilar characters off the court, exhibited wildly contrasting behavior on the court and who, though they were roughly equal in ability, competed with strikingly different degrees of success. 1

Mutt usually won — sometimes against opponents who looked like better athletes and who seemed far more intent on winning than Mutt was. Mutt played as hard as anybody, yet there was always at the heart of his effort a sort of amused relaxation, a casualness that tended to disconcert his do-or-die rivals. Watching Mutt smilingly dispatch opponents, applauding their good shots and ceding them all close calls, one came to a new understanding of the expression "killing with kindness." 2

Jeff was another story. A sweetheart till you put a racket in his hand, Jeff would become — to put it bluntly — a bit of a jerk when 3 the score was being kept. He'd become downright paranoid about the rules; in tough situations he actually seemed to be suffering out there. It didn't help that he usually lost — sometimes to players with less talent and who seemed to have far less at stake.

One evening — after a team match in which a successful play by Mutt had given us high hopes, which hopes had then gone down the tubes with Jeff — another teammate and I commiserated over beers and tried to pin down the differences in temperament that made one of our players such a finisher and the other such a choke artist. After some preliminary groping, my teammate put it this way: "It's simple. Mutt loves to win."

"Deep," I said. "*Everybody* loves to win."

My teammate shook his head and rattled his glass for emphasis. "Not Jeff," he said. "Jeff hates to lose."

For a moment I pondered the distinction. Sure it was catchy, but I wasn't convinced it really meant anything.

"There's a very real difference there," my teammate went on, addressing my skeptical expression. "Why do you think they talk about 'the thrill of victory and the agony of defeat' on TV every weekend? It's not just the outcome they're talking about, it's the attitude."

But it wasn't until we'd talked through the implications of the distinction that I realized how basic a contrast this was. It was the difference between being motivated by joy and driven by dread — and an awful lot of what made Mutt 6–1 and respected around the league and made Jeff 2–5 with a reputation as a head case seemed to follow directly from the crucial skewing of outlook.

It explained why Mutt seemed relaxed even at moments of peak effort, while Jeff seemed tense even between points: attuned to the joy of winning, Mutt could savor his striving, looking ahead to a well-earned beer and a good night's sleep; hounded by the dread of losing, Jeff was like a man in a dentist's chair, braced for the pain before the pain arrived, making himself miserable in the meantime. It explained why Mutt was gracious to his opponents, while Jeff couldn't help being surly: motivated by joy, Mutt regarded his rivals as allies of a sort, helping to mold the situation that would make one of the contestants feel like a million bucks and that would at least give the other the excitement of going for it. Goaded by the specter of defeat, Jeff found it difficult not to cast his opponents in the very differerent role of enemies — the agents of his humiliation. And finally, the distinction helped explain why Mutt usually succeeded, while Jeff screwed up: loving to win, Mutt regarded the game as a medium that buoyed his spirits, that held him up and let him swim with all the grace that he could muster; hating to lose, Jeff seemed to see the contest as a vicious whirlpool whose purpose was to drag him down. Accordingly, he didn't swim through it, he thrashed, which of course is the world's worst way to stay afloat.

Now, if the distinction we're talking about applied only to squash players or even just to athletes, there wouldn't be a whole lot more to say. But one of the glorious things about sports — in which the rules and objects are clear and one may be relatively confident that the outcome will be just — is that they often provide clues to how things work in the less-well-defined arenas of the real world. 11

I have recently heard a story concerning two young men who work in advertising. Having similar credentials and experience, they came due for promotion at roughly the same time. Now, the irony of this situation was that it wasn't a competitive one — one man's promotion had little or nothing to do with the other's, and as to who got moved up first, that was more a question of circumstances within the agency than of preferment. Still, one of the men involved — clearly a Jeff — seemed determined to regard the whole business as a contest, a race. In a perverse sort of way, this made perfect sense: it is part of the burden of a man who hates to lose that he tends to imagine battles where none exist, that he puts his ego on the line even when no line has been drawn. 12

"I really couldn't understand it," said the other man, a friend of mine who I believe qualifies as a Mutt. "This fellow and I had been fairly close colleagues. But as soon as we found out we were both being groomed to move up, his whole attitude changed. No more skull sessions — like he was afraid I'd pirate his ideas. No more wise-assing together — like he was paranoid that I'd use it against him. Hell, I didn't want *his* promotion — I wanted *my* promotion. 13

"Then it got back to me," my friend continued, "that he'd been subtly running me down in certain quarters. Jesus Christ, I thought, he's playing hardball and I'm not even playing!" 14

Well, of *course* he wasn't. Being a Mutt — that is, being privy to the joy of winning — he knew there was no true satisfaction in games that were contrived out of thin air. You could make yourself miserable over imagined contests; to feel good, though, you needed something real. And if the game was not based on something fair 15 and actual, the wiser course was just to wait it out on the sidelines. Which is what this Mutt did.

But the real world being neither quite logical nor always just, it turned out that the Jeff of this pair got his promotion first. My friend — the "loser" — got his a few weeks later.

"What was really strange," he recalled, "was how the guy changed back once the business was settled. On the day I got moved up, he came over to me with a big handshake and this look in his eyes that said, 'The struggle's over, we both survived, so let's be buddies again.' And I realized in that moment that the poor bastard hadn't *meant* to be petty or malicious. He had just gone into panic mode, out of control. I felt sorry for him but I made it clear I intended to keep my distance from then on. I had no doubt he'd do the exact same thing next time. How can you trust a guy like that?"

The answer is, you can't.

But the truly corrosive effect of living in terror of defeat has less to do with the forfeit of others' trust and esteem than with the abdication of those feelings toward oneself. The man who hates to lose is hamstrung by the fear of making mistakes. He fluctuates between a joyless caution and the sort of flaming recklessness that comes not from courage but from the simple reflex of too much restraint finally blowing its cork. Unequipped to embrace the notion of risk, the man who hates to lose makes things riskier than they have to be; he tries to step so lightly that he falls all over himself.

I was discussing this pattern with a friend of mine when she suddenly blurted out: "Horse shows."

"Horse shows?" I said.

"Yeah," she said. "A perfect illustration of what you're saying is what happens in the performance of five-gaited horses."

"That's fascinating," I said, "but I think we're talking about people."

"Exactly," she countered, "and what you see at shows is the character of the rider as reflected in the horse — almost as though the rider's brain, or even soul, was grafted on to the animal's body, like in the old idea of the centaur."

I rolled my eyes.

"I'm serious," she insisted. "It's amazing how much of human nature gets revealed. A horse is bigger, after all, and knows fewer tricks for hiding its feelings — it's easier to read. Now bear with me . . ."

And she went on to explain that the horses are judged on five 27 different gaits of increasing difficulty, each of which — with a little of the old suspension of disbelief — might be said to correspond to some aspect of the riders' lives. The first gait is a simple walk, which corresponds, say, to mundane, low-pressure affairs. My friend observed: "The horses whose riders are worried about losing will show something a little tentative in their stride, a bit too much concern with 'How'm I doin'?' After the walk comes the trot, where the pace is picked up and the adrenaline starts to flow; not surprisingly, the confident riders put the adrenaline to good advantage, while the nervous ones start showing the first signs of overload.

"Where it really gets good, though," my friend continued, "is 28 the canter, where the centaurs have to strut."

Cantering is showing off, no bones about it; it's making witty 29 chatter at a cocktail party, wining and dining colleagues or lovers. The riders who love to win, my friend maintained, canter with measure and charm; the ones who hate to lose try too hard and cross that line between flair and bluster, concern and desperation.

Next comes the slow gait, a totally artificial way of moving, a 30 skill that the horses must be taught against the grain of their natural instincts. "Corresponds rather neatly to the demands placed on people in most careers. Wouldn't you agree?" my friend said wryly.

"Slow gait," she went on, "is where the centaurs with the losing 31 attitudes really start to come unstuck. They get paralyzed with options, like the centipede who stops to wonder which leg to move first. They can't just cut loose and *do* it. By the time they come to rack" — which is slow gait brought up to blurring speed, and which corresponds to peak demands, the situations that really separate the Mutts from the Jeffs: deadlines to meet! confrontations with the boss! — "the horses that are distracted by fear are a pretty sorry spectacle. Their eyes look terrified, as if they were trapped in burning barns."

"Sounds grim," I said. "But what about the other side? What's it 32 like when one of your centaurs is confident?"

Her answer was quick and simple. "Then it can be a thing of 33 beauty," she said. "Then it gives you an incredibly refreshing sense of possibilities, of difficult tasks performed with elegance and calm."

At the very least, this equine analogy does suggest a thing or 34 two about the self-fulfilling tendencies of both joy and dread, and perhaps provides a clue to what is at the heart of that previous quantity we call the thrill of victory. The satisfaction lies not so much in victory itself as in the spirit-flexing exercise of those powers that can *lead* to victory, in the airing of that robustness that allows one to strive and to savor — win or lose — the salty tang of one's own effort.

And if you doubt there's joy in that, ask a centaur.   3

Meanings and Values

1a. According to this essay, what are the qualities of a "Mutt"?

 b. What are the qualities of a "Jeff"?

2. In talking about the phrase used on television, "the thrill of victory and the agony of defeat," the author's teammate says, "It's not just the outcome they're talking about, it's the attitude" (par. 8). What does the teammate mean?

3a. The author claims that sports "often provide clues to how things work in the less-well-defined arenas of the real world" (par. 11). In what ways are sports and everyday activities similar?

 b. In what ways are they different?

4a. Is the story of the two advertising executives an example of irony of situation as Shames suggests (par. 12)? (See Guide to Terms: *Irony*.)

 b. If not, is the story ironic in any way? Explain.

5. Why would Shames believe you can't trust a person like the "Jeff" in the story of the advertising executives?

6. What is the "equine analogy" mentioned in paragraph 34, and what does it contribute to our understanding of human behavior? Explain. (See the introduction to Section 4, "Analogy.")

7a. On the basis of your experience, does Shames's treatment of people as "Mutts" or "Jeffs" seem justified?

 b. If you feel it is not justified, is it because you find his perspective oversimplified? Explain your answer.

Expository Techniques

1a. What are the three main sections of this essay? Be specific.

 b. In what ways are the beginnings and endings of each section signalled to the reader? (Guide: *Transition*.)

 c. What is the purpose of each section, and what does each contribute to the overall purpose of the essay? (Guide: *Purpose* and *Unity*.)

2. Discuss how the author uses parallel structures in paragraphs 9, 10, and 29 to emphasize the contrasts he is presenting. (Guide: *Parallel Structure*.)

3. The author uses a purposely abrupt transition to introduce the analogy between people and horses performing in shows. (For a discussion of analogy — a special form of comparison — see the introduction to Section 4.) Why would the author choose to make the transition so abrupt and surprising and to emphasize these qualities in paragraphs 20–25? (Guide: *Transition*.)

4. This essay contains a number of short paragraphs. What reasons might the author have had for using them, and is their use justified? (Guide: *Evaluation*.)

5. Which of the standard closing techniques are used in this essay? (Guide: *Closings*.)

Diction and Vocabulary

1a. Identify a number of the places in this essay where Shames uses slang or colloquial expressions. (Guide: *Colloquial Expressions*.)

 b. If you consider these expressions appropriate despite the relative formality of the essay, explain what they add to the effectiveness of the essay.

 c. If you consider them inappropriate, explain why.

2. Identify as many examples as you can of the following figures of speech in this essay and discuss their use: allusion; simile; metaphor. (Guide: *Figures of Speech*.)

3. In what way can the centaur be viewed as a symbol of the relationship between our attitudes and our actions? (Guide: *Symbol*.)

4. Familiarize yourself with the following words and their meanings, consulting a dictionary as needed: disconcert, ceding (par. 2); commiserated (4); skewing (9); attuned, goaded, specter, medium (10); preferment (12); fluctuates (19); gaits, mundane (27).

Suggestions for Writing and Discussion

1. What experiences have you had that can be explained by the "Mutt-and-Jeff" distinction that Shames makes in his essay? Develop an expository essay of your own on this theme using your own experiences as a source of examples.

2. Choose a sport (skiing or baseball, for example) or a hobby (making model airplanes, gardening) that reveals interesting contrasts in human behavior and develop an essay from it using either comparison or classification as a pattern for your writing.

3.   If you believe that Shames's view of winners and losers is oversimplified or incorrect in some other way, argue against it, making sure to provide examples to support your opinion.

(NOTE: Suggestions for topics requiring development by COMPARISON and CONTRAST follow.)

Writing Suggestions for Section 3
Comparison and Contrast

Base your central theme on one of the following, and develop your composition primarily by use of comparison and/or contrast. Use examples liberally for clarity and concreteness, chosen always with your purpose and reader-audience in mind.

1. Two kinds of home life.
2. The sea at two different times.
3. The innate qualities needed for success in two careers.
4. The natural temperaments of two acquaintances.
5. Two poets.
6. The teaching techniques of two instructors or former teachers.
7. Two methods of parental handling of teenage problems.
8. Two family attitudes toward the practice of religion.
9. Two "moods" of the same town at different times.
10. The personalities (or atmospheres) of two cities or towns of similar size.
11. Two acquaintances who exemplify different ways of serving humanity.
12. Two acquaintances who seem to symbolize different philosophies of life.
13. Two different attitudes toward the same thing or activity: one "practical," the other romantic or aesthetic.
14. The beliefs and practices of two religions or denominations concerning *one* aspect of religion.
15. Two courses on the same subject: one in high school and one in college.
16. The differing styles of two players of some sport or game.
17. The hazards of frontier life and those of life today.
18. The views of two recent presidents concerning the trappings of high office.

4

Using *Analogy* as an Expository Device

Analogy is a special form of comparison that is used for a specific purpose: to explain something abstract or difficult to understand by showing its similarity to something concrete or easy to understand. A much less commonly used technique than logical comparison (and contrast), analogy is, nonetheless, a highly efficient means of explaining some difficult concepts or of giving added force to the explanations.

Logical comparison is made between two members of the same general class, usually assuming the same kind of interest in the subject matter of both. But in analogy we are really concerned only with the subject matter of one, using a second just to help explain the first. The two subjects, quite incomparable in most respects, are never of the same general class; if they are, we then have logical comparison, not analogy.

If the analogy is to be effective, the writer should be able to assume that the reader is familiar enough with the easier subject, or can quickly be made so, that it really helps explain the more difficult one. A common example is the explanation of the human circulatory system, which we may have trouble comprehending, by comparing the heart and arteries with a pump forcing water through the pipes of a plumbing system. This analogy has been carried further to liken the effect of cholesterol deposits on the inner walls of the arteries to mineral deposits that accumulate inside water pipes and eventually close them entirely. Although there is little logical similarity between a steel pipe and a human artery, the *analogical* similarity would be apparent to most readers — but the analogy might cause even greater confusion for anyone who did not know about pumps.

Distinguishing between analogy and metaphor is sometimes difficult. The difference is basically in their purpose: the function of a metaphor is merely *to describe*, to create a brief, vivid image for the reader; the function of analogy is primarily one of exposition, *to explain*, rather than to describe. In this sense, however, the function of a metaphor is actually *to suggest* an analogy: instead of showing the similarities of the heart and the pump, a metaphor might simply refer to "that faithful pump inside my chest," implying enough of a comparison to serve its purpose as description. (We can see here why some people refer to analogy as "extended" metaphor.) The analogist, when trying to explain the wide selection of college subjects and the need for balance in a course of study, could use the easily understood principle of a cafeteria, which serves Jell-o and lemon meringue pie, as well as meat and potatoes. If his purpose had been only to create an image, to describe, he might have referred simply to the bewildering variety in "the cafeteria of college courses" — and that would have been a metaphor. (For still another example of the more conventional type of analogy, see the explanation of *Unity*, in "Guide to Terms.")

But as useful as analogy can be in exposition, it is a difficult technique to use in logical argument. The two subjects of an analogy, although similar in one or more ways useful for illustration, may be basically too different for any reliable conclusions to be drawn from their similarity.

Sample Paragraph (Analogy)

Sets up, in first sentence, the *analogical* comparison. (They cannot form a logical comparison, however, as towns and a family are of different classes.)

("Broad" is a slang term, usually further classified as a vulgarity. Suitable only for very informal writing.)

Sometimes the local poets-at-heart think of Valley towns as members of a family — diverse, scrappy, but loyal and loving too, each with its own characteristics. Casey, for instance, is the plain old daddy of all, unimaginative, hard-working, but also a notorious brawler on paycheck nights. The eldest daughter is Riverton, a pale and beautiful woman with her head bowed in prayer. But across the river is a pretty lady of a different sort: sister Eden, a good-hearted broad

If used for descriptive rather than explanatory, purposes, various portions of the analogy could be classed as metaphors: e.g., "plain old daddy" and "head bowed in prayer."

("Fellow": colloquial.)

("Kid": colloquial.)

("Picks on" is colloquial and would not be suitable in formal writing.)

with lips painted red and earrings clinking, living on the verge of scandal but never quite in it. And there's Waldoville, the wise older brother, a prosperous country type but tolerant of diversities, first to sail in with both fists flying when any of the rest is attacked. But off to the north lives the peculiar brother, Camelot, an artistic fellow, not much for socializing, mostly content in his own little world. And several smaller stepchildren are scattered around: like Rejoice, that untidy kid who is probably anemic as well; Little Lost Ben, still nearly lost in the woods; New Cambria, a pretty little retarded lass; and, on the far south side, sturdy young Stephen's Mill, who may be the best athlete of all. True, this country family may fight and bicker among themselves — but woe to the outside bully who picks on any one of them.

JAMES C. RETTIE

> JAMES C. RETTIE was an employee of the National Forest Service's experimental station at Upper Darby, Pennsylvania, in 1948 when he adapted this fable from a United States Department of Agriculture pamphlet entitled "To Hold This Soil." At the time, he was a member of The Society of the Friends of the Land and an ardent conservationist.

"But a Watch in the Night": A Scientific Fable

> "But a Watch in the Night"[1] is a highly innovative analogy and illustrates, among other things, the extreme versatility of this pattern of exposition. The analogy itself (a "scientific fable," as the author has called it) is composed almost entirely of narration (a pattern to be studied further in Section 9). While Rettie has taken numerous creative liberties not often available to the student in ordinary college writing, he apparently was very much aware of the same goal we all need to keep in mind when writing: the desired effect, for *his* purposes, on *his* reader-audience.

Out beyond our solar system there is a planet called Copernicus. It   1
came into existence some four or five billion years before the birth of

"But a Watch in the Night" by James C. Rettie from *Forever the Land*, edited by Russell and Kate Lord. Copyright 1950 by Harper & Row, Publishers, Inc. Reprinted by permission of Harper & Row, Publishers, Inc.

[1]From the Bible, Psalm 90, apparently either slightly altered or using a translation other than the King James version, which reads:

Lord, thou hast been our dwelling place
In all generations.
Before the mountains were brought forth,
Or ever thou hadst formed the earth and the world,
Even from everlasting to everlasting, thou art God.
Thou turnest man to destruction;
And sayest, "Return, ye children of men."
For a thousand years in thy sight
Are but as yesterday when it is past,
And as a watch in the night. . . .

114

our Earth. In due course of time it became inhabited by a race of intelligent men.

About 750 million years ago the Copernicans had developed the motion picture machine to a point well in advance of the stage that we have reached. Most of the cameras that we now use in motion picture work are geared to take twenty-four pictures per second on a continuous strip of film. When such film is run through a projector, it throws a series of images on the screen and these change with a rapidity that gives the visual impression of normal movement. If a motion is too swift for the human eye to see it in detail, it can be captured and artificially slowed down by means of the slow-motion camera. This one is geared to take many more shots per second — ninety-six or even more than that. When the slow-motion film is projected at the normal speed of twenty-four pictures per second, we can see just how the jumping horse goes over a hurdle. 2

What about motion that is too slow to be seen by the human eye? That problem has been solved by the use of the time-lapse camera. In this one, the shutter is geared to take only one shot per second, or one per minute, or even one per hour — depending upon the kind of movement that is being photographed. When the time-lapse film is projected at the normal speed of twenty-four pictures per second, it is possible to see a bean sprout growing up out of the ground. Time-lapse films are useful in the study of many types of motion too slow to be observed by the unaided, human eye. 3

The Copernicans, it seems, had time-lapse cameras some 757 million years ago and they also had superpowered telescopes that gave them a clear view of what was happening upon this Earth. They decided to make a film record of the life history of Earth and to make it on the scale of one picture per year. The photography has been in progress during the last 757 million years. 4

In the near future, a Copernican interstellar expedition will arrive upon our Earth and bring with it a copy of the time-lapse film. Arrangements will be made for showing the entire film in one continuous run. This will begin at midnight of New Year's eve and continue day and night without a single stop until midnight of December 31. The rate of projection will be twenty-four pictures per second. Time on the screen will thus seem to move at the rate of 24 years per second; 1,440 years per minute; 86,400 years per hour; approximately 2 million years per day; and 62 million years per 5 month. The normal life-span of individual man will occupy about three seconds. The full period of Earth history that will be unfolded on the screen (some 757 million years) will extend from what the geologists call Pre-Cambrian times up to the present. This will, by no means, cover the full time-span of the Earth's geological history, but it will embrace the period since the advent of living organisms.

During the months of January, February and March the picture 6
will be desolate and dreary. The shape of the land masses and the oceans will bear little or no resemblance to those that we know. The violence of geological erosion will be much in evidence. Rains will pour down on the land and promptly go booming down to the seas. There will be no clear streams anywhere except where the rains fall upon hard rock. Everywhere on the steeper ground the stream channels will be filled with boulders hurled down by rushing waters. Raging torrents and dry stream beds will keep alternating in quick succession. High mountains will seem to melt like so much butter in the sun. The shifting of land into the seas, later to be thrust up as new mountains, will be going on at a grand scale.

Early in April there will be some indication of the presence of 7
single-celled living organisms in some of the warmer and sheltered coastal waters. By the end of the month it will be noticed that some of these organisms have become multicellular. A few of them, including the Trilobites, will be encased in hard shells.

Toward the end of May, the first vertebrates will appear, but 8
they will still be aquatic creatures. In June about 60 percent of the land area that we know as North America will be under water. One broad channel will occupy the space where the Rocky Mountains now stand. Great deposits of limestone will be forming under some of the shallower seas. Oil and gas deposits will be in process of formation — also under shallow seas. On land there will still be no sign of vegetation. Erosion will be rampant, tearing loose particles and chunks of rock and grinding them into sand and silt to be spewed out by the streams into bays and estuaries.

About the middle of July the first land plants will appear and 9
take up the tremendous job of soil building. Slowly, very slowly, the mat of vegetation will spread, always battling for its life against the power of erosion. Almost foot by foot, the plant life will advance, lacing down with its root structures whatever pulverized rock material it can find. Leaves and stems will be giving added protection

against the loss of the soil foothold. The increasing vegetation will pave the way for the land animals that will live upon it.

Early in August the seas will be teeming with fish. This will be what geologists call the Devonian period. Some of the races of these fish will be breathing by means of lung tissue instead of through gill tissues. Before the month is over, some of the lung fish will go ashore and take on a crude lizard-like appearance. Here are the first amphibians.   10

In early September the insects will put in their appearance. Some will look like huge dragon flies and will have a wingspread of 24 inches. Large portions of the land masses will now be covered with heavy vegetation that will include the primitive spore-propagating trees. Layer upon layer of this plant growth will build up, later to appear as the coal deposits. About the middle of this month, there will be evidence of the first seed-bearing plants and the first reptiles. Heretofore, the land animals will have been amphibians that could reproduce their kind only by depositing a soft egg mass in quiet waters. The reptiles will be shown to be freed from the aquatic bond because they can reproduce by means of a shelled egg in which the embryo and its nurturing liquids are sealed in and thus protected from destructive evaporation. Before September is over, the first dinosaurs will be seen — creatures destined to dominate the animal realm for about 140 million years and then to disappear.   11

In October there will be a series of mountain uplifts along what is now the eastern coast of the United States. A creature with feathered limbs — half bird and half reptile in appearance — will take itself into the air. Some small and rather unpretentious animals will be seen to bring forth their young in a form that is a miniature replica of the parents and to feed these young on milk secreted by mammary glands in the female parent. The emergence of this mammalian form of animal life will be recognized as one of the great events in geologic time. October will also witness the high water mark of the dinosaurs — creatures ranging in size from that of the modern goat to monsters like Brontosaurus that weighed some 40 tons. Most of them will be placid vegetarians, but a few will be hideous-looking carnivores, like Allosaurus and Tyrannosaurus. Some of the herbivorous dinosaurs will be clad in bony armor for protection against their flesh-eating comrades.   12

November will bring pictures of a sea extending from the Gulf   13

of Mexico to the Arctic in space now occupied by the Rocky Mountains. A few of the reptiles will take to the air on bat-like wings. One
of these, called Pteranodon, will have a wingspread of 15 feet. There
will be a rapid development of the modern flowering plants, modern trees, and modern insects. The dinosaurs will disappear. Toward the end of the month there will be a tremendous land disturbance in which the Rocky Mountains will rise out of the sea to assume
a dominating place in the North American landscape.

As the picture runs on into December, it will show the mam-   14
mals in command of the animal life. Seed-bearing trees and grasses
will have covered most of the land with a heavy mantle of vegetation. Only the areas newly thrust up from the sea will be barren.
Most of the streams will be crystal clear. The turmoil of geologic
erosion will be confined to localized areas. About December 25 will
begin the cutting of the Grand Canyon of the Colorado River.
Grinding down through layer after layer of sedimentary strata, this
stream will finally expose deposits laid down in Pre-Cambrian
times. Thus in the walls of that canyon will appear geological forma-
tions dating from recent times to the period when the earth had no
living organisms upon it.

The picture will run on through the latter days of December and   15
even up to its final day with still no sign of mankind. The spectators
will become alarmed in the fear that man has somehow been left
out. But not so; sometime about noon on December 31 (one million
years ago) will appear a stooped, massive creature of man-like
proportions. This will be Pithecanthropus, the Java ape man. For
tools and weapons he will have nothing but crude stone and
wooden clubs. His children will live a precarious existence
threatened on the one side by hostile animals and on the other by
tremendous climatic changes. Ice sheets — in places 4000 feet
deep — will form in the northern parts of North America and Eura-
sia. Four times this glacial ice will push southward to cover half the
continents. With each advance the plant and animal life will be
swept under or pushed southward. With each recession of the ice,
life will struggle to reestablish itself in the wake of the retreating
glaciers. The wooly mammoth, the musk ox, and the caribou all will
fight to maintain themselves near the ice line. Sometimes they will
be caught and put into cold storage — skin, flesh, blood, bones and
all.

The picture will run on through supper time with still very little   16 evidence of man's presence on the Earth. It will be about 11 o'clock when Neanderthal man appears. Another half hour will go by before the appearance of Cro-Magnon man living in caves and painting crude animal pictures on the walls of his dwelling. Fifteen minutes more will bring Neolithic man, knowing how to chip stone and thus produce sharp cutting edges for spears and tools. In a few minutes more it will appear that man has domesticated the dog, the sheep and, possibly, other animals. He will then begin the use of milk. He will also learn the arts of basket weaving and the making of pottery and dugout canoes.

The dawn of civilization will not come until about five or six minutes before the end of the picture. The story of the Egyptians, the Babylonians, the Greeks, and the Romans will unroll during the fourth, the third and the second minute before the end. At 58 minutes and 43 seconds past 11:00 P.M. (just 1 minute and 17 seconds before the end) will come the beginning of the Christian era. Columbus will discover the new world 20 seconds before the end. The Declaration of Independence will be signed just 7 seconds before the final curtain comes down.

In those few moments of geologic time will be the story of all that has happened since we became a nation. And what a story it will be! A human swarm will sweep across the face of the continent and take it away from the primitive red men. They will change it far more radically than it has ever been changed before in a comparable time. The great virgin forests will be seen going down before ax and fire. The soil, covered for aeons by its protective mantle of trees and grasses, will be laid bare to the ravages of water and wind erosion. Streams that had been flowing clear will, once again, take up a load of silt and push it toward the seas. Humus and mineral salts, both vital elements of productive soil, will be seen to vanish at a terrifying rate. The railroads and highways and cities that will spring up may divert attention, but they cannot cover up the blight of man's recent activities. In great sections of Asia, it will be seen that man must utilize cow dung and every scrap of available straw or grass for fuel to cook his food. The forests that once provided wood for this purpose will be gone without a trace. The use of these agricultural wastes for fuel, in place of returning them to the land, will be leading to increasing soil impoverishment. Here and there will be seen a dust storm darkening the landscape over an area a thousand miles across. Man-creatures will be shown counting their wealth in terms of bits of printed paper representing other bits of a scarce but comparatively useless yellow metal that is kept buried in strong vaults. Meanwhile, the soil, the only real wealth that can keep mankind alive on the face of this Earth, is savagely being cut loose from its ancient moorings and washed into the seven seas.

We have just arrived upon this Earth. How long will we stay?   19█

Meanings and Values

1a.   What is the significance of the quotation, as it is used in the title of this essay?

b.   Is the title itself an allusion? Why, or why not? (See Guide to Terms: *Figures of Speech.*)

c.   Explain why you personally do, or do not, like the title.

2a.   What do you find ironic in the latter part of paragraph 18? (Guide: *Irony.*)

b.   What kind of irony is it?

3a.   Compare the effectiveness of Rettie's unique handling of the soil-loss problem with the methods commonly used for environmental propaganda.

b.   Could he have enlarged it effectively to include other environmental problems? Why, or why not?

Expository Techniques

1a.   In what respects does "But a Watch in the Night" qualify as analogy?

b.   Why could the author not have achieved his purpose as well by showing us more simply, in actual year spans, the brevity of human existence on earth, rather than by this condensed movie version?

2a.   The author devotes five paragraphs just to setting up his analogy. In what way, or ways, might this slow beginning be justified?

b.   Does the analogy benefit by such a detailed explanation of the camera's capabilities? Why, or why not?

c.   Why do you suppose Rettie created a fictional planet?

d.   Should he have told us at some point that the whole thing is make-believe? Why, or why not?

3a.   Why do you think the author took the trouble to work out the rate of projection to fit exactly into one year?

b.   What is gained, or lost, by learning as early as paragraph 5 that the normal life span of individual man would occupy only about three seconds?

4a. What did you believe at first to be the central theme? (Guide: *Unity*.)

b. How did your impression of the theme become modified in paragraph 5?

c. In view of the overall essay, state what you now believe to have been the author's theme.

d. Does the composition have unity — i.e., do all parts serve as tributaries, however indirect, into the central theme?

5a. Explain fully, in terms of "emphasis," why this slow unfolding of the real theme helps, or hinders, in achieving the author's apparent purpose. (Guide: *Emphasis*.)

b. This is a more "creative" piece than most expositions. Why would such a slow unfolding be inappropriate to most college and workaday writing?

6. What advantage is gained, if any, by the parallel beginnings of most paragraphs? (Guide: *Parallel Structure*.)

7a. What criteria did Rettie apparently use in selecting, from among thousands, the details to be included in the various time periods?

b. Would it have been better to use some other criteria? Why, or why not?

8a. A rhetorical question is used here in a highly strategic position. Where is it? (Guide: *Rhetorical Questions*.)

b. How effective is its use?

Diction and Vocabulary

1a. The naming of the planet makes use, rather indirectly, of an allusion. To what does it refer? (Guide: *Figures of Speech*.)

b. Why is it appropriate, or inappropriate, for this piece?

2a. What kind of figure of speech do you find in paragraph 6?

b. In paragraph 17 there is a figure of speech that is also a cliché. What is it? (Guide: *Figures of Speech* and *Clichés*.)

c. What kind of figure of speech is it?

d. Why is it also classifiable as a cliché?

Suggestions for Writing and Discussion

1. What practical steps could be taken now to prevent the rest of our "only real wealth" from being washed into the sea? What are the chances of such steps being taken seriously enough, soon enough?

2.   Assuming that our food-production technology continues to advance rapidly, is it conceivable that humankind might manage to survive without much soil? Discuss this possibility.

3.   If you are particularly interested in the Bible, for either literary or religious reasons, discuss more fully the meanings of the part of Psalm 90 quoted in the introduction. If you like, you may enlarge your discussion to include the entire psalm.

(NOTE: Suggestions for topics requiring development by use of ANALOGY are on page 140, at the end of this section.)

TOM WOLFE

TOM WOLFE was born in 1931 and grew up in Richmond, Virginia, was graduated from Washington and Lee University, and took his doctorate at Yale. After working for several years as a reporter for *The Washington Post*, he joined the staff of the New York *Herald Tribune* in 1962. He has won two Washington Newspaper Guild Awards, one for humor and the other for foreign news. Wolfe has been a regular contributor to *New York*, *Esquire*, and other magazines. His books include *The Kandy-Kolored Tangerine-Flake Streamline Baby* (1965), *The Electric Kool-Aid Acid Test* (1968), *Radical Chic and Mau-Mauing the Flak Catchers* (1970), *The New Journalism* (1973), *The Painted Word* (1975), *The Right Stuff* (1977), *In Our Time* (1980), *Underneath the I-Beams: Inside the Compound* (1981), and *From Bauhaus to Our House* (1981).

O Rotten Gotham —
Sliding Down into the Behavioral Sink

"O Rotten Gotham — Sliding Down into the Behavioral Sink," as used here, is excerpted from a longer selection by that title in Wolfe's book *The Pump House Gang* (1968). Here, as he frequently does, the author investigates an important aspect of modern life — seriously, but in his characteristic and seemingly free-wheeling style. It is a style that is sometimes ridiculed by scholars but is far more often admired. (Wolfe, as the serious student will discover, is always in complete control of his materials and methods, using them to create certain effects, to reinforce his ideas.) In this piece his analogy is particularly noteworthy for the extensive usage he is able to get from it.

I just spent two days with Edward T. Hall, an anthropologist, 1
watching thousands of my fellow New Yorkers short-circuiting

themselves into hot little twitching death balls with jolts of their own adrenalin. Dr. Hall says it is overcrowding that does it. Overcrowding gets the adrenalin going, and the adrenalin gets them queer, autistic, sadistic, barren, batty, sloppy, hot-in-the-pants, chancred-on-the-flankers, leering, puling, numb — the usual in New York, in other words, and God knows what else. Dr. Hall has the theory that overcrowding has already thrown New York into a state of behavioral sink. Behavioral sink is a term from ethology, which is the study of how animals relate to their environment. Among animals, the sink winds up with a "population collapse" or "massive die-off." O rotten Gotham.

It got to be easy to look at New Yorkers as animals, especially   2
looking down from some place like a balcony at Grand Central at the rush hour Friday afternoon. The floor was filled with the poor white humans, running around, dodging, blinking their eyes, making a sound like a pen full of starlings or rats or something.

"Listen to them skid," says Dr. Hall.   3

He was right. The poor old etiolate animals were out there   4
skidding on their rubber soles. You could hear it once he pointed it out. They stop short to keep from hitting somebody or because they are disoriented and they suddenly stop and look around, and they skid on their rubber-soled shoes, and a screech goes up. They pour out onto the floor down the escalators from the Pan-Am Building, from 42nd Street, from Lexington Avenue, up out of subways, down into subways, railroad trains, up into helicopters —

"You can also hear the helicopters all the way down here," says   5
Dr. Hall. The sound of the helicopters using the roof of the Pan-Am Building nearly fifty stories up beats right through. "If it weren't for this ceiling" — he is referring to the very high ceiling in Grand Central — "this place would be unbearable with this kind of crowding. And yet they'll probably never 'waste' space like this again."

They screech! And the adrenal glands in all those poor white   6
animals enlarge, micrometer by micrometer, to the size of cantaloupes. Dr. Hall pulls a Minox camera out of a holster he has on his belt and starts shooting away at the human scurry. The Sink!

Dr. Hall has the Minox up to his eye — he is a slender man,   7
calm, 52 years old, young-looking, an anthropologist who has worked with Navajos, Hopis, Spanish-Americans, Negroes, Trukese. He was the most important anthropologist in the government during the crucial years of the foreign aid program, the 1950's.

He directed both the Point Four training program and the Human Relations Area Files. He wrote *The Silent Language* and *The Hidden Dimension*, two books that are picking up the kind of "underground" following his friend Marshall McLuhan started picking up about five years ago. He teaches at the Illinois Institute of Technology, lives with his wife, Mildred, in a high-ceilinged town house on one of the last great residential streets in downtown Chicago, Astor Street; he has a grown son and daughter, loves good food, good wine, the relaxed, civilized life — but comes to New York with a Minox at his eye to record! — perfect — The Sink.

We really got down in there by walking down into the Lexington Avenue line subway stop under Grand Central. We inhaled those nice big fluffy fumes of human sweat, urine, effluvia, and sebaceous secretions. One old female human was already stroked out on the upper level, on a stretcher, with two policemen standing by. The other humans barely looked at her. They rushed into line. They bellied each other, haunch to paunch, down the stairs. Human heads shone through the gratings. The species North European tried to create bubbles of space around themselves, about a foot and a half in diameter —

"See, he's reacting against the line," says Dr. Hall.

— but the species Mediterranean presses on in. The hell with bubbles of space. The species North European resents that, this male human behind him presses forward toward the booth . . . *breathing* on him, he's disgusted, he pulls out of the line entirely, the species Mediterranean resents him for resenting it, and neither of them realizes what the hell they are getting irritable about exactly. And in all of them the old adrenals grow another micrometer.

Dr. Hall whips out the Minox. Too perfect! The bottom of The Sink.

It is the sheer overcrowding, such as occurs in the business sections of Manhattan five days a week and in Harlem, Bedford-Stuyvesant, southeast Bronx every day — sheer overcrowding is converting New Yorkers into animals in a sink pen. Dr. Hall's argument runs as follows: all animals, including birds, seem to have a built-in inherited requirement to have a certain amount of territory, space, to lead their lives in. Even if they have all the food they need, and there are no predatory animals threatening them, they cannot tolerate crowding beyond a certain point. No more than two hundred wild Norway rats can survive on a quarter acre of ground,

for example, even when they are given all the food they can eat.
They just die off.

But why? To find out, ethologists have run experiments on all   13
sorts of animals, from stickleback crabs to Sika deer. In one major
experiment, an ethologist named John Calhoun put some domesticated white Norway rats in a pen with four sections to it, connected
by ramps. Calhoun knew from previous experiments that the rats
tend to split up into groups of ten to twelve and that the pen,
therefore, would hold forty to forty-eight rats comfortably, assuming they formed four equal groups. He allowed them to reproduce
until there were eighty rats, balanced between male and female, but
did not let it get any more crowded. He kept them supplied with
plenty of food, water, and nesting materials, In other words, all
their more obvious needs were taken care of. A less obvious need —
space — was not. To the human eye, the pen did not even look
especially crowded. But to the rats, it was crowded beyond endurance.

The entire colony was soon plunged into a profound behavioral   14
sink. "The sink," said Calhoun, "is the outcome of any behavioral
process that collects animals together in unusually great numbers.
The unhealthy connotations of the term are not accidental: a behavioral sink does act to aggravate all forms of pathology that can be
found within a group."

For a start, long before the rat population reached eighty, a   15
status hierarchy had developed in the pen. Two dominant male rats
took over the two end sections, acquired harems of eight to ten
females each, and forced the rest of the rats into the two middle
pens. All the overcrowding took place in the middle pens. That was
where the "sink" hit. The aristocrat rats at the end grew bigger,
sleeker, healthier, and more secure the whole time.

In The Sink, meanwhile, nest building, courting, sex behavior,   16
reproduction, social organization, health — all of it went to pieces.
Normally, Norway rats have a mating ritual in which the male
chases the female, the female ducks down into a burrow and sticks
her head up to watch the male. He performs a little dance outside
the burrow, then she comes out, and he mounts her, usually for a
few seconds. When The Sink set in, however, no more than three
males — the dominant males in the middle sections — kept up the
old customs. The rest tried everything from satyrism to homosexuality or else gave up on sex altogether. Some of the subordinate

males spent all their time chasing females. Three or four might chase one female at the same time, and instead of stopping at the burrow entrance for the ritual, they would charge right in. Once mounted, they would hold on for minutes instead of the usual seconds.

Homosexuality rose sharply. So did bisexuality. Some males   17
would mount anything — males, females, babies, senescent rats, anything. Still other males dropped sexual activity altogether, wouldn't fight and, in fact, would hardly move except when the other rats slept. Occasionally, a female from the aristocrat rats' harems would come over the ramps and into the middle sections to sample life in The Sink. When she had had enough, she would run back up the ramp. Sink males would give chase up to the top of the ramp, which is to say, to the very edge of the aristocratic preserve. But one glance from one of the king rats would stop them cold and they would return to The Sink.

The slumming females from the harems had their adventures   18
and then returned to a placid, healthy life. Females in The Sink, however, were ravaged, physically and psychologically. Pregnant rats had trouble continuing pregnancy. The rate of miscarriages increased significantly, and females started dying from tumors and other disorders of the mammary glands, sex organs, uterus, ovaries, and Fallopian tubes. Typically, their kidneys, livers, and adrenals were also enlarged or diseased or showed other signs associated with stress.

Child-rearing became totally disorganized. The females lost the   19
interest or the stamina to build nests and did not keep them up if they did build them. In the general filth and confusion, they would not put themselves out to save offspring they were momentarily separated from. Frantic, even sadistic competition among the males was going on all around them and rendering their lives chaotic. The males began unprovoked and senseless assaults upon one another, often in the form of tail-biting. Ordinarily, rats will suppress this kind of behavior when it crops up. In The Sink, male rats gave up all policing and just looked out for themselves. The "pecking order" among males in The Sink was never stable. Normally, male rats set up a three-class structure. Under the pressure of overcrowding, however, they broke up into all sorts of unstable subclasses, cliques, packs — and constantly pushed, probed, explored, tested one another's power. Anyone was fair game, except for the aristocrats in the end pens.

Calhoun kept the population down to eighty, so that the next   20
stage, "population collapse" or "massive die-off," did not occur. But
the autopsies showed that the pattern — as in the diseases among
the female rats — was already there.

The classic study of die-off was John J. Christian's study of Sika   21
deer on James Island in the Chesapeake Bay, west of Cambridge,
Maryland. Four or five of the deer had been released on the island,
which was 280 acres and uninhabited, in 1916. By 1955 they had
bred freely into a herd of 280 to 300. The population density was
only about one deer per acre at this point, but Christian knew that
this was already too high for the Sikas' inborn space requirements,
and something would give before long. For two years the number of
deer remained 280 to 300. But suddenly, in 1958, over half the deer
died; 161 carcasses were recovered. In 1959 more deer died and the
population steadied at about 80.

In two years, two-thirds of the herd had died. Why? It was not   22
starvation. In fact, all the deer collected were in excellent condition,
with well-developed muscles, shining coats, and fat deposits between the muscles. In practically all the deer, however, the adrenal
glands had enlarged by 50 percent. Christian concluded that the
die-off was due to "shock following severe metabolic disturbance,
probably as a result of prolonged adrenocortical hyperactivity. . . .
There was no evidence of infection, starvation, or other obvious
cause to explain the mass mortality." In other words, the constant
stress of overpopulation, plus the normal stress of the cold of
the winter, had kept the adrenalin flowing so constantly in the deer
that their systems were depleted of blood sugar and they died of
shock.

Well, the white humans are still skidding and darting across the   2
floor of Grand Central. Dr. Hall listens a moment longer to the
skidding and the darting noises, and then says, "You know, I've
been on commuter trains here after everyone has been through one
of these rushes, and I'll tell you, there is enough acid flowing in the
stomachs in every car to dissolve the rails underneath."

Just a little invisible acid bath for the linings to round off the
day. The ulcers the acids cause, of course, are the one disease people
have already been taught to associate with the stress of city life. But
overcrowding, as Dr. Hall sees it, raises a lot more hell with the body
than just ulcers. In everyday life in New York — just the usual,
getting to work, working in massively congested areas like 42nd

Street between Fifth Avenue and Lexington, especially now that the Pan-Am Building is set in there, working in cubicles such as those in the editorial offices at Time-Life, Inc., which Dr. Hall cites as typical of New York's poor handling of space, working in cubicles with low ceilings and, often, no access to a window, while construction crews all over Manhattan drive everybody up the Masonite wall with air-pressure generators with noises up to the boil-a-brain decibel level, then rushing to get home, piling into subways and trains, fighting for time and for space, the usual day in New York — the whole now-normal thing keeps shooting jolts of adrenalin into the body, breaking down the body's defenses and winding up with the work-a-daddy human animal stroked out at the breakfast table with his head apoplexed like a cauliflower out of his $6.95 semi-spread Pima-cotton shirt, and nosed over into a plate of No-Kloresto egg substitute, signing off with the black thrombosis, cancer, kidney, liver, or stomach failure, and the adrenals ooze to a halt, the size of eggplants in July.

One of the people whose work Dr. Hall is interested in on this score is Rene Dubos at the Rockefeller Institute. Dubos's work indicates that specific organisms, such as the tuberculosis bacillus or a pneumonia virus, can seldom be considered "the cause" of a disease. The germ or virus, apparently, has to work in combination with other things that have already broken the body down in some way — such as the old adrenal hyperactivity. Dr. Hall would like to see some autopsy studies made to record the size of adrenal glands in New York, especially of people crowded into slums and people who go through the full rush-hour-work-rush-hour cycle every day. He is afraid that until there is some clinical, statistical data on how overcrowding actually ravages the human body, no one will be willing to do anything about it. Even in so obvious a thing as air pollution, the pattern is familiar. Until people can actually see the smoke or smell the sulphur or feel the sting in their eyes, politicians will not get excited about it, even though it is well known that many of the lethal substances polluting the air are invisible and odorless. For one thing, most politicians are like the aristocrat rats. They are insulated from The Sink by practically sultanic buffers — limousines, chauffeurs, secretaries, aides-de-camp, doormen, shuttered houses, high-floor apartments. They almost never ride subways, fight rush hours, much less live in the slums or work in the Pan-Am Building.

Meanings and Values

1a.   Who are members of the "species Mediterranean"?

  b.   Who belong to the "species North European"?

  c.   What could account for their difference in space requirements (pars. 8–10)?

2.   Is this writing primarily objective or subjective? (See Guide to Terms: *Objective/Subjective.*) Why?

3a.   Do you get the impression that the author is being unkind, "making fun" of the harried New Yorkers?

  b.   How, if at all, does he prevent such an impression?

4a.   Compare Wolfe's style, tone, and point of view with those of Catton or Roiphe (Sec. 3). (Guide: *Style/Tone* and *Point of View.*)

  b.   Do these features necessarily make one author less effective than another in achieving his purposes? Explain.

Expository Techniques

1a.   Using whatever criteria we have available for judging the success of analogy, appraise the effectiveness of this one.

  b.   Does the author work it *too* hard? Be prepared to defend your answer.

2.   What are the benefits of the frequent return to what Dr. Hall is doing or saying (e.g., in pars. 3, 5, 7, 9, 11, 23)?

3.   Paragraph 12 has a useful function beyond the simple information it imparts — a sort of organic relation to the coming development. Explain how this is accomplished.

4.   How is the switch to Sika deer (par. 21) prepared for, and a bumpy transition avoided?

5.   The preceding three questions are related in some manner to the problems of transition. How, if at all, are such problems also matters of coherence? (Guide: *Coherence.*)

6.   Wolfe is adept at creating just the effect he wants, and the careful student of writing can detect a subtle change of style and pace with each change of subpurpose. (Guide: *Style/Tone.*)

  a.   Analyze stylistic differences, with resulting effects, between the description of chaos at Grand Central and the information about Dr. Hall in paragraph 7.

  b.   Analyze such differences between the Grand Central scene and the account of the laboratory experiment with rats.

  c.   Analyze the differences between the Grand Central scene and the final paragraph.

7.   Explain how the style of the more descriptive portions is also a matter of emphasis. (Guide: *Emphasis.*)

8a.   Illustrate as many as possible of the elements of effective syntax (itself a matter of style) by examples from this selection. (Guide: *Syntax.*)

b.   What is gained or lost by the unusual length and design of the last sentence of paragraph 24? (We can be sure that it did not "just happen" to Wolfe — and equally sure that one of such length would be disastrous in most writing.)

Diction and Vocabulary

1.   What is the significance of the word "Gotham"?

2a.   Why do you think the author refers (deliberately, no doubt) to "my fellow New Yorkers" in the first sentence?

b.   What soon could have been the effect if he had not taken such a step?

3.   Why does he consistently, after paragraph 2, refer to the people as "poor white humans," "poor human animals," etc?

4.   In paragraph 14 he refers to the connotations of the word "sink." What are its possible connotations? (Guide: *Connotation/Denotation.*)

5.   Cite examples of verbal irony to be found in paragraphs 5, 8, 24. (Guide: *Irony.*)

6.   Which of the elements of style mentioned in your answer to question 4a of "Meanings and Values" are also matters of diction?

7.   Consult your dictionary as needed for full understanding of the following words: autistic, puling (par. 1); etiolate (4); effluvia, sebaceous (8); pathology (14); satyrism (16); senescent (17); decibel, thrombosis (24); lethal (25).

Suggestions for Writing and Discussion

1.   Carrying Wolfe's analogy still further, trace the steps by which a rise in serious crime must result from the overcrowding of "poor human animals."

2.   If you are familiar with another city, particularly during rush hours, which appears to you much like New York in this respect, describe it.

3.   If you are familiar with some area of high-density population that has solved its problem of overcrowding, explain the solution.

4.   What practical steps can the *individual* take, if forced to live and/or work in overcrowded conditions, to avoid becoming the victim of his or her own adrenals?

(NOTE: Suggestions for topics requiring development by use of ANALOGY are on page 140, at the end of this section.)

ANNIE DILLARD

ANNIE DILLARD was born in 1945 in Pittsburgh, Pennsylvania. She received a B.A. and an M.A. from Hollins College and has been professor of English at Western Washington State University and writer in residence at Wesleyan University. Her book *Pilgrim at Tinker Creek* (1974), based on her experiences living in the Roanoke Valley of Virginia, was awarded the Pulitzer Prize for general nonfiction. She has also published a book of poems, *Tickets for a Prayer Wheel* (1974); a volume of literary criticism, *Living by Fiction* (1982); and two collections of brief narratives and meditations on nature and experience, *Holy the Firm* (1978) and *Teaching a Stone to Talk* (1982).

Sojourner

This essay, from *Teaching a Stone to Talk*, is typical of Dillard's approach: a sharply observed event or natural scene becomes the source for a commentary on human life and its relationship to the world at large. The vivid description of floating islands that opens this selection helps make an unusual phenomenon seem familiar and provides the basis for the analogy around which the essay is structured. Though many of the words used here will seem unfamiliar, they do not affect the essay's readability and instead give a richness and freshness to the writing.

If survival is an art, then mangroves are artists of the beautiful: not 1 only that they exist at all — smooth-barked, glossy-leaved, thickets of lapped mystery — but that they can and do exist as floating islands, as trees upright and loose, alive and homeless on the water.

I have seen mangroves, always on tropical ocean shores, in 2 Florida and in the Galápagos. There is the red mangrove, the yellow, the button, and the black. They are all short, messy trees, waxy-leaved, laced all over with aerial roots, woody arching butt-resses, and weird leathery berry pods. All this tangles from a black muck soil, a black muck matted like a mud-sopped rag, a muck without any other plants, shaded, cold to the touch, tracked at the water's edge by herons and nosed by sharks.

It is these shoreline trees which, by a fairly common accident, can become floating islands. A hurricane flood or a riptide can wrest a tree from the shore, or from the mouth of a tidal river, and hurl it into the ocean. It floats. It is a mangrove island, blown.

There are floating islands on the planet; it amazes me. Credu-lous Pliny[1] described some islands thought to be mangrove islands floating on a river. The people called these river islands *the dancers*, "because in any consort of musicians singing, they stir and move at the stroke of the feet, keeping time and measure."

Trees floating on rivers are less amazing than trees floating on the poisonous sea. A tree cannot live in salt. Mangrove trees exude salt from their leaves; you can see it, even on shoreline black man-groves, as a thin white crust. Lick a leaf and your tongue curls and coils; your mouth's a heap of salt.

Nor can a tree live without soil. A hurricane-born mangrove island may bring its own soil to the sea. But other mangrove trees make their own soil — and their own islands — from scratch. These are the ones which interest me. The seeds germinate in the fruit on the tree. The germinated embryo can drop anywhere — say, onto a dab of floating muck. The heavy root end sinks; a leafy plumule unfurls. The tiny seedling, afloat, is on its way. Soon aerial roots shooting out in all directions trap debris. The sapline's net-works twine, the interstices narrow, and water calms in the lee. Bacteria thrive on organic broth; amphipods swarm. These crea-tures grow and die at the trees' wet feet. The soil thickens, accumu-lating rainwater, leaf rot, seashells, and guano; the island spreads.

More seeds and more muck yield more trees on the new island. A society grows, interlocked in a tangle of dependencies. The island rocks less in the swells. Fish throng to the backwaters stilled in snarled roots. Soon, Asian mudskippers — little four-inch fish — clamber up the mangrove roots into the air and peer about from periscope eyes on stalks, like snails. Oysters clamp to submersed

[1]Pliny the Elder (A.D. 23–79), Roman scholar and author of *Natural History*. — EDS.

roots, as do starfish, dog whelk, and the creatures that live among tangled kelp. Shrimp seek shelter there, limpets a holdfast, pelagic birds a rest.

And the mangrove island wanders on, afloat and adrift. It [8] walks teetering and wanton before the wind. Its fate and direction are random. It may bob across an ocean and catch on another mainland's shores. It may starve or dry while it is still a sapling. It may topple in a storm, or pitchpole. By the rarest of chances, it may stave into another mangrove island in a crash of clacking roots, and mesh. What it is most likely to do is drift anywhere in the alien ocean, feeding on death and growing, netting a makeshift soil as it goes, shrimp in its toes and terns in its hair.

We could do worse. [9]

I alternate between thinking of the planet as home — dear and [10] familiar stone hearth and garden — and as a hard land of exile in which we are all sojourners. Today I favor the latter view. The word "sojourner" occurs often in the English Old Testament. It invokes a nomadic people's sense of vagrancy, a praying people's knowledge of estrangement, a thinking people's intuition of sharp loss: "For we are strangers before thee, and sojourners, as were all our fathers: our days on the earth are as a shadow, and there is none abiding."

We don't know where we belong, but in times of sorrow it [11] doesn't seem to be here, here with these silly pansies and witless mountains, here with sponges and hard-eyed birds. In times of sorrow the innocence of the other creatures — from whom and with whom we evolved — seems a mockery. Their ways are not our ways. We seem set among them as among lifelike props for a tragedy — or a broad lampoon — on a thrust rock stage.

It doesn't seem to be here that we belong, here where space is [12] curved, the earth is round, we're all going to die, and it seems as wise to stay in bed as budge. It is strange here, not quite warm enough, or too warm, too leafy, or inedible, or windy, or dead. It is not, frankly, the sort of home for people one would have thought of — although I lack the fancy to imagine another.

The planet itself is a sojourner in airless space, a wet ball flung [13] across nowhere. The few objects in the universe scatter. The coherence of matter dwindles and crumbles toward stillness. I have read, and repeated, that our solar system as a whole is careering through space toward a point east of Hercules. Now I wonder: what could that possible mean, east of Hercules? Isn't space curved? When we get "there," how will our course change, and why? will we slide down the universe's inside arc like mud slung at a wall? Or what sort of welcoming shore is this east of Hercules? Surely we don't anchor there, and disembark, and sweep into dinner with our host. Does someone cry "Last stop, last stop"? At any rate, east of Hercules, like east of Eden, isn't a place to call home. It is a course without direction; it is "out." And we are cast.

These are enervating thoughts, the thoughts of despair. They crowd back, unbidden, when human life as it unrolls goes ill, when we lose control of our lives or the illusion of control, and it seems that we are not moving toward any end but merely blown. Our life seems cursed to be a wiggle merely, and a wandering without end. Even nature is hostile and poisonous, as though it were impossible for our vulnerability to survive on these acrid stones.

Whether these thoughts are true or not I find less interesting than the possibilities for beauty they may hold. We are down here in time, where beauty grows. Even if things are as bad as they could possibly be, and as meaningless, then matters of truth are themselves indifferent; we may as well please our sensibilities and, with as much spirit as we can muster, go out with a buck and wing.

The planet is less like an enclosed spaceship — spaceship earth — than it is like an exposed mangrove island beautiful and loose. We the people started small and have since accumulated a great and solacing muck of soil, of human culture. We are rooted in it; we are bearing it with us across nowhere. The word "nowhere" is our cue: the consort of musicians strikes up, and we in the chorus stir and move and start twirling our hats. A mangrove island turns drift to dance. It creates its own soil as it goes, rocking over the salt sea at random, rocking day and night round the sun, rocking round the sun and out toward east of Hercules.

Meanings and Values

1a.   A sojourner is a person who lives in a place for only a brief time. Using this definition and Dillard's review of the term's connotations (par. 10), discuss the ways mangroves can be considered sojourners. (See Guide to Terms: *Connotation/Denotation*.)

b. Discuss the ways human beings can be considered sojourners.

2. As with many analogies, the points of comparison between the two subjects of this essay (floating islands and human life) are numerous. List as many of their similarities as you can, including those that are not mentioned directly in the essay.

3a. Summarize the central theme of this essay. (Because the second half of the essay is relatively abstract, the theme may be a bit more difficult to summarize than the themes of other essays in this collection.) (Guide: *Unity*.)

b. Are there places in the essay where the author sums up the meaning of the analogy and thereby hints at the central theme? Specify.

4a. What is the author's point of view? Does it change in the course of the essay? (Guide: *Point of View*.)

b. How would you describe the overall tone in this selection? (Guide: *Style/Tone*.)

c. Is the tone in paragraph 1–8 different from that in paragraphs 9–16?

5. Dillard calls attention to the statement "We could do worse" by making it a one-sentence paragraph. Clarify the meaning or meanings of the statement.

6. Who might the "host" in paragraph 13 be?

7. Where would you place this essay on an objective-to-subjective continuum? Why? (Guide: *Objective/Subjective*.)

8a. In what way are floating islands (par. 1) an example of paradox? (Guide: *Paradox*.)

b. What other examples of paradox can you find in this selection?

c. How are the paradoxes related to the theme of the essay? (Guide: *Unity*.)

9. Some people claim that Dillard's writing is often sentimental. Look at the passages where she describes feelings we often have about the meaninglessness of life (par. 14) or the lack of fit between our hopes and desires and the world we live in (pars. 11–12), and decide whether or not she has managed to avoid sentimentality. (Guide: *Sentimentality*.)

Expository Techniques

1a. The opening paragraph of this essay tries not only to interest readers in the topic but also to highlight the aspects of it that are most directly related to the author's theme. What devices of emphasis does the author use to accomplish these goals? (Guide: *Emphasis*.)

b. Keeping in mind both the essay's purpose and the potential reader-audience, indicate whether this is a successful introduction. (Guide: *Evaluation*.)

c.   If you do not think it is successful, discuss how it might be improved.

2.   Many instructors want their students to avoid using the pronoun "you" to address the reader unless they use it consistently throughout an essay. Dillard, however, introduces "you" abruptly in paragraph 5. Why does she do this? Is this use of "you" justified and effective?

3a. Where does the second part of the essay begin, and how does Dillard signal its beginning to the reader?

b.   If you answered "yes" to question 4c in "Meanings and Values," indicate what changes in style Dillard uses to help change the tone. (Guide: *Style/Tone.*)

4a. Is the first part of this essay easier to read than the second part? Why, or why not?

b.   Did you find the essay as a whole or any parts of it hard to read? If so, what caused you the most difficulty?

c.   Could the author have made the essay easier to read without destroying its effect or changing its purpose? Explain.

5a. The transitions between paragraphs in this essay are less obvious than those in some of the other essays in this book. Identify the transitional devices linking the following pairs of paragraphs and state why you think the author chose to use them: paragraphs 3 and 4, 4 and 5, 5 and 6, 11 and 12. (Guide: *Transition.*)

b.   Do the transitional devices help unify the essay while at the same time helping the author achieve the essay's purposes? (Guide: *Unity* and *Evaluation.*)

6a. In paragraphs 10 and 16, Dillard suggests two analogies different from the one used to organize the essay. What are they?

b.   Why does she suggest them only to reject them in favor of the analogy between human life and the floating mangrove islands?

Diction and Vocabulary

1a. Is the diction in the first part of this essay more concrete or more abstract than that in the second part? More specific or more general. (Guide: *Concrete/Abstract* and *Specific/General.*)

b.   In what other ways does the diction in the first part differ from that in the second part?

2a. In paragraph 2 the author uses what are known as "cumulative" sentences, that is, sentences that begin with a subject and predicate and then add a variety of modifiers at the end in order to explain, amplify, or illustrate. Identify the cumulative sentences in paragraph 2. (Guide: *Syntax*.)

b.   In what ways are cumulative sentences particularly appropriate to the author's purpose in paragraph 2?

c.   Identify cumulative sentences elsewhere in the selection and discuss their uses.

3a.   This selection uses unusual words and puts common words to unusual uses. Using a dictionary if necessary, discuss the meaning of the following phrases and indicate what they contribute to the passages from which they are taken and to the essay as a whole: "a leafy plumule unfurls" (par. 6); "organic broth" (6); "limpets a holdfast, pelagic birds a rest" (7); "these silly pansies and witless mountains," (11); "hard-eyed birds" (11).

b.   Do such words and phrases make the essay hard to read? Why, or why not?

c.   What, if anything, do such words and phrases add to the essay?

4.   Consult your dictionary as needed to determine the meanings of the following words: lapped (par. 1); buttresses (2); riptide, wrest (3); credulous, consort (4); exude (5); plumule, interstices, lee, amphipods, guano (6); whelk, kelp, limpets, pelagic, (7); wanton, pitchpole, stave (8); nomadic (10); lampoon (11); careering, disembark (13); enervating, acrid (14); indifferent, buck (15).

Suggestions for Writing and Discussion

Plan and discuss, in oral and written form, one of the following passages, clarifying its meanings and implications.

1.   "We the people started small and have since accumulated a great and solacing muck of soil, of human culture" (par. 16).

2.   "The coherence of matter dwindles and crumbles toward stillness" (par. 13).

3.   "Even if things are as bad as they could possibly be, and as meaningless, then matters of truth are themselves indifferent; we may as well please our sensibilities and, with as much spirit as we can muster, go out with a buck and wing" (par. 15).

4.   "It doesn't seem to be here that we belong, here where space is curved, the earth is round, we're all going to die, and it seems as wise to stay in bed as budge" (par. 12).

(NOTE: Suggestions for topics requiring development by use of ANALOGY follow.)

Writing Suggestions for Section 4
Analogy

In any normal situation, the analogy is chosen to help explain a theme-idea that already exists — such as those in the first group below. But for classroom training, which even at best is bound to be somewhat artificial, it is sometimes permissible to work from the other direction, to develop a theme that fits some preselected analogy-symbol. Your instructor will indicate which of the groups to use.

1. State a central theme about one of the following general topics or a suitable one of your own, and develop it into a composition by use of an analogy of your own choosing.

   a. A well-organized school system or business establishment.
   b. Starting a new business or other enterprise.
   c. The long-range value of programs for underprivileged children.
   d. The complexity of narcotics control.
   e. The need for cooperation between management and labor.
   f. Today's intense competition for success.
   g. Women's liberation in a "man's world."
   h. The results of ignorance.
   i. The dangers of propaganda.

2. Select an analogy-symbol from the following list and fashion a worthwhile theme that it can illustrate. Develop your composition as instructed.

   a. A freeway at commuting time.
   b. Building a road through a wilderness.
   c. Building a bridge across a river.
   d. A merry-go-round.
   e. A wedding.
   f. A car wash.
   g. Flood destruction of a levee.
   h. The tending of a young orchard.
   i. An animal predator stalking prey.
   j. A medical clinic.
   k. A juggling act.
   l. An oasis.

Explaining through *Process Analysis*

Process analysis explains how the steps of an operation lead to its completion. Although in one narrow sense it may be considered a kind of narration, process analysis has an important difference in purpose, and hence in approach. Other narration is mostly concerned with the story itself, or with a general concept illustrated by it, but process tells of methods that end in specified results. We might narrate a story about a rifle — its purchase, its role in colorful episodes, perhaps its eventual retirement from active servce. (We could, for other purposes, *define* "rifle," or *classify* the types of rifles, and no doubt *compare* and *contrast* these types and *illustrate* by examples.) But showing how a rifle works, or how it is manufactured, or how it should be cared for — this is process, and it sometimes becomes the basic pattern of an exposition.

Most writers are especially concerned with two kinds of process, both of them apparent in the preceding example of rifles: the directional, which explains how to *do* something (how to shoot a gun or how to clean it); and the informational, which explains how something is or was *done* (how guns are manufactured). The directional process can range from the instructions on a shampoo bottle to a detailed plan showing how to make the United Nations more effective, and will often contain detailed justification for individual steps or for the process itself. The informational process, on the other hand, might explain the steps of a wide variety of operations or actions, of mental or evolutionary processes, with no how-to-do-it purpose at all — how someone went about choosing a college or how the planet Earth was formed. Informational process analysis has been seen in earlier selections: Douglas explained how ants are an essential link in the development of the European blue butterfly, and Wolfe explained how the experiment with Norway rats was conducted.

Most process analyses are explained in simple, chronological steps. Indeed, the exact order is sometimes of greatest importance, as in a recipe. But occasionally there are problems in organization. The step-by-step format may need to be interrupted for descriptions, definitions, and other explanatory asides. If the process is a proposed solution, part of a problem-solution argument, then it may be necessary to justify each of the steps in turn and dismiss alternatives. And, still more of a problem, some processes defy a strict chronological treatment, because several things occur simultaneously. To explain the operating process of a gasoline engine, for example, the writer would be unable to convey at once everything that happens at the same time. Some way must be found to present the material in *general* stages, organized as subdivisions, so that the reader can see the step-by-step process through the confusion of interacting relationships.

Another difficulty in explaining by process analysis is estimating what knowledge the reader may already have. Presuming too little background may quickly lead to boredom or even irritation, with a resulting communication block; presuming too much will almost certainly leave the reader bewildered. Like a chain dependent on its weakest link for its strength, the entire process analysis can fail because of just one unclear point that makes the rest incomprehensible.

Sample Paragraph (Process Analysis)

Background information. *Process* objective is specified.

("Sort of": colloquial.)

Outsiders marvel at how Valley people are always of one opinion on public matters. But locally it's called "predisposition," a process having no legal status but used since early days when the Caseys still ran things. (In valley isolation, folks had developed a sort of poor-cousins complex, had become highly defensive against Outside

143

Begins *informational process* itself, how the specified objective is achieved. Uses simple chronological steps.

Authority.) The process begins with ten local forums throughout the Valley, where everyone can voice an opinion. Arguments are loud, sometimes physical, but in the end each major faction at each meeting elects its own share of delegates to the District Assembly. This convenes later in Grange Hall — and it all starts over, but on a generally more decorous level. Once the final vote is taken, that verdict becomes THE Valley opinion, come what may, with no exceptions. Anyone wanting to be an exception, in public, will certainly never want to again — like that new realtor in

Ends *informational process.*

Example, used to illustrate generality in preceding sentence.

("Guy": slang expression, not suitable in formal writing.)

Eden. Recently the State decided to put a four-lane road through the Valley, a move opposed by local "predisposition." But this guy went to a hearing in Bayport to relate how much the road was needed. A month later, when his last realty listings had evaporated, he changed his mind and went back to the city. And the State, recalling past experience, wisely decided not to mess around just now with those Valley hornets.

Result of the process.

("Mess around": colloquial.) ("Hornets" is used metaphorically.)

DONALD M. MURRAY

DONALD M. MURRAY, born in 1924 in Boston, is himself a writer and currently teaches writing at the University of New Hampshire. He has served as an editor of *Time* and, in 1954, was awarded the Pulitzer Prize for editorials written for the Boston *Herald*. Among his published works are novels, books of nonfiction, stories, poetry, and both a textbook and articles on the teaching of writing.

The Maker's Eye:
Revising Your Own Manuscripts

"The Maker's Eye: Revising Your Own Manuscripts," first published in slightly different form in *The Writer*, provides an example of directional process. The author presents his information in chronological steps, most of them supported by direct quotations from professional writers. Much of the advice is applicable to student writing as well as to professional work.

When students complete a first draft, they consider the job of writing done — and their teachers too often agree. When professional writers complete a first draft, they usually feel that they are at the start of the writing process. When a draft is completed, the job of writing can begin.

That difference in attitude is the difference between amateur and professional, inexperience and experience, journeyman and craftsman. Peter F. Drucker, the prolific business writer, calls his first draft "the zero draft" — after that he can start counting. Most writers share the feeling that the first draft, and all of those which follow, are opportunities to discover what they have to say and how best they can say it.

"The Maker's Eye: Revising Your Own Manuscripts" by Donald M. Murray, from *The Writer* (October 1973). Revised version reprinted by permission of International Creative Management. Copyright © 1973 by Donald M. Murray.

To produce a progression of drafts, each of which says more 3
and says it more clearly, the writer has to develop a special kind of
reading skill. In school we are taught to decode what appears on the
page as finished writing. Writers, however, face a different category
of possibility and responsibility when they read their own drafts. To
them the words on the page are never finished. Each can be changed
and rearranged, can set off a chain reaction of confusion or clarified
meaning. This is a different kind of reading, which is possibly more
difficult and certainly more exciting.

Writers must learn to be their own best enemy. They must 4
accept the criticism of others and be suspicious of it; they must
accept the praise of others and be even more suspicious of it. Writers
cannot depend on others. They must detach themselves from their
own pages so that they can apply both their caring and their craft to
their own work.

Such detachment is not easy. Science fiction writer Ray Brad- 5
bury supposedly puts each manuscript away for a year to the day
and then rereads it as a stranger. Not many writers have the discipline or the time to do this. We must read when our judgment may
be at its worst, when we are close to the euphoric moment of
creation.

Then the writer, counsels novelist Nancy Hale, "should be 6
critical of everything that seems to him most delightful in his style.
He should excise what he most admires, because he wouldn't thus
admire it if he weren't . . . in a sense protecting it from criticism."
John Ciardi, the poet, adds, "The last act of the writing must be to
become one's own reader. It is, I suppose, a schizophrenic process,
to begin passionately and to end critically, to begin hot and to end
cold; and, more important, to be passion-hot and critic-cold at the
same time."

Most people think that the principal problem is that writers are 7
too proud of what they have written. Actually, a greater problem for
most professional writers is one shared by the majority of students.
They are overly critical, think everything is dreadful, tear up page
after page, never complete a draft, see the task as hopeless.

The writer must learn to read critically but constructively, to cut 8
what is bad, to reveal what is good. Eleanor Estes, the children's
book author, explains: "The writer must survey his work critically,
coolly, as though he were a stranger to it. He must be willing to
prune, expertly and hard-heartedly. At the end of each revision, a

manuscript may look . . . worked over, torn apart, pinned together, added to, deleted from, words changed and words changed back. Yet the book must maintain its original freshness and spontaneity."

Most readers underestimate the amount of rewriting it usually takes to produce spontaneous reading. This is a great disadvantage to the student writer, who sees only a finished product and never watches the craftsman who takes the necessary step back, studies the work carefully, returns to the task, steps back, returns, steps back, again and again. Anthony Burgess, one of the most prolific writers in the English-speaking world, admits, "I might revise a page twenty times." Roald Dahl, the popular children's writer, states, "By the time I'm nearing the end of a story, the first part will have been reread and altered and corrected at least 150 times. . . . Good writing is essentially rewriting. I am positive of this."

Rewriting isn't virtuous. It isn't something that ought to be done. It is simply something that most writers find they have to do to discover what they have to say and how to say it. It is a condition of the writer's life.

There are, however, a few writers who do little formal rewriting, primarily because they have the capacity and experience to create and review a large number of invisible drafts in their minds before they approach the page. And some writers slowly produce finished pages, performing all the tasks of revision simultaneously, page by page, rather than draft by draft. But it is still possible to see the sequence followed by most writers most of the time in rereading their own work.

Most writers scan their drafts first, reading as quickly as possible to catch the larger problems of subject and form, then move in closer and closer as they read and write, reread and rewrite.

The first thing writers look for in their drafts is *information*. They know that a good piece of writing is built from specific, accurate, and interesting information. The writer must have an abundance of information from which to construct a readable piece of writing.

Next writers look for *meaning* in the information. The specifics must build to a pattern of significance. Each piece of specific information must carry the reader toward meaning.

Writers reading their own drafts are aware of *audience*. They put themselves in the reader's situation and make sure that they deliver information which a reader wants to know or needs to know in a manner which is easily digested. Writers try to be sure that they anticipate and answer the questions a critical reader will ask when reading the piece of writing.

Writers make sure that the *form* is appropriate to the subject and the audience. Form, or genre, is the vehicle which carries meaning to the reader, but form cannot be selected until the writer has adequate information to discover its significance and an audience which needs or wants that meaning.   16

Once writers are sure the form is appropriate, they must then look at the *structure*, the order of what they have written. Good writing is built on a solid framework of logic, argument, narrative, or motivation which runs through the entire piece of writing and holds it together. This is the time when many writers find it most effective to outline as a way of visualizing the hidden spine by which the piece of writing is supported.   17

The element on which writers may spend a majority of their time is *development*. Each section of a piece of writing must be adequately developed. It must give readers enough information so that they are satisfied. How much information is enough? That's as difficult as asking how much garlic belongs in a salad. It must be done to taste, but most beginning writers underdevelop, underestimating the reader's hunger for information.   18

As writers solve development problems, they often have to consider questions of *dimension*. There must be a pleasing and effective proportion among all the parts of the piece of writing. There is a continual process of subtracting and adding to keep the piece of writing in balance.   19

Finally, writers have to listen to their own voices. *Voice* is the force which drives a piece of writing forward. It is an expression of the writer's authority and concern. It is what is between the words on the page, what glues the piece of writing together. A good piece of writing is always marked by a consistent, individual voice.   20

As writers read and reread, write and rewrite, they move closer and closer to the page until they are doing line-by-line editing. Writers read their own pages with infinite care. Each sentence, each line, each clause, each phrase, each word, each mark of punctuation, each section of white space between the type has to contribute to the clarification of meaning.   21

Slowly the writer moves from word to word, looking through language to see the subject. As a word is changed, cut, or added, as   22 a construction is rearranged, all the words used before that moment and all those that follow that moment must be considered and reconsidered.

Writers often read aloud at this stage of the editing process, muttering or whispering to themselves, calling on the ear's experience with language. Does this sound right — or that? Writers edit, shifting back and forth from eye to page to ear to page. I find I must do this careful editing in short runs, no more than fifteen or twenty minutes at a stretch, or I become too kind with myself. I begin to see what I hope is on the page, not what actually is on the page.

This sounds tedious if you haven't done it, but actually it is fun. Making something right is immensely satisfying, for writers begin to learn what they are writing about by writing. Language leads them to meaning, and there is the joy of discovery, of understanding, of making meaning clear as the writer employs the technical skills of language.

Words have double meanings, even triple and quadruple meanings. Each word has its own potential for connotation and denotation. And when writers rub one word against the other, they are often rewarded with a sudden insight, an unexpected clarification.

The maker's eye moves back and forth from word to phrase to sentence to paragraph to sentence to phrase to word. The maker's eye sees the need for variety and balance, for a firmer structure, for a more appropriate form. It peers into the interior of the paragraph, looking for coherence, unity, and emphasis, which make meaning clear.

I learned something about this process when my first bifocals were prescribed. I had ordered a larger section of the reading portion of the glass because of my work, but even so, I could not contain my eyes within this new limit of vision. And I still find myself taking off my glasses and bending my nose towards the page, for my eyes unconsciously flick back and forth across the page, back to another page, forward to still another, as I try to see each evolving line in relation to every other line.

When does this process end? Most writers agree with the great Russian writer Tolstoy, who said, "I scarcely ever reread my published writings, if by chance I come across a page, it always strikes me: all this must be rewritten; this is how I should have written it."

The maker's eye is never satisfied, for each word has the poten- 29
tial to ignite new meaning. This article has been twice written all the
way through the writing process, and it was published four years
ago. Now it is to be republished in a book. The editors make a few
small suggestions, and then I read it with my maker's eye. Now it
has been re-edited, re-revised, re-read, re-re-edited, for each piece
of writing to the writer is full of potential and alternatives.

A piece of writing is never finished. It is delivered to a deadline, 30
torn out of the typewriter on demand, sent off with a sense of
accomplishment and shame and pride and frustration. If only there
were a couple more days, time for just another run at it, perhaps
then . . .

Meanings and Values

1a. What is the author's point of view in this selection? (See Guide to
Terms: *Point of View.*)

 b. What is the relationship between his tone and the point of view?
(Guide: *Style/Tone.*)

2a. What, if anything, prevents this selection from being as fascinating
to read as some of the other pieces already studied?

 b. Could (or should) Murray have done anything else to enliven his
process analysis? If so, what might it be?

3a. What was the author's purpose in writing this selection? (Guide:
Evaluation.)

 b. How well did he succeed?

 c. Was it worth doing?

Expository Techniques

1a. What standard techniques of introduction does this author use in
his opening paragraph? (Guide: *Introductions.*)

 b. How well does this paragraph meet the requirements of a good
introduction?

2. Into which of the two basic types of process analysis can this selection be classed? Why?

3. What, if anything, is gained by the frequent use of quotations from
professional writers?

4a. Are the distinctions among his eight steps of rewriting (pars. 13–20)
made clear enough? Be specific.

b.   Does anything about the order of these eight steps seem peculiar to you? If so, explain.

5a. Cite examples of parallel structure from paragraphs 21 and 26. (Guide: *Parallel Structure.*)

b.   What is gained by such usage?

Diction and Vocabulary

1a. Cite several uses of figurative language and state what kind they are. (Guide: *Figures of Speech.*)

b.   What is the main advantage in their use?

2a. What, if anything, do you find unusual about saying "a majority of their time" (par. 18)?

b.   What other way, if any, do you prefer?

3.   Is it clear to you how "each word has its own potential for connotation and denotation" (par. 25)? (Guide: *Connotation/Denotation.*) If it is, explain the assertion.

4.   Use the dictionary as necessary to understand the meanings of the following words: prolific (par. 2); euphoric (5); excise, schizophrenic (6); spontaneity (8); genre (16); potential (29).

Suggestions for Writing and Discussion

1a. Who was the reader-audience the author apparently had in mind in writing this process analysis?

b.   Explain fully why it would, or would not, be worth all the suggested time and trouble just to produce papers for your college courses?

2.   Discuss the assertion that "writers begin to learn what they are writing about by writing" (par. 24). If it seems more logical (for you) to learn what you are writing about some other way, what is it?

(NOTE: Suggestions for topics requiring development by PROCESS ANALYSIS are on page 174, at the end of this section.)

ALEXANDER PETRUNKEVITCH

ALEXANDER PETRUNKEVITCH (1875–1964), a Russian-born zoologist, taught at several leading American universities and received honors from others. He was one of the world's foremost authorities on spiders, and his first important book, published in 1911, was *Index Catalogue of Spiders of North, Central, and South America.* He later achieved distinction for his writings on zoological subjects as well as for his translations of English poetry into Russian and Russian poetry into English. Two of his other books are *Choice and Responsibility* (1947) and *Principles of Classification* (1952).

The Spider and the Wasp

"The Spider and the Wasp" was first published in the August 1952 issue of *Scientific American*, and it is reproduced here almost in its entirety. This essay should be particularly interesting to students of composition because it demonstrates not only exposition of natural process but also semiscientific writing that has been made understandable, perhaps even fascinating, for completely nonscientific readers. It is also a good illustration of the successful interweaving of several expository techniques.

1 In the feeding and safeguarding of their progeny insects and spiders exhibit some interesting analogies to reasoning and some crass examples of blind instinct. The case I propose to describe here is that of the tarantula spiders and their archenemy, the digger wasps of the genus *Pepsis.* It is a classic example of what looks like intelligence pitted against instinct — a strange situation in which the victim, though fully able to defend itself, submits unwittingly to its destruction.

2 Most tarantulas live in the tropics, but several species occur in the temperate zone and a few are common in the southern U.S.

Some varieties are large and have powerful fangs with which they can inflict a deep wound. These formidable-looking spiders do not, however, attack man; you can hold one in your hand, if you are gentle, without being bitten. Their bite is dangerous only to insects and small mammals such as mice; for man it is no worse than a hornet's sting.

Tarantulas customarily live in deep cylindrical burrows, from which they emerge at dusk and into which they retire at dawn. Mature males wander about after dark in search of females and occasionally stray into houses. After mating, the male dies in a few weeks, but a female lives much longer and can mate several years in succession. In a Paris museum is a tropical specimen which is said to have been living in captivity for 25 years.

A fertilized female tarantula lays from 200 to 400 eggs at a time; thus it is possible for a single tarantula to produce several thousand young. She takes no care of them beyond weaving a cocoon of silk to enclose the eggs. After they hatch, the young walk away, find convenient places in which to dig their burrows and spend the rest of their lives in solitude. The eyesight of tarantulas is poor, being limited to a sensing of change in the intensity of light and to the perception of moving objects. They apparently have little or no sense of hearing, for a hungry tarantula will pay no attention to a loudly chirping cricket placed in its cage unless the insect happens to touch one of its legs.

But all spiders, and especially hairy ones, have an extremely delicate sense of touch. Laboratory experiments prove that tarantulas can distinguish three types of touch: pressure against the body wall, stroking of the body hair, and riffling of certain very fine hairs on the legs called trichobothria. Pressure against the body, by the finger or the end of a pencil, causes the tarantula to move off slowly for a short distance. The touch excites no defensive response unless the approach is from above where the spider can see the motion, in which case it rises on its hind legs, lifts its front legs, opens its fangs and holds this threatening posture as long as the object continues to move.

The entire body of a tarantula, especially its legs, is thickly clothed with hair. Some of it is short and wooly, some long and stiff. Touching this body hair produces one of two distinct reactions. When the spider is hungry, it responds with an immediate and swift attack. At the touch of a cricket's antennae the tarantula seizes the insect so swiftly that a motion picture taken at the rate of 64 frames per second shows only the result and not the process of capture. But when the spider is not hungry, the stimulation of its hairs merely causes it to shake the touched limb. An insect can walk under its hairy belly unharmed.

The trichobothria, very fine hairs growing from disklike mem-   7
branes on the legs, are sensitive only to air movement. A light breeze makes them vibrate slowly, without disturbing the common hair. When one blows gently on the trichobothria, the tarantula reacts with a quick jerk of its four front legs. If the front and hind legs are stimulated at the same time, the spider makes a sudden jump. This reaction is quite independent of the state of its appetite.

These three tactile responses — to pressure on the body wall,   8
to moving of the common hair, and to flexing of the trichobothria — are so different from one another that there is no possibility of confusing them. They serve the tarantula adequately for most of its needs and enable it to avoid most annoyances and dangers. But they fail the spider completely when it meets its deadly enemy, the digger wasp *Pepsis*.

These solitary wasps are beautiful and formidable creatures.   9
Most species are either a deep shiny blue all over, or deep blue with rusty wings. The largest have a wing span of about 4 inches. They live on nectar. When excited, they give off a pungent odor — a warning that they are ready to attack. The sting is much worse than that of a bee or common wasp, and the pain and swelling last longer. In the adult stage the wasp lives only a few months. The female produces but a few eggs, one at a time at intervals of two or three days. For each egg the mother must provide one adult tarantula, alive but paralyzed. The mother wasp attaches the egg to the paralyzed spider's abdomen. Upon hatching from the egg, the larva is many hundreds of times smaller than its living but helpless victim. It eats no other food and drinks no water. By the time it has finished its single Gargantuan meal and become ready for wasphood, nothing remains of the tarantula but its indigestible chitinous skeleton.

The mother wasp goes tarantula-hunting when the egg in her   10
ovary is almost ready to be laid. Flying low over the ground late on a sunny afternoon, the wasp looks for its victim or for the mouth of a tarantula burrow, a round hole edged by a bit of silk. The sex of the spider makes no difference, but the mother is highly discriminating as to species. Each species of *Pepsis* requires a certain species of

tarantula, and the wasp will not attack the wrong species. In a cage with a tarantula which is not its normal prey, the wasp avoids the spider and is usually killed by it in the night.

Yet when a wasp finds the correct species, it is the other way   11
about. To identify the species the wasp apparently must explore the spider with her antennae. The tarantula shows an amazing tolerance to this exploration. The wasp crawls under it and walks over it without evoking any hostile response. The molestation is so great and so persistent that the tarantula often rises on all eight legs, as if it were on stilts. It may stand this way for several minutes. Meanwhile the wasp, having satisfied itself that the victim is of the right species moves off a few inches to dig the spider's grave. Working vigorously with legs and jaws, it excavates a hole 8 to 10 inches deep with a diameter slightly larger than the spider's girth. Now and again the wasp pops out of the hole to make sure that the spider is still there.

When the grave is finished, the wasp returns to the tarantula to   12
complete her ghastly enterprise. First she feels it all over once more with her antennae. Then her behavior becomes more aggressive. She bends her abdomen, protruding her sting, and searches for the soft membrane at the point where the spider's legs join its body — the only spot where she can penetrate the horny skeleton. From time to time, as the exasperated spider slowly shifts ground, the wasp turns on her back and slides along with the aid of her wings, trying to get under the tarantula for a shot at the vital spot. During all this maneuvering, which can last for several minutes, the tarantula makes no move to save itself. Finally the wasp corners it against some obstruction and grasps one of its legs in her powerful jaws. Now at last the harassed spider tries a desperate but vain defense. The two contestants roll over and over on the ground. It is a terrifying sight and the outcome is always the same. The wasp finally manages to thrust her sting into the soft spot and holds it there for a few seconds while she pumps in the poison. Almost immediately the tarantula falls paralyzed on its back. Its legs stop twitching; its heart stops beating. Yet it is not dead, as is shown by the fact that if taken from the wasp it can be restored to some sensitivity by being kept in a moist chamber for several months.

After paralyzing the tarantula, the wasp cleans herself by drag-   13
ging her body along the ground and rubbing her feet, sucks a drop of blood oozing from the wound in the spider's abdomen, then grabs a leg of the flabby, helpless animal in her jaws and drags it

down to the bottom of the grave. She stays there for many minutes, sometimes for several hours, and what she does all that time in the dark we do not know. Eventually she lays her egg and attaches it to the side of the spider's abdomen with a sticky secretion. Then she emerges, fills the grave with soil carried bit by bit in her jaws, and finally tramples the ground all around to hide any trace of the grave from prowlers. Then she flies away, leaving her descendant safely started in life.

In all this the behavior of the wasp evidently is qualitatively 14 different from that of the spider. The wasp acts like an intelligent animal. This is not to say that instinct plays no part or that she reasons as man does. But her actions are to the point; they are not automatic and can be modified to fit the situation. We do not know for certain how she identifies the tarantula — probably it is by some olfactory or chemo-tactile sense — but she does it purposefully and does not blindly tackle a wrong species.

On the other hand, the tarantula's behavior shows only confu- 15 sion. Evidently the wasp's pawing gives it no pleasure, for it tries to move away. That the wasp is not simulating sexual stimulation is certain because male and female tarantulas react in the same way to its advances. That the spider is not anesthetized by some odorless secretion is easily shown by blowing lightly at the tarantula and making it jump suddenly. What, then, makes the tarantula behave as stupidly as it does?

No clear, simple answer is available. Possibly the stimulation 16 by the wasp's antennae is masked by a heavier pressure on the spider's body, so that it reacts as when prodded by a pencil. But the explanation may be much more complex. Initiative in attack is not in the nature of tarantulas; most species fight only when cornered so that escape is impossible. Their inherited patterns of behavior apparently prompt them to avoid problems rather than attack them. For example, spiders always weave their webs in three dimensions, and when a spider finds that there is insufficient space to attach certain threads in the third dimension, it leaves the place and seeks another, instead of finishing the web in a single plane. This urge to escape seems to arise under all circumstances, in all phases of life, and to take the place of reasoning. For a spider to change the pattern of its web is as impossible as for an inexperienced man to build a bridge across a chasm obstructing his way.

In a way the instinctive urge to escape is not only easier but 17 often more efficient than reasoning. The tarantula does exactly what is most efficient in all cases except in an encounter with a ruthless and determined attacker dependent for the existence of her own species on killing as many tarantulas as she can lay eggs. Perhaps in this case the spider follows its usual pattern of trying to escape, instead of seizing and killing the wasp, because it is not aware of its danger. In any case, the survival of the tarantula species as a whole is protected by the fact that the spider is much more fertile than the wasp.

Meanings and Values

1. Briefly summarize the "qualitative" differences between the behavior of the tarantula and that of the wasp.

2. What is the likelihood that some humans also have inherited patterns of behavior that "prompt them to avoid problems rather than attack them" (par. 16)? Use concrete examples, if possible, to support your views.

3. What parallels to the tarantula-wasp relationship can you find in the history of nations? Be specific and explain.

4a. Describe the type, or types, of readers to whom you think *Scientific American* is meant to appeal. (Do not jump to conclusions: if not familiar with the magazine, you may have to browse through a few issues.)

b. If you were the editor, why would you have chosen (or not chosen) to publish this piece?

Expository Techniques

1a. Where does the author state his central theme?

b. Is this a desirable location? Why, or why not?

2a. What is the primary function of the process analysis in relation to the central theme?

b. How successfully does it accomplish its purpose?

3. In paragraph 9 the author goes from pure description of the wasp into the narrative account that involves both wasp and spider. How does he arrange the content itself to provide smooth and natural transition, hence ensuring coherence? (See Guide to Terms: *Transition* and *Coherence*.)

4. The author also usually arranges his subject materials to help achieve effective *inter*paragraph transitions so that one gets an echo

of the last part of one paragraph when reading the topic sentence of the next. List or mark the uses of this transitional device.

5. Effective coherence also depends to a great extent on smooth sentence-to-sentence transitions. In describing events in a time sequence, it is sometimes hard to avoid a dull list that runs on "and then . . . and then . . . ." List or mark the eight introductory devices showing time relationship in paragraph 12, and notice their variety.

6a. How many paragraphs constitute the closing?

b. What function do they serve in addition to concluding the selection?

7. This essay utilizes, to varying extents, the expository patterns of cause and effect, definition, induction, and description. It can also be used to illustrate three patterns we have already studied.

a. What are the patterns?

b. Explain their use in this essay.

Diction and Vocabulary

1. Do such informal expressions as "pops out of the hole" (par. 11), "for a shot at the vital spot," and "pumps in the poison" (12) help or hinder the essay's success? Why?

2. Consider such expressions as "beautiful and formidable creatures" (par. 9), "ghastly enterprise," and "terrifying sight" (12).

a. Are these expressions objective or subjective? (Guide: *Objective/ Subjective.*) Explain why.

b. Why would they be, or not be, suitable in a scientific report?

c. What useful purpose, if any, do they serve here?

3a. What do your answers to questions 1 and 2 indicate about the author's tone? (Guide: *Style/Tone.*)

b. How would you describe his tone?

c. Explain why it is, or is not, suitable to his subject matter and to his audience.

4. Any specialist writing on a technical subject for a lay audience (as much of *Scientific American*'s audience is) has a problem with professional terminology. Consider this author's use of "trichobothria" (par. 5), "chitinous" (9), "olfactory," and "chemo-tactile" (14).

a. Does there seem to be an excessive use of technical language?

b. Do you think these words could have been avoided without weakening scientific exactness? If so, how?

c. Does their use create a communication block for the lay reader, or does the author succeed in avoiding this fault?

d.   Why has he bothered to define "trichobothria" — even repeating his definition — but not the others?

5.   The use of "Gargantuan" (par. 9) is an allusion. (Guide: *Figures of Speech.*) Find the source to which the author alludes and explain the word's meaning in this essay.

6.   Consult the dictionary as needed for a full understanding of the following words, especially as used in this essay: progeny, archenemy, classic (par. 1); formidable (2); perception (4); riffling (5); disklike (7); tactile (8); pungent, chitinous (9); discriminating (10); evoking, molestation (11); harassed (12); secretion (13); qualitatively, olfactory, chemo-tactile (14); ruthless (17).

Suggestions for Writing and Discussion

1.   Use the tarantula-wasp relationship as the basis of an analogy to explain the relationship between two persons that you know.

2.   Use analogy as suggested above to explain the historical relationship between two specific countries.

3.   Using patterns of illustration and comparison, distinguish between intellectual and instinctive human behavior.

4.   Compare or contrast humans' motives for killing with those of animals. Some use of classification might also be helpful in this assignment.

(NOTE: Suggestions for topics requiring development by PROCESS ANALYSIS are on page 174, at the end of this section.)

ROBERT L. VENINGA and JAMES P. SPRADLEY

ROBERT L. VENINGA, born in 1941, in Milwaukee, Wisconsin, received his Ph.D. from the University of Minnesota and is associate professor in the Program of Health Education there. He has written on health education and health administration and is a frequent speaker at conventions in these fields.

JAMES P. SPRADLEY (1933–1983) was born in Baker, Oregon, and raised in Los Angeles. He received his Ph.D. in anthropology from the University of Washington and wrote more than a dozen books, including a widely adopted textbook, *Conformity and Conflict: Readings in Cultural Anthropology*. His scholarly books and articles covered such topics as skid-row alcoholics, cocktail-waitress culture, American family life, Kwakiutl Indian culture, childhood deafness, and the relationship between culture and stress. He taught at Seattle Pacific College and the University of Washington Medical School. At the time of his death he was DeWitt Wallace Professor of Anthropology at Macalester College, St. Paul, Minnesota.

The Stress Response

"The Stress Response" (editors' title), a selection from *The Work-Stress Connection: How to Cope with Job Burnout* (1981), is a good example of informational process. As is appropriate with a discussion of human behavior, the selection makes effective use of narrative, so that readers can see how their own behaviors are similar to those being discussed in the essay.

One of the most remarkable discoveries of modern science is that human beings have a general response to all forms of stress. Your body switches on the stress response whether you suffer from third-degree burns or receive an eviction notice. The pattern follows a similar course and it has a single goal: *to bring relief from the stress.* The stress response has evolved over millions of years and gives us, along with other mammals, a definite survival advantage.

During an earlier period of human existence, many daily stresses posed a direct threat to survival. One's life depended on an appropriate response executed with the greatest speed. The vast majority of strategies used by the earliest humans for dealing with threat depended on *muscular activity.* Like our primate ancestors before them, early hunter-gatherers depended exclusively on immediately available natural resources. They roamed about within a specific territory, chasing game animals, moving with wet and dry seasons to sources of food and water, fighting off predators, and protecting themselves against severe weather. The ability to use physical strength, speed, agility, and stamina was an important selective advantage. Through the long process of evolution, human beings came to share with other mammals this generalized stress response. It seeks to bring relief from stress *by means of vigorous muscular activity.*

Dr. Walter Cannon, an American physiologist, initiated the study of this stress response during the 1920s. Scientific research since then has supported the general outline of his theory, although we now know far more about the biochemical nature of this response pattern. Dr. Cannon called it the "fight-or-flight" response. He argued that it played an important role in survival. "If fear always paralyzed it would result in danger of destruction," he wrote. "But fear and aggressive feeling, as anticipatory responses to critical situations, make ready for action and thereby they have had great survival values."

The stress response actually involves four closely related processes. It begins when your body undergoes a rapid *mobilization,* a preparation for muscular activity. Consider the stress response of Ron Dorsey, a patrolman on the graveyard shift of a large city police department. On a cold night in January 1979, shortly after three o'clock, a call came over his radio. "Burglary in process at Sixteen hundred Grand Avenue." "That's mine!" he shouted to himself and at the same instant felt his heart begin to pound. Tense with fear, even though he had been on the force for six years, Ron sped to the address, an apartment building a few blocks away. As he skidded into the snow-covered alley behind the building, he saw a dark figure rush out the back door, dash across the alley, and run between two houses. "Stop or I'll shoot!" Ron yelled as he jumped from his car and started after the person. "I had no intention of shooting," Ron admitted later, "but I wanted to scare that guy into stopping." And stop he did, hands high in the air. In a moment Ron had him pushed up against the side of the house, frisked him for weapons, and then walked him back to his patrol car where he radioed for help. Less than four minutes had passed since Ron had first heard the call.

Like all of us under stress, Ron was keenly aware of his feelings, thoughts, and actions — what we call the behavioral aspects of the stress response. However, hidden from view, a host of endocrine and automatic-nervous-system functions had also taken place. A dramatic biochemical change had coursed through Ron's body. Hundreds of scientific studies have confirmed that the human body, anticipating the necessity of fight or flight, begins to mobilize almost instantly. And this happens whether you're chasing a criminal, denied a promotion, working under unrealistic deadlines, or ground down by an autocratic boss. . . . 5

It all starts in the hypothalamus, a tiny bundle of nerve cells at the center of the brain. Messages race from that command post and spread the alarm throughout the nervous system. Muscles tense. Blood vessels constrict. The tiny capillaries under the skin shut down altogether. The pituitary gland sends out two hormones that move through the bloodstream to stimulate the thyroid and adrenal glands. Thyroid hormones increase the energy supply you need to cope physically with the stress. The adrenals send some thirty additional hormones to nearly every organ in the body. This automatic stress response causes the pulse rate to shoot up; blood pressure soars. The stomach and intestines stop all the busy activity of digestion. Hearing and smell become more acute. Hundreds of other physical changes occur without us even knowing it. 6

The second process, one which starts immediately, is a sharp *increase in energy consumption*. The alarm reaction that puts the entire body in a state of readiness burns up considerable energy. That's why, in the aftermath of an auto accident or other sudden stress, even people who suffered no injuries will feel completely drained. It also helps to explain why people can sometimes perform feats of 7 exceptional strength in stress situations. Ron Dorsey's body began to burn up energy at a rapid rate the moment he received the call. His feelings of lassitude from several hours of dull routine disappeared with the changes in body chemistry.

Dr. Hans Selye, the pioneering endocrinologist and father of stress research, believes that under stress we use up a special fuel source, what he calls "adaptation energy." This energy provides power to mobilize the body; it also appears to give us strength for the fight-or-flight reaction. The way our body consumes this adaptation energy is critical to our understanding of job burnout. After four decades of stress research, Dr. Selye concluded that each human being has a finite amount of adaptation energy available at the time we encounter stress. After burning up part or all that is available, we need an opportunity to replenish the available supply by removing ourselves from the stress. When stress continues for a prolonged period, the available adaptation energy burns up and exhuastion sets in.

The third process that makes up part of our stress response is the *muscular action involved in fight or flight.* All the mobilization and energy consumption has this end in sight: taking some vigorous action to eliminate or escape the stress. The fight-or-flight adaptation worked well for early human beings, and it works well for us today, but only in certain situations. Taking quick and skillful action enabled Ron Dorsey to apprehend a suspected criminal. His stress response could hardly have been designed to carry out its job more efficiently. If you've ever had to jump out of the way of an oncoming automobile, swerve or hit your brakes to avoid a collision, stay up all night with a sick child, or rush someone to a hospital emergency room, you know the value of the fight-or-flight response.

Finally, the stress response ends with the *return of the body to a state of equilibrium.* Within a few hours Ron was back on the street, cruising in his patrol car. He felt tired but relaxed. That morning Ron went to bed early and slept for nine hours. He woke up feeling great. His adaptation energy had been renewed. Once again he was prepared to respond calmly to emergency situations. During the next few days, his body would continue to build up the supply of adaptation energy. Fortunately, nature has designed these relatively stable periods, including sleep, to restore our adaptation-energy level, leaving us prepared for future stress.

Meanings and Values

1. In your own words define the stress response as these authors present it. Make sure you identify each of its major elements, but keep your definition as brief as you can.

2a. According to the authors, the stress response developed over millions of years as a way "to bring relief from stress *by means of vigorous muscular activity.*" Is it still of use in a modern setting, where much of our activity is mental rather than physical? Provide illustrations to support your answer.

b. In what modern settings is the response particularly appropriate?

c. Particularly inappropriate?

3. How would you describe the tone of this essay? (See Guide to Terms: *Style/Tone.*)

4a. What practical value might this selection have for readers? (Might it explain, for example, why many people need to take a nap after a stressful day at work?)

b. Is the authors' purpose to provide practical advice? If not, how would you describe their purpose? (Guide: *Purpose.*)

Expository Techniques

1a. What transitional devices do the authors use to indicate where their explanations of each element in the stress response begin? (Guide: *Transition.*)

b. Are transitional devices used effectively in this essay? (Guide: *Evaluation.*)

2a. Would you describe this piece as a step-by-step explanation of a process? Explain.

b. If not, how would you describe the organization of the selection?

c. Why do you think the authors chose to organize the piece in the way they did?

3. The second paragraph is devoted to a discussion of the evolution of the stress response rather than to a direct explanation of how it works. What role does this paragraph play in the overall development of the selection? (Guide: *Unity.*)

4. What patterns other than process are used in this piece?

5a. What is gained or lost by presenting a single long example in paragraph 4 and using it rather than a number of shorter examples as the primary means for discussing the different elements of the stress response?

b.   Are most expository essays that follow a process pattern likely to use one well-developed example or multiple examples? Explain. (If you have read the Murray, Petrunkevitch, and/or Mitford essays in this section, you may wish to turn to them for examples to support your answer.)

Diction and Vocabulary

1a.   Who were "early hunter-gatherers" (par. 2)?

b.   What is the "graveyard shift" (par. 4)?

c.   What is the "fight-or-flight" response (par. 3)?

2.   This selection reports on scientific research about the stress response. Does it contain as many technical terms as you might expect in writing of this sort, or fewer?

3.   Consult your dictionary as needed to determine the meaning of the following words: primate, predators, agility, stamina, generalized (par. 2); physiologist, anticipatory (3); behavioral, endocrine, autonomic, coursed, autocratic (5); lassitude (7); adaptation, finite (8); equilibrium (10).

Suggestions for Writing and Discussion

1.   Even a normal day in the life of a student, a businessperson, or a parent can be stress-filled. Discuss just how stressful an average day can be for one of these kinds of people using examples to illustrate events that can set off the stress response.

2.   Certain professions or jobs cause more stress than the average occupation. Describe some of these stressful occupations and explain why they cause so much stress.

3.   Many diseases, including heart attacks and strokes, have been traced to excessive stress. Describe some stressful situations that occur in everyday life and propose ways to avoid setting of the stress response in these situations. (You may find it useful to classify the causes of stress.)

4.   Consider what other human behavior patterns besides the "fight-or-flight" response may have accounted for our success as a species over the long process of evolution. Choose one or more of these behaviors and argue whether they are or are not still appropriate in modern society. Comparison might be a useful pattern for this discussion. (As a starting point you might consider what role our behaviors in raising children played in our survival as a species.)

(NOTE: Suggestions for topics requiring development by PROCESS ANALYSIS are on page 174, at the end of this section.)

JESSICA MITFORD

Jessica Mitford was born in 1917, the daughter of an English peer. Her brother was sent to Eton, but she and her six sisters were educated at home by their mother. At the age of nineteen Mitford left home, eventually making her way to the United States in 1939. Since 1944 she has been an American citizen, and is now living in San Francisco. She did not begin her writing career until she was thirty-eight. Her books are *Lifeitselfmanship* (1956); her autobiography, *Daughters and Rebels* (1960); the best-seller *The American Way of Death* (1963); *The Trial of Dr. Spock* (1969); *Kind and Usual Punishment* (1973), a devastating study of the American penal system; *A Fine Old Conflict* (1977); and *Poison Penmanship* (1979). Mitford's articles have appeared in *The Atlantic Monthly*, *Harper's*, and *McCall's*.

To Dispel Fears of Live Burial

"To Dispel Fears of Live Burial" (editors' title) is a portion of *The American Way of Death*, a book described in *The New York Times* as a "savagely witty and well-documented exposé." The "savagely witty" style, evident in this selection, does not obscure the fact of its being a tightly organized, step-by-step process analysis.

Embalming is indeed a most extraordinary procedure, and one must wonder at the docility of Americans who each year pay hundreds of millions of dollars for its perpetuation, blissfully ignorant of what it is all about, what is done, how it is done. Not one in ten thousand has any idea of what actually takes place. Books on the subject are extremely hard to come by. They are not to be found in most libraries or bookshops. 1

In an era when huge television audiences watch surgical opera- 2 tions in the comfort of their living rooms, when, thanks to the animated cartoon, the geography of the digestive system has become familiar territory even to the nursery school set, in a land where the satisfaction of curiosity about almost all matters is a national pastime, the secrecy surrounding embalming can, surely, hardly be attributed to the inherent gruesomeness of the subject. Custom in this regard has within this century suffered a complete reversal. In the early days of American embalming, when it was performed in the home of the deceased, it was almost mandatory for some relative to stay by the embalmer's side and witness the procedure. Today, family members who might wish to be in attendance would certainly be dissuaded by the funeral director. All others, except apprentices, are excluded by law from the preparation room.

A close look at what does actually take place may explain in   3
large measure the undertaker's intractable reticence concerning a procedure that has become his major *raison d'être*. It is possible he fears that public information about embalming might lead patrons to wonder if they really want this service? If the funeral men are loath to discuss the subject outside the trade, the reader may, understandably, be equally loath to go on reading at this point. For those who have the stomach for it, let us part the formaldehyde curtain. . . .

The body is first laid out in the undertaker's morgue — or   4
rather, Mr. Jones is reposing in the preparation room — to be readied to bid the world farewell.

The preparation room in any of the better funeral establish-   5
ments has the tiled and sterile look of a surgery, and indeed the embalmer-restorative artist who does his chores there is beginning to adopt the term "dermasurgeon" (appropriately corrupted by some mortician-writers as "demisurgeon") to describe his calling. His equipment, consisting of scalpels, scissors, augers, forceps, clamps, needles, pumps, tubes, bowls and basins, is crudely imitative of the surgeon's as is his technique, acquired in a nine- or twelve-month post-high-school course in an embalming school. He is supplied by an advanced chemical industry with a bewildering array of fluids, sprays, pastes, oils, powders, creams, to fix or soften tissue, shrink or distend it as needed, dry it here, restore the moisture there. There are cosmetics, waxes and paints to fill the cover features, even plaster of Paris to replace entire limbs. There are ingenious aids to prop and stabilize the cadaver: A Vari-Pose Head

Rest, the Edwards Arm and Hand Positioner, the Repose Block (to support the shoulders during the embalming), and the Throop Foot Positioner, which resembles an old-fashioned stocks.

Mr. John H. Eckels, president of the Eckels College of Mortuary   6
Science, thus describes the first part of the embalming procedure: "In the hands of a skilled practitioner, this work may be done in a comparatively short time and without mutilating the body other than by slight incision — so slight that it scarcely would cause serious inconvenience if made upon a living person. It is necessary to remove the blood, and doing this not only helps in the disinfecting, but removes the principal cause of disfigurements due to discoloration."

Another textbook discusses the all-important time element: 7
"The earlier this is done, the better, for every hour that elapses between death and embalming will add to the problems and complications encountered. . . ." Just how soon should one get going on the embalming? The author tells us, "On the basis of such scanty information made available to this profession through its rudimentary and haphazard system of technical research, we must conclude that the best results are to be obtained if the subject is embalmed before life is completely extinct — that is, before cellular death has occurred. In the average case, this would mean within an hour after somatic death." For those who feel that there is something a little rudimentary, not to say haphazard, about this advice, a comforting thought is offered by another writer. Speaking of fears entertained in early days of premature burial, he points out, "One of the effects of embalming by chemical injection, however, has been to dispel fears of live burial." How true; once the blood is removed, chances of live burial are indeed remote.

To return to Mr. Jones, the blood is drained out through the   8
veins and replaced by embalming fluid pumped in through the arteries. As noted in *The Principles and Practices of Embalming*, "Every operator has a favorite injection and drainage point — a fact which becomes a handicap only if he fails or refuses to forsake his favorites when conditions demand it." Typical favorites are the carotid artery, femoral artery, jugular vein, subclavian vein. There are various choices of embalming fluid. If Flextone is used, it will produce a "mild, flexible rigidity. The skin retains a velvety softness, the tissues are rubbery and pliable. Ideal for women and children." It may be blended with B. and G. Products Company's

Lyf-Lyk tint, which is guaranteed to reproduce "nature's own skin texture . . . the velvety appearance of living tissue." Suntone comes in three separate tints: Suntan; Special Cosmetic Tint, a pink shade "especially indicated for young female subjects"; and Regular Cosmetic Tint, moderately pink.

About three to six gallons of dyed and perfumed solution of formaldehyde, glycerin, borax, phenol, alcohol and water are soon circulating through Mr. Jones, whose mouth has been sewn together with a "needle directed upward between the upper lip and gum and brought out through the left nostril," with the corners raised slightly "for a more pleasant expression." If he should be bucktoothed, his teeth are cleaned with Bon Ami and coated with colorless nail polish. His eyes, meanwhile, are closed with flesh-tinted eye caps and eye cement.

The next step is to have at Mr. Jones with a thing called a trocar. This is a long, hollow needle attached to a tube. It is jabbed into the abdomen, poked around the entrails and chest cavity, the contents of which are pumped out and replaced with "cavity fluid." This done, and the hole in the abdomen sewn up, Mr. Jones's face is heavily creamed (to protect the skin from burns which may be caused by leakage of the chemicals), and he is covered with a sheet and left unmolested for a while. But not for long — there is more, much more, in store for him. He has been embalmed, but not yet restored, and the best time to start the restorative work is eight to ten hours after embalming, when the tissues have become firm and dry.

The object of all this attention to the corpse, it must be remembered, is to make it presentable for viewing in an attitude of healthy repose. "Our customs require the presentation of our dead in the semblance of normality . . . unmarred by the ravages of illness, disease or mutilation," says Mr. J. Sheridan Mayer in his *Restorative Art*. This is rather a large order since few people die in the full bloom of health, unravaged by illness and unmarked by some disfigurement. The funeral industry is equal to the challenge: "In some cases the gruesome appearance of a mutilated or disease-ridden subject may be quite discouraging. The task of restoration may seem impossible and shake the confidence of the embalmer. This is the time for intestinal fortitude and determination. Once the formative work is begun and affected tissues are cleaned or removed, all doubts of success vanish. It is surprising and gratifying to discover the results which may be obtained."

The embalmer, having allowed an appropriate interval to 12 elapse, returns to the attack, but now he brings into play the skill and equipment of sculptor and cosmetician. Is a hand missing? Casting one in plaster of Paris is a simple matter. "For replacement purposes, only a cast of the back of the hand is necessary; this is within the ability of the average operator and is quite adequate." If a lip or two, a nose or an ear should be missing, the embalmer has at hand a variety of restorative waxes with which to model replacements. Pores and skin texture are simulated by stippling with a little brush, and over this cosmetics are laid on. Head off? Decapitation cases are rather routinely handled. Ragged edges are trimmed, and head joined to torso with a series of splints, wires and sutures. It is a good idea to have a little something at the neck — a scarf or high collar — when time for viewing comes. Swollen mouth? Cut out tissue as needed from inside the lips. If too much is removed, the surface contour can easily be restored by padding with cotton. Swollen necks and cheeks are reduced by removing tissue through vertical incisions made down each side of the neck. "When the deceased is casketed, the pillow will hide the suture incisions . . . as an extra precaution against leakage, the suture may be painted with liquid sealer."

The opposite condition is more likely to present itself — that of 13 emaciation. His hypodermic syringe now loaded with massage cream, the embalmer seeks out and fills the hollowed and sunken areas by injection. In this procedure the backs of the hands and fingers and the under-chin area should not be neglected.

Positioning the lips is a problem that recurrently challenges the 14 ingenuity of the embalmer. Closed too tightly, they tend to give a stern, even disapproving expression. Ideally, embalmers feel, the lips should give the impression of being ever so slightly parted, the upper lip protruding slightly for a more youthful appearance. This takes some engineering, however, as the lips tend to drift apart. Lip drift can sometimes be remedied by pushing one or two straight pins through the inner margin of the lower lip and then inserting them between the two front upper teeth. If Mr. Jones happens to have no teeth, the pins can just as easily be anchored in his Armstrong Face Former and Denture Replacer. Another method to maintain lip closure is to dislocate the lower jaw, which is then held in its new position by a wire run through holes which have been drilled through the upper and lower jaws at the midline. As the French are fond of saying, *il faut souffrir pour être belle.*[1]

If Mr. Jones has died of jaundice, the embalming fluid will very likely turn him green. Does this deter the embalmer? Not if he has intestinal fortitude. Masking pastes and cosmetics are heavily laid on, burial garments and casket interiors are color-correlated with particular care, and Jones is displayed beneath rose-colored lights. Friends will say, "How *well* he looks." Death by carbon monoxide, on the other hand, can be rather a good thing from the embalmer's viewpoint: "One advantage is the fact that this type of discoloration is an exaggerated form of a natural pink coloration." This is nice because the healthy glow is already present and needs but little attention.

The patching and filling completed, Mr. Jones is now shaved, washed and dressed. Cream-based cosmetic, available in pink, flesh, suntan, brunette and blond, is applied to his hands and face, his hair is shampooed and combed (and, in the case of Mrs. Jones, set), his hands manicured. For the horny-handed son of toil special care must be taken; cream should be applied to remove ingrained grime, and the nails cleaned. "If he were not in the habit of having them manicured in life, trimming and shaping is advised for better appearance — never questioned by kin."

Jones is now ready for casketing (this is the present participle of the verb "to casket"). In this operation, his right shoulder should be depressed slightly "to turn the body a bit to the right and soften the appearance of lying flat on the back." Positioning the hands is a matter of importance, and special rubber positioning blocks may be used. The hands should be cupped slightly for a more lifelike, relaxed appearance. Proper placement of the body requires a delicate sense of balance. It should lie as high as possible in the casket, yet not so high that the lid, when lowered, will hit the nose. On the other hand, we are cautioned, placing the body too low "creates the impression that the body is in a box."

Jones is next wheeled into the appointed slumber room where a few last touches may be added — his favorite pipe placed in his hand or, if he was a great reader, a book propped into position. (In

[1]You have to suffer if you want to be beautiful. — Eds.

the case of little Master Jones a Teddy bear may be clutched.) Here he will hold open house for a few days, visiting hours 10 A.M. to 9 P.M.

Meanings and Values

1a. What is the author's tone? (See Guide to Terms: *Style/Tone*.)

b. Try to analyze the effect this tone had, at first reading, on your impressions of the subject matter itself.

c. Form a specific comparison between this effect of tone and the effect of "tone of voice" in spoken language.

2. Why was it formerly "almost mandatory" for some relative to witness the embalming procedure (par. 2)?

3a. Do you believe that public information about this procedure would cost mortuaries much embalming business (par. 3)? Why, or why not?

b. Why *do* people subject their dead to such a process?

4. Use the three-part system of evaluation to judge the success of this process analysis. (Guide: *Evaluation*.)

Expository Techniques

1a. What is the central theme? (Guide: *Unity*.)

b. Which parts of the writing, if any, do not contribute to the theme, thus damaging unity?

c. What other elements of the writing contribute to, or damage, unity?

2a. Beginning with paragraph 4, list or mark the transitional devices that help to bridge paragraphs. (Guide: *Transition*.)

b. Briefly explain how coherence is aided by such interparagraph transitions.

3. In this selection, far more than in most, emphasis can best be studied in connection with style. In fact, the two are almost indistinguishable here, and few, if any, of the other methods of achieving emphasis are used at all. (Guide: *Emphasis* and *Style/Tone*.) Consider each of the following stylistic qualities (some may overlap; others are included in diction) and illustrate, by examples, how each creates emphasis.

a. Number and selection of details — e.g., the equipment and "aids" (par. 5).

b. Understatement — e.g., the "chances of live burial" (par. 7).

c. Special use of quotations — e.g., "that the body is in a box" (par. 17).

d. Sarcasm and/or other forms of irony — e.g., "How *well* he looks" (par. 15). (Guide: *Irony.*)

Diction and Vocabulary

1. Much of the essay's unique style (with resulting emphasis) comes from qualities of diction. Use examples to illustrate the following. (Some may be identical to those of the preceding answer, but they need not be.)

a. Choice of common, low-key words to achieve sarcasm through understatement — e.g., "This is nice . . ." (par. 15).

b. Terms of violence — e.g., "returns to the attack" (par. 12).

c. Terms of the living — e.g., "will hold open house" (par. 18).

d. The continuing use of "Mr. Jones."

2a. Illustrate the meaning of "connotation" with examples of quotations from morticians. (Guide: *Connotation/Denotation.*)

b. Are these also examples of "euphemism"?

c. Show how the author uses these facts to her own advantage — i.e., again, to achieve emphasis.

3a. Comment briefly on the quality and appropriateness of the metaphor that ends the introduction. (Guide: *Figures of Speech.*)

b. Is this, in any sense, also an allusion? Why, or why not?

4. Use the dictionary as needed to understand the meanings of the following words: docility, perpetuation (par. 1); inherent, mandatory (2); intractable, reticence, *raison d'être* (3); ingenious (5); rudimentary, cellular, somatic (7); carotid artery, femoral artery, subclavian vein (8); semblance (11); simulated, stippling, sutures (12); emaciation (13); dispel (7, title).

Suggestions for Writing and Discussion

1. What evidence can you find that "the satisfaction of curiosity about almost all matters is a national pastime" (par. 2)? Is this a good thing or not? Why?

2. Burial customs differ widely from country to country, sometimes from area to area in this country. If you can, describe one of the more distinctive customs and, if possible, show its sources — e.g., the climate, "old country" tradition.

3. What do you foresee as near- and far-future trends or radical changes in American burial practices? Why?

4.   You may wish to develop further your answers to question 3 of "Meanings and Values" — the rationale of a large majority of people who do use this mortuary "service" for their departed relatives.

5.   If you like, explain your personal preferences and the reasons for them.

(NOTE: Suggestions for topics requiring development by PROCESS ANALYSIS follow.)

Writing Suggestions for Section 5
Process Analysis

1. From one of the following topics develop a central theme into an *informational* process analysis, showing:
   a. How you selected a college.
   b. How you selected your future career or major field of study.
   c. How your family selected a home.
   d. How a potential riot was stopped.
   e. How religious faith is achieved.
   f. How gasoline is made.
   g. How the air in _____ becomes polluted.
   h. How lightning kills.
   i. How foreign policy is made.
   j. How political campaigns are financed.
   k. How _____ Church was rebuilt.
   l. How fruit blossoms are pollinated.
   m. How an unusual sport is played.

2. Select a specific reader-audience and write a *directional* process analysis on one of the following topics, showing:
   a. How to *do* any of the processes suggested by topics 1a–e. (This treatment will require a different viewpoint, completely objective, and may require a different organization.)
   b. How to overcome shyness.
   c. How to overcome stage fright.
   d. How to make the best use of study time.
   e. How to write a college composition.
   f. How to sell an ugly house.
   g. How to prepare livestock or any other entry for a fair.
   h. How to start a club (or some other kind of recurring activity).
   i. How to reduce the number of highway accidents in an area.
   j. How to survive a tornado (or other natural disaster).
   k. How to select a car.
   l. How to develop moral (or physical) courage.
   m. How to set up a fish tank and keep the fish alive and healthy.

6

Analyzing *Cause and Effect* Relationships

Unlike process analysis, which merely tells *how*, causal analysis seeks to explain *why*. The two may be combined, but they need not be — many people have driven a car successfully after being told how to do it, never knowing or caring why the thing moved when they turned a key and worked a pedal or two.

Some causes and effects are not very complicated; at least their explanation requires only a simple statement. A car may sit in the garage for a while because its owner has no money for a license tag, and sometimes this is explanation enough. But frequently a much more thorough analysis is required, and this may even become the basic pattern of an exposition.

To explain fully the causes of a war or a depression or election results, the writer must seek not only *immediate* causes (the ones encountered first) but also *ultimate* causes (the basic, underlying factors that help to explain the more apparent ones). Business or professional people, as well as students, often have a pressing need for this type of analysis. How else could they fully understand or report on a failing sales campaign, diminishing church membership, a local increase in traffic accidents, or teenage use of hard drugs? The immediate cause of a disastrous warehouse fire could be faulty electrical wiring, but this might be attributed in turn to the company's unwise economy measures, which might be traced even further to undue pressures on the management to show large profits. The written analysis might logically stop at any point, of course, depending entirely on its purpose and the reader-audience for which it is intended.

Similarly, both the immediate and ultimate *effects* of an action or situation may, or may not, need to be fully explored. If a 5 percent pay raise is granted, what will be the immediate effect on the cost of production, leading to what ultimate effects on prices and, in some cases, on the economy of a business, a town, or perhaps the entire nation?

In earlier selections of this book we have seen several examples of causal analysis. In Section 1, for instance, Buckley gives some attention to both immediate and ultimate causes of American apathy, and in Section 4, Wolfe is concerned with both immediate and ultimate effects of overcrowding.

Causal analysis is one of the chief techniques of reasoning; and if the method is used at all, the reader must always have confidence in its thoroughness and logic. Here are some ways to avoid the most common faults in causal reasoning:

1. Never mistake the fact that something happens with or after another occurrence as evidence of a causal relationship — for example, that a black cat crossing the road caused the flat tire a few minutes later, or that a course in English composition caused a student's nervous breakdown that same semester.

2. Consider all possibly relevant factors before attributing causes. Perhaps studying English did result in a nervous breakdown, but the cause may also have been ill health, trouble at home, or the anguish of a love affair. (The composition course, by providing an "emotional" outlet, may even have helped *postpone* the breakdown!)

3. Support the analysis by more than mere assertions: offer evidence. It would not often be enough to *tell* why Shakespeare's wise Othello believed the villainous Iago — the dramatist's lines should be used as evidence, possibly supported by the opinions of at least one literary scholar. If you are explaining that capital punishment deters crime, do not expect the reader to take your word for it — give before-and-after statistics or the testimony of reliable authorities.

4. Be careful not to omit any links in the chain of causes or effects unless you are certain that the readers for whom the writing is intended will automatically make the right connections themselves — and this is frequently a dangerous assumption. To unwisely omit one or more of the links might leave the reader with only a vague, or even erroneous, impression of the causal connec-

tion, possibly invalidating all that follows and thus making the entire writing ineffective.

5. Be honest and objective. Writers (or thinkers) who bring their old prejudices to the task of causal analysis, or who fail to see the probability of *multiple* causes or effects, are almost certain to distort their analyses or to make them so superficial, so thin, as to be almost worthless.

Ordinarily the method of causal analysis is either to work logically from the immediate cause (or effect) down toward the most basic, or to start with the basic and work up toward the immediate. But after at least analyzing the subject and deciding what the purpose requires in the paragraph or entire composition, the writer will usually find that a satisfactory pattern suggests itself.

Sample Paragraph (Cause/Effect)

("Time-hallowed" is used in a somewhat ironic sense.)
("They've," "fiddling around," and "rap session" are colloquial and would not be suitable in more formal writing.)

On analysis, this first *immediate cause* is made up of three causes fitting into each other: the kids get into less trouble *because* they have less time *because* they have to work *because* they live in the country. ("Kids" is colloquial.)

Three *immediate causes*.

Most members of Ilona Principals' League agree that Valley young people are far better behaved than most they've encountered. Except for time-hallowed vices — like sneaking a smoke or a beer, or a little fiddling around between sexes — juvenile delinquency is rare. Why? At their last rap session the educators decided these are the most obvious causes: First, being in a basically rural area, most children grow up with work to do, leaving less time and energy for trouble. Because country kids predominate, working has long been "in" among even "townies" who might otherwise be less subject to it. Second, a much higher percentage of families here remain intact, more likely to keep a traditional value system. (Even the swingers of Eden, when they begin to raise families, usually settle down and establish rules.) Third, the small,

178

The *ultimate cause*: the Valley's isolation.

[One paragraph does not permit much support for the assertions. The use of principals, however, does give the assertions some authority.]

close-knit communities are mostly well stocked with relatives, interested in keeping misbehavior in check. But basic to all of these is the fact of the Valley's isolation, more psychological now than physical, but nonetheless real. By the time kids reach their upper teens, get driver's licenses, and begin to mix freely at school affairs outside the Valley, character is generally well enough formed to take some exposure to the drug-and-crime culture of the "other world."

CAROL TAVRIS

Carol Tavris earned her Ph.D. in social psychology from the University of Michigan and currently teaches at the Human Relations Center of the New School for Social Research in New York. She is the author of *Anger: The Misunderstood Emotion* (1982), co-author of *The Longest War: Sex Differences in Perspective* (1977), and a contributing editor of *American Health* magazine. She has also published articles in a variety of popular magazines, including *Psychology Today, Vogue, Ms., Redbook, New York, Geo,* and *Human Nature.*

Seeing Red

"Seeing Red," excerpted from a chapter of the same title in *Anger: The Misunderstood Emotion,* shows why it is often necessary to go beyond the most obvious explanations to get at the real causes of human behavior. The causal analysis in this selection is sometimes complicated, but the author's effective use of example and other patterns of exposition make the piece interesting and easy to follow.

[When reason] is asleep, then the wild beast within us, gorged with meat or drink, starts up and having shaken off sleep, goes forth to satisfy his desires; and there is no conceivable folly or crime it won't commit.

— *Plato*

It is a perfect spring day in New York, a day to banish winter surliness. 1
Buoyant and happy, my husband and I emerge from the Museum of Modern Art late in the afternoon, when we realize that our sojourn has delayed us in meeting friends for dinner. Every phone booth on the block is occupied. We walk down several streets, but apparently the rest of New York City is going to be late for dinner, too. We see a young couple standing at a pair of public telephones, and as the woman finishes her conversation and is about to start

another I ask her politely whether I might make the briefest of calls. Sudden-
ly, the young man, a natty fellow in a business suit and gold chains, whirls
around and spits obscenities at us. He is so vicious, and his anger so
unexpected, that we feel physically violated.

For the next hour we have vivid fantasies of retaliation: what we should 2
have said, what we should have done. As we tell our dinner companions
about the experience our anger returns, and I am astonished by my desire to
slap the arrogance out of that young man's contorted, ugly face. I am also
astonished by the depth of feeling this trivial incident produces.

Brief rages like this are familiar experiences for most city dwell- 3
ers. They erupt when the already high level of stimulation that
urban life produces is ignited by people who behave unexpectedly
or who heed their own rules of conduct. Of course, there are plenty
of outrageous events that will make us feel angry — threats,
assaults, heartless murders, injustices — but the question here is
the way provocations intersect with the background buzz of our
lives.

For example, suppose that a couple goes to see a pornographic 4
movie and are turned on by it. Now suppose they get into an
argument about finances on the way home. Their heightened emotional arousal from the movie is likely to inflame their quarrel,
making them feel angrier with each other than if they hadn't seen
the movie. But what if they have the quarrel on the way *to* the
movie? Now the film is likely to act as a diverson, redirecting their
angry arousal into feelings of sexual stimulation. (Three psychologists, Edward and Marcia Donnerstein and R. Evans, have actually
conducted the experiment that demonstrated this.)

Clearly, the answer to such questions as "How does pornogra- 5
phy affect its viewers?" is complicated. So is the answer to "What
provocations make you angry?" because anger will often depend on
whether your level of physiological arousal occurs before or after a
specific provocation. Anger depends on some things you are aware
of (such as the rude young man at the phone booth) and others that
you are not aware of (such as your heart rate and adrenaline level).
This is why events that you may find amusing on Tuesday seem
infuriating on Friday, or why the mannerisms of your beloved that
you usually find charming are today grating on your nerves.

If you put a few rats together in a small cage, it is easy to set up 6 circumstances that will soon have them at each other's throats. You can blast them with loud, incessant noise. You can crowd them together like rush-hour commuters. You can give them the rat equivalent of a long hot summer. Rats are physiologically human-ish, which is why they are used reliably to test our foods for cancer and our stresses for disease. But human beings differ from rats in (at least) one respect: the things that will agitate a rat will anger a person only under certain psychological conditions.

In today's conservative climate, where much effort is being made to demonstrate the genetic (and by inference ineradicable) components of human behavior, I think it is especially important to try to specify those psychological conditions. If frustration is dangerous, we best be careful not to place obstructions in the way of our children, lovers, friends or co-workers; indeed, we'd better be certain not to let our own frustrations mount up. If noise and crowds generate aggression, there's not much point in trying to improve urban conditions; it's urban life itself that is making us miserable. If aggression in sports is at least one way to absorb our city rages, then let's encourage those hockey and tennis players who celebrate violence. If people are not responsible for their actions when they drink, then we and our laws might as well continue to forgive drunk drivers, abusive spouses, and assaultive individuals who "only had a couple too many." In the examples that follow, a pattern is apparent. Frustration, noise, crowds, alcohol, and sports do not instinctively generate or "release" anger; they generate physical arousal which, when coupled with a psychological provocation, can *become* the feeling of anger. Conversely, the same arousal, when coupled with a happier interpretation of events, can become the feeling of exhilaration. The failure to understand the connections between arousal, attitude, and aggression has led to a host of misunderstandings in our laws, entertainment, love affairs, and daily lives. . . . 7

New York is a noisy place; Los Angeles is not. New York is filled with the sounds of drills and car honks and sirens, shouters and singers and musicians, blaring radios and shrill arguments. Los Angeles is filled with the sounds of warbling birds and the gentle whizz of traffic, which hardly ever honks. I can sleep through almost anything in New York. In Los Angeles, the sound of a 8 neighbor's whirring air conditioner and the raucous caw of a single bird will rouse me grumbling. A New Yorker I know inhales the sounds of sirens as if they were magnolia blossoms. "I love that noise," he says. "It means someone is racing to the rescue. It means help. It means the city is working." "I hate sirens," his wife says, "that AW-oo, AW-oo at an intolerably loud and piercing level. A siren is a shriek that means another disaster."

The sound, therefore, is not always the fury. The anger provoked by noise has much to do with what the noise represents. For instance, many New Yorkers are angry about the blaring tape decks — the "singing briefcase," as one wit called them — that some teenagers carry with them on the street, in subways, in parks. The music is usually disco, played at full blast; and the kids who strut around with these weighty machines are usually black or Hispanic. Middle-class citizens regard the noise of street stereos as acts of thoughtlessness at best and open hostility to whites at worst. Both explanations are possible. But it is also possible that the singing briefcases are a fad, a mark of status like the zoot suit, DA haircut, or souped-up jalopies, all of which infuriated the elders of their day. And the folks who hate this music and its intrusion on their private reveries often go home to apartments that usually have excellent stereo systems, where they play, at top volume, their preferences in rock, jazz, and classical. It's not noise alone that angers. It's what the noise means.

Loud sounds are arousing: they produce an increase in adrenaline that may feel uncomfortable. ("My father's loud Wagner operas made my mother feel she was going to cry," one woman told me. "He never believed her, though. He just thought she was out to deprive him of one of his few great pleasures.") This arousal, when coupled with a provocation, generates anger. Noise alone does not make people angry or aggressive, but noise *increases the likelihood* of anger when a catalyst is added.

To distinguish the effects of noise from the effects of human offensiveness, Vladimir Konečni asked 120 young men and women to participate in what they thought was an experiment on learning. Each student worked on an anagram test with Konečni's confederate; sometimes the confederate kept up a patter of insults and irritating mannerisms, sometimes he behaved himself and worked quietly on the anagrams. In the next phase of the study, each student read fifty words to the confederate, who had to give a one-word free-association answer. If the student thought the answer was "creative," he pushed a button marked *good*; otherwise, he pushed a button that supposedly administered shock.

All through this "learning" procedure, the students wore earphones and listened to a steady stream of music. Well, it wasn't exactly music. Because Konečni wanted to control the precise degree of complexity and loudness of the noise without contaminating these factors by the students musical preferences, he programmed a computer to generate tones. The "music" ranged in complexity from nursery-song level to the highly avant-garde, and from the soft (about 73 decibels) to loud (about 97 decibels). So some of the students heard computer compositions that were loud and simple (rather than disco); others got a soft and simple version (like Muzak); others, loud and complex (like jazz); and others, soft and complex (analogous, perhaps, to a Bach fugue). A control group heard no sounds at all during the experiment. 12

Konečni found that people, unlike rats, need more than noise to provoke aggression. The students who had not been insulted by the stooge were completely unaffected by the noise. They dealt between eleven and thirteen shocks, on the average, whether they were listening to loud and complicated noise, soft and pleasant noise, or no noise at all. The students who had been insulted but who were not aroused by the music gave about fifteen shocks, not appreciably more than the noninsulted students. But when the music was loud *or* complex, and especially when it was loud *and* complex, the insulted students felt the angriest of all groups and readily seized the chance to get back at their offender. They blasted him with an average of five shocks more than anyone else gave. 13

Inadvertently, Konečni discovered the truth of one cliché, while adding a modern modification. The students who listened to the simple, quiet tones were the least likely to be provoked by the offensive partner. They didn't retaliate angrily against him when they had the chance. They didn't rise to his bait. Apparently it isn't just any music that soothes the savage breast, but Muzak. 14

The sheer decibel level of the noise around us is not enough to make us cranky, irritable, or aggressive. (It can, however, affect our mental and physical health, which is another matter.) Suppose a new highway is built near your house and now you have to put up with the rumble and buzz of traffic all day long. Does the noise annoy you? According to research, the answer is no if you be- 15 lieve that the road has brought economic benefits to your community — jobs and services — and therefore increased the value of your house. The answer is yes if you believe your property values have been diminished and if you bought the house in the first place to live in a remote spot. Even people who live near the deafening roar of airports are not irritated by the noise of airplanes if they believe in the importance and benefit of airports to their own economic health. Once again, actual anger depends on what the noise means to you. . . .

Not long ago, a fashionable explanation of urban violence was population density. Comparing clustered people to trapped rats, some observers argued that crowded cities would turn into urban sinks. They produced statistics that correlated measures of density (such as number of people per residential acre or average number of individuals per room) with juvenile delinquency, infant mortality, VD, crime, and other forms of social pathology. The evidence looked good at first, but the theory subsequently fell into disrepute. The association between density and pathology disintegrates when income, education, and ethnicity are taken into account. Among the poor in America, it is poverty, not crowding per se, that causes crime and other problems. In Tokyo, where population density exceeds that of any U.S. city, crowding is not associated with social pathology. In spacious Los Angeles, where you can drive for blocks and not see a pedestrian, the crime rate exceeds that of New York.

Further, some crowds are wonderful, even an essential part of the fun, such as at baseball games, carnivals, summer concerts in the park, jazz clubs, bars, and New Year's celebrations. One hundred scattered fans at a football game are depressing to viewers and players alike, and few would want to eat at a restaurant if only three of twenty tables were occupied. Crowded conditions in steerage, for immigrants fulfilling a life's dream to come to America, did not produce the rage that crowded conditions in prisons do.

So it is not crowding itself that creates anger, but one's perceptions about the crowd. Does a crowd make you feel trapped, or do you know how to get around in spite of it? Did you choose to join the crowd, or did it join you? Is it temporary or permanent? What have your experience and culture taught you about crowds? Most of all, do you have control over your actions when you are in a crowd, or does the sheer force of numbers keep you from doing what you want?

The mere presence of many other people is indeed arousing — 19
to a lesser extent, so is the presence of one other person — but
whether that arousal is transformed into pleasure or anger depends
less on whether you *are* crowded than on whether you *feel* crowded.
Density itself does not make you angry until it curtails your sense of
freedom and control. For example, when people are able to work
effectively and without interruptions in a densely packed room,
they feel less crowded than if they work with interruptions in the
same room with fewer people. The same number of persons per
square foot will feel pleasant in a cozy pub and frightening in a
stalled subway. The dreadful failure of housing projects such as
Pruitt-Igoe, which was nearly destroyed by its inhabitants before
the city of St. Louis tore it down, was not a result of overcrowding
but of bad design. Cold, impersonal, alienating structures can make
people feel unhappy living or working in them, especially if they
aren't designed to make human connections easy and regular; it is
the mismanagement of density that creates the problem, not the
density.

At the upper limits of density, of course, such as a traffic jam or 20
a rock concert, crowding and loss of control are synonymous. But in
everyday life, people learn how to work their own crowds; it's only
unfamiliar crowds that unsettle them. Dense living conditions that
are normal to a Japanese would be cramped to a Chicagoan, and
Chicago's density would be intolerable to a Nebraskan. The teeming
streets of Fez, where native Moroccans know how to dodge the
animals and each other to get where they are going, make me feel
anxious, excited, and, if I'm jostled, irritated; the teeming streets of
the Lower East Side, where I know how to find bargains and
blintzes, make me feel energetic, happy, and, if I'm jostled, tolerant.

The arousal of crowds may break into anger if the usual rules 21
that govern crowd action are violated. Arabs and Latin Americans
stand closer to each other in conversation than Americans do,
taking detailed note of facial expressions and mannerisms. An
American who does not know this is likely to feel "pushed" and
annoyed when an Arab stands too close for comfort; he misinter-
prets the Arab's stance as a provocation. By and large, middle-class
Americans have a greater need for distance and privacy than many
other groups do. This is a learned, social need, not a biological one.
Many Americans who visit China cannot understand how the

Chinese can "crowd" several generations into small quarters. The Chinese are equally astonished to learn that American parents, who frequently give each of their children a separate room, would feel crowded if grandparents and other relatives lived with them. The Chinese and the Americans have entirely different family structures, values, and beliefs about crowding.

Feeling angry about being crowded also depends on what you have relative to what you used to have, as a famous old Jewish story teaches. It seems a poor man complained to his rabbi about the overcrowding in his house: a wife, six children, a mother-in-law, and a boarder were driving him crazy. The rabbi listened and offered one sentence of advice: "Bring your goat into the house." "My goat?" "Your goat."   22

A week later the poor man returned, complaining about the stench and dirt of the goat in addition to the crowd in his house. The rabbi said: "Bring your chickens into the house." "Oy, rabbi, my chickens?" "Your chickens."   23

A week later the poor man was a nervous wreck. "Rabbi," he moaned, "you have to help me." The rabbi listened. "Put out the goat." "Only the goat?" "Only the goat."   24

The poor man did as he was told, and returned to the rabbi in a few days. "It's better, Rabbi," he said, "but a house full of nine people and three chickens . . ." "Put out the chickens," said the rabbi.   25

A week later the man returned to the rabbi. "Rabbi, you're a genius!" he said. "Now my house is as roomy as a mansion!"   26

Meanings and Values

1. Do you have confidence in this author's facts and reasoning? Why, or why not?

2a. In this selection the author tries to distinguish between provocations that can cause anger and conditions that contribute to it. How successful is she in making this distinction and in supporting it with examples? (See Guide to Terms: *Evaluation*.)

  b. Think back over the last two weeks about times you got angry and describe the events, trying to identify both the provocation and the contributing conditions.

  c. Besides noise and crowding, what conditions can you think of that might contribute to anger? (Be ready to provide an illustration of each.)

3a. Specify at least two ways in which an understanding of how a variety of conditions can contribute to anger might be of value to individuals in dealing with their own anger.

b. In dealing with the anger of others.

4a. Where would you place this piece on an objective-to-subjective continuum? Why? (Guide: *Objective/Subjective.*)

b. What is the author's point of view? (Guide: *Point of View.*)

5a. If you have read the Wolfe essay in Section 4, contrast Tavris's treatment of the effects of crowding with Wolfe's.

b. Which essay presents the better evidence to support its conclusions?

6a. Where in this selection does the author make use of humor?

b. Does this use of humor weaken the selection by conflicting with its generally serious tone? (Guide: *Style/Tone.*)

c. If not, how does the humor add to the effectiveness of the selection?

7. In your own words, sum up the distinction the author makes between humans and rats with regard to anger (par. 6).

8a. What elements of a formal essay does this selection contain? (Guide: *Essay.*)

b. What elements of an informal essay?

c. Taken as a whole, is this selection a formal or an informal essay? Why?

Expository Techniques

1a. How long is the introduction to this essay? (Guide: *Introductions.*)

b. Which of the standard introductory techniques are used in this selection?

c. Does the opening of this selection perform the three essential functions of an introduction? If it is unsuccessful in any way, point out the flaws.

2a. Where in this piece does the author announce the central theme?

b. What is the central theme?

c. Explain how each of the following examples contributes to the development of the theme: the "singing briefcases" (par. 9); Konečni's experiment (11–14); the story of the poor man and his house (22–26).

d. Does the wide variety of examples Tavris uses strengthen the points she makes or do they harm the unity of the essay by distracting the reader's attention from the central theme? Explain. (Guide: *Unity.*)

3a. How often does Tavris use examples from her own experience? Specify.

b.   Do these personal examples add authority to what she has to say or do they undermine her credibility?

4a.   What expository patterns besides causal analysis does the author use, and where does she use them?

b.   What role do these other patterns play in the success (or failure) of the piece? (Guide: *Evaluation.*)

Diction and Vocabulary

1a.   What is the cliché the author refers to in paragraph 14? (Guide: *Clichés.*)

b.   Is this an allusion? (Guide: *Figures of Speech.*)

c.   Does the paragraph contain any other figures of speech?

2.   To what fads is the author referring in this passage: "a mark of status like the zoot suit, DA haircut, or souped-up jalopies" (par. 9)?

3.   If you are unfamiliar with any of the following words, consult your dictionary as necessary: buoyant, sojourn, natty (par. 1); retaliation, arrogance, contorted (2); adrenaline, mannerisms (5); incessant, physiologically (6); reveries (9); catalyst (10); anagram (11); decibels, fugue (12); stooge (13); sinks, pathology, ethnicity (16); density, alienating (19); synonymous, blintzes (20).

Suggestions for Writing and Discussion

1.   How might factors like noise, crowding, poverty, and stress at work contribute to crimes like child abuse, spouse-beating, or violent fights among friends and neighbors? Give examples to help explain your answer.

2.   Besides anger, can other human emotions like love or envy be affected by the general psychological condition of a person? Explain.

3.   Tavris attacks a number of common beliefs either directly or indirectly. Among these are the belief that New York must be a difficult place to live because of the high level of noise (par. 8) and that overcrowding is in itself dangerous to psychological health (pars. 16–26). Indicate why you agree or disagree with her position on these or any other issues, drawing support from your own experience if possible.

(NOTE: Suggestions for topics requiring development by analysis of CAUSE AND EFFECT are on page 209, at the end of this section.)

GAIL SHEEHY

GAIL SHEEHY (born 1937) is a native New Yorker. After graduating from the University of Vermont, she was a department store consumer representative, a fashion coordinator, newspaper fashion editor, and women's feature writer for the New York *Herald Tribune*. Since 1968 Sheehy has been a contributing editor for *New York* magazine. Her articles have appeared in numerous magazines, including *McCall's, Cosmopolitan, Holiday, Glamour, Good Housekeeping*, and *The New York Times Magazine*. Her books are *Lovesounds* (1970), *Speed Is of the Essence* (1971), *Panthermania* (1971), *Hustling* (1973), and *Passages* (1976), which was on the nation's best-seller lists for many months.

$70,000 a Year, Tax Free

"$70,000 a Year, Tax Free" (editors' title) was written for NBC's "Comment" series, but the material was incorporated into *Hustling*. Its brevity, due to time limitations on the original presentation, obviously precluded a really thorough analysis of the topic. Observing how the author did use the time at her disposal provides some of the value of studying the selection here.

How many women do you know who can take home seventy   1
thousand dollars a year? A psychiatrist? She might take home half
that. A congresswoman? Shirley Chisholm's salary is forty-two-
five.

No, the quickest way for a woman to get ahead in this country is   2
to take up the oldest profession: prostitution.

As one veteran streetwalker explained to a runaway she was   3
breaking in: "You have no status, no power, and no way to get it
except by using your body. Why give it away? You're sitting on a
gold mine."

And so, every summer, in New York City, the hue and cry goes   4
up: Crack down on prostitution! Close the massage parlors! But why
has New York become a boomtown for hustlers? Not because of the
increased use of drugs, as most people assume. It began with a
change in New York's penal code four years ago. Loitering for the
purpose of prostitution was reduced by former Police Commissioner Leary from a misdemeanor to a violation. Even girls found guilty
on the more serious "pross collar" rarely go to jail. Most judges let
them go for a twenty-five to fifty dollar fine — and a week to pay. It
amounts to a license.

Word of this change spread with interest through the pimp   5
grapevine around the country: New York was wide open. Today,
you'd hardly guess which four states have the largest pipeline
shipping prostitutes to New York: in order, they are Minnesota,
Massachusetts, Michigan, and Ohio. There are lots of fair haired
girls from Minnesota with street names like Little Tiffany, and
Marion the Librarian. But why do they come? It couldn't be a more
American phenomenon: The prostitute's dream is the most upward
mobile, middle class, American pie dream of all.

Number one: she wants money — high-style clothes, a model   6
apartment, candy color wigs and her teeth capped.

Number two: she's looking for a "family." Most of the girls have   7
one or two children — illegitimate. On top of that, the girl is often
white and her illegitimate child is black. Back home in Minneapolis,
she was already a social pariah, and she couldn't make a go of living
and working while dragging a baby from room to rented room. So
she comes to New York, looking for a new kind of family — exactly
what the pimp provides.

He puts up his stable of three or four girls in a high-rise apart-   8
ment, pays their rent, buys their clothes, foots their doctor bills. Top
woman in this "family" — the pimp's favorite, who brings in the
most money — is called his "wife." The rest are known as "wife-in-
laws." Remarkably enough, they all get along quite well. The tie that
really binds is the baby sitter — the girls share one for seventy-five
dollars a week and this is what frees them to work.

As a midtown hooker from Virginia put it to me: "Most of the   9
girls are here doing it for their kids. I don't want my daughter to
have the kind of childhood I had. She's going to have the best!"

So now the prostitute has money, a family, a baby sitter. The   1
other thing she craves is "glamour and excitement," things she

probably dreamed of finding in a career as a model or actress. But those fields are fiercely competitive. Besides, as a prostitute sees it, models and actresses are treated like dress hangers or pieces of meat: they give their bodies away to advance their careers, while so-called straight women exchange sex for the financial security of marriage. A "working girl," as the prostitute refers to herself, is the only honest one: she sets the price, delivers the goods, and concludes her business within the hour — no romantic nonsense about it.

And finally, after she is on the street for a few months, the pace of peeping and hiding, the game of stinging johns and ducking police vans, becomes a way of life. It gets into the blood like gambler's fever. 11

The hooker with the heart of gold? That's a male myth. Many of our street girls can be as vicious and money mad as any corporation president. Moreover, they can be less emotional than men in conducting acts of personal violence. The bulk of their business is not the dispensation of pleasure: it is to mug, rob, swindle, knife and possibly even murder their patrons. Police drags against them are about as effective as pacification programs in Vietnam. Apply police pressure to streetwalkers and robberies generally go up. If a girl doesn't bring in that fixed amount, two hundred and fifty a night, she'll go home to a beating from her pimp. 12

People are puzzled: why this boom in prostitution when young America is bursting with sexual freedom? They forget about men over forty, men who learned their sexual fantasies from nudie calendars in the gas station. To be fun, the bedmate must be a no-no. "You can't fantasize about your wife or girlfriend," one man explained. "The woman has to be an unknown." And where is this illicit thrill of forbidden flesh still to be found? On the black market, of course. Furthermore, the prostitute makes no emotional demands. She would never call his office the next day. It is her stock in trade to encourage men's sexual fantasies and exploit them. How else can a girl make seventy thousand dollars a year, tax free? 13

Meanings and Values

1a. Briefly summarize the author's reasons for a girl's becoming a prostitute.

b.   Do you consider these ultimate or immediate causes — or would you classify them somewhere in between? Why?

2a.   Why does the author consider these motivations as an "American pie dream" (par. 5)?

b.   To which of the causes, if any, does the description seem to you not to apply? Why?

3.   Why does she assume that we'd "hardly guess" which four states have the largest pipelines into New York prostitution (par. 5)?

4.   Do you see anything ironic in the prostitute's comments in paragraph 9? (See Guide to Terms: *Irony*.) If so, explain.

5a.   How can perpetuation of the "male myth" (par. 12) be explained?

b.   Why would it be more difficult to "fantasize" about one's wife or girlfriend (par. 13)?

6a.   Where would you locate this selection on a objective-to-subjective continuum? (Guide: *Objective/Subjective*.)

b.   Is the author guilty of any sentimentality? (Guide: *Sentimentality*.) If so, where?

Expository Techniques

1a.   In which paragraphs does the author explain why prostitution has increased greatly in New York City?

b.   Does this seem to be a thorough cause-and-effect analysis?

c.   Is it sufficient for the purpose? Why, or why not?

2a.   In paragraphs 6–11 the author outlines a different set of causes. Would they have been more effective for her purpose if she had gone deeper into the more ultimate causes?

b.   Why do you think she did not?

c.   What function is served by the first sentence of paragraph 10? Why would the author have considered it a useful device in this particular exposition?

3a.   What is Sheehy's central theme? (Guide: *Unity*.)

b.   Do all portions of the essay serve as tributaries into this theme, thus giving unity to the writing? If not, what are the exceptions?

4a.   Which of the standard techniques of introduction does the author use? (Guide: *Introductions*.)

b.   Why do they seem particularly well chosen, considering the basic purpose of this exposition?

5a.   The last sentence is a good example of at least one standard technique of closing. (Guide: *Closings*.) What is it?

b.   Suggest a different kind of closing and compare the relative effectiveness of the two.

6.   Which of the patterns of exposition already studied does Sheehy employ in paragraph 10?

7.   In your opinion, would any of her statements have benefited by further qualification? (Guide: *Qualification.*) If so, explain why.

Diction and Vocabulary

1.   Illustrate the meaning of the following terms by use of one or more examples from this selection.
   a.   Colloquialism. (Guide: *Colloquial Expressions.*)
   b.   Simile. (Guide: *Figures of Speech.*)
   c.   Cliché. (Guide: *Clichés.*)

2.   What is a "social pariah" (par. 7)?

3.   Considering this exposition's original purpose, why do you think the author used few, if any, "dictionary-type" words?

Suggestions for Writing and Discussion

1.   The author says most people assume that the increase in prostitution is related to an increased use of drugs. How logical does this assumption appear to you? Explain.

2.   Explore parallels in other, more legitimate fields in which motivation may be provided by the "upwardly mobile, middle class, American pie dream" (par. 5).

3.   In view of the five reasons for a girl's becoming a prostitute — all seeming to be fairly common desires — why is it that even more girls do not engage in prostitution?

4.   Which of her five reasons do you think would also apply to the thriving business (in some cities especially) of male prostitution? Are there other reasons that apply here?

5.   How logical and/or just do you consider the move in many areas toward "equal guilt" laws, whereby the male is considered as guilty as the prostitute he employs?

6.   Should there even *be* laws prohibiting prostitution?

7.   The word "prostitution" is often used with broader meaning than in Sheehy's analysis — e.g., "prostitution of talent" or "prostitution of science." Select one such usage and examine motivations in terms of this author's "upward mobility" theories.

(NOTE: Suggestions for topics requiring development by analysis of CAUSE AND EFFECT are on page 209, at the end of this section.)

MARGARET HALSEY

MARGARET HALSEY was born in Yonkers, New York, in 1910. A
graduate of Skidmore College and Teachers College of Columbia
University, she wrote her first book after living in England for a
year. *With Malice Towards Some*, a comic study of the English, was
a runaway best-seller in 1938. During World War II, she worked at
the famous Stage Door Canteen in New York's Times Square, one
of only two canteens in the country open to black as well as white
servicemen. Her book about this experiment in racial integration,
Color Blind, was published in 1946. Halsey is the author of four
other books, including *No Laughing Matter: The Autobiography of a
WASP* (1977).

What's Wrong with "Me, Me, Me"?

"What's Wrong with 'Me, Me, Me'?" was first published in *Newsweek*. Here Halsey is concerned with both immediate and ultimate
effects, as she examines the popular cult of "Inner Wonderfulness." The author uses sarcasm as one subtle but important
device by which to show the basic error of the "human-potential
industry" and the "me" generation's attempts to find themselves.

Tom Wolfe has christened today's young adults the "me" generation, and the 1970s — obsessed with things like consciousness expansion and self-awareness — have been described as the decade
of the new narcissism. The cult of "I," in fact, has taken hold with
the strength and impetus of a new religion. But the joker in the pack
is that it is all based on a false idea.

The false idea is that inside every human being, however unprepossessing, there is a glorious, talented and overwhelmingly

Reprinted from *Newsweek*, April 17, 1978, by permission of International Creative
Management. Copyright © 1978 by Margaret Halsey.

attractive personality. This personality — so runs the erroneous belief — will be revealed in all its splendor if the individual just forgets about courtesy, cooperativeness and consideration for others and proceeds to do exactly what he or she feels like doing.

Nonsense.

Inside each of us is a mess of unruly primitive impulses, and these can sometimes, under the strenuous self-discipline and dedication of art, result in notable creativity. But there is no such thing as a pure, crystalline and well-organized "native" personality, though a host of trendy human-potential groups trade on the mistaken assumption that there is. And backing up the human-potential industry is the advertising profession, which also encourages the idea of an Inner Wonderfulness that will be unveiled to a suddenly respectful world upon the purchase of this or that commodity.

However, an individual does not exist in a vacuum. A human being is not an isolated, independent thing-in-itself, but inevitably reflects the existence of others. The young adults of the "me" generation would never have lived to grow up if a great many parents, doctors, nurses, farmers, factory workers, teachers, policemen, firemen and legions of others had not ignored their human potential and made themselves do jobs they did not perhaps feel like doing in order to support the health and growth of children.

And yet, despite the indulgence of uninhibited expression, the "self" in self-awareness seems to cause many new narcissists and members of the "me" generation a lot of trouble. This trouble emerges in talk about "identity." We hear about the search for identity and a kind of distress called an identity crisis.

"I don't know who I am." How many bartenders and psychiatrists have stifled yawns on hearing that popular threnody for the thousandth time!

But this sentence has no meaning unless spoken by an amnesia victim, because many of the people who say they do not know who they are, actually *do* know. What such people really mean is that they are not satisfied with who they are. They feel themselves to be timid and colorless or to be in some way or other fault-ridden, but they have soaked up enough advertising and enough catch-penny ideas of self-improvement to believe in universal Inner Wonderfulness. So they turn their backs on their honest knowledge of themselves — which with patience and courage could start them on the road to genuine development — and embark on a quest for a will-o'-the wisp called "identity."

But a *search* for identity is predestined to fail. Identity is not found, the way Pharaoh's daughter found Moses in the bulrushes. Identity is built. It is built every day and every minute throughout the day. The myriad choices, small and large, that human beings make all the time determine identity. The fatal weakness of the currently fashionable approach to personality is that the "self" of the self-awareness addicts, the self of Inner Wonderfulness, is static. Being perfect, it does not need to change. But genuine identity changes as one matures. If it does not, if the 40-year-old has an identity that was set in concrete at the age of 18, he or she is in trouble.

The idea of a universal Inner Wonderfulness that will be apparent to all beholders after a six-week course in self-expression is fantasy.

But how did this fantasy gain wide popular acceptance as a realizable fact?

Every society tries to produce a prevalent psychological type that will best serve its ends, and that type is always prone to certain emotional malfunctions. In early capitalism, which was a producing society, the ideal type was acquisitive, fanatically devoted to hard work and fiercely repressive of sex. The emotional malfunctions to which this type was liable were hysteria and obsession. Later capitalism, today's capitalism, is a consuming society, and the psychological type it strives to create, in order to build up the largest possible markets, is shallow, easily swayed and characterized much more by self-infatuation than self-respect. The emotional malfunction of this type is narcissism.

It will be argued that the cult of "I" has done some individuals a lot of good. But at whose expense? What about the people to whom these "healthy" egotists are rude or even abusive? What about the people over whom they ride roughshod? What about the people they manipulate and exploit? And — the most important question of all — how good a preparation for inevitable old age and death is a deliberately cultivated self-love? The psychologists say that the full-blown classic narcissists lose all dignity and go mad with fright as they approach their final dissolution. Ten or fifteen years from now — when the young adults of the "me" generation hit middle age — will be the time to ask whether "self-awareness" really does people any good.

A long time ago, in a book called "Civilization and Its Discontents," Freud pointed out that there is an unresolvable conflict between the human being's selfish, primitive, infantile impulses and the restraint he or she must impose on those impulses if a stable society is to be maintained. The "self" is not a handsome god or goddess waiting coyly to be revealed. On the contrary, its complexity, confusion and mystery have proved so difficult that throughout the ages men and women have talked gratefully about *losing* themselves. They *lose* the self in contemplating a great work of art, or in nature, or in scientific research, or in writing poetry, or in fashioning things with their hands or in projects that will benefit others rather than themselves.   14

The current glorification of self-love will turn out in the end to be a no-win proposition, because in questions of personality or "identity," what counts is not who you are, but what you do. "By their fruits, ye shall know them." And by their fruits, they shall know themselves.   15

Meanings and Values

1a.   What irony is involved in Halsey's comments on people's "search for identity"? (See Guide to Terms: *Irony*.)

   b.   Why is it ironic?

   c.   What kind of irony is it?

2a.   What is the author's point of view? (Guide: *Point of View*.)

   b.   Is it too extreme to be most effective?

3a.   Would the essay benefit by greater use of qualification? (Guide: *Qualification*.)

   b.   If so, how could the author have gone about it?

   c.   If not, explain why the writing is better as it is.

4.   Is it really necessary for today's capitalism to create the psychological type described in paragraph 12? Use specific advertising examples to illustrate your points.

5.   Use the three-point system to evaluate the success of this selection. (Guide: *Evaluation*.)

Expository Techniques

1a. Which of the standard techniques are used for the introduction? (Guide: *Introductions.*)

  b. How successful are they in fulfilling the three basic requirements of a good introduction?

2. One of the most interesting aspects of this essay is the manner of alternating between a cause/effect analysis and other patterns of exposition.

  a. What is the primary pattern used in paragraphs 2 and 3, and the first part of paragraph 4?

  b. What pattern is used in the latter part of paragraph 4?

  c. Are the effects considered in paragraphs 6–8 better classified as immediate or ultimate? Why?

  d. What is the primary pattern of paragraph 9?

  e. Paragraph 12 analyzes the causes of today's "fantasy," but it also makes good use of another basic pattern of exposition. What is it?

  f. The real climax of the writing comes in paragraph 13. Do you think the author is more concerned here with immediate or ultimate effects? Why?

3a. Are the questions of paragraph 13 classifiable as "rhetorical"? (Guide: *Rhetorical Questions.*) Why, or why not?

  b. Do they provide an effective way of presenting the climactic material of the paragraph?

4a. The closing consists of the last two paragraphs. What standard techniques are used? (Guide: *Closings.*)

  b. Does it perform the basic function of a good closing?

Diction and Vocabulary

1a. Cite the figures of speech in paragraphs 1, 4, and 9.

  b. Are they well chosen?

2. What are the rhetorical benefits of the one-word paragraph 3?

3. Explain the source and meaning of "narcissism" (or "narcissists"), as used in several paragraphs of this essay.

4. For various reasons Halsey's uses of "Inner Wonderfulness" gain much desired emphasis. (Guide: *Emphasis.*) List all the factors that contribute to this effect.

5. Consult your dictionary as needed to determine meanings of the following words: impetus (par. 1); unprepossessing (2); crystalline (4); threnody (7); acquisitive (12).

Suggestions for Writing and Discussion

1. If you consider the "me generation" too broad a generalization, in view of the many obvious exceptions, explain why. Be as specific as possible.

2. Explore the possibility that a search for identity might *lead* one to be more considerate of and involved with others.

3. Discuss in depth the ideas suggested by one or more of the following quotations:

   a. "Inside each of us is a mess of unruly primitive impulses" (par. 4).

   b. Identity "is built every day and every minute throughout the day" (par. 9).

   c. "Throughout the ages men and women have talked gratefully about *losing* themselves" (par. 14).

(NOTE: Suggestions for topics requiring development by analysis of CAUSE AND EFFECT are on page 209, at the end of this section.)

ROBERT C. CHRISTOPHER

Robert C. Christopher was born in 1924 in Thomaston, Connecticut. He has had a distinguished career as a journalist, serving as senior editor at *Time*, foreign editor and executive editor at *Newsweek*, and the first editor of *Newsweek International*. He earned a degree in oriental studies from Yale and has written articles about Japan for *The New York Times Magazine*, the *London Sunday Times*, *Asia*, and *Foreign Affairs*. He is currently administrator of the Pulitzer Prizes.

The Fruits of Industry

In "The Fruits of Industry," part of a chapter from his book *The Japanese Mind* (1983), Christopher examines and rejects several explanations for Japan's industrial success before suggesting that the real cause lies in the social structure of Japan. The pattern of causal analysis followed by this essay is a common and useful one, and the author also draws on comparison, process analysis, and examples to explore his subject thoroughly.

It was ten thirty at night, and on the stool next to mine in the Orchid Bar of Tokyo's Hotel Okura a British businessman was sipping moodily at a snifter of brandy. He was, he explained, about to head home to London empty-handed, having failed to land a big contract because the product his company made did not meet the standards of reliabilty insisted upon by a potential Japanese client. In due course, the Englishman ordered a second brandy and savored it in silence, all the while staring intently at a pair of Japanese bartenders who were deftly mixing and dispensing a bewildering variety of drinks to forty or fifty customers. Finally, his snifter empty, the

Englishman abruptly jumped up off his bar stool and, just before disappearing into the night, said loudly to no one in particular: "They are so damned efficient, these people, that it's bloody frightening."

In so saying, the frustrated Briton was of course voicing a sentiment now shared by most of the world's non-Japanese population. Only fifteen years ago, eminent Europeans like France's Jean-Jacques Servan-Schreiber were pointing with alarm to "the American challenge" and glumly predicting the imminent economic takeover of the world by U.S.-controlled multinational corporations. Today all that is forgotten and it is the Japanese challenge that obsesses businessmen, labor leaders and politicians all the way from Detroit to Düsseldorf. How do they do it? Westerners ask in anguished wonderment. How have the inhabitants of a relatively small country with virtually no natural resources managed to build in so short a time the world's second-largest industrial economy? What are the secrets that have enabled Japan to surpass the once-impregnable United States in automobile production, rival it in steel production and unleash upon the world at large a torrent of consumer goods so high in quality and reasonable in price that in one field after another, the developed nations of the West have fallen back upon protectionism, overt or disguised, as the only way to prevent destruction of their domestic industries?

Back in the '60s and early '70s, when they had not yet perceived the full dimensions of the Japanese challenge, most Western businessmen and politicians were inclined to attribute the superior competitiveness of so many Japanese products to some kind of Oriental trickery. Cheap labor was the explanation, they said. Or more darkly yet, they accused the Japanese of widespread dumping — selling goods abroad at prices below their cost of production.

But as the years went by and Japan's great modern corporations steadily expanded their foreign beachheads in one industry after another, the charge of unfair competition became harder and harder to sustain as the primary explanation for Japan's export successes. Clearly, no manufacturer, not even an inscrutable Oriental one, can go on, decade in and decade out, continually selling his products at a loss. And the cheap-labor argument, though still frequently heard, does not stand up to close examination either. For one thing, Japan's most successful manufacturers have for some time been steadily reducing their dependence on human labor: Japan's newer steel mills, auto plants and TV assembly lines are considerably more automated and "robotized" than most comparable Western facilities. In any case, overall labor costs in Japan now equal or surpass those prevailing in most of Western Europe and in some instances actually surpass those in the United States itself. Yet Japanese automakers now sell more cars in the United States than all their European competitors combined.

Faced with these awkward facts, realists in the West began to search for more sophisticated explanations for the superior competitiveness of the Japanese. One reason for it, some people suggested, was that Japanese industry had been fortunate enough to have most of its plants bombed off the face of the earth during World War II and thus, unlike American industry, had been left with no choice but to replace obsolescent factories and mills with more modern and efficient ones. An even more intriguing suggestion was the concept of "Japan, Inc." developed by American business consultant James Abegglen. This was a vision of the Japanese economy as a kind of seamless web in which politicians, bureaucrats and businessmen all worked industriously toward mutually agreed-upon ends. As oversimplified by some of its popularizers, however, it was often reduced to the proposition that unlike the U.S. Government, the Government of Japan invariably seeks, by fair means or foul, to strengthen private industry and advance its interests.

There was some truth to both these suggestions, but again, as time wore on, it became clear that neither of them by itself could fully account for the Japanese miracle. World War II bomb damage, extensive as it was, has very little relevance to the current efficiency of the Japanese auto industry, which existed only in rudimentary form in the 1940s, and it has none whatsoever to Japanese dominance of consumer electronics, an industry which did not exist at all then. And while the Japanese Government has indeed played a vital role in the nurturing of Japanese industry, that role does not, as many Americans appear to believe, involve extraordinarily, heavy financial aid to industry. In one important respect, in fact, Tokyo is actually less openhanded than Washington: where the U.S. Government underwrites close to 50 percent of all the research and development efforts of American corporations — including more than 35 percent of all nonmilitary research — only about 25 percent of the R&D money spent in Japan comes from government agencies.

In short, if one is intellectually honest, it is very difficult to find 7
an ego-salving set of excuses for the fact that American industry in
recent years has so frequently been outperformed by Japanese industry. In recognition of this, an increasing number of
Americans — perhaps the most influential being Harvard professor
Ezra Vogel, the author of *Japan as Number One: Lessons for America* —
have come up with a revisionist interpretation of the Japanese
challenge. The real explanation of the Japanese success story, the
revisionists say, is that in a number of respects — social, economic
and administrative — Japan operates more intelligently and efficiently than Western societies do. The basic message preached by
the revisionists, at least as it gets through to most American
businessmen, bureaucrats and politicians, is a simple one: observe
what the Japanese do and then try your damnedest to do likewise.

If only because it reflects a sensible degree of modesty — a 8
virtue that has never loomed large in the American national
character — the revisionists' approach surely represents a step in
the right direction. But as a prescription for concrete action it also
carries some inherent risks. To determine what if any economic
devices the United States can reasonably hope to borrow from
Japan, it is first necessary to arrive at a clear understanding of how
big Japanese corporations actually operate — and why they can and
do operate that way.

A half century ago, my great-uncle Will Lee lived in a small 9
Connecticut town owned by the Talcotts, an old Yankee family
whose ancestors had reputedly acquired the place from a sachem
called Uncas the Mohegan.

When I say that the Talcotts owned Talcottville, I mean exactly 10
that. They were more than just the owners of the woolen mill that
was the heart of the community and gave employment to most of
Talcottville's men. They also owned every house in town, had built
the local school and in the manner of eighteenth-century English
squires, had appointed the rector of the local church. Talcottville, in
short, was at once a business enterprise and a community.

Today, like most of the scores of other such communities that 11
once dotted the United States, Talcottville is no longer a company
town — and most Americans would not regret the change. On the
contrary, nearly all of us in this country regard the increasing rarity
of communities owned or dominated by a single company as a sign

of progress. To be dependent on your employer not only for your income but also for your housing, your recreation and even, in a sense, your social life is, by contemporary American standards, an unacceptable infringement on personal freedom. It is therefore somewhat disconcerting to discover that in up-and-coming Japan the state of affairs is almost exactly the reverse. Since World War II, in fact, Japan's major business enterprises have increasingly developed into something approaching self-contained communities. This is not to say that Japan has become simply one vast collection of company towns. What has been happening there is something considerably more complex — something first drawn to my attention by Isamu Yamashita, the chairman of Mitsui Zosen (or, as it is known in English, the Mitsui Engineering and Shipbuilding Company). . . .

. . . [W]hen I asked him a cliché Harvard Business School question — what basic line of business did Mitsui Zosen consider itself to be in — Yamashita suddenly waxed philosophical. Mitsui Zosen, he allowed, was essentially in the business of surviving.

"You have to remember," he went on, "that only fifty years ago we Japanese were still living in an essentially feudal system. As a general thing, people in those days stuck to the communities where they were born. But after World War II, when Japan began reindustrializing, people started to flock to the big industrial complexes, and the old sense of geographic community largely broke down. In a very real way, we in industry spoiled the old community life of Japan, and something had to replace it. So in today's Japan, companies like ours are the new communities, and their managers have a responsibility to create conditions in which people can enjoy a community life. Above all, of course, we managers have the overriding responsibility of keeping the community alive."

At first blush this seemed an interesting but slightly artificial construct — the sort of thing thrown out by a young sociologist desperately seeking a topic for a Ph.D. thesis. But just how true it really is was driven home to me a couple of weeks later when I spent an afternoon with Toru Iijima, a foreman in the Nissan Motor company's Oppama assembly plant, which sits on the western shore of Tokyo Bay near the great naval base of Yokosuka.

At thirty-seven, Toru Iijima is a lean, handsome man of uncommon dignity and self-possession. I have, in fact, rarely met anyone who struck me as being more in command of his own soul than Iijima. Yet for him the sun rises and sets on Nissan.

A car nut since childhood, Iijima passed up public high school 16 to attend the Nissan Vocational School. From there he went directly to the stamping shop of the Oppama plant. Today, twenty years later, he is still in the stamping shop, but now he has fifteen people working under him.

When he first went to work at Oppama, Iijima lived in a bache- 17 lor dormitory that Nissan maintains at Oppama. In due course he married a girl who also worked at Nissan, and for a while they lived in a company-owned apartment. Then a baby came along — today the Iijimas have two sons, thirteen and ten — and Iijima decided to buy his own home. With the help of Nissan's real estate subsidiary, he was able to do so at considerably less than the exorbitant price that housing in the Tokyo megalopolis normally commands. And his payments are relatively easy to handle because of the installment savings program Nissan makes available to its employees — a kind of credit union that pays higher interest than ordinary banks and lends money more cheaply.

A devoted father, Iijima spends much of his free time on barbe- 18 cues and hikes with his family. But he is also a keen athlete who makes frequent use of the plant gymnasium at Oppama, competing with other Nissan workers in a variety of sports. On vacations he usually drives his wife and children to the mountains in his Nissan Sunny (Datsun 210) — which he bought at an employee discount.

If all this makes Toru Iijima sound like a mindless creation of 19 Nissan, it does him a great injustice. When I asked him if he wanted his sons to go to university so they could become Nissan engineers, he threw me a cool, level look. "I hope they will do whatever they want," he said. "They have to have their own way of life."

Nonetheless, Nissan provides Iijima with the same sense of 20 belonging that Talcottville gave to my great-uncle Will. The thought of looking for a better job elsewhere or, more to the point, of being cast adrift by Nissan literally never crosses Iijima's mind. He knows that unless he commits some heinous offense, he will never be fired. And he knows, too, that if the Oppama plant were ever obliged to reduce production drastically, Nissan would make every effort to find useful employment for any redundant personnel. . . .

For Toru Iijima, Nissan is more than the source of his income. It 21 is a living organism with which he identifies to a degree surpassed only by his identification with his family and his country. "Nissan," he told me, sounding remarkably like Isamu Yamashita, "must survive for long, long years, and the quality of its work must be maintained through all those years." . . .

Meanings and Values

1a. What causes of Japan's industrial success does the author consider and then reject?

b. Are his reasons for rejecting them convincing? Why, or why not? (See Guide to Terms: *Evaluation.*)

c. What does he consider the real reason for Japan's success?

d. Do you find his explanation convincing? Why, or why not?

2a. What is the author's apparent purpose in this selection? (Guide: *Purpose.*)

b. Is this purpose stated clearly anywhere in the selection? Be specific.

c. Does the author accomplish his apparent purpose? Explain.

3a. Does Christopher admire the Japanese, or is his attitude closer to that of the Englishman described in the first paragraph? Support your answer with examples from the selection.

b. How, then, would you describe the tone of the piece? (Guide: *Style/Tone.*)

c. Where would you place this essay on a objective-to-subjective continuum? (Guide: *Objective/Subjective.*)

4a. What does it mean to say that a company is "essentially in the business of surviving" (par. 12)?

b. Is this true of most American or European companies? Of companies in Latin America or the rest of the Third World?

5a. Why does the author find it necessary to say of the man who works for Nissan Motor Company, "I have, in fact, rarely met anyone who struck me as being more in command of his own soul than Iijima" (par. 15)?

b. Why would the description of Iijima's career and family life (pars. 16–18) make him seem like a "mindless creature" (par. 19) rather than a hard-working person and a devoted parent? Explain.

c. Is Iijima being ironic when he says, " 'Nissan . . . must survive for long, long years, and the quality of its work must be maintained through all those years' "(par. 21)? (Guide: *Irony.*)

d. If an American worker said something similar, would it probably be ironic? Explain.

6a. Do you believe that American workers would be likely to accept the system and attitudes that the author identifies as the reasons for Japan's success? Be ready to defend your answer.

b. Does the author believe the United States or other countries should adopt the Japanese model of industrial organization? Why, or why not?

Expository Techniques

1a. What standard introductory techniques does the author use? (Guide: *Introductions.*)

b. What other things besides introducing the topic does the author do in the opening of the selection? For example, does he get the reader emotionally involved in the search for causes?

2a. Is the author justified in spending so much time at the beginning of the section discussing explanations he feels are at best only partially correct? (Guide: *Evaluation.*)

b. What advantage, if any, is there in this strategy?

c. Is the movement from unsatisfactory explanations to a satisfactory one a common way to organize causal analysis? (Give examples if you can.)

d. Is the organization of this piece similar in any way to the organization of the other essays in this section?

3. In paragraph 2, Christopher asks, "How do they do it?" Does this question indicate that the basic pattern of the essay is process analysis, or is this simply an interesting way to introduce the search for causes? Be ready to defend your answer.

4a. If the basic pattern in this selection is cause/effect analysis, why does the author spend time comparing life in American "company towns" with the current situation in Japan (pars. 9–11, 20)?

b. What patterns other than cause and effect and comparison are used in this piece?

c. How does each of the patterns contribute to the overall purpose and theme of the selection? (Guide: *Unity.*)

5a. In explaining the motivations of Japanese workers and companies, the author uses extended examples. Would a variety of shorter examples have been more effective? Why, or why not?

b. Instead of examples, should the author have relied on statistical studies demonstrating the loyalty of Japanese workers? Explain.

c. Do you find the examples believable? Do they seem characteristic of the attitudes of Japanese workers? Why?

Diction and Vocabulary

1. What elements of diction does the author use in the first paragraph of this selection to get and hold the reader's attention? (Guide: *Diction.*)

2a. Are the questions in paragraph 2 rhetorical questions? (Guide: *Rhetorical Questions.*)

b. What is the function of the questions?

3a. In what ways are paragraphs 3–6 parallel? (Guide: *Parallel Structure.*)

b. What kind of emphasis does the author achieve through the use of parallel sentences and other parallel structures in paragraphs 2, 11, and 20? (Guide: *Emphasis.*)

4. If you are unfamiliar with any of the following words, consult your dictionary as necessary: deftly, bloody (par. 1); impregnable, protectionism (2); beachheads, inscrutable (4); realists, obsolescent (5); rudimentary, nurturing (6); salving, revisionist (7); inherent, (8); sachem (9); squires (10); disconcerting (11); waxed (12); construct (14); subsidiary, exorbitant (17); heinous, redundant (20).

Suggestions for Writing and Discussion

1. Why do you think Japanese industry has captured such a large share of the world market? Are its products better? Cheaper? Support your answer with specific examples.

2. Taking into account the Japanese model as Christopher presents it, suggest what American industry can do to become more competitive. Organize your suggestions into an oral or written composition.

3. Explore how your life would change if this country adopted Japanese ideas of loyalty to a particular company and of the responsibility of companies to support community life.

4. Are you surprised or irritated by the attitudes of Japanese workers? Do you admire their values? Explore your reactions and be ready to explain them.

5. Are Japanese companies taking unfair advantage of their workers, or does everyone benefit from the system? Be ready to defend your answer.

6. Besides Talcottville, there are many examples of company towns in this country, such as the Pullman section of Chicago. If there is a company town in your area, look into its history and try to identify the reasons for its success or failure. (If there is no company town in your area, history books can provide plenty of examples.)

(NOTE: Suggestions for topics requiring development by analysis of CAUSE AND EFFECT follow.)

Writing Suggestions for Section 6
Cause and Effect

Analyze the immediate and ultimate causes and/or effects of one of the following subjects, or another suggested by them. (Be careful that your analysis does not develop into a mere listing of superficial "reasons.")

1. The ethnic makeup of a neighborhood.
2. Some *minor* discovery or invention.
3. The popularity of some modern singer or other celebrity admired especially by young people.
4. The popularity of some fad of clothing or hair style.
5. The widespread fascination for antique cars (or guns, furniture, dishes, etc.).
6. The widespread enjoyment of fishing or hunting.
7. Student cheating.
8. Too much pressure (on you or an acquaintance) for good school grades.
9. Your being a member of some minority ethnic or religious group.
10. Your association, as an outsider, with members of such a group.
11. The decision of some close acquaintance to enter the religious life.
12. Some unreasonable fear or anxiety that afflicts you or someone you know well.
13. Your need to conform.
14. Your tendency toward individualism.
15. The popularity of video games.
16. The mainstreaming of handicapped children.
17. The growing importance of computers.

7

Using *Definition* to Help Explain

Few writing faults can cause a more serious communication block between writer and reader than using key terms that can have various meanings or shades of meaning. To be useful rather than detrimental, such terms must be adequately defined.

Of the two basic types of definition, only one is our special concern as a pattern of exposition. But the other, the simpler form, is often useful to clarify meanings of concrete or noncontroversial terms. This simple process is similar to that used most in dictionaries: either providing a synonym (for example, cinema: a motion picture), or placing the word in a class and then showing how it differs from others of the same class (for example, metheglin: an alcoholic liquor made of fermented honey — here the general class is "liquor," and the differences between metheglin and other liquors are that it is "alcoholic" and "made of fermented honey").

Berne, for instance, sees the need to define several of his key terms in the process of classifying — e.g., viscerotonic endomorph, somatotonic mesomorph, and cerebrotonic ectomorph; and Jastrow defines some of the basic elements of brains and computers.

With many such abstract, unusual, or coined terms, typical readers are too limited by their own experiences and opinions (and no two sets are identical) for writers to expect understanding of the exact sense in which the terms are used. They have a right, of course, to use such abstract words any way they choose — as long as their readers know what that way is. The importance of making this meaning clear becomes crucial when the term is used as a key element of the overall explanation. And sometimes the term being defined is even more than a key element: it may be the subject itself, either for purposes of explanation or argument.

Extended definition, unlike the simple, dictionary type, follows no set and formal pattern. Often readers are not even aware of the process. Because it is an integral part of the overall subject, extended definition is written in the same tone as the rest of the exposition (or argument), usually with an attempt to interest the readers, as well as to inform or persuade them.

There are some expository techniques peculiar to definition alone. The purpose may be served by giving the background of the term. Or the definition may be clarified by negation, sometimes called "exclusion" or "differentiation," by showing what is *not* meant by the term. Still another way is to enumerate the characteristics of what is defined, sometimes isolating an essential one for special treatment.

To demonstrate the possibilities in these patterns, we can use the term "juvenile delinquency," which might need defining in some contexts since it certainly means different things to different people. (Where do we draw the line, for instance, between "boyish pranks" and antisocial behavior, or between delinquent and nondelinquent experimentation with sex or marijuana?) We might show how attitudes toward juvenile crime have changed: "youthful high spirits" was the label for some of our grandfathers' activities that would be called "delinquency" today. Or we could use negation, eliminating any classes of juvenile wrongdoing not considered delinquency in the current discussion. Or we could simply list characteristics of the juvenile delinquent or isolate one of these — disrespect for authority or lack of consideration for other people — as a universal.

But perhaps the most dependable techniques for defining are the basic expository patterns already studied. Writers could illustrate their meaning of "juvenile delinquency" by giving *examples* from their own experience, from newspaper accounts, or from other sources. (Every one of the introductions to the eleven sections of this book, each a definition, relies greatly on illustration by example.) They could analyze the subject by *classification* of types or degrees of delinquency. They could use the process of *comparison* and *contrast*, perhaps between delinquent and nondelinquent youth. Showing the *causes* and *effects* of juvenile crime could help explain their attitudes toward it, and hence its meaning for them.

They might choose to use *analogy*, perhaps comparing the child to a young tree growing grotesque because of poor care and attention. Or a step-by-step analysis of the *process* by which a child becomes delinquent might, in some cases, help explain the intended meaning.

Few extended definitions would use all these methods, but the extent of their use must always depend on three factors: (1) the term itself, since some are more elusive and subject to misunderstanding than others; (2) the function the term is to serve in the writing, since it would be foolish to devote several pages to defining a term that serves only a casual or unimportant purpose; and (3) the prospective reader-audience, since writers want to avoid insulting the intelligence or background of their readers, yet want to go far enough to be sure of their understanding.

But this, of course, is a basic challenge in any good writing — analyzing the prospective readers and writing for the best effect on *them.*

Sample Paragraph (Definition)

We are tipped off in the first sentence to what will be defined.

Some of the *characteristics.*

(Irony by understatement.)

Negation, or *exclusion*, to let us know what is not meant.

Background of the term.

One rare treat the visitor can anticipate is an introduction to Ilona Valley sorghum molasses — on hot biscuits, or in taffy or gingerbread, to name a few of the delights. Rich in iron, moreover, molasses with sulphur is still a standard spring tonic in some older families. (This is generally considered less delightful than taffy.) But sorghum molasses must never, never be confused with ordinary store-bought molasses. The latter is typically made of sugar cane from which much of the sugar has been boiled off and removed. ("Blackstrap" has given up practically *all* the sugar.) But Valley molasses is made of sorghum, a different plant entirely, akin to Indian corn but containing a sweet pith in the stalk. Introduced here by the Caseys,

Another important *characteristic*.

Process analysis to help define.

(An example, used to illustrate the general, abstract term "prestige.")

it must have found an ideal climate and soil; most ranches now have at least a small patch of sorghum. Of four known varieties, only one, sugar (or saccharin) sorghum, is used for making molasses — really a syrup, as all the sugar is left in it. Harvested in late summer, ground or chopped by hand or machine, it is then boiled in vats over outdoor fires. The stirring, straining, fire-tending, and jugging are an all-hands operation, but the result has wide prestige: several folks who grew up here (one as far away as Tokyo) have a few gallons shipped to them every fall.

MARIE WINN

MARIE WINN was born in Czechoslovakia, and emigrated with her
family to the United States, where she attended the New York
City schools. She was graduated from Radcliffe College and also
attended Columbia University. Winn has written eleven books,
all of them about children, and been a frequent contributor to *The
New York Times* and various other newspapers and periodicals.

Television Addiction

"Television Addiction" is the title of a chapter in Marie Winn's
highly regarded book *The Plug-In Drug* (1977), and our selection is
an excerpt from that chapter. It will be seen that a careful definition of the term "addiction," and a careful application of it to TV
viewing, particularly by the young, is of utmost importance to the
author's main point, as indicated by the book's title. It is a fairly
typical use of extended definition.

The word "addiction" is often used loosely and wryly in conversa- 1
tion. People will refer to themselves as "mystery book addicts" or
"cookie addicts." E. B. White writes of his annual surge of interest in
gardening: "We are hooked and are making an attempt to kick the
habit." Yet nobody really believes that reading mysteries or ordering seeds by catalogue is serious enough to be compared with
addictions to heroin or alcohol. The word "addiction" is here used
jokingly to denote a tendency to overindulge in some pleasurable
activity.

People often refer to being "hooked on TV." Does this, too, fall 2
into the lighthearted category of cookie eating and other pleasures
that people pursue with unusual intensity, or is there a kind of
television viewing that falls into the more serious category of destructive addiction?

When we think about addiction to drugs or alcohol, we frequently focus on negative aspects, ignoring the pleasures that accompany drinking or drug-taking. And yet the essence of any serious addiction is a pursuit of pleasure, a search for a "high" that normal life does not supply. It is only the inability to function without the addictive substance that is dismaying, the dependence of the organism upon a certain experience and an increasing inability to function normally without it. Thus a person will take two or three drinks at the end of the day not merely for the pleasure drinking provides, but also because he "doesn't feel normal" without them.

An addict does not merely pursue a pleasurable experience and need to experience it in order to function normally. He needs to *repeat* it again and again. Something about that particular experience makes life without it less than complete. Other potentially pleasurable experiences are no longer possible, for under the spell of the addictive experience, his life is peculiarly distorted. The addict craves an experience and yet he is never really satisfied. The organism may be temporarily sated, but soon it begins to crave again.

Finally a serious addiction is distinguished from a harmless pursuit of pleasure by its distinctly destructive elements. A heroin addict, for instance, leads a damaged life: his increasing need for heroin in increasing doses prevents him from working, from maintaining relationships, from developing in human ways. Similarly an alcoholic's life is narrowed and dehumanized by his dependence on alcohol.

Let us consider television viewing in the light of the conditions that define serious addictions.

Not unlike drugs or alcohol, the television experience allows the participant to blot out the real world and enter into a pleasurable and passive mental state. The worries and anxieties of reality are as effectively deferred by becoming absorbed in a television program as by going on a "trip" induced by drugs or alcohol. And just as alcoholics are only inchoately aware of their addiction, feeling that they control their drinking more than they really do ("I can cut it out any time I want — I just like to have three or four drinks before dinner"), people similarly overestimate their control over television watching. Even as they put off other activities to spend hour after hour watching television, they feel they could easily resume living in a different, less passive style. But somehow or other while the television set is present in their homes, the click doesn't sound. With television pleasures available, those other experiences seem less attractive, more difficult somehow.

A heavy viewer (a college English instructor) observes: 8

"I find television almost irresistible. When the set is on, I cannot 9
ignore it. I can't turn it off. I feel sapped, will-less, enervated. As I reach out to turn off the set, the strength goes out of my arms. So I sit there for hours and hours."

The self-confessed television addict often feels he "ought" to do 10
other things — but the fact that he doesn't read and doesn't plant his garden or sew or crochet or play games or have conversations means that those activities are no longer as desirable as television viewing. In a way a heavy viewer's life is as imbalanced by his television "habit" as a drug addict's or an alcoholic's. He is living in a holding pattern, as it were, passing up the activities that lead to growth or development or a sense of accomplishment. This is one reason people talk about their television viewing so ruefully, so apologetically. They are aware that it is an unproductive experience, that almost any other endeavor is more worthwhile by any human measure.

Finally it is the adverse effect of television viewing on the lives 11
of so many people that defines it as a serious addiction. The television habit distorts the sense of time. It renders other experiences vague and curiously unreal while taking on a greater reality for itself. It weakens relationships by reducing and sometimes eliminating normal opportunities for talking, for communicating.

And yet television does not satisfy, else why would the viewer 12
continue to watch hour after hour, day after day? "The measure of health," writes Lawrence Kubie, "is flexibility . . . and especially the freedom to cease when sated."[1] But the television viewer can never be sated with his television experiences — they do not provide the true nourishment that satiation requires — and thus he finds that he cannot stop watching.

[1]Lawrence Kubie, *Neurotic Distortion and the Creative Process* (Lawrence: University of Kansas Press, 1958).

Meanings and Values

1. Would you classify this as formal or informal writing? Why? (See Guide to Terms: *Essay.*)
2. Is it primarily objective or subjective? Why? (Guide: *Objective/Subjective.*)
3. Using our three-question method, evaluate this selection, giving particular attention to the third question. (Guide: *Evaluation.*)
4a. What do you think would be Winn's reply to the assertion that television is such an important element in contemporary culture that time spent watching it is seldom wasted?
   b. Do you think you would agree with her answer? Explain.

Expository Techniques

1a. What is the first technique of definition used in this selection? Where is it used?
   b. Why is it important to get this aspect of the subject over first?
2a. Which paragraphs are devoted to an enumeration of the characteristics of addiction?
   b. How many are there, according to the author?
3a. What major pattern of exposition does the latter half of the selection utilize?
   b. How important is definition of the term prior to this development? Why?
   c. Would it have been better if the author had presented a more orderly, point-by-point discussion of this latter material? Why, or why not?

Diction and Vocabulary

1a. Is there anything distinctive about Winn's diction, as demonstrated in this piece? (Guide: *Diction.*) (You may wish to compare it with that of such authors as Thurber in Section 1 or Wolfe in Section 4.)
   b. Does your answer to question 1a indicate that Winn's style is inferior in some way? Explain.
2. Use the dictionary as necessary to understand the meanings of the following words: wryly (par. 1); organism (3); sated (4); inchoately (7); enervated (9).

Suggestions for Writing and Discussion

1. Even assuming that a person has a terrible TV habit, what does it really matter (to the person or to others) whether the habit qualifies as an addiction?

2. What other pastimes can you think of that fit, or nearly fit, Winn's criteria for addiction? Do they have any redeeming qualities that TV viewing does not offer?

3. Why do people often worry about the amount of time spent watching TV but seldom about the amount of time spent reading books or magazines? Explain.

(NOTE: Suggestions for topics requiring development by use of DEFINITION are on page 238, at the end of this section.)

ROGER CARAS

ROGER CARAS was born in 1928, in Methuen, Massachusetts. He attended Northeastern University and the University of Southern California, from which he received his B.A. He has written radio, television, and film scripts, and his articles on natural history and anthropology have appeared in a variety of magazines. He is also a contributing editor of *Geo* magazine and the author of numerous books for adults and children, including *Antarctica: Land of Frozen Time* (1962), *Dangerous to Man* (1964), *North American Mammals* (1967), *The Private Lives of Animals* (1974), *Venomous Animals of the World* (1974), *Monarch of Deadman Bay: The Life and Death of a Kodiak Bear* (1977), and *The Forest* (1979).

What's a Koala?

This essay, first published in *Geo* magazine, shows how an extended definition can give fresh insight into a subject. The author's lively style and use of interesting illustrations add to the essay's appeal.

To the Australian aborigines, the Dreamtime was the time of crea- 1
tion. It was then that the creatures of the earth, including man, came into being. There are many legends about that mystical period, but unfortunately, the koala does not fare too well in any of them. Slow-witted though it is in life, the koala is generally depicted in myth and folklore as a trickster and a thief.

One tale tells of how the koala was forced to live among the 2
newly created people of the earth. His hosts did not treat him well and refused to give him water in a time of drought, so the koala stole all the tribe's water and hid it at the top of a very tall tree, which he

220

had caused to spring up from a mere bush. In another story, a koala joins forces with a starfish, a bird and another animal to steal a whale's canoe.

However illogical the notion of a canoe-owning whale might seem, the koala itself, zoologically, seems hardly more logical. It is one of the world's two favorite teddy bears. The other, of course, is the panda, although neither the panda nor the koala is a bear at all. In fact, unlike the panda — which is a kind of cousin twice removed to the bears of the world — the koala doesn't even come close. It is related to the wombat distantly, to the kangaroo even more distantly, and to the opossum. It is a marsupial, pouch and all. But then again, it isn't a run-of-the-mill marsupial: the typical marsupial pouch runs transversely, across the body, while the koala's pouch opens to the rear and extends upward and forward. That, apparently, keeps it from getting snagged on tree limbs.

The koala, all 10 to 30 pounds and two to three feet of it (there is an amazing range in size among adults), is a beast of tall trees. Koalas live most of their lives high up in any one of 35 species of eucalyptus, or gum tree. They subsist on eucalyptus leaves, which they can't digest on their own. They rely on microorganisms in their digestive tract to do it for them. They can also handle some mistletoe leaves and some leaves from a tree known as the box.

With so particular a diet, the first koalas in captivity died because no one knew what to feed them. Until recently, very little, if anything, was known about the biology of the koala. And the knowledge we now have has come from field studies using animals that have been captured, marked and released. Situated on the marsupial family tree somewhere between the opossum and the tunneling wombat (koalas have cheek pouches to help them handle their tough, fibrous diet, and wombats have traces of the same kind of pouch), the koalas are a kind of zoological dead end. Their diet and their need to stay high in their gum trees have made them so specialized that they would be incapable of handling any marked change in their habitat or food supply.

On occasion the koala does come down to the ground, usually to shuffle over to another tree, generally taking the opportunity along the way to lick up some gravel to aid in digestion. It is then that koalas are most vulnerable to their foremost natural enemy, the feral Australian dog we call the dingo. How much trouble they have with snakes is not really known, but Australia's pythons could give them a problem.

Koalas may be solitary, or a mature male may assemble a small harem, which he guards jealously. Mating occurs every other year from September to January, and gestation is abbreviated. (All marsupials have brief pregnancies. Even the great gray kangaroo, at 175 pounds, has a gestation period of less than 40 days.) For koalas, it is anywhere from 25 to 30 days. At birth, the single offspring weighs a barely believable one fifth of an ounce — or even a little less — and it must remain in its mother's pouch on one of her two nipples for six months if it is to have any chance at all of surviving. It is entirely dependent on its mother for at least a year. Once on its own, however, unless a dingo happens to get it during a transit between two trees, the koala is likely to live to be almost 20.

During the mating period, the increasingly bellicose male displays a surprising range of noises. (For some reason, people tend to think of koalas as virtually mute animals, except for those few that speak English on TV in Australian airline commercials.) The territorial, harem-guarding male may issue a startling guttural roar, mew like a dyspeptic cat or make a staccato sneezing sound that can be confused with the distress of a human suffering from a head cold. On rare occasions, apparently when it is in a really foul mood, the koala makes a very loud and rapid ticking noise — like a time bomb counting down. All in all, the koala has a fairly extensive, and expressive, vocabulary.

To add some emphasis to their noisemaking, the males discharge an oily substance from glands in their chest. This makes a mess of their fur, but it also gives pungent notice of prior claims to a tree and to breedable females. The noisy, musty belligerence of a koala during the mating season takes people by surprise; it just doesn't seem in keeping with the animal's cuddly appearance. Koalas are, in fact, less cuddly than they look. Most wild animals are.

The koala sleeps the day away tucked up high on its perch and then feeds for most of the night, which makes it difficult to see koalas, much less study them. White settlers were in koala country in eastern Australia for more than 10 years before they reported seeing their first specimen. In Australia today, the koala has a variety of names, including — quite pardonably — teddy bear and native bear. They are also known as bangaroos, koolewongs, narnagoons and buidelbeers. The latter four names, of course, are not likely to be used in everyday conversation outside of Australia.

The European discovery of the koala occurred in 1798. John 11
Price, a servant of Captain John Hunter, the governor, went exploring with an ex-convict named James Wilson. Southwest of Sydney, they encountered a koala, which Wilson likened to a South American sloth (the poor koala, it seems, has always had an identity crisis). The next explorer to report seeing a koala was a French ensign named Barrallier, who came across one in 1802 and said it was a kind of monkey. He traded some spears and axes with the natives for the "monkey's" four feet, which he sent off to his boss in a bottle of brandy. Slowly but surely, with family affiliations in a perfect muddle, the koala made its way into the European consciousness. That's when the killing started. The koala's dense gray pelt is luxuriously soft and fine, and by the early decades of this century, the animal had been hunted almost to extinction. The koala is now protected wherever it is found.

No one knows how many koalas there once were, how many 12
there should be or, indeed, how many there are today. It is hard to get much of a fix on the word *endangered*, but the International Union for the Conservation of Nature and Natural Resources (IUCN), the internationally recognized arbiter of the status of species, does not list the koala as endangered, threatened or even rare. Protection has evidently been working, and the only precarious perch that the koala may now be astride is the branch on which it sits as it sleeps away its days.

It was not always that way. As recently as 1924, nearly 2 million 13
koala skins were exported from Australia's eastern states. Three years later, 10,000 licensed trappers exported more than 600,000 pelts from Sydney alone. Public outrage at the massacre led to the enactment of protectionary measures. Today, killing a koala in Australia is considered only slightly less offensive than doing in your neighbor or spouse.

In the wild, koalas are about as inoffensive to human interests 14
as animals can be. They don't bother agricultural enterprises, and there are no reports of attacks on man. But a koala in hand is quite a different thing from one in the bush. They have well-developed claws — as their arboreal life would naturally require — and they bite with a particularly unpleasant grinding action. To look at its perennially sleepy eyes, its bulbous patent-leather nose and white-

rimmed furry ears, one would not think of a koala capable of any
offense at all. Still, if one has to handle a koala — and most of us
never have to — it's advisable to wear gloves and lift the animal
from behind, under the armpits.

The early European interest shown in the koala is not difficult to
understand. All the animals of Australia were oddities to Europeans
who were just becoming aware of the little-known continent. Kan-
garoos, wombats, wallabies and the particularly dangerous snakes
of the area attracted a great deal of attention. Australian animals still
do, but none more affectionately than the koala. It is one of the most
primitive mammals in the world and would probably make one of
the least satisfactory pets (and one of the most difficult to feed). Yet
each night its toy likeness is hugged to sleep by millions of children
around the world. The koala that we grew up hugging is far more
legend than zoological fact. The koala that exists in fact is far more
interesting than its legend. It is ancient, it is secretive, and it acts in
ways no one would expect it to act. Belying our first impressions and
preconceived notions, the koala — the mythic trickster of the
Dreamtime — is something of a trickster after all.

Meanings and Values

1a.   List the things most people believe about koala bears (and that you
      may have believed before you read this essay). Then look over the
      essay to see how many of these beliefs Caras deliberately sets out to
      modify or contradict.

 b.   Would it be appropriate to say that the purpose of this essay is to
      change the way people view koala bears, in effect, to redefine the
      term "koala"? (See Guide to Terms: *Purpose*.)

2a.   Is the contrast between the information the essay presents on the
      unsuitableness of koalas as pets and the popularity of toy koalas
      among children (par. 15) an example of irony of situation? Why, or
      why not? (Guide: *Irony*.)

 b.   Does the essay contain other examples of irony?

3.   What tone does the author adopt to avoid irritating readers as he
      tries to change many of their beliefs about koalas? (Guide: *Style/
      Tone*.)

4.   What is the author's point of view? (Guide: *Point of View*.)

5a.   Caras uses the term "marsupial" a number of times in the essay, but
      instead of defining the term, he merely reminds readers of one of the

characteristics of a marsupial when he says, "It is a marsupial, pouch and all" (par. 3). Is Caras correct in assuming that most readers will have a general idea of what a marsupial is, or should he have provided a full definition of the term?

b. The magazine for which this article was written, *Geo,* is a popular magazine directed toward people interested in natural history and the sciences. Would the readers of this magazine be likely to know what a marsupial is?

c. Where else in the essay is it possible that Caras assumes a greater knowledge of the natural world than his readers are likely to possess?

6. What would Caras be likely to say to anyone who thinks koala bears are cuddly and who might think of keeping a koala or some other wild animal as a pet? (Be ready to point to specific statements in the essay as the basis for your answer.)

Expository Techniques

1a. How long is the introduction to this essay? (Guide: *Introductions.*)

b. Should the title be considered part of the introduction?

c. If the author wants to present an extended definition of the koala bear (as the title seems to indicate), why would he begin the essay by retelling legends rather than by moving as quickly as possible to a discussion of the koala's characteristics?

d. How many of the essential functions of an introduction are performed by the opening of this essay? Explain.

2. In what ways does the closing echo the introduction? Why? (Guide: *Closings.*)

3. Instead of making a direct statement like "Killing a koala is considered a serious crime," the author chose to say, "Today, killing a koala in Australia is considered only slightly less offensive than doing in your neighbor or spouse" (par. 13). Why?

4a. Identify the places where this essay defines by negation, or exclusion, and explain why this technique is used so often in this essay.

b. What other expository techniques peculiar to definition alone are used in this essay?

c. In what paragraphs may they be found?

d. Are any of the basic expository patterns used in the essay as well? If so, where?

5a. If you have read Winn's essay "Television Addiction," discuss the ways her use of the definition pattern differs from Caras's.

b.   Can the differences be attributed to the subject matter of the essays, to the purpose, or to the authors' styles of writing?

6.   What devices for achieving emphasis does Caras use in paragraphs 3, 5, and 8, and why does he use them? (Guide: *Emphasis.*)

7.   What features of syntax make Caras's style distinctive? (Guide: *Syntax.*)

Diction and Vocabulary

1.   What figures of speech are used in paragraph 8? (Guide: *Figures of Speech.*)

2a. How is qualification used in paragraphs 5–7 and 12–13? (Guide: *Qualification.*)

b.   What purposes is it used for?

3.   Explain what the author means when he says, "the koalas are a kind of zoological dead end" (par. 5).

4.   Use the dictionary as necessary to become familiar with the following words: aborigines (par. 1); zoologically, wombat, marsupial (3); subsist (4); fibrous, habitat (5); feral (6); gestation, transit (7); bellicose, guttural, dyspeptic (8); pungent, belligerence (9); ensign (11); arbiter (12); arboreal, bulbous (14).

Suggestions for Writing and Discussion

1.   Think of some other animals (panda, zebra, giraffe), places (Death Valley, Alaska), or things (computers, a kind of job) that would benefit from redefinition in the same way as the koala does in Caras's essay, and then prepare a written or oral composition that redefines your subject in an interesting manner.

2.   Why is it worth protecting animals like the koala even if they serve no apparent purpose? (If you have read the Douglas essay in Section 1, you may wish to refer to it in your discussion.)

3.   What qualities of animals like the koala, the panda, and the kangaroo capture our imagination and affection? Why are snakes, alligators, and weasels less attractive to us?

(NOTE: Suggestions for topics requiring development by use of DEFINITION are on page 238, at the end of this section.)

D. H. LAWRENCE

DAVID HERBERT LAWRENCE (1885–1930), British novelist, poet, essayist, and playwright, was for many years a controversial literary figure because of his frank and, for his time, obsessive treatment of sex in some of his novels. The son of a coal miner, Lawrence began his career as a schoolmaster, and with the success of his first novel, *The White Peacock* (1911), he decided to live by writing. His books include *Sons and Lovers* (1913), *The Rainbow* (1915), *Women in Love* (1921), and *Lady Chatterly's Lover* (1928). Lawrence has been admired by many for his insightful and artistic power in prose. E. M. Forster referred to him as "the greatest imaginative novelist of our generation."

Pornography

"Pornography" is excerpted from *Pornography and Obscenity*, first published in 1930. Providing us with one man's definition of a still highly controversial term, this selection also illustrates the naturalness and vivid spontaneity of style characteristic of Lawrence's writing.

What is pornography to one man is the laughter of genius to 1
another.

The word itself, we are told, means "pertaining to harlots" — 2
the graph of the harlot. But nowadays, what is a harlot? If she was a woman who took money from a man in return for going to bed with him — really, most wives sold themselves, in the past, and plenty of harlots gave themselves, when they felt like it, for nothing. If a woman hasn't got a tiny streak of harlot in her, she's a dry stick as a rule. And probably most harlots had somewhere a streak of womanly generosity. Why be so cut and dried? The law is a dreary thing, and its judgments have nothing to do with life. . . .

One essay on pornography, I remember, comes to the conclu- 3
sion that pornography in art is that which is calculated to arouse
sexual desire, or sexual excitement. And stress is laid on the fact,
whether the author or artist *intended* to arouse sexual feelings. It is
the old vexed question of intention, become so dull today, when we
know how strong and influential our unconscious intentions are.
And why a man should be held guilty of his conscious intentions,
and innocent of his unconscious intentions, I don't know, since
every man is more made up of unconscious intentions than of
conscious ones. I am what I am, not merely what I think I am.

However! We take it, I assume, that *pornography* is something 4
base, something unpleasant. In short, we don't like it. And why
don't we like it? Because it arouses sexual feelings?

I think not. No matter how hard we may pretend otherwise, 5
most of us rather like a moderate rousing of our sex. It warms us,
stimulates us like sunshine on a grey day. After a century or two of
Puritanism, this is still true of most people. Only the mob-habit of
condemning any form of sex is too strong to let us admit it naturally.
And there are, of course, many people who are genuinely repelled
by the simplest and most natural stirrings of sexual feeling. But
these people are perverts who have fallen into hatred of their fellow-
men; thwarted, disappointed, unfulfilled people, of whom, alas,
our civilisation contains so many. And they nearly always enjoy
some unsimple and unnatural form of sex excitement, secretly.

Even quite advanced art critics would try to make us believe 6
that any picture or book which had "sex appeal" was *ipso facto* a bad
book or picture. This is just canting hypocrisy. Half the great poems,
pictures, music, stories, of the whole world are great by virtue of the
beauty of their sex appeal. Titian or Renoir, the Song of Solomon or
Jane Eyre, Mozart or "Annie Laurie," the loveliness is all interwoven
with sex appeal, sex stimulus, call it what you will. Even Michel-
angelo, who rather hated sex, can't help filling the Cornucopia with
phallic acorns. Sex is a very powerful, beneficial and necessary
stimulus in human life, and we are all grateful when we feel its
warm, natural flow through us, like a form of sunshine. . . .

Then what is pornography, after all this? It isn't sex appeal or 7
sex stimulus in art. It isn't even a deliberate intention on the part of
the artist to arouse or excite sexual feelings. There's nothing wrong
with sexual feelings in themselves, so long as they are straightforward and not sneaking or sly. The right sort of sex stimulus is

invaluable to human daily life. Without it the world grows grey. I would give everybody the gay Renaissance stories to read; they would help to shake off a lot of grey self-importance, which is our modern civilised disease.

But even I would censor genuine pornography, rigorously. It would not be very difficult. In the first place, genuine pornography is almost always underworld, it doesn't come into the open. In the second, you can recognise it by the insult it offers, invariably, to sex and to the human spirit. 8

Pornography is the attempt to insult sex, to do dirt on it. This is unpardonable. Take the very lowest instance, the picture postcard sold underhand, by the underworld, in most cities. What I have seen of them have been of an ugliness to make you cry. The insult to the human body, the insult to a vital human relationship! Ugly and cheap they make the human nudity, ugly and degraded they make the sexual act, trivial and cheap and nasty. 9

It is the same with the books they sell in the underworld. They are either so ugly they make you ill, or so fatuous you can't imagine anybody but a cretin or a moron reading them, or writing them. 10

It is the same with the dirty limericks that people tell after dinner, or the dirty stories one hears commercial travellers telling each other in a smoke-room. Occasionally there is a really funny one, that redeems a great deal. But usually they are just ugly and repellent, and the so-called "humour" is just a trick of doing dirt on sex. 11

Now the human nudity of a great many modern people is just ugly and degraded, and the sexual act between modern people is just the same, merely ugly and degrading. But this is nothing to be proud of. It is the catastrophe of our civilisation. I am sure no other civilisation, not even the Roman, has showed such a vast proportion of ignominious and degraded nudity, and ugly, squalid dirty sex. Because no other civilisation has driven sex into the underworld, and nudity to the w.c. 12

The intelligent young, thank heaven, seem determined to alter in these two respects. They are rescuing their young nudity from the stuffy, pornographical hole-and-corner underworld of their elders, and they refuse to sneak about the sexual relation. This is a change the elderly grey ones of course deplore, but it is in fact a very great change for the better, and a real revolution. 13

But it is amazing how strong is the will in ordinary, vulgar 14 people, to do dirt on sex. It was one of my fond illusions, when I was young, that the ordinary healthy-seeming sort of men in railway carriages, or the smoke-room of an hotel or a pullman, were healthy in their feelings and had a wholesome rough devil-may-care attitude towards sex. All wrong! All wrong! Experience teaches that common individuals of this sort have a disgusting attitude towards sex, a disgusting contempt of it, a disgusting desire to insult it. If such fellows have intercourse with a woman, they triumphantly feel that they have done her dirt, and now she is lower, cheaper, more contemptible than she was before.

It is individuals of this sort that tell dirty stories, carry indecent picture postcards, and know the indecent books. This is the great pornographical class — the really common men-in-the-street and women-in-the-street. They have as great a hate and contempt of sex as the greyest Puritan, and when an appeal is made to them, they are always on the side of the angels. They insist that a film-heroine shall be a neuter, a sexless thing of washed-out purity. They insist that real sex-feeling shall only be shown by the villain or villainess, low lust. They find a Titian or a Renoir really indecent, and they don't want their wives and daughters to see it.

Why? Because they have the grey disease of sex-hatred, coupled with the yellow disease of dirt-lust. The sex functions and the excrementory functions in the human body work so close together, yet they are, so to speak, utterly different in direction. Sex is a creative flow, the excrementory flow is towards dissolution, de-creation, if we may use such a word. In the really healthy human being the distinction between the two is instant, our profoundest instincts are perhaps our instincts of opposition between the two flows.

But in the degraded human being the deep instincts have gone dead, and then the two flows become identical. *This* is the secret of really vulgar and of pornographical people: the sex flow and the excrement flow is the same to them. It happens when the psyche deteriorates, and the profound controlling instincts collapse. Then sex is dirt and dirt is sex, and sexual excitement becomes a playing with dirt, and any sign of sex in a woman becomes a show of her dirt. This is the condition of the common, vulgar human being whose name is legion, and who lifts his voice and it is the *Vox populi, vox Dei*. And this is the source of all pornography.

Meanings and Values

1. Does this selection better illustrate subjective or objective writing? (See Guide to Terms: *Objective/Subjective*.) Justify your answer, citing specific examples.

2. Would you classify it as formal or informal writing? (Guide: *Essay*.) Why?

3a. Do you think that a person should, in general, be held responsible for "unconscious intentions" (par. 3)?

   b. Does the law do so?

4a. Does it seem to you that the author may be overgeneralizing in the last sentence of paragraph 5?

   b. If such forms of sex excitement are enjoyed "secretly," how could he know enough about the matter to make such a broad assertion?

5. What, if anything, is paradoxical in the fact that the type of men described early in paragraph 14 have the "grey disease" (par. 16)? (Guide: *Paradox*.)

Expository Techniques

1a. In developing his definition of pornography, Lawrence uses negation, or exclusion. What is negated?

   b. Which paragraphs are devoted to negation?

   c. Why do you suppose he considers them important enough for so much attention? Do you agree?

2a. Which of the other methods of extended definition does he use?

   b. In which paragraphs may they be found?

3. In your estimation, are rhetorical questions overused in this selection? (Guide: *Rhetorical Questions*.) Be prepared to justify your answer.

4a. Cite examples of as many as possible of the standard methods of achieving emphasis. (Guide: *Emphasis*.)

   b. What, to you, is the overall effect?

5. Several of the most noticeable features of Lawrence's style are also matters of syntax. (Guide: *Style/Tone* and *Syntax*.) Illustrate as many of these as possible by examples from the writing.

Diction and Vocabulary

1a. In the second paragraph is a metaphor that is also a cliché. (Guide: *Clichés*.) What is it?

b.   How, if at all, can its use be justified?

2.   Cite at least two other examples of metaphor and one of simile.
       (Guide: *Figures of Speech.*)

3.   What is the meaning of w.c. (par. 12)?

4a.   What is the meaning of *ipso facto* (par. 6)?

b.   Why is it italicized?

5.   What is the meaning of "*Vox populi, vox Dei*" (par. 17)?

6a.   In at least five paragraphs Lawrence uses a euphemism. (Guide:
       Connotation/Denotation.) What is it?

b.   In which paragraphs do you find it used?

c.   If sex-hatred is the "grey disease," why do you suppose Lawrence
       chose "yellow" to describe the disease of "dirt-lust"?

7.   How do you account for the unusual spelling of several words in this
       essay, e.g., *grey* and *civilisation*?

8.   Consult your dictionary as necessary for the meaning of the follow-
       ing words: canting, phallic (par. 6); fatuous, cretin (10); ignominious
       (12).

Suggestions for Writing and Discussion

1.   Select one or more of the artists or works of art listed in paragraph 6,
       analyze, and explain fully why you agree or disagree that "the
       loveliness is all interwoven with sex appeal [or] sex stimulus."

2.   The "intelligent young" of 1930 (par. 13) are now the gray "establish-
       ment" of parents and grandparents against whom the intelligent
       young of the 1960s and 1970s staged their so-called sexual revolu-
       tion. Trace the process by which such an ironic reversal came about.
       Do you believe this is an inevitable result of generation-aging —
       e.g., will *your* children and grandchildren also be engaging in sexual
       revolution?

3.   Both of the author's "negated" definitions have been used repeated-
       ly by others in the attempt to get a fair and workable *legal* distinction
       between pornography and nonpornography. Usually these
       attempts failed, and no one felt that the problem had been really
       solved. How well would Lawrence's definition work as a legal
       definition — perhaps with some modification you can suggest?

4.   What, if anything, do you think should be done about "hard-core"
       pornography?

(NOTE: Suggestions for topics requiring development by use of DEFINITION
       are on page 238, at the end of this section.)

MICHAEL KORDA

MICHAEL KORDA was born in London in 1933, and he served with the Royal Air Force from 1952 to 1954. After holding various editorial positions with Simon and Schuster, book publishers, Korda is now editor-in-chief. He is also an author in his own right. His books are *Male Chauvinism: How It Works* (1973), *Power: How to Get It, How to Use It* (1975), *Charmed Lives* (1979), and a novel entitled *Worldly Goods* (1982).

What It Takes to Be a Leader

"What It Takes to Be a Leader," first published in *Newsweek*, is hardly a detailed set of instructions, but it is a forthright statement of qualities (and circumstances) that seem to the author to be most associated with leadership. Point by point he builds his definition and, in so doing, illustrates some interesting uses of this pattern of exposition.

At a moment when we are waiting to see whether we have elected a President or a leader,[1] it is worth examining the differences between the two. For not every President is a leader, but every time we elect a President we hope for one, especially in times of doubt and crisis. In easy times we are ambivalent — the leader, after all, makes demands, challenges the status quo, shakes things up. 1

Leadership is as much a question of timing as anything else. The leader must appear on the scene at a moment when people are looking for leadership, as Churchill did in 1940, as Roosevelt did in 1933, as Lenin did in 1917. And when he comes, he must offer a simple, eloquent message. 2

Great leaders are almost always great simplifiers, who cut 3

Reprinted from *Newsweek*, January 5, 1981, by permission of the author. Copyright © 1981 by Michael Korda.

[1]"What It Takes to Be a Leader" was published on January 5, 1981, before Reagan had taken office.

through argument, debate and doubt to offer a solution everybody can understand and remember. Churchill warned the British to expect "blood, toil, tears and sweat"; FDR told Americans that "the only thing we have to fear is fear itself"; Lenin promised the war-weary Russians peace, land and bread. Straightforward but potent messages.

We have an image of what a leader ought to be. We even recognize the physical signs: leaders may not necessarily be tall, but they must have bigger-than-life, commanding features — LBJ's nose and ear lobes, Ike's broad grin. A trademark also comes in handy: Lincoln's stovepipe hat, JFK's rocker. We expect our leaders to stand out a little, not to be like ordinary men. Half of President Ford's trouble lay in the fact that, if you closed your eyes for a moment, you couldn't remember his face, figure or clothes. A leader should have an unforgettable identity, instantly and permanently fixed in people's minds.

It also helps for a leader to be able to do something most of us can't: FDR overcame polio; Mao swam the Yangtze River at the age of 72. We don't want our leaders to be "just like us." We want them to be like us but better, special, more so. Yet if they are *too* different, we reject them. Adlai Stevenson was too cerebral. Nelson Rockefeller, too rich.

Even television, which comes in for a lot of knocks as an image builder that magnifies form over substance, doesn't altogether obscure the qualities of leadership we recognize, or their absence. Television exposed Nixon's insecurity, Humphrey's fatal infatuation with his own voice.

A leader must know how to use power (that's what leadership is about), but he also has to have a way of showing that he does. He has to be able to project firmness — no physical clumsiness (like Ford), no rapid eye movements (like Carter).

A Chinese philosopher once remarked that a leader must have the grace of a good dancer, and there is a great deal of wisdom to this. A leader should know how to appear relaxed and confident. His walk should be firm and purposeful. He should be able, like Lincoln, FDR, Truman, Ike and JFK, to give a good, hearty, belly laugh, instead of the sickly grin that passes for good humor in Nixon or Carter. Ronald Reagan's training as an actor showed to good effect in the debate with Carter, when by his easy manner and apparent affability, he managed to convey the impression that in fact he was the President and Carter the challenger.

If we know what we're looking for, why is it so difficult to find? The answer lies in a very simple truth about leadership. People can only be led where they want to go. The leader follows, though a step ahead. Americans *wanted* to climb out of the Depression and needed someone to tell them they could do it, and FDR did. The British believed that they could still win the war after the defeats of 1940, and Churchill told them they were right. 9

A leader rides the waves, moves with the tides, understands the deepest yearnings of his people. He cannot make a nation that wants peace at any price go to war, or stop a nation determined to fight from doing so. His purpose must match the national mood. His task is to focus the people's energies and desires, to define them in simple terms, to inspire, to make what people already want seem attainable, important, within their grasp. 10

Above all, he must dignify our desires, convince us that we are taking part in the making of great history, give us a sense of glory about ourselves. Winston Churchill managed, by sheer rhetoric, to turn the British defeat and the evacuation of Dunkirk in 1940 into a major victory. FDR's words turned the sinking of the American fleet at Pearl Harbor into a national rallying cry instead of a humiliating national scandal. A leader must stir our blood, not appeal to our reason. 11

For this reason, businessmen generally make poor leaders. They tend to be pragmatists who think that once you've explained why something makes sense, people will do it. But history shows the fallacy of this belief. When times get tough, people don't want to be told what went wrong, or lectured, or given a lot of complicated statistics and plans (like Carter's energy policy) they don't understand. They want to be moved, excited, inspired, consoled, uplifted — in short, led! 12

A great leader must have a certain irrational quality, a stubborn refusal to face facts, infectious optimism, the ability to convince us that all is not lost even when we're afraid it is. Confucius suggested that while the advisers of a great leader should be as cold as ice, the leader himself should have fire, a spark of divine madness. 13

He won't come until we're ready for him, for the leader is like a mirror, reflecting back to us our own sense of purpose, putting into 14 words our own dreams and hopes, transforming our needs and fears into coherent policies and programs.

Our strength makes him strong; our determination makes him determined; our courage makes him a hero; he is, in the final analysis, the symbol of the best in us, shaped by our own spirit and will. And when these qualities are lacking in us, we can't produce him; and even with all our skill at image building, we can't fake him. He is, after all, merely the sum of us.

Meanings and Values

1. Precisely what is meant by the allegation that, for some people, the television appearance of a leader or would-be leader "magnifies form over substance" (par. 6)?

2a. Is this selection mostly specific or general? Why? (See Guide to Terms: *Specific/General.*)

 b. Where, if at all, does it change in this respect?

3. Can the various references to presidents be classified as rhetorical allusions? Why, or why not? (Guide: *Figures of Speech.*)

4. Is this a formal, informal, or familiar essay? Why? (Guide: *Essay.*)

5a. How can a leader *follow* "a step *ahead*" (par. 9)?

 b. Is this statement a paradox? Why, or why not? (Guide: *Paradox.*)

6. The author seems to classify Johnson as a leader (par. 4). How, then, can you account for Johnson's loss of support for United States involvement in Vietnam?

7. Has the country found out yet whether we "elected a President or a leader" (par. 1)? Which did we elect?

8. Do Korda's criteria apply only to "good" leaders? Or can they also apply to evil leaders, coming forth when people are ready for them? If the latter, use at least one example (not necessarily in the United States) to illustrate.

9. If you have read the Barber piece in Section 2, into which class do you think a leader — as defined by Korda — would be most likely to fit? Why?

Expository Techniques

1a. Which two methods of definition has Korda used extensively?

 b. Why, if at all, do they work well together?

 c. Cite at least one paragraph in which both are used.

2a. What third method of definition is used in paragraph 12? Explain.

b. Cite other minor uses of this method.

3. Is the last sentence of paragraph 11 an example of parallel structure? Why, or why not? (Guide: *Parallel Structure.*)

4. Does paragraph 14 contain a logical comparison, an analogy, or a simile? Why do you so classify it? (Guide: *Analogy* and *Figures of Speech.*)

5a. How successful do you consider Korda's closing? Why? (Guide: *Closings.*)

b. Which, if any, of the standard methods of closing does he use?

Diction and Vocabulary

1a. What kind of figures of speech are found in paragraph 10? (Guide: *Figures of Speech.*)

b. In paragraph 13?

2. In paragraph 15, does Korda use the word "symbol" in exactly the same sense as described in this book? (Guide: *Symbol.*) If not, what is the difference?

3. Use the dictionary as necessary to become familiar with the following words: ambivalent, status quo (par. 1); cerebral (5); pragmatists, fallacy (12).

Suggestions for Writing and Discussion

1. Select one of the numerous characteristics of a leader (as Korda sees them) to discuss further. Organize your ideas to present a coherent oral or written composition.

2. If you prefer, disagree with the author on one or more of the characteristics, but try to keep your discussion nonpolitical.

3. Clarify (as though for someone slow to grasp such subtleties) and build upon the paradox in paragraph 9.

4. Is there any reason to assume that a woman would be less likely than a man to possess all these qualities of good leadership? Discuss fully — and fairly.

5. What do you consider the possibility of a young man's deliberately *developing* all of the characteristics and then becoming president?

(NOTE: Suggestions for topics requiring development by use of DEFINITION follow.)

Writing Suggestions for Section 7
Definition

Develop a composition for a specified purpose and audience, using whatever methods and expository patterns will help convey a clear understanding of your meaning of one of the following terms:

1. Country rock music.
2. Conscience.
3. Religion.
4. Bigotry.
5. Rationalization.
6. Empathy.
7. Altruism.
8. Hypocrisy.
9. Humor.
10. Sophistication.
11. Naiveté.
12. Cowardice.
13. Wisdom.
14. Integrity.
15. Morality.
16. Sin.
17. Social poise.
18. Intellectual (the person).
19. Pornography (if your opinions differ appreciably from D. H. Lawrence's).

Explaining with the Help of *Description*

Exposition, as well as argument, can be made more vivid, and hence more understandable, with the support of description. Most exposition does contain some elements of description, and at times description carries almost the entire burden of the explanation, becoming a basic pattern for the expository purpose.

Description is most useful in painting a word-picture of something concrete, such as a scene or a person. Its use is not restricted, however, to what we can perceive with our senses; we can also describe (or attempt to describe) an abstract concept, such as an emotion or a quality or a mood. But most attempts to describe fear, for instance, still resort to the physical — a "coldness around the heart," perhaps — and in such concrete ways communicate the abstract to the reader.

In its extreme forms, description is either *objective* or *impressionistic* (subjective), but most of its uses are somewhere between these extremes. Objective description is purely factual, uncolored by any feelings of the author; it is the type used for scientific papers and most business reports. But impressionistic description, as the term implies, at least tinges the purely factual with the author's personal impressions; instead of describing how something *is*, objectively, the author describes how it *seems*, subjectively. Such a description might refer to the "blazing heat" of an August day. Somewhat less impressionistic would be "extreme heat." But the scientist would describe it precisely as "115 degrees Fahrenheit," and this would be purely objective reporting, unaffected by the impressions of the author. (No examples of the latter are included in this section, but many textbooks for other courses utilize the technique of pure objective description, as do encyclopedias. The Petrunkevitch essay in Section 5 provides some good examples of objective description, although not entirely unmixed with colorful impressionistic details.)

The first and most important job in any descriptive endeavor is to select the details to be included. There are usually many from which to choose, and writers must constantly keep in mind the kind of picture they want to paint with words — for *their* purpose and *their* audience. Such a word-picture need not be entirely visual; in this respect writers have more freedom than artists, for writers can use strokes that will add the dimensions of sound, smell, and even touch. Such "strokes," if made to seem natural enough, can help create a vivid and effective image in the reader's mind.

Most successful impressionistic description focuses on a single *dominant impression.* Of the many descriptive details ordinarily available for use, the author selects those which will help create a mood or atmosphere or emphasize a feature or quality. But more than the materials themselves are involved, for even diction can often assist in creating the desired dominant impression. Sometimes syntax is also an important factor, as in the use of short, hurried sentences to help convey a sense of urgency or excitement.

Actual structuring of passages is perhaps less troublesome in description than in most of the other patterns. But some kind of orderliness is needed for the sake of both readability and a realistic effect. (Neither objective nor impressionistic description can afford not to be realistic, in one manner or another.) In visual description, orderliness is usually achieved by presenting details as the eye would find them — that is, as arranged in space. We could describe a person from head to toe, or vice versa, or begin with the most noticeable feature and work from there. A scenic description might move from near to far or from far to near, from left to right or from right to left. It might also start with a broad, overall view, gradually narrowing to a focal point, probably the most significant feature of the scene. These are fairly standard kinds of description; but as the types and occasions for using description vary widely, so do the possibilities for interesting treatment. In many cases, writers are limited only by their own ingenuity.

But ingenuity should not be allowed to produce *excessive* description, an amazingly certain path to reader boredom. A few well-chosen details are better than profusion. Economy of words is desirable in any writing, and description is no exception. Appropriate use of figurative language and careful choice of strong nouns and verbs will help prevent the need for strings of modifiers, which are wasteful and can seem amateurish.

Even for the experienced writer, however, achieving good description remains a constant challenge; the beginner should not expect to attain this goal without working at it.

Sample Paragraph (Description)

Leads off with *impressionistic* details. "Barren," "junk-cluttered," and "tired" all are how the area is perceived by the author.

Along South Road, after miles of barren hills and crossing Suicide Creek, the road rounds a bend and levels along a junk-cluttered ravine; and there is Rejoice, lined up in one tired row of buildings facing Colman's Gulch. According to legend, both

Background information.

gulch and town owe their names to Ezra Colman, who had come to settle. Ezra and his wife, Ivy, were just plodding along when Ez found a rock he thought was gold. Mrs. Colman asked how to help, and he shouted to get the hell out of the way, to go rejoice unto the Lord or something. By the time his gold fever eased (with no gold but quite a pile of rocks), Ivy had planted potatoes, so that's where they

Transitional, between background and coming description.

built a cabin. It still stands there back of Nettie's Gas, still the straightest building in town; but that's not saying

"Leans toward the gulch" is an *objective* detail (how it *is*); "to keep watch . . ." is purely *impressionistic* (how it *seems*).

much: most of Rejoice leans toward the gulch, as though to keep watch on Ezra's rocks. There's one block of

These are mostly *objective* details, but selected no doubt to contribute to a *dominant impression* of poverty, dejection.

mostly empty stores and a church, another four blocks of houses. Large or small, they are all unpainted and have broken windows stuffed with faded jeans. Each has a cat dozing against the door, and children spirit-

"Fragrant," which is *impressionistic*, involves another sense in the otherwise visual description.

Primarily *objective*, but meant as contrast to the *dominant impression*, perhaps making the dismal scene more poignant by contrast to roses.

lessly playing drag-race in a rusty heap in the yard. But Rejoice is fragrant: rose vines, gone wild, blooming pink everywhere, climbing over every sagging barn and stump and even the Galilee Church and the old Colman cabin.

SHARON CURTIN

SHARON CURTIN, a native of Douglas, Wyoming, was raised in a family of ranchers and craftspeople. Curtin, a women's liberationist and political leftist, has worked as a nurse in New York and California but now devotes most of her time to writing and to operating a small farm in Virginia. Her current projects include a book about industrial development in the western Great Plains.

Aging in the Land of the Young

"Aging in the Land of the Young" is the first part of Curtin's article by that title, as it appeared in the *Atlantic Monthly* in July 1972. It is largely a carefully restructured composite of portions of her book *Nobody Ever Died of Old Age,* also published in 1972. It illustrates the subjective form of description, generally known as impressionistic description.

Old men, old women, almost 20 million of them. They constitute 10 percent of the total population, and the percentage is steadily growing. Some of them, like conspirators, walk all bent over, as if hiding some precious secret, filled with self-protection. The body seems to gather itself around those vital parts, folding shoulders, arms, pelvis like a fading rose. Watch and you see how fragile old people come to think they are. 1

Aging paints every action gray, lies heavy on every movement, imprisons every thought. It governs each decision with a ruthless and single-minded perversity. To age is to learn the feeling of no longer growing, of struggling to do old tasks, to remember familiar actions. The cells of the brain are destroyed with thousands of unfelt tiny strokes, little pockets of clotted blood wiping out memories and 2 abilities without warning. The body seems slowly to give up, randomly stopping, sometimes starting again as if to torture and tease with the memory of lost strength. Hands become clumsy, frail transparencies, held together with knotted blue veins.

Sometimes it seems as if the distance between your feet and the 3 floor were constantly changing, as if you were walking on shifting and not quite solid ground. One foot down, slowly, carefully force the other foot forward. Sometimes you are a shuffler, not daring to lift your feet from the uncertain earth but forced to slide hesitantly forward in little whispering movements. Sometimes you are able to "step out," but this effort — in fact the pure exhilaration of easy movement — soon exhausts you.

The world becomes narrower as friends and family die or move 4 away. To climb stairs, to ride in a car, to walk to the corner, to talk on the telephone; each action seems to take away from the energy needed to stay alive. Everything is limited by the strength you hoard greedily. Your needs decrease, you require less food, less sleep, and finally less human contact; yet this little bit becomes more and more difficult. You fear that one day you will be reduced to the simple acts of breathing and taking nourishment. This is the ultimate stage you dread, the period of helplessness and hopelessness, when independence will be over.

There is nothing to prepare you for the experience of growing 5 old. Living is a process, an irreversible progression toward old age and eventual death. You see men of eighty still vital and straight as oaks; you see men of fifty reduced to gray shadows in the human landscape. The cellular clock differs for each one of us, and is profoundly affected by our own life experiences, our heredity, and perhaps most important, by the concepts of aging encountered in society and in oneself.

The aged live with enforced leisure, on fixed incomes, subject 6 to many chronic illnesses, and most of their money goes to keep a roof over their heads. They also live in a culture that worships youth.

A kind of cultural attitude makes me bigoted against old peo- 7 ple; it makes me think young is best; it makes me treat old people like outcasts.

Hate that gray? Wash it away! 8
Wrinkle cream. 9

Monkey glands. 10
Face-lifting. 11
Look like a bride again. 12
Don't trust anyone over thirty. 13
I fear growing old. 14
Feel Young Again! 15

I am afraid to grow old — we're all afraid. In fact, the fear of 16
growing old is so great that every aged person is an insult and a
threat to the society. They remind us of our own death, that our
body won't always remain smooth and responsive, but will some-
day betray us by aging, wrinkling, faltering, failing. The ideal way
to age would be to grow slowly invisible, gradually disappearing,
without causing worry or discomfort to the young. In some ways
that does happen. Sitting in a small park across from a nursing home
one day, I noticed that the young mothers and their children
gathered on one side, and the old people from the home on the
other. Whenever a youngster would run over to the "wrong" side,
chasing a ball or just trying to cover all the available space, the old
people would lean forward and smile. But before any communication could be established, the mother would come over, murmuring
embarrassed apologies, and take her child back to the "young" side.

Now, it seemed to me that the children didn't feel any particu- 17
lar fear and the old people didn't seem to be threatened by the
children. The division of space was drawn by the mothers. And the
mothers never looked at the old people who lined the other side of
the park like so many pigeons perched on the benches. These
well-dressed young matrons had a way of sliding their eyes over,
around, through the old people; they never looked at them directly.
The old people may as well have been invisible; they had no reality
for the youngsters, who were not permitted to speak to them, and
they offended the aesthetic eye of the mothers.

My early experiences were somewhat different; since I grew up 18
in a small town, my childhood had more of a nineteenth-century
flavor. I knew a lot of old people, and considered some of them
friends. There was no culturally defined way for me to "relate" to
old people, except the rules of courtesy which applied to all adults.
My grandparents were an integral and important part of the family
and of the community. I sometimes have a dreadful fear that mine
will be the last generation to know old people as friends, to have a

sense of what growing old means, to respect and understand man's mortality and his courage in the face of death. Mine may be the last generation to have a sense of living history, of stories passed from generation to generation, of identity established by family history.

Meanings and Values

1. What is the general tone of this writing? (See Guide to Terms: *Style/Tone.*)

2. If you find it depressing to read about aging, try to analyze why (especially in view of the fact that you are very likely many years from the stage of "a fading rose").

3. Why do you suppose it is more likely to be the mothers than the children who shun old people (pars. 16–17)?

4a. Has this author avoided the excesses of sentimentality? (Guide: *Sentimentality.*)

  b. If not, where does she fail? If she does avoid sentimentality, try to discover how.

Expository Techniques

1a. Why should this writing be classed as primarily impressionistic, rather than objective?

  b. What is the dominant impression?

2a. Analyze the role that selection of details plays in creating the dominant impression.

  b. Provide examples of the type of details that could have been included but were not.

  c. Are such omissions justifiable?

3a. Paragraph 5 ends the almost pure description to begin another phase of the writing. What is it?

  b. How has the author provided for a smooth transition between the two? (Guide: *Transition.*)

4a. What particular method of gaining emphasis has been used effectively in one portion of the selection? (Guide: *Emphasis.*)

  b. How might the material have been presented if emphasis were not desired?

5. Which previously studied patterns of exposition are also used in this writing? Cite paragraphs where each may be found.

Diction and Vocabulary

1a. The author sometimes changes person — e.g., "they" to "you" after paragraph 2. Analyze where the changes occur.

 b. What justification, if any, can you find for each change?

2a. Which two kinds of figure of speech do you find used liberally to achieve this description? (Guide: *Figures of Speech.*)

 b. Cite three or more examples of each.

 c. As nearly as you can tell, are any of them clichés? (Guide: *Clichés.*)

Suggestions for Writing and Discussion

1. If Curtin is correct in her fears expressed in the last two sentences, what could be the consequences for society in general?

2. Discuss the pros and cons of placing senile old people in rest homes, rather than letting them live alone or taking them to live with the family. What other alternatives, if any, does the family have?

3. If you know some very old person who (apparently) is not as affected by aging as the ones the author describes, what seems to account for this difference?

4. If you are familiar with the Gray Panther movement, or others like it, discuss what exactly it is that the movement hopes to accomplish.

5. If many people at age sixty-five to seventy are still efficient at their jobs, as is often argued, what practical reasons are there for forcing retirement at that age?

(NOTE: Suggestions for topics requiring development by use of DESCRIP-TION are on page 276, at the end of this section.)

E. B. WHITE

E. B. WHITE, distinguished essayist, was born in Mount Vernon, New York, in 1899. A graduate of Cornell University, White has worked as a reporter and advertising copywriter, and in 1926 he joined the staff of *The New Yorker* magazine. Since 1937 he has done most of his writing at his farm in Maine, for many years contributing a regular column, "One Man's Meat," to *Harper's* magazine and freelance editorials for the "Notes and Comments" column of *The New Yorker*. White has also written children's books, two volumes of verse, and, with James Thurber, *Is Sex Necessary?* (1929). With his wife Katherine White, he compiled *A Subtreasury of American Humor* (1941). Collections of his own essays include *One Man's Meat* (1942), *The Second Tree from the Corner* (1953), *The Points of My Compass* (1962), and *Essays of E. B. White* (1977). In 1959 he revised and enlarged William Strunk's *The Elements of Style*, a textbook still widely used in college class-rooms. White has received many honors and writing awards for his crisp, highly individual style and his sturdy independence of thought.

Once More to the Lake

In this essay White relies primarily on description to convey his sense of the passage of time and the power of memory. The vivid scenes and the clear yet expressive prose in this essay are charac-teristic of his writing.

August 1941

One summer, along about 1904, my father rented a camp on a lake in 1
Maine and took us all there for the month of August. We all got ringworm from some kittens and had to rub Pond's Extract on our arms and legs night and morning, and my father rolled over in a

canoe with all his clothes on; but outside of that the vacation was a success and from then on none of us ever thought there was any place in the world like that lake in Maine. We returned summer after summer — always on August 1 for one month. I have since become a salt-water man, but sometimes in summer there are days when the restlessness of the tides and the fearful cold of the sea water and the incessant wind that blows across the afternoon and into the evening make me wish for the placidity of a lake in the woods. A few weeks ago this feeling got so strong I bought myself a couple of bass hooks and a spinner and returned to the lake where we used to go, for a week's fishing and to revisit old haunts.

I took along my son, who had never had any fresh water up his 2 nose and who had seen lily pads only from train windows. On the journey over to the lake I began to wonder what it would be like. I wondered how time would have marred this unique, this holy spot — the coves and streams, the hills that the sun set behind, the camps and the paths behind the camps. I was sure that the tarred road would have found it out, and I wondered in what other ways it would be desolated. It is strange how much you can remember about places like that once you allow your mind to return into the grooves that lead back. You remember one thing, and that suddenly reminds you of another thing. I guess I remembered clearest of all the early mornings, when the lake was cool and motionless, remembered how the bedroom smelled of the lumber it was made of and of the wet woods whose scent entered through the screen. The partitions in the camp were thin and did not extend clear to the top of the rooms, and as I was always the first up I would dress softly so as not to wake the others, and sneak out into the sweet outdoors and start out in the canoe, keeping close along the shore in the long shadows of the pines. I remembered being very careful never to rub my paddle against the gunwale for fear of disturbing the stillness of the cathedral.

The lake had never been what you would call a wild lake. There 3 were cottages sprinkled around the shores, and it was in farming country although the shores of the lake were quite heavily wooded. Some of the cottages were owned by nearby farmers, and you would live at the shore and eat your meals at the farmhouse. That's what our family did. But although it wasn't wild, it was a fairly large and undisturbed lake and there were places in it that, to a child at least, seemed infinitely remote and primeval.

I was right about the tar: it led to within half a mile of the shore. But when I got back there, with my boy, and we settled into a camp near a farmhouse and into the kind of summertime I had known, I could tell that it was going to be pretty much the same as it had been before — I knew it, lying in bed the first morning, smelling the bedroom and hearing the boy sneak quietly out and go off along the shore in a boat. I began to sustain the illusion that he was I, and therefore, by simple transposition, that I was my father. This sensation persisted, kept cropping up all the time we were there. It was not an entirely new feeling, but in this setting it grew much stronger. I seemed to be living a dual existence. I would be in the middle of some simple act, I would be picking up a bait box or laying down a table fork, or I would be saying something, and suddenly it would be not I but my father who was saying the words or making the gesture. It gave me a creepy sensation.

We went fishing the first morning. I felt the same damp moss covering the worms in the bait can, and saw the dragonfly alight on the tip of my rod as it hovered a few inches from the surface of the water. It was the arrival of this fly that convinced me beyond any doubt that everything was as it always had been, that the years were a mirage and that there had been no years. The small waves were the same, chucking the rowboat under the chin as we fished at anchor, and the boat was the same boat, the same color green and the ribs broken in the same places, and under the floorboards the same fresh-water leavings and débris — the dead helgramite, the wisps of moss, the rusty discarded fishhook, the dried blood from yesterday's catch. We stared silently at the tips of our rods, at the dragonflies that came and went. I lowered the tip of mine into the water, tentatively, pensively dislodging the fly, which darted two feet away, poised, darted two feet back, and came to rest again a little farther up the rod. There had been no years between the ducking of this dragonfly and the other one — the one that was part of memory. I looked at the boy, who was silently watching his fly, and it was my hands that held his rod, my eyes watching. I felt dizzy and didn't know which rod I was at the end of.

We caught two bass, hauling them in briskly as though they were mackerel, pulling them over the side of the boat in a businesslike manner without any landing net, and stunning them with a blow on the back of the head. When we got back for a swim before lunch, the lake was exactly where we had left it, the same number of inches from the dock, and there was only the merest suggestion of a breeze. This seemed an utterly enchanted sea, this lake you could leave to its own devices for a few hours and come back to, and find that it had not stirred, this constant and trustworthy body of water. In the shallows, the dark, water-soaked sticks and twigs, smooth and old, were undulating in clusters on the bottom against the clean ribbed sand, and the track of the mussel was plain. A school of minnows swam by, each minnow with its small individual shadow, doubling the attendance, so clear and sharp in the sunlight. Some of the other campers were in swimming, along the shore, one of them with a cake of soap, and the water felt thin and clear and unsubstantial. Over the years there had been this person with the cake of soap, this cultist, and here he was. There had been no years.

Up to the farmhouse to dinner through the teeming, dusty 7 field, the road under our sneakers was only a two-track road. The middle track was missing, the one with the marks of the hooves and the splotches of dried, flaky manure. There had always been three tracks to choose from in choosing which track to walk in; now the choice was narrowed down to two. For a moment I missed terribly the middle alternative. But the way led past the tennis court, and something about the way it lay there in the sun reassured me; the tape had loosened along the backline, the alleys were green with plantains and other weeds, and the net (installed in June and removed in September) sagged in the dry noon, and the whole place steamed with midday heat and hunger and emptiness. There was a choice of pie for dessert, and one was blueberry and one was apple, and the waitresses were the same country girls, there having been no passage of time, only the illusion of it as in a dropped curtain — the waitresses were still fifteen; their hair had been washed, that was the only difference — they had been to the movies and seen the pretty girls with the clean hair.

Summertime, oh, summertime, pattern of life indelible, the 8 fade-proof lake, the woods unshatterable, the pasture with the sweetfern and the juniper forever and ever, summer without end; this was the background, and the life along the shore was the design, their tiny docks with the flagpole and the American flag floating against the white clouds in the blue sky, the little paths over the roots of the trees leading from camp to camp and the paths leading back to the outhouses and the can of lime for sprinkling, and at the souvenir counters at the store the miniature birch-bark canoes and the postcards that showed things looking a little better than they looked. This was the American family at play, escaping the city heat, wondering whether the newcomers in the camp at the head of the cove were "common" or "nice," wondering whether it was true that the people who drove up for Sunday dinner at the farmhouse were turned away because there wasn't enough chicken.

It seemed to me, as I kept remembering all this, that those times and those summers had been infinitely precious and worth saving. There had been jollity and peace and goodness. The arriving (at the beginning of August) had been so big a business in itself, at the railway station the farm wagon drawn up, the first smell of the pine-laden air, the first glimpse of the smiling farmer, and the great importance of the trunks and your father's enormous authority in such matters, and the feel of the wagon under you for the long ten-mile haul, and at the top of the last long hill catching the first view of the lake after eleven months of not seeing this cherished body of water. The shouts and cries of the other campers when they saw you, and the trunks to be unpacked, to give up their rich burden. (Arriving was less exciting nowadays, when you sneaked up in your car and parked it under a tree near the camp and took out the bags and in five minutes it was all over, no fuss, no loud wonderful fuss about trunks.)

Peace and goodness and jollity. The only thing that was wrong now, really, was the sound of the place, an unfamiliar nervous sound of the outboard motors. This was the note that jarred, the one thing that would sometimes break the illusion and set the years moving. In those other summertimes all motors were inboard; and when they were at a little distance, the noise they made was a sedative, an ingredient of summer sleep. They were one-cylinder and two-cylinder engines, and some were make-and-break and some were jump-spark, but they all made a sleepy sound across the lake. The one-lungers throbbed and fluttered, and the twin-cylinder ones purred and purred, and that was a quiet sound, too. But now the campers all had outboards. In the daytime, in the hot mornings, these motors made a petulant, irritable sound; at night, in the still evening when the afterglow lit the water, they whined about one's ears like mosquitoes. My boy loved our rented outboard, and his great desire was to achieve single-handed mastery over it, and authority, and he soon learned the trick of choking it a little (but not too much), and the adjustment of the needle valve. Watching him I would remember the things you could do with the old one-cylinder engine with the heavy flywheel, how you could have it eating out of your hand if you got really close to it spiritually. Motorboats in those days didn't have clutches, and you would make a landing by shutting off the motor at the proper time and coasting in with a dead rudder. But there was a way of reversing them, if you learned the trick, but cutting the switch and putting it on again exactly on the final dying revolution of the flywheel, so that it would kick back against compression and begin reversing. Approaching a dock in a strong following breeze, it was difficult to slow up sufficiently by the ordinary coasting method, and if a boy felt he had complete mastery over his motor, he was tempted to keep it running beyond its time and then reverse it a few feet from the dock. It took a cool nerve, because if you threw the switch a twentieth of a second too soon you would catch the flywheel when it still had speed enough to go up past center, and the boat would leap ahead, charging bull-fashion at the dock.

We had a good week at the camp. The bass were biting well and 11 the sun shone endlessly, day after day. We would be tired at night and lie down in the accumulated heat of the little bedrooms after the long hot day and the breeze would stir almost imperceptibly outside and the smell of the swamp drift in through the rusty screens. Sleep would come easiy and in the morning the red squirrel would be on the roof, tapping out his gay routine. I kept remembering everything, lying in bed in the mornings — the small steamboat that had a long rounded stern like the lip of a Ubangi, and how quietly she ran on the moonlight sails, when the older boys played their mandolins and the girls sang and we ate doughnuts dipped in sugar, and how sweet the music was on the water in the shining night, and what it had felt like to think about girls then. After breakfast we would go up to the store and the things were in the same place — the minnows in a bottle, the plugs and spinners disarranged and pawed over by the youngsters from the boys' camp, the Fig Newtons and the Beeman's gum. Outside, the road was tarred and cars stood in front of the store. Inside, all was just as it had always been, except there was more Coca-Cola and not so much Moxie and root beer and birch beer and sarsaparilla. We would walk out with the bottle of pop apiece and sometimes the pop would backfire up our noses and hurt. We explored the streams, quietly, where the turtles slid off the sunny logs and dug their way into the soft bottom; and we lay on the town wharf and fed worms to the tame bass. Everywhere we went I had trouble making out which was I, the one walking at my side, the one walking in my pants.

One afternoon while we were there at that lake a thunderstorm came up. It was like the revival of an old melodrama that I had seen long ago with childish awe. The second-act climax of the drama of the electrical disturbance over a lake in America had not changed in any important respect. This was the big scene, still the big scene. The whole thing was so familiar, the first feeling of oppression and heat and a general air around camp of not wanting to go very far away. In mid-afternoon (it was all the same) a curious darkening of the sky, and a lull in everything that had made life tick; and then the way the boats suddenly swung the other way at their moorings with the coming of a breeze out of the new quarter, and the premonitory rumble. Then the kettle drum, then the snare, then the bass drum and cymbals, then crackling light against the dark, and the gods grinning and licking their chops in the hills. Afterward the calm, the rain steadily rustling in the calm lake, the return of light and hope and spirits, and the campers running out in joy and relief to go swimming in the rain, their bright cries perpetuating the deathless joke about how they were getting simply drenched, and the children screaming with delight at the new sensation of bathing in the rain, and the joke about getting drenched linking the generations in a strong indestructible chain. And the comedian who waded in carrying an umbrella.

When the others went swimming, my son said he was going in, too. He pulled his dripping trunks from the line where they had hung all through the shower and wrung them out. Languidly, and with no thought of going in, I watched him, his hard little body, skinny and bare, saw him wince slighty as he pulled up around his vitals the small, soggy, icy garment. As he buckled the swollen belt, suddenly my groin felt the chill of death.

Meanings and Values

1a.   Why does White decide to return to the lake?

  b.   Can the lake be considered a personal symbol for White? (See Guide to Terms: *Symbol.*)

c. If so, what does it symbolize?

2a. In what ways has the lake and its surroundings remained the same since White's boyhood? Be specific.

b. In what ways has it changed?

3a. At one point in the essay White says, "I seemed to be living a dual existence" (par. 4). What is the meaning of this statement?

b. How does this "dual existence" affect his point of view in the essay? (Guide: *Point of View.*)

c. Is the "dual existence" emphasized more in the first half of the essay or the second half? Why?

4a. Where would you place this essay on an objective-to-subjective continuum? (Guide: *Objective/Subjective.*)

b. Is this a formal or an informal essay? Explain. (Guide: *Essay.*)

5a. After spending a day on the lake, White remarks, "There had been no years" (par. 6). What other direct or indirect comments does he make about time and change? Be specific.

b. How are these comments related to the central theme of the essay? (Guide: *Unity.*)

6a. What is the tone of the essay? (Guide: *Style/Tone.*)

b. Does the tone change or remain the same throughout the essay?

7a. What is meant by the closing phrase of the essay, "suddenly my groin felt the chill of death" (par. 13)?

b. Is this an appropriate way to end the essay? Why, or why not?

Expository Techniques

1a. If you agree that the lake is a personal symbol for White, explain how he enables readers to understand its significance. (Guide: *Symbol.*)

b. Is he successful in doing this? (Guide: *Evaluation.*)

2a. In the first part of the essay White focuses on the unchanged aspects of the lake; in the second part he begins acknowledging the passage of time. Where does this shift in attitude take place?

b. What strategies, including transitional devices, does White use to signal to the reader the shift in attitude? Be specific.

3a. How does White use the discussion of outboard motors and inboard motors (par. 10) to summarize the differences between life at the lake in his youth and at the time of his return with his son? Explain.

4. Many of the descriptive passages in this essay convey a dominant impression, usually an emotion or mood. Choose a paragraph from the essay and discuss how the author's choice of details, variety of

syntax, and diction help create a dominant impression. Be specific. (Guide: *Syntax* and *Diction*.)

5a.   In many places the author combines description and comparison. Select a passage from the essay and discuss in detail how he combines the patterns.

 b.   In what ways is the combination of description and comparison appropriate to the theme and the point of view of the essay?

6.   White has often been praised for the clarity and variety of his prose style. To what extent are these qualities the result of syntax and of the variety of strategies he uses to achieve emphasis? (Choose a sample paragraph, such as 6, 9, or 12, to illustrate your answer.) (Guide: *Emphasis* and *Syntax*.)

Diction and Vocabulary

1.   To what extent are the qualities of White's style mentioned in your answer to question 6 of "Expository Techniques" matters of diction? (Guide: *Diction*.)

2a.   How much do the connotations of the words used in paragraph 8 contribute to the dominant impression the author is trying to create? (Guide: *Connotation/Denotation*.)

 b.   In paragraph 10?

3a.   Why would the author refer to the person with the cake of soap as "this cultist" (par. 6)?

 b.   In what sense can a tennis court steam "with midday heat and hunger and emptiness" (par. 7)?

4.   What kind of paradox is presented in this passage: " . . . the waitresses were the same country girls, there having been no passage of time, only the illusion of it as in a dropped curtain — the waitresses were still fifteen; their hair had been washed, that was the only difference — they had been to the movies and seen the pretty girls with the clean hair" (par. 7). (Guide: *Paradox*.)

5a.   Is the diction in this passage sentimental: "Summertime, oh, summertime, pattern of life indelible, the fade-proof lake, the woods unshatterable, the pasture with the sweetfern and the juniper forever and ever, summer without end. . . ." (par. 8)? (Guide: *Sentimentality*.)

 b.   If so, why would the author choose to use this style in the passage?

 c.   Does the passage contain an allusion? If so, what is alluded to and why? (Guide: *Figures of Speech*.)

6.   Study the author's uses of the following words, consulting the dictionary as needed: incessant, placidity (par. 1); gunwale (2);

primeval (3); transposition (40; helgramite, pensively (5); petulant (10); premonitory (12); languidly (13).

Suggestions for Writing and Discussion

1. Choose some place you remember from your childhood and have seen recently and write a description of it comparing its present appearance with your memories of it.

2. Prepare a description of some object or place that symbolizes the passage of time and try to control the tone of your description so it reflects your attitudes toward time and change.

3. Discuss your relationship with your parents (or your children) in so far as that relationship includes experiences similar to the ones White describes in "Once More to the Lake."

4. If you have taken a summer vacation like the one recorded by White, compare your experiences and the setting to those in the essay. How much have our civilization — and our vacations — changed since the time of the events in the essay?

(NOTE: Suggestions for topics requiring development by use of DESCRIPTION are on page 276, at the end of this section.)

MARTIN HOFFMAN

MARTIN HOFFMAN, born in 1935, is a staff psychiatrist at the Center for Special Problems at the San Francisco Health Department. He received a grant from the National Institute of Mental Health for the study of male homosexuals in the San Francisco Bay area and has taught a course on sexual deviance at both the undergraduate and graduate levels at the University of California, Berkeley. He is also experienced in psychoanalytic theory.

The Gay Bar

"The Gay Bar" is a portion of Hoffman's book *The Gay World* (1968), the controversial report on his three-year study of the homosexual scene in the San Francisco Bay area. In it, according to *Publisher's Weekly*, Hoffman "does for the homosexual subculture, its causes and patterns, what Vance Packard has done in more conventional areas." This selection provides us with a far different type of description than have the preceding two.

The gay bar has almost become a social institution in America. It is the central public place around which gay life revolves and is to be found in all large and medium-sized cities across the country. We would like to describe here the "typical gay bar," although, of course, there is no such thing, any more than there is a "typical straight bar." Perhaps, narrowing our focus a bit, what we want to describe is what I call the "middle-class" gay bar, by which I mean not that all its members are necessarily middle-class socioeconomically, but rather that middle-class proprieties are observed and that there is nothing unique or specialized about the bar. We will not, for example, be concerned with the leather-jacket motorcycle bars, nor

From *The Gay World* by Martin Hoffman, © 1968 by Basic Books, Inc., Publishers, New York. Reprinted by permission of the publisher.

with the hustler bars so beautifully described by Rechy,[1] nor with those bars which provide entertainment such as drag shows and male go-go dancers.

Perhaps the most important fact about a gay bar is that it is a sexual marketplace. That is, men go there for the purpose of seeking sexual partners, and if this function were not served by the bar there would be no gay bars, for, although homosexuals also go there to drink and socialize, the search for sexual experience is in some sense the core of the interaction in the bar. It should, however, be obvious that there must be more going on in the bar than simply people meeting and leaving; otherwise the bar could not exist as a commercial enterprise. People have to come there for a time long enough to drink, in order to make it profitable to the management to run these bars. And gay bars are very profitable and have sprung up in large numbers. It is estimated that there are about 60 gay bars in Los Angeles and about 40 in San Francisco. A number of heterosexuals have converted their own taverns into gay bars simply because they have found it more profitable to run a gay bar, even though they are sometimes not particularly delighted with the clientele. The gay bar plays a central role in the life of very many homosexuals — one which is much more important than the role played by straight bars in the life of all but a few heterosexuals. This is connected intimately with the use of the gay bar as a sexual marketplace and, of course, with the fact that homosexuals, as homosexuals, have really no place else where they can congregate without disclosing to the straight world that they are homosexual.

What does a gay bar look like? In the first place, unlike most middle-class straight bars, it is almost exclusively populated by males. Sometimes non-homosexuals accidentally walk into a gay bar and it is usually this lack of women that makes them aware that they may have inadvertently walked into a homosexual setting. There are a few bars in which lesbians congregate along with male homosexuals, especially in cities which are not large enough to support a lesbian bar. But even in the larger cities, lesbian bars are not very common. They are never as large as the large metropolitan male gay bars. This is because female homosexuals are much less promiscuous than male homosexuals and really not able to support a sexual marketplace on the scale that males do.

[1]John Rechy, *City of Night* (1963).

Occasionally, "fruit flies," i.e., women who like to associate with male homosexuals, are found in gay bars, although they are not a very prominent part of any gay bar scene. Why a woman who is not a lesbian would like to associate with male homosexuals is a question which cannot be altogether answered in general, except to say that some of these women obviously find homosexual men a lot less threatening than heterosexual men, since the former are not interested in them sexually. Since these women are not potential sexual partners for the males, they are not potential sources of rejection for them either, and thereby they find themselves the subject of much attention by the male clientele. Consequently, they are the beneficiaries of a great deal of sociability without being objects of seduction. Some women find this a very appealing position.

In the gay world there is a tremendous accent on youth and this is reflected in the composition of the bar clientele. Youth is very much at a premium and young men will go to the bars as soon as they have passed the legal age limit. This varies from state to state; it is 18 in New York and 21 in California. Along with the younger men, there are somewhat older men who are trying to look young. They attempt to accomplish this primarily by dress. The typical bar costume is the same style of dress that an average college undergraduate might wear. It would consist of a sport shirt, Levis, and loafers or sneakers. In this "typical" middle-class gay bar which I am attempting to describe, extremely effeminate dress and mannerisms are not well tolerated. Nevertheless, it would not be correct to say that the scene in a gay bar looks like a fraternity stag party. There is a tendency toward effeminacy in the overall impression one gets from observing the bar, although this may not necessarily be anything striking or flagrant. There is a certain softness or absence of stereotypical masculine aggression present in the conversations and behavior of the bar patrons. Also, in spite of the fact that the model bar costume is very much like that one would see on a college campus, there is a good deal of special attention paid by the bar patrons to their dress, so that they seem almost extraordinarily well groomed. There is thus a feeling of fastidiousness about the appearance of the young men in the bar which, along with their muted demeanor, rather clearly differentiates the overall *Gestalt* of the gay bar from that which would be experienced upon entering a gathering of young male heterosexuals. There are usually a few clearly identifiable homosexuals, although the majority of individuals in the bar are not identifiable and would not be thought homosexual in another setting. It seems to be the general consensus of gay bar observers that fights are less likely to break out in a gay than in a straight bar. This is, I think, probably attributable to the psychological characteristics of the clientele rather than to anything about the structure of the bar itself. Male homosexuals would certainly rather make love than war.

One of the clearest differences between the gay and the straight   6
bar is that in the gay bar the attention of the patrons is focused directly on each other. In a gay bar, for example, the patrons who are sitting at the bar itself usually face away from the bar and look toward the other people in the room and toward the door. When a new patron walks in, he receives a good deal of scrutiny, and people engaged in conversation with each other just naturally assume that their interlocutors will turn away from them to watch each new entering patron. All this is, of course, part of the pervasive looking and cruising which goes on in the bar.

There is a great deal of milling about in the bar and individuals   7
tend to engage in short, superficial conversations with each other. They try to make the circuit around the bar to see everyone in it, perhaps stopping to chat with their friends but usually not for very long. In a way, the shortness and superficiality of the conversations in the bar mirror that same brevity and shallowness of interpersonal relations which characterize gay life as a whole.

Heterosexual observers and even homosexuals who are not   8
habitués of the bar scene often express great perplexity about the bars — they cannot quite understand what's going on there. They seem to be bewildered by the sight of all these young men standing around and communicating so little with one another. The patrons stand along the walls, it seems, for hours, without speaking. They move around the room and talk at length with almost no one. One heterosexual observer said that he felt as if everyone in the room were standing around waiting for some important figure to come in, but, of course, he never comes. He likened the scene to a reception for a foreign ambassador, where everyone stands around simply marking time until the dignitary arrives. In a sense, this observer was correct, for the young men *are* waiting for some important person to arrive, one who will never arrive — but it is not a foreign ambassador. Each is waiting for a handsome young prince to come

and carry him off in his arms. They're waiting for the ideal sexual object, and if they don't find him they may very well go home alone, in spite of the fact that there are sometimes hundreds of other attractive young men right there in the bar.

The gay bar, then, in a sense may be thought of as a stage on which is played out a fantasy in which the hero never arrives. The reason why heterosexuals and even some homosexuals cannot understand what is going on is because they are not a party to this fantasy. They imagine that if you are going to a place to seek a sexual partner, you go in, look around a little bit, walk up to somebody that you like, engage in a conversation, and then go out together. And sometimes this is precisely what does occur in the gay bar. Very often, in fact, but the bewildering problem which confronts the uninitiated observer is why this does not happen more often: why, in fact, all these good-looking and well-dressed young men are standing around uncommunicative.

Sherri Cavan[2] has made the suggestion that in the homosexual pickup bar it may happen that encounters are never begun because each party is waiting for the other to offer the first words of greeting. This is presumably due to the fact that when the situation involves two males, it is not clear who is expected to make the initial overture. One cannot deny the saliency of this observation. Nevertheless, I do not think it alone accounts fully for the strange situation in the gay bar, since one would expect the reverse to occur just as well, i.e., since both parties can make the initial overture, one would think that at least one of the members of the hypothetical pair could overcome his shyness. I think the sociological explanation fails to take into account the psychological factors involved. As many observers have noted, homosexuals are very much afraid of rejection, and hence, have an inordinate hesitancy about making an approach. I think this is due to the following reason: the only aspect of their self which male homosexuals are able to adequately present in a bar situation is their physical appearance. If they are rejected in making a conversational opening, this is interpreted (probably correctly) to mean a rejection of that crucial part of themselves, namely, their desirability as a sexual partner. Hence, their self-esteem is very much at stake and they have a great deal to lose by being rejected.

It must be remembered that in the gay world the only real

---

[2] Sherri Cavan, *Liquor License: An Ethnography of Bar Behavior* (1966), p. 192.

criterion of value is physical attractiveness; consequently, a rejection by a desired partner is a rejection of the only valued part of one's identity in that world. When we understand this, I think we understand why the fear of rejection is so prevalent among homosexual men.

The gay bar, is, then, a lot less licentious than people who are not aware of what is going on there might be inclined to think. When heterosexual men enter a gay bar for the first time for the purpose of simply visiting it, they often seem afraid that somehow they will be rapidly approached, or perhaps even attacked, by the sexual deviants present inside the bar. This, of course, is about as far from reality as it is possible to imagine. It would not be unusual if none of the patrons would engage them in conversation during the entire course of the evening. If they are not young and handsome, they may well have great difficulty in communicating with anyone after even a great deal of effort on their part. 12

A word should be said, I suppose, about the function of the gay bar as a source of group solidarity and as a place where one can meet one's friends and exchange gossip. I think, however, that this function is obvious and that it need not be elaborated upon. Many homosexuals frequent gay bars for reasons other than seeking sexual partners. If sex eventuates from the bar interaction, this is fine, but it is not the reason they went there in the first place. They went there for sociability. And yet this too must be qualified, for in the back of their minds is usually the thought that perhaps that special person will walk through the door tonight and they will meet him and go home with him. 13

The "cosmetic" quality of the gay bar is a result, in large part, of the need for anonymity which pervades all the public places of the gay world. If one can only present the visible and nonidentifying aspect of one's identity, one's physical appearance will be the central aspect that can be displayed to others. If homosexuals could meet *as homosexuals* in the kinds of social settings in which heterosexuals can (e.g., at school, at work) where the emphasis on finding sexual partners is not the controlling force behind all the social interaction which transpires, a great deal of the anonymous promiscuity which now characterizes homosexual encounters would be replaced by a more "normal" kind of meeting between two persons. Perhaps, then, the sexual relationships which develop would become more stable. Maybe the gay bar itself would not change — 14 this can only be a matter for conjecture — but, at any rate, it would not be so central to gay life.

Meanings and Values

1a.   Where would you place this writing on an objective–subjective continuum? (See Guide to Terms: *Objective/Subjective.*)

b.   Is there a dominant impression? If so, what is it?

c.   If there is a dominant impression, is it sufficient to give the description desirable unity?

2a.   Explain more fully the meaning of "stereotypical masculine aggression" (par. 5).

b.   If you have had some experience in a "typical straight bar," or in a similar setting, do you think one necessarily finds such "aggression" there? Explain.

3a.   Clarify the author's meaning of the sentence beginning, "If homosexuals could meet . . ." (par. 14).

b.   Do you think that this is a valid observation? (Consider, for instance, whether even heterosexuals ordinarily meet *as* heterosexuals in "social settings.")

4.   At the outset the author states that his purpose is to "describe" the gay bar (par. 1), but description was obviously not his only purpose, perhaps not even his primary one.

a.   What other purpose or purposes do you think he had?

b.   How well did he succeed?

c.   Was it a worthwhile endeavor? Why, or why not? (Guide: *Evaluation.*)

Expository Techniques

1.   What useful functions are served by the introductory paragraph, other than simply providing a way to start the essay?

2a.   A rhetorical question begins the actual physical description. What is it? (Guide: *Rhetorical Questions.*)

b.   Why is it rhetorical?

3a.   How effective do you think the author's choice of details is for his purposes?

b.   If you think other details would have improved his descriptive analysis, what are they? Why are they needed?

c.   Give several examples of details that might be desirable if the purpose had been to create a highly impressionistic description.

4a.   What other patterns of exposition are used in this essay?

b.   Cite two examples of each.

5a.   Some of the paragraphs here are somewhat longer than those in most modern writing. Are they too long? If so, what is the disadvantage?

b.   Select one of the longest, locate its topic sentence, and consider whether or not all parts of the paragraph are related to it. What, if anything, does this tell you about its unity? (Guide: *Unity.*)

c.   If unity is lacking, how might this weakness be overcome? Be specific.

Diction and Vocabulary

1a.   In the first paragraph Hoffman uses the editorial "we." Is this advantageous, or not? Why?

b.   Why do you think he did not continue its use throughout the essay?

2a.   The seemingly excess wordiness of numerous passages in this essay might be criticized. Do any seem too wordy to you? (Guide: *Diction* and *Syntax.*)

b.   If so, cite as many specific examples as you can.

c.   Select one of these and rewrite it with the same exact meaning but with greater economy of language and therefore, perhaps, with greater clarity and more effective syntax.

3a.   Hoffman uses several colloquial expressions, some so new that they cannot be found in some dictionaries. Cite five that you would classify as colloquial. (Guide: *Colloquial.*)

b.   Why do they not alter the generally serious tone of the essay?

c.   Would the writing be better, however, without them? Why, or why not?

4a.   Why is "*Gestalt*" printed in italics (par. 5)?

b.   What does it mean, as used here?

c.   Is it really needed here, or would a more common word have done as well? If the latter, suggest one.

5.   Study the author's uses of the following words, consulting the dictionary as needed: proprieties (par. 1); heterosexuals (2, and others); inadvertently, promiscuous (3); flagrant, fastidiousness, demeanor, consensus (5); interlocutors, pervasive (6); habitués (8); saliency, hypothetical, inordinate, crucial (10); criterion (11); licentious (12); eventuates (13); transpires, conjecture (14).

Suggestions for Writing and Discussion

1.   If, through observation or serious reading, you have noticed any changes of public attitude toward homosexuality, describe such changes and what you believe to be the reasons for them. If you wish, project these trends into the future.

2.   What do you think should be the function of law in attempting to regulate private morality — e.g., between "consenting adults"?

3.   What possible cause/effect relationship, if any, do you see between "hard-core" pornography and sexual deviation?

4.   If you have read or heard authoritative and recent discussions on the causes of homosexuality, explain one or more of these theories. If you wish, compare two of them.

5.   Some religions have traditionally taught that homosexuality is a "sin against nature." How would you interpret the meaning of this dictum?

(NOTE: Suggestions for topics requiring development by use of DESCRIP-TION are on page 276, at the end of this section.)

GEORGE SIMPSON

GEORGE SIMPSON, born in Virginia in 1950, received his B.A. in journalism from the University of North Carolina. He has been employed at *Newsweek* since 1972 and in 1978 became public affairs director for that magazine. Before joining *Newsweek*, Simpson worked for two years as a writer and editor for the *Carolina Financial Times* in Chapel Hill, North Carolina, and as a reporter for the *News-Gazette* in Lexington, Virginia. He received the Best Feature Writing award from Sigma Delta Chi in 1972 for a five-part investigative series on the University of North Carolina football program. He has written stories for *The New York Times*, *Sport*, *Glamour*, the *Winston-Salem Journal*, and *New York*.

The War Room at Bellevue

"The War Room at Bellevue" was first published in *New York* magazine. The author chose, for good reason, to stay strictly within a time sequence as he described the emergency ward. This essay is also noteworthy for the cumulative descriptive effect, which was accomplished almost entirely with objective details.

Bellevue. The name conjures up images of an indoor war zone: the wounded and bleeding lining the halls, screaming for help while harried doctors in blood-stained smocks rush from stretcher to stretcher, fighting a losing battle against exhaustion and the crushing number of injured. "What's worse," says a longtime Bellevue nurse, "is that we have this image of being a hospital only for . . ." She pauses, then lowers her voice; "for crazy people."

Though neither battlefield nor Bedlam is a valid image, there is something extraordinary about the monstrous complex that spreads for five blocks along First Avenue in Manhattan. It is said best by the head nurse in Adult Emergency Service: "If you have any chance for

1

2

survival, you have it here." Survival — that is why they come. Why do injured cops drive by a half-dozen other hospitals to be treated at Bellevue? They've seen the Bellevue emergency team in action.

9:00 P.M. It is a Friday night in the Bellevue emergency room. The after-work crush is over (those who've suffered through the day, only to come for help after the five-o'clock whistle has blown) and it is nearly silent except for the mutter of voices at the admitting desk, where administrative personnel discuss who will go for coffee. Across the spotless white-walled lobby, ten people sit quietly, passively, in pastel plastic chairs, waiting for word of relatives or to see doctors. In the past 24 hours, 300 people have come to the Bellevue Adult Emergency Service. Fewer than 10 percent were true emergencies. One man sleeps fitfully in the emergency ward while his heartbeat, respiration, and blood pressure are monitored by control consoles mounted over his bed. Each heartbeat trips a tiny bleep in the monitor, which attending nurses can hear across the ward. A half hour ago, doctors in the trauma room withdrew a six-inch stiletto blade from his back. When he is stabilized, the patient will be moved upstairs to the twelve-bed Surgical Intensive Care Unit.

9:05 P.M. An ambulance backs into the receiving bay, its red and yellow lights flashing in and out of the lobby. A split second later, the glass doors burst open as a nurse and an attendant roll a mobile stretcher into the lobby. When the nurse screams, "Emergent!" the lobby explodes with activity as the way is cleared to the trauma room. Doctors appear from nowhere and transfer the bloodied body of a black man to the treatment table. Within seconds his clothes are stripped away, revealing a tiny stab wound in his left side. Three doctors and three nurses rush around the victim, each performing a task necessary to begin treatment. Intravenous needles are inserted into his arms and groin. A doctor draws blood for the lab, in case surgery is necessary. A nurse begins inserting a catheter into the victim's penis and continues to feed in tubing until the catheter reaches the bladder. Urine flows through the tube into a plastic bag. Doctors are glad not to see blood in the urine. Another nurse records pulse and blood pressure.

The victim is in good shape. He shivers slightly, although the trauma room is exceedingly warm. His face is bloodied, but shows no major lacerations. A third nurse, her elbow propped on the treatment table, asks the man a series of questions, trying to quickly outline his medical history. He answers abruptly. He is drunk. His left side is swabbed with yellow disinfectant and a doctor injects a local anesthetic. After a few seconds another doctor inserts his finger into the wound. It sinks in all the way to the knuckle. He begins to rotate his finger like a child trying to get a marble out of a milk bottle. The patient screams bloody murder and tries to struggle free.

Meanwhile in the lobby, a security guard is ejecting a derelict 6
who has begun to drink from a bottle hidden in his coat pocket. "He's a regular, was in here just two days ago," says a nurse. "We checked him pretty good then, so he's probably okay now. Can you believe those were clean clothes we gave him?" The old man, blackened by filth, leaves quietly.

9:15 P.M. A young Hispanic man interrupts, saying his preg- 7
nant girl friend, sitting outside in his car, is bleeding heavily from her vagina. She is rushed into an examination room, treated behind closed doors, and rolled into the observation ward, where, much later in the night, a gynecologist will treat her in a special room — the same one used to examine rape victims. Nearby, behind curtains, the neurologist examines an old white woman to determine if her headaches are due to head injury. They are not.

9:45 P.M. The trauma room has been cleared and cleaned mer- 8
cilessly. The examination rooms are three-quarters full — another overdose, two asthmatics, a young woman with abdominal pains. In the hallway, a derelict who has been sleeping it off urinates all over the stretcher. He sleeps on while attendants change his clothes. An ambulance — one of four that patrol Manhattan for Bellevue from 42nd Street to Houston, river to river — delivers a middle-aged white woman and two cops, the three of them soaking wet. The woman has escaped from the psychiatric floor of a nearby hospital and tried to drown herself in the East River. The cops fished her out. She lies on a stretcher shivering beneath white blankets. Her eyes stare at the ceiling. She speaks clearly when an administrative worker begins routine questioning. The cops are given hospital gowns and wait to receive tetanus shots and gamma globulin — a hedge against infection from the befouled river water. They will hang around the E.R. for another two hours, telling their story to as many as six other policemen who show up to hear it. The woman is rolled into an examination room, where a male nurse speaks gently: "They tell me you fell into the river." "No," says the woman, "I

jumped. I have to commit suicide." "Why?" asks the nurse. "Because I'm insane and I can't help [it]. I have to die." The nurse gradually discovers the woman has a history of psychological problems. She is given dry bedclothes and placed under guard in the hallway. She lies on her side, staring at the wall.

The pace continues to increase. Several more overdose victims arrive by ambulance. One, a young black woman, had done a striptease on the street just before passing out. A second black woman is semiconscious and spends the better part of her time at Bellevue alternately cursing at and pleading with the doctors. Attendants find a plastic bottle coated with methadone in the pocket of a Hispanic O.D. The treatment is routinely the same, and sooner or later involves vomiting. Just after doctors begin to treat the O.D., he vomits great quantities of wine and methadone in all directions. "Lovely business, huh?" laments one of the doctors. A young nurse confides that if there were other true emergencies, the overdose victims would be given lower priority. "You can't help thinking they did it to themselves," she says, "while the others are accident victims."

10:30 P.M. A policeman who twisted his knee struggling with an "alleged perpetrator" is examined and released. By 10:30, the lobby is jammed with friends and relatives of patients in various stages of treatment and recovery. The attendant who also functions as a translator for Hispanic patients adds chairs to accommodate the overflow. The medical walk-in rate stays steady — between eight and ten patients waiting. A pair of derelicts, each with battered eyes, appear at the admitting desk. One has a dramatically swollen face laced with black stitches.

11:00 P.M. The husband of the attempted suicide arrives. He thanks the police for saving his wife's life, then talks at length with doctors about her condition. She continues to stare into the void and does not react when her husband approaches her stretcher.

Meanwhile, patients arrive in the lobby at a steady pace. A young G.I. on leave has lower-back pains; a Hispanic man complains of pains in his side; occasionally parents hurry through the adult E.R. carrying children to the pediatric E.R. A white woman of about 50 marches into the lobby from the walk-in entrance. Dried blood covers her right eyebrow and upper lip. She begins to perform. "I was assaulted on 28th and Lexington, I was," she says grandly, "and I don't have to take it *anymore*. I was a bride 21 years ago and, God, I was beautiful then." She has captured the attention of all present. "I was there when the boys came home — on Memorial Day — and I don't have to take this kind of treatment."

As midnight approaches, the nurses prepare for the shift change. They must brief the incoming staff and make sure all reports are up-to-date. One young brunet says, "Christ, I'm gonna go home and take a shower — I smell like vomit." 13

11:50 P.M. The triage nurse is questioning an old black man about chest pains, and a Hispanic woman is having an asthma attack, when an ambulance, its sirens screaming full tilt, roars into the receiving bay. There is a split-second pause as everyone drops what he or she is doing and looks up. Then all hell breaks loose. Doctors and nurses are suddenly sprinting full-out toward the trauma room. The glass doors burst open and the occupied stretcher is literally run past me. Cops follow. It is as if a comet has whooshed by. In the trauma room it all becomes clear. A half-dozen doctors and nurses surround the lifeless form of a Hispanic man with a shotgun hole in his neck the size of your fist. Blood pours from a second gaping wound in his chest. A respirator is slammed over his face, making his chest rise and fall as if he were breathing. "No pulse," reports one doctor. A nurse jumps on a stool and, leaning over the man, begins to pump his chest with her palms. "No blood pressure," screams another nurse. The ambulance driver appears shaken. "I never thought I'd get here in time," he stutters. More doctors from the trauma team upstairs arrive. Wrappings from syringes and gauze pads fly through the air. The victim's eyes are open yet devoid of life. His body takes on a yellow tinge. A male nurse winces at the gunshot wound. "This guy really pissed off somebody," he says. This is no ordinary shooting. It is an execution. IV's are jammed into the body in the groin and arms. One doctor has been plugging in an electrocardiograph and asks everyone to stop for a second so he can get a reading. "Forget it," shouts the doctor in charge. "No time." "Take it easy, Jimmy," someone yells at the head physician. It is apparent by now that the man is dead, but the doctors keep trying injections and finally they slit open the chest and reach inside almost up to their elbows. They feel the extent of the damage and suddenly it is all over. "I told 'em he was dead," says one nurse, withdrawing. "They didn't listen." The room is very still. The doctors are momentarily disgusted, then go on about their business. The room clears quickly. Finally there is only a male nurse 14 and the still-warm body, now waxy-yellow, with huge ribs exposed on both sides of the chest and giant holes in both sides of the neck. The nurse speculates that this is yet another murder in a Hispanic political struggle that has brought many such victims to Bellevue. He marvels at the extent of the wounds and repeats, "This guy was really blown away."

Midnight. A hysterical woman is hustled through the lobby into an examination room. It is the dead man's wife, and she is nearly delirious. "I know he's dead, I know he's dead," she screams over and over. Within moments the lobby is filled with anxious relatives of the victim, waiting for word on his condition. The police are everywhere asking questions, but most people say they saw nothing. One young woman says she heard six shots, two louder than the other four. At some point, word is passed that the man is, in fact, dead. Another woman breaks down in hysterics; everywhere young Hispanics are crying and comforting each other. Plainclothes detectives make a quick examination of the body, check on the time of pronouncement of death, and begin to ask questions, but the bereaved are too stunned to talk. The rest of the uninvolved people in the lobby stare dumbly, their injuries suddenly paling in light of a death.

12:30 A.M. A black man appears at the admissions desk and says he drank poison by mistake. He is told to have a seat. The ambulance brings in a young white woman, her head wrapped in white gauze. She is wailing terribly. A girl friend stands over her, crying, and a boyfriend clutches the injured woman's hands, saying, "I'm here, don't worry, I'm here." The victim has fallen downstairs at a friend's house. Attendants park her stretcher against the wall to wait for an examination room to clear. There are eight examination rooms and only three doctors. Unless you are truly an emergency, you will wait. One doctor is stitching up the eyebrow of a drunk who's been punched out. The friends of the woman who fell down the stairs glance up at the doctors anxiously, wondering why their friend isn't being treated faster.

1:10 A.M. A car pulls into the bay and a young Hispanic asks if a shooting victim has been brought here. The security guard blurts out, "He's dead." The young man is stunned. He peels his tires leaving the bay.

1:20 A.M. The young woman of the stairs is getting stitches in a small gash over her left eye when the same ambulance driver who brought in the gunshot victim delivers a man who has been stabbed in the back on East 3rd Street. Once again the trauma room goes from 0 to 60 in five seconds. The patient is drunk, which helps him endure the pain of having the catheter inserted through his penis into his bladder. Still he yells, "That hurts like a bastard," then adds sheepishly, "Excuse me, ladies." But he is not prepared for what comes next. An X-ray reveals a collapsed right lung. After just a shot of local anesthetic, the doctor slices open his side and inserts a long plastic tube. Internal bleeding had kept the lung pressed down and prevented it from reinflating. The tube releases the pressure. The ambulance driver says the cops grabbed the guy who ran the eight-inch blade into the victim's back. "That's not the one," says the man. "They got the wrong guy." A nurse reports that there is not much of the victim's type blood available at the hospital. One of the doctors says that's okay, he won't need surgery. Meanwhile blood pours from the man's knife wound and the tube in his side. As the nurses work, they chat about personal matters, yet they respond immediately to orders from either doctor. "How ya doin'?" the doctor asks the patient. "Okay," he says. His blood spatters on the floor.

So it goes into the morning hours. A Valium overdose, a woman who fainted, a man who went through the windshield of his car. More overdoses. More drunks with split eyebrows and chins. The doctors and nurses work without complaint. "This is nothing, about normal, I'd say," concludes the head nurse. "No big deal." 19

Meanings and Values

1a.   What is the author's point of view? (See Guide to Terms: *Point of View*.)

  b.   How is this reflected by the tone? (Guide: *Style/Tone.*)

2a.   Does Simpson ever slip into sentimentality — a common failing when describing the scenes of death and tragedy? (Guide: *Sentimentality.*)

  b.   If so, where? If not, how does he avoid it?

3a.   Cite at least six facts learned from reading this piece that are told, not in general terms, but by specific, concrete details — e.g., that a high degree of cleanliness is maintained at Bellevue, illustrated by "the spotless white-walled lobby" (par. 3) and "the trauma room has been cleared and cleaned mercilessly" (par. 8).

b. What are the advantages of having facts presented in this way?

4. If you have read the Halsey selection in Section 6, tell how the Bellevue staff members (many of them undoubtedly young) apparently avoided the "new narcissism" that afflicts so many of their generation.

Expository Techniques

1. How do you think the author went about selecting details, from among the thousands that must have been available to him?

2a. Do you consider the writing to be primarily objective or impressionistic?

b. Clarify any apparent contradictions.

c. What is the dominant impression, if any?

3. What is the value of using a timed sequence in such a description?

4. Does it seem to you that any of this description is excessive — i.e., unnecessary to the task at hand?

5a. List, in skeletal form, the facts learned about the subject from reading the two-paragraph introduction.

b. How well does it perform the three basic purposes of an introduction? (Guide: *Introductions.*)

6a. What is the significance of the rhetorical question in paragraph 2? (Guide: *Rhetorical Questions.*)

b. Why is it rhetorical?

7. Is the short closing effective? (Guide: *Closings.*) Why, or why not?

Diction and Vocabulary

1a. Cite the clichés in paragraphs 4, 5, 8, and 14. (Guide: *Clichés.*)

b. What justification, if any, can you offer for their use?

2. Cite the allusion in paragraph 2, and explain its meaning and source. (Guide: *Figures of Speech.*)

3a. Simpson uses some slang and other colloquialisms. Cite as many of these as you can. (Guide: *Colloquial Expressions.*)

b. Is their use justified? Why, or why not?

4. Why is "alleged perpetrator" placed in quotation marks (par. 10)?

Suggestions for Writing and Discussion

1. Explain why "neither battlefield nor Bedlam is a valid image" of the emergency room at Bellevue (pars. 1, 2).

2. Do you think it is right and/or understandable that ODs should be given lower priorities than "true emergencies" (par. 9)? Defend your views.

3. If you have had a job that to the outsider might seem hectic or hazardous, or both, were the personnel also able to "chat about personal matters" while the work was in progress? What were the circumstances?

(NOTE: Suggestions for topics requiring development by use of DESCRIPTION follow.)

Writing Suggestions for Section 8
Description

1. Primarily by way of impressionistic description that focuses on a single dominant impression, show and explain the mood, or atmosphere of one of the following:

   a. A county fair.

   b. A ball game.

   c. A rodeo.

   d. A wedding.

   e. A funeral.

   f. A riot.

   g. A ghost town.

   h. A cave.

   i. A mine.

   j. An antique shop.

   k. A party.

   l. A family dinner.

   m. A traffic jam.

   n. Reveille.

   o. An airport (or a bus depot).

   p. A drag race (or a horse race).

   q. A home during one of its rush hours.

   r. The last night of Christmas shopping.

   s. A natural scene at a certain time of day.

   t. The campus at examination time.

   u. A certain person at a time of great emotion — e.g., joy, anger, grief.

2. Using objective description as your basic pattern, explain the functional qualities or the significance of one of the following:

   a. A house for sale.

   b. A public building.

   c. A dairy barn.

   d. An ideal workshop (or hobby room).

   e. An ideal garage.

   f. A commune.

   g. The layout of a town (or airport).

   h. The layout of a farm.

   i. A certain type of boat.

9

Using *Narration* as an Expository Technique

Attempts to classify the functions of narration seem certain to develop difficulties and end in arbitrary and sometimes fuzzy distinctions. These need not distress us, however, if we remember that narration remains narration — a factual or fictional report of a sequence of events — and that our only reason for trying to divide it into categories is to find some means of studying its uses.

In a sense, as we have already seen in Section 5, exposition by process analysis makes one important, if rather narrow, use of narration, since it explains in sequence how specific steps lead to completion of some process. At the other extreme is narration that has very little to do with exposition: the story itself is the important thing, and instead of a series of steps leading obviously to a completed act, events *develop* out of each other and build suspense, however mild, through some kind of conflict. This use of narration includes the novel and short story, as well as some news and sports reporting. Because we are studying exposition, however, we must avoid getting too involved with these uses of narration; they require special techniques, the study of which would require a whole course or, in fact, several courses.

Between the extremes of a very usable analysis of process and very intriguing narration for the story's sake — and often seeming to blur into one or the other — is narration for *explanation's* sake, to explain a concept that is more than process and that might have been explained by one of the other patterns of exposition. Here only the form is narrative; the function is expository.

Fortunately, the average student seldom needs to use narration for major explanatory purposes, as it has been used in each of the following selections. But to learn the handling of even minor or localized narration, the best procedure (short of taking several college courses, or at least one that concentrates on the narrative form) is simply to observe how successful writers use it to perform various functions. Localized narration can sometimes be helpful in developing any of the other major patterns of exposition — e.g., as in the Buckley essay (Section 1), or Catton's (Section 3).

The most common problems can be summarized as follows:

1. *Selection of details.* As in writing description, the user of narration always has far more details available than can or should be used. Good unity demands the selection of only those details that are most relevant to the purpose and the desired effect.

2. *Time order.* The writer can use straight chronology, relating events as they happen (the usual method in minor uses of narration), or the flashback method, leaving the sequence temporarily in order to go back and relate some now-significant happening of a time prior to the main action. If flashback is used, it should be deliberate and for a valid reason — not merely because the episode was neglected at the beginning.

3. *Transitions.* The lazy writer of narration is apt to resort to the transitional style of a three-year-old: " . . . and then we . . . and then she . . . and then we. . . ." Avoiding this style may tax the ingenuity, but invariably the result is worth the extra investment of time and thought.

4. *Point of view.* This is a large and complex subject if dealt with fully, as a course in narration would do. Briefly, however, the writer should decide at the beginning whether the reader is to experience the action through a character's eyes (and ears and brain) or from an overall, objective view. This decision makes a difference in how much can be told, whose thoughts or secret actions can be included. The writer must be consistent throughout the narrative and include only information that could logically be known through the adopted point of view.

5. *Dialogue.* Presumably the writer already knows the mechanics of using quotations. Beyond these, the problems are to make conversation as natural-sounding as possible and yet to keep it from

rambling through many useless details — to keep the narrative moving forward by *means* of dialogue.

As in most patterns of writing, the use of expository narration is most likely to be successful if the writer constantly keeps the purpose and audience in mind, remembering that the only reason for using the method in the first place — for doing *any* writing — is to communicate ideas. Soundness, clarity, and interest are the best means of attaining this goal.

Sample Paragraph (Narration)

The author has used a straight sequential time order and selected only those details that will carry the narrative forward.

The overall point of view is objective, not seen through the eyes of any of the characters. There is no dialogue.

("Kid: a colloquialism.)

The Valley was dense with fir when Joseph Casey brought his wife and eleven children upriver on a crude log raft. They landed in a storm on a gravel spit, but the raft broke up and headed, in pieces, back toward the sea with most of their belongings. But Joe Casey saved his tools, and the older boys built a cabin — not much of one, but the first house in Ilona Valley. After several trips back to the settlement for supplies, Casey managed to set up a sawmill, and from then on the family prospered. (Bayport was growing, providing a good market for lumber.) But Mrs. Casey was a city person and never got used to flies and babies. Soon after the youngest, little Ben, wandered off into the woods one day, never to be seen again, Lula Casey, now forty-six and sure she was pregnant again, became hysterical. Casey tried to be comforting: he patted her stomach and said the new kid would be a fine replacement for little lost Ben. This ended the shrieking;

but sometime that night Lula got up, took the new oar-boat, and apparently rowed frantically for hours upstream, against the current. The boat came merrily back downstream, empty, passing the Casey place at sunrise. And days later the boys found the body in the backwater brush at the mouth of what later was known as Suicide Creek.

MARTIN GANSBERG

MARTIN GANSBERG, born in Brooklyn, New York, in 1920, received a Bachelor of Social Sciences degree from St. John's University. He has been an editor and reporter for *The New York Times* since 1942, including a three-year period as editor of its international edition in Paris. He also served on the faculty of Fairleigh Dickinson University for fifteen years. Gansberg has written for many magazines, including *Diplomat*, *Catholic Digest*, *Facts*, and *U.S. Lady*.

38 Who Saw Murder Didn't Call the Police

"38 Who Saw Murder . . ." was written for *The New York Times* in 1964, and for obvious reasons it has been anthologized frequently since then. Cast in a deceptively simple news style, it still provides material for serious thought, as well as a means of studying the use and technique of narration.

For more than half an hour 38 respectable, law-abiding citizens in Queens watched a killer stalk and stab a woman in three separate attacks in Kew Gardens. 1

Twice their chatter and the sudden glow of their bedroom lights interrupted him and frightened him off. Each time he returned, sought her out, and stabbed her again. Not one person telephoned the police during the assault; one witness called after the woman was dead. 2

That was two weeks ago today. 3

Still shocked is Assistant Chief Inspector Frederick M. Lussen, in charge of the borough's detectives and a veteran of 25 years of homicide investigations. He can give a matter-of-fact recitation on many murders. But the Kew Gardens slaying baffles him — not 4 because it is a murder, but because the "good people" failed to call the police.

"As we have reconstructed the crime," he said, "the assailant had three chances to kill this woman during a 35-minute period. He returned twice to complete the job. If we had been called when he first attacked, the woman might not be dead now."

This is what the police say happened beginning at 3:20 A.M. in the staid, middle-class, tree-lined Austin Street area:

Twenty-eight-year-old Catherine Genovese, who was called Kitty by almost everyone in the neighborhood, was returning home from her job as manager of a bar in Hollis. She parked her red Fiat in a lot adjacent to the Kew Gardens Long Island Rail Road Station, facing Mowbray Place. Like many residents of the neighborhood, she had parked there day after day since her arrival from Connecticut a year ago, although the railroad frowns on the practice.

She turned off the lights of her car, locked the door, and started to walk the 100 feet to the entrance of her apartment at 82–70 Austin Street, which is in a Tudor building, with stores in the first floor and apartments on the second.

The entrance to the apartment is in the rear of the building because the front is rented to retail stores. At night the quiet neighborhood is shrouded in the slumbering darkness that marks most residential areas.

Miss Genovese noticed a man at the far end of the lot, near a seven-story apartment house at 82–40 Austin Street. She halted. Then, nervously, she headed up Austin Street toward Lefferts Boulevard, where there is a call box to the 102nd Police Precinct in nearby Richmond Hill.

She got as far as a street light in front of a bookstore before the man grabbed her. She screamed. Lights went on in the 10-story apartment house at 82–67 Austin Street, which faces the bookstore. Windows slid open and voices punctuated the early-morning stillness.

Miss Genovese screamed: "Oh, my God, he stabbed me! Please help me! Please help me!"

From one of the upper windows in the apartment house, a man called down: "Let that girl alone!"

The assailant looked up at him, shrugged and walked down

Austin Street toward a white sedan parked a short distance away. Miss Genovese struggled to her feet.

Lights went out. The killer returned to Miss Genovese, now trying to make her way around the side of the building by the parking lot to get to her apartment. The assailant stabbed her again. 15

"I'm dying!" she shrieked. "I'm dying!" 16

Windows were opened again, and lights went on in many apartments. The assailant got into his car and drove away. Miss Genovese staggered to her feet. A city bus, Q–10, the Lefferts Boulevard line to Kennedy International Airport, passed. It was 3:35 A.M. 17

The assailant returned. By then, Miss Genovese had crawled to the back of the building, where the freshly painted brown doors to the apartment house held out hope for safety. The killer tried the first door; she wasn't there. At the second door, 82–62 Austin Street, he saw her slumped on the floor at the foot of the stairs. He stabbed her a third time — fatally. 18

It was 3:50 by the time the police received their first call, from a man who was a neighbor of Miss Genovese. In two minutes they were at the scene. The neighbor, a 70-year-old woman, and another woman were the only persons on the street. Nobody else came forward. 19

The man explained that he had called the police after much deliberation. He had phoned a friend in Nassau County for advice and then he had crossed the roof of the building to the apartment of the elderly woman to get her to make the call. 20

"I didn't want to get involved," he sheepishly told the police. 21

Six days later, the police arrested Winston Moseley, a 29-year-old business-machine operator, and charged him with homicide. Moseley had no previous record. He is married, has two children and owns a home at 133–19 Sutter Avenue, South Ozone Park, Queens. On Wednesday, a court committed him to Kings County Hospital for psychiatric observation. 22

When questioned by the police, Moseley also said that he had slain Mrs. Annie May Johnson, 24, of 146–12 133rd Avenue, Jamaica, on Feb. 29 and Barbara Kralik, 15, of 174–17 140th Avenue, Springfield Gardens, last July. In the Kralik case, the police are holding Alvin L. Mitchell, who is said to have confessed to that slaying. 23

The police stressed how simple it would have been to have 24
gotten in touch with them. "A phone call," said one of the detectives, "would have done it." The police may be reached by dialing
"O" for operator or SPring 7–3100.

Today witnesses from the neighborhood, which is made up of 25
one-family homes in the $35,000 to $60,000 range with the exception
of the two apartment houses near the railroad station, find it difficult to explain why they didn't call the police.

A housewife, knowingly if quite casually, said, "We thought it 26
was a lover's quarrel." A husband and wife both said, "Frankly, we
were afraid." They seemed aware of the fact that events might have
been different. A distraught woman, wiping her hands on her
apron, said, "I didn't want my husband to get involved."

One couple, now willing to talk about that night, said they 27
heard the first screams. The husband looked thoughtfully at the
bookstore where the killer first grabbed Miss Genovese.

"We went to the window to see what was happening," he said, 28
"but the light from our bedroom made it difficult to see the street."
The wife, still apprehensive, added: "I put out the light and we were
able to see better."

Asked why they hadn't called the police, she shrugged and 29
replied: "I don't know."

A man peeked out from the slight opening in the doorway to his 30
apartment and rattled off an account of the killer's second attack.
Why hadn't he called the police at the time? "I was tired," he said
without emotion. "I went back to bed."

It was 4:25 A.M. when the ambulance arrived to take the body of 31
Miss Genovese. It drove off. "Then," a solemn police detective said,
"the people came out."

Meanings and Values

1a. What is Gansberg's central (expository) theme?

b. How might he have developed this theme without using narration
    at all? Specify what patterns of exposition he could have used
    instead.

c. Would any of them have been as effective as narration *for the pur-
    pose*? Why, or why not?

2. Show how this selection could be used as an illustration in an explanatory discussion of abstract and concrete writing. (See Guide to Terms: *Concrete/Abstract.*)

3a. Why has this narrative account of old news (the murder made its only headlines in 1964) retained its significance to this day?

b. Are you able to see in this event a paradigm of any larger condition or situation? If so, explain, using examples as needed to illustrate your ideas.

4. If you have read Wolfe's essay (Sec. 4), do you think Dr. Hall would have been very surprised at this New York case of noninvolvement? Why, or why not?

Expository Techniques

1a. What standard introductory technique is exemplified in the first paragraph? (Guide: *Introductions.*)

b. How effective do you consider it?

c. If you see anything ironic in the fact stated there, explain the irony. (Guide: *Irony.*)

2a. Where does the main narration begin?

b. What, then, is the function of the preceding paragraphs?

3a. Study several of the paragraph transitions within the narration itself to determine Gansberg's method of advancing the time sequence (to avoid overuse of "and then"). What is the technique?

b. Is another needed? Why, or why not?

4a. What possible reasons do you see for the predominant use of short paragraphs in this piece?

b. Does this selection lose any effectiveness because of the short paragraphs?

5. Undoubtedly, the author selected with care the few quotations from witnesses that he uses. What principle or principles do you think applied to his selection?

6. Explain why you think the quotation from the "solemn police detective" was, or was not, deliberately and carefully chosen to conclude the piece. (Guide: *Closings.*)

7a. Briefly identify the point of view of the writing. (Guide: *Point of View.*)

b. Is it consistent throughout?

c. Show the relation, as you see it, between this point of view and the author's apparent attitude toward his subject matter.

8a.   Does he permit himself any sentimentality? If so, where? (Guide: *Sentimentality*.)

b.   If not, specifically what might he have included that would have slipped into melodrama or sentimentality?

Diction and Vocabulary

1a.   Why do you think the author used no difficult words in this narration?

b.   Do you find the writing at all belittling to college people because of this fact? Why, or why not?

Suggestions for Writing and Discussion

1.   Use both developed and undeveloped examples to show the prevalence, among individuals, of an anti-involvement attitude today. Or, if you prefer, show that this accusation is unjustified.

2.   If this narration can be regarded as a paradigm (see question 3b of "Meanings and Values"), select one example from the larger subject and develop it on whatever theme you choose. Your example could be from international affairs, if you like (and if you don't mind becoming the center of a controversy) — e.g., the recent cries of "Murder!" from numerous small countries. If you prefer, go into more distant (and therefore less controversial) history for your example.

3.   If such a crime as the Genovese murder were happening in an area or a situation where police were not so instantly available, what do you think an observer should do about it? What would *you* do? Justify your stand fully.

(NOTE: Suggestions for topics requiring development by NARRATION are on page 311, at the end of this section.)

BOB GREENE

BOB GREENE, born in 1947 in Columbus, Ohio, is a columnist for the *Chicago Tribune*. His daily reports and commentary are syndicated to more than 120 other newspapers in the United States, Canada, Latin America, and Japan. He is the winner of the 1977 National Headliner Award as best columnist in the United States. His articles have appeared in *Newsweek, Harper's, Rolling Stone, Sport, New Times,* and *The New York Times,* and his commentary has been featured on the CBS television and radio networks. Greene has written five books: *We Didn't Have None of Them Fat Funky Angels on the Wall of Heartbreak Hotel, and Other Reports from America* (1971), *Running: A Nixon-McGovern Campaign Journal* (1973), *Billion Dollar Baby* (1974), *Johnny Deadline, Reporter: The Best of Bob Greene* (1976), and *Bagtime* (1977).

That's Entertainment

"That's Entertainment," first published in *Esquire*, is not only a skillful narrative but also the means of making some interesting observations on human nature. Greene's bold and (apparently) nearly emotionless style is well equipped to handle this coverage of a memorable "fight" scene — and the crowd's behavior — in a Dayton, Ohio, arena.

Steve Caudill, a twenty-three-year-old air-freight handler, bled   1
from his nose, mouth, and eyes. The blood formed a mask over his face; with each breath he took, the bleeding grew worse. As he moved to avoid getting hit one more time, a paper cup full of beer dropped from the darkness and splashed his legs.

"Kill somebody!" came a voice from high in the arena, but it was   2
hard to make out individual voices amid the animal chant. More beer was thrown into the ring. Caudill's opponent — David

Guidugli, twenty-six, a construction worker — was also losing blood, but the sound of the crowd seemed to make him afraid to stop.

This was in a place called Hara Arena, a converted ice rink on the outskirts of Dayton, Ohio. The evening had not been promoted as a boxing match, and indeed it was something . . . different. These two contestants were not boxers; neither were the thirty-four other local men who were providing the entertainment for the audience of almost four thousand.

The crowd was excited to see Caudill and Guidugli spill their blood, yes, but if the truth be told, they had been even happier several minutes earlier, when Stanton Long, a machine operator, had staggered to the side of the ring and, in great pain, vomited the entire contents of his stomach onto the concrete floor below. And they had laughed mightily when Raymond Morris, a forty-five-year-old bartender, had convulsed on the mat after taking a beating from a man twenty-two years his junior.

The arena had been chilly before the people had arrived, but now it was steaming. You could feel the heat.

Three weeks earlier, the posters had gone up in the bars and factories around Dayton. HOW TOUGH ARE YOU? read the headline that stood next to a large drawing of a man's fist. The subhead: "We're looking for the toughest man in the Southwest Ohio area. Could it be you?"

The poster solicited "bar bouncers, construction workers, bar brawlers, truck drivers, policemen, factory workers, firemen, farmers, etc., etc." Professional boxers were not welcome. Tickets for the two evenings would be scaled from $6 to $10. The winner would receive $1,000, the runner-up $500. The others would receive nothing.

This was the Toughman Contest. If you live in New York or Chicago or Los Angeles, you may have never heard of this phenomenon; it does not travel to most major metropolitan areas. But virtually every weekend of the year, a Toughman Contest is held somewhere in the United States — in Wheeling, West Virginia; in Savannah, Georgia; in Grand Rapids, Michigan; in Green Bay, Wisconsin.

The premise — as devised by Arthur Dore, the entrepreneur from Bay City, Michigan, who invented Toughman in 1979 — is

simple. People in towns that have not been able to support professional boxing for years will pack the nearest arenas and fairgrounds
and coliseums to see the local braggarts and barroom bullies try to
hurt one another. And the meanest men in these towns will fight —
most of them for free — out of some vague dream of glory.

The word *boxing* is almost never used in promoting the Toughman Contest. It's too tame a phrase and would turn off potential
customers; besides, it doesn't come close to describing what goes on
in the Toughman ring. Sure, there are boxing gloves and three
two-minute rounds and a panel of judges to select a winner if both
contestants go the distance. But almost no one does. Most matches
end with one contestant either on the floor or begging for someone
to stop the beating. There is fear and cruelty and humiliation in that
ring. There are 300-pound men punching 175-pound men to the
canvas and then snorting aloud as they punch them some more.
There are men who, finding themselves unable to back up the
bravado that brought them there in the first place, weep as they are
repeatedly slammed against the ropes. There are painfully out-of-
shape men being tortured by men tough enough to maim them. On
the final night, a contestant who continues to win his matches may
be required to fight four different opponents. These elimination
bouts go on until there is only one man left.

No, *boxing* doesn't cover it. The Toughman competition has
more to do with professional wrestling, except that this is not the
illusion of blood and violence but the fact of blood and violence; it
has more to do with *The Music Man*,[1] except that the local pride that
Art Dore has come to town to exploit comes from a darker side of the
human spirit.

"This is what people want to see," Dore said. A bearded man of
forty-three, he was sitting in a room in the concrete bowels of Hara
Arena a few hours before the Dayton show was to begin. "It's a
macho thing. It's for real. They know it's not fake. There's no
bobbing or weaving or dancing. These people want action. They
want to see a guy who's always boasting that he can whip someone's ass go out and prove it.

"I don't try to analyze it," Dore said with a shrug. "I just try to
sell it."

---

[1]A Broadway musical (1957), written by Meredith Willson, adapted for a film
version (1962).

And the men who would do the bleeding? They had sent résumés to the arena, listing their physical dimensions and their occupations: carpenter, Frigidaire worker, city parks maintenance man, Pepsi delivery agent. Many had simply noted "Unemployed." For two nights they would step into the ring with strangers, while other strangers screamed at them from the seats and Art Dore, at the microphone, egged them on with insults and exhortations.

Between elimination bouts they waited in a small room on the arena's first floor. The men wore cut-off Levis and tank tops, T-shirts and swimming trunks. Some looked like motorcycle gang members; others would have seemed more at home next to a gas station pump. Here was a man with a ring in his left ear; there was another with an obscenity tattooed on the back of his hand. Most of the Toughman contestants waiting backstage could not precisely define what made them want to do this. They seemed to be drawn by the promise of the one thing that had eluded them all their lives: success. They were all small-town, small-job boys; none had attempted to make it in the larger world. They had accepted that, and lived with it. Since grade school they had known that they had certain . . . limitations. And then Art Dore had come to town with his promise: You don't need talent. You don't need grace. You don't need ambition. All you need is the meanness that has been your little secret all your life, and if you're mean enough, you're going to be a star. Success? Bleed for it, and it can finally be yours.

"I don't know," said Harlan Glassburn, a twenty-five-year-old construction worker, whose entry form listed him at six feet five inches and 245 pounds. "I just want to see what I can do in there. I've been in a few barroom brawls, but you get hit with a pool stick and you ain't going to be standing up too long. I know I ain't going to make it all the way to the end of this, but at least I got more guts than the people sitting up in the stands. They just want to see blood, and I ain't afraid to bleed."

Stanton Long, the twenty-three-year-old machine operator who would later vomit before the delighted crowd, said, "All my buddies at work were talking about this. You know, there's a lot of crazy people walking around Dayton, a lot of people carrying guns. I've beat up many guys with my fists, but I don't carry a gun. I'm a pretty mellow guy, but if there's a fight, someone's got to do the fighting."

After winning his first-round match, Bruce Niles, thirty-two years old and 330 pounds, a stockman for International Harvester, came into the room. The noise from the crowd followed him in. 18

"The fights I've been in on the street, there's been a lot of kicking and biting," he said. "You know, you drink a lot of beer and your head gets all buzzed up. Out there just now, I knocked the guy over the ropes, and I don't know what got into me . . . I wanted to kill him. The referee kept pulling me off, but I got on top of the guy. I don't know what it is . . . when you get excited . . . you just want to blow it out of your gourd . . . finish the job. . . ." 19

High in the arena, fueled by beer, the crowd was on its feet and screaming. This was the second night of the Toughman Contest. Although the fighters were being led into the ring one pair after another, the pace was not fast enough for some members of the audience. "Bring on the meat!" a voice called out. A number of fistfights had broken out in the stands, the frequency of these brawls increasing as the night grew longer. 20

"Those are everyday people out there," said Jerry Johnson, a carpenter who had paid his way into both nights of the contest. "They're people just like us, mashing each other's noses and mouths up. There's no rules, just good action." 21

Johnson's tone was flat and even, betraying not a trace of irony. He seemed to be enjoying a casual night out. If another visitor to Hara Arena felt a different set of emotions — a sick creeping in the pit of the stomach, an unclean film on the soul that seemed to grow thicker with each new roar from the crowd, with each new bloodletting — that visitor was clearly in the minority. The people in the arena seemed to feel no revulsion. They felt only an urgent tingling. 22

The crowd was mostly male, but the women who were in the audience seemed to be enjoying the show even more than the men. "I think it must be exciting to hit someone like that," said Rosa Ginter, thirty-three, a nursing home employee. "I don't think it's true that women don't like violence. I'd like to see even more action, if you want to know the truth." 23

About halfway back on the main floor, a twenty-year-old woman named Tonya Hopkins — a cashier at a local K mart — sat with her husband, watching a particularly bloody exchange. Her 24 eyes were alive. Asked if she wanted to sit at ringside, she left her husband to accompany a reporter to the card table that had been set up against the ring. Up close, she could hear each punch tear at flesh, watch each spurt of blood spatter from the mouths and noses of the fighters. She did not take her eyes away from them; her breathing became irregular, and her chest heaved.

"I like it," she said, her eyes still on the men. "I really like it. These guys can really take a lot of stuff. I didn't realize . . . I like the way they look in each other's eyes. It's so physical . . . I think it's more the taking that gets to me than the giving. I can't stop looking in their faces. It's so beautiful."

"There's almost seven hundred pounds of men in that ring," Art Dore shouted into the ringside microphone as two huge contestants belted each other toward the end of the evening.

The Dayton Toughman Contest was nearly over. It had played itself out almost without incident. Oh, there was one problem when a group of men from the audience lured an arena security guard into a men's rest room, where their companions waited for him, split his head open, beat him, and left him on the floor. But generally, Dore was happy with the way the two evenings had gone.

David Guidugli won the title of Toughest Man in Southwest Ohio; he was presented with a check for $1,000 and Dore played a cassette tape of the theme from *Rocky* into the microphone as Guidugli stood, cut and weary, in the center of the ring.

Hara Arena emptied as quickly as it had filled. Several of the Toughman contestants stayed around, as if there might be something else waiting for them, but when no one spoke to them they quietly departed.

The heat was gone, too. Once again, the arena was just a chilly ice rink that for some reason had a boxing ring set up in the middle. Streaks of blood remained on the white floor of the ring, but other than that there was no reminder of what had occurred during the past two nights.

Art Dore closed his briefcase. He walked toward the box office of the arena to check the night's receipts. In the morning he would be on a plane; he had work to do. Dayton was over; he was on his way to find the toughest man in Sioux City, Iowa.

Meanings and Values

1a. What is the author's point of view? (See Guide to Terms: *Point of View*.)

b. Show how it would have been an entirely different narrative if written from the point of view of one of the crowd.

c. Of one of the contestants.

2a. Do you think the title of this selection is meant to be satirical? (Guide: *Satire*.)

b. Can the selection itself be classified as satire?

3a. Describe briefly the author's attitude toward his subject matter.

b. Cite several passages on which you base your answer.

c. In which paragraph does he come nearest to telling us outright of his own reactions to the contest? (Notice the technique by which he avoids a first-person declaration.)

d. Show how, in this essay at least, attitude and tone are closely related. (Guide: *Style/Tone*.)

4a. What is the general effect of being told the job of each contestant mentioned?

b. Of learning that Jerry Johnson (par. 21) is a carpenter?

5a. What generality do you think the quotations in paragraphs 23–25 are meant to illustrate?

b. If a broader observation is implied by these, what is it?

6a. How could you explain whether this piece is primarily objective or subjective? (Guide: *Objective/Subjective*.)

b. What seems to be the biggest difficulty in making such an assessment about "That's Entertainment"?

c. Does the existence of this problem indicate a defect in the piece? Why, or why not?

7a. What is this "darker side of the human spirit" that Dore came to exploit (par. 11)?

b. What is the strong implication of paragraph 29?

Expository Techniques

1. Any good narrative depends largely on the author's *selection* of details. (They seldom just happen along.) Consider the following and state briefly why you think each was included: (a) the cup of beer dropped from the darkness (par. 1); (b) the several references to

the loss of blood (1, 2); (c) the fact that none of the contestants were boxers (3); (d) details of the misfortunes of the four injured men in paragraph 4; (e) the steaming heat (5); (f) Dore's shrug (13); (g) the tattooed obscenity (15); (h) the "delighted" crowd (17); (i) the final sentence of the Niles quotation (19); (j) the final sentence of the Johnson quotation (21); (k) the physical description of Tonya Hopkins as she sat at ringside (24); (l) Dore's shouted comment in paragraph 26; (m) the "problem" in the men's rest room (27); (n) the fact that "the heat was gone, too" (30).

2. Cite descriptive details by which Greene characterizes the crowd.

3a. Which paragraphs can be used to demonstrate the flashback method of time ordering.

 b. Why did the author not disclose this information before beginning his major chronology?

4a. Which of the other patterns of exposition could have been used instead of narration to achieve the author's purpose? How?

 b. Would such treatment have been as successful?

5. Which of the standard techniques is used to introduce this selection? (Guide: *Introductions.*)

6. How fitting do you consider the closing? Why? (Guide: *Closings.*)

Diction and Vocabulary

1a. More than mere exuberance (like baseball's classic "Kill the bum!"), what connotation does "Kill somebody!" soon take on as you read this selection (par. 2)? (Guide: *Connotation/Denotation.*)

 b. What significance do you attach to "Bring on the meat!" as used in this context (par. 20)?

 c. What is the connotation, in *this* context, of "animal chant" (par. 2)? Of "steaming" and "heat" (par. 5)?

2. Why might the author have assumed that Johnson would betray "a trace of irony" (par. 11)? (Guide: *Irony.*)

3. Greene uses figures of speech sparingly, but the ones he does use are apt and colorful. Cite the figures of speech in the following paragraphs and indicate what kind they are: 11, 18, 19, 20, 22. (Guide: *Figures of Speech.*)

4. If you are unfamiliar with any of the following words, consult your dictionary as necessary: phenomenon (par. 8); premise, entrepreneur (9); potential, bravado (10); exploit (11); exhortations (14); eluded (15).

Suggestions for Writing and Discussion

1.   Discuss the possibility that this "darker side of the human spirit" (par. 11) is present in all of us. If so, how do most people manage to keep it under control? If not, do these 4,000 spectators represent a kind of throwback to a more barbaric age? And if that is it, what of those in Sioux City, in Wheeling and Savannah, Grand Rapids and Green Bay?

2.   If you prefer, consider the possibility that Dore is right, that "this is what people want to see" — e.g., the "fact of blood and violence" (par. 11) and the "fear and cruelty and humiliation" (par. 10) demonstrated in the ring. Is Rosa Ginter right when she says that women do like violence (par. 23)? Or is she the exception?

3.   We have laws prohibiting bullfights and cockfights, presumably because they are cruel to animals. Should we also have laws preventing such spectacles as the Toughman Contest — because they are cruel to humans? If not, what basic difference do you see?

(NOTE: Suggestions for topics requiring development by NARRATION are on page 311, at the end of this section.)

GEORGE ORWELL

GEORGE ORWELL (1903–1950), whose real name was Eric Blair, was a British novelist and essayist, well known for his satire. He was born in India and educated at Eton in England; he was wounded while fighting in the Spanish Civil War. Later he wrote the books *Animal Farm* (1945), a satire on Soviet history, and *1984* (1949), a vivid picture of life in a projected totalitarian society. He was, however, also sharply aware of injustices in democratic societies and was consistently socialistic in his views. Many of Orwell's essays are collected in *Critical Essays* (1946), *Shooting an Elephant and Other Essays* (1950), and *Such, Such Were the Joys* (1953).

A Hanging

"A Hanging" is typical of Orwell's essays in its setting — Burma — and in its subtle but biting commentary on colonialism, on capital punishment, even on one aspect of human nature itself. Although he is ostensibly giving a straightforward account of an execution, the author masterfully uses descriptive details and dialogue to create atmosphere and sharply drawn characterizations. The essay gives concrete form to a social message that is often delivered much less effectively in abstract generalities.

It was in Burma, a sodden morning of the rains. A sickly light, like 1
yellow tinfoil, was slanting over the high walls into the jail yard. We were waiting outside the condemned cells, a row of sheds fronted with double bars, like small animal cages. Each cell measured about ten feet by ten and was quite bare within except for a plank bed and a pot for drinking water. In some of them brown, silent men were squatting at the inner bars, with their blankets draped round them.

These were the condemned men, due to be hanged within the next week or two.

One prisoner had been brought out of his cell. He was a Hindu, 2 a puny wisp of a man, with a shaven head and vague liquid eyes. He had a thick, sprouting mustache, absurdly too big for his body, rather like the mustache of a comic man on the films. Six tall Indian warders were guarding him and getting him ready for the gallows. Two of them stood by with rifles and fixed bayonets, while the others handcuffed him, passed a chain through his handcuffs and fixed it to their belts, and lashed his arms tight to his sides. They crowded very close about him, with their hands always on him in a careful, caressing grip, as though all the while feeling him to make sure he was there. It was like men handling a fish which is still alive and may jump back into the water. But he stood quite unresisting, yielding his arms limply to the ropes, as though he hardly noticed what was happening.

Eight o'clock struck and a bugle call, desolately thin in the wet 3 air, floated from the distant barracks. The superintendent of the jail, who was standing apart from the rest of us, moodily prodding the gravel with his stick, raised his head at the sound. He was an army doctor, with a grey toothbrush mustache and a gruff voice. "For God's sake, hurry up, Francis," he said irritably. "The man ought to have been dead by this time. Aren't you ready yet?"

Francis, the head jailer, a fat Dravidian in a white drill suit and 4 gold spectacles, waved his black hand. "Yes sir, yes sir," he bubbled. "All iss satisfactorily prepared. The hangman iss waiting. We shall proceed."

"Well, quick march, then. The prisoners can't get their break- 5 fast till this job's over."

We set out for the gallows. Two warders marched on either side 6 of the prisoner, with their rifles at the slope; two others marched close against him, gripping him by arm and shoulder, as though at once pushing and supporting him. The rest of us, magistrates and the like, followed behind. Suddenly, when we had gone ten yards, the procession stopped short without any order or warning. A dreadful thing had happened — a dog, come goodness knows whence, had appeared in the yard. It came bounding among us with a loud volley of barks and leapt round us wagging its whole body, wild with glee at finding so many human beings together. It was a large woolly dog, half Airedale, half pariah. For a moment it pranced around us, and then, before anyone could stop it, it had made a dash for the prisoner, and jumping up tried to lick his face. Everybody stood aghast, too taken aback even to grab the dog.

"Who let that bloody brute in here?" said the superintendent angrily. "Catch it, someone!"

A warder detached from the escort, charged clumsily after the dog, but it danced and gambolled just out of his reach, taking everything as part of the game. A young Eurasian jailer picked up a handful of gravel and tried to stone the dog away, but it dodged the stones and came after us again. Its yaps echoed from the jail walls. The prisoner, in the grasp of the two warders, looked on incuriously, as though this was another formality of the hanging. It was several minutes before someone managed to catch the dog. Then we put my handkerchief through its collar and moved off once more, with the dog still straining and whimpering.

It was about forty yards to the gallows. I watched the bare brown back of the prisoner marching in front of me. He walked clumsily with his bound arms, but quite steadily, with that bobbing gait of the Indian who never straightens his knees. At each step his muscles slid neatly into place, the lock of hair on his scalp danced up and down, his feet printed themselves on the wet gravel. And once, in spite of the men who gripped him by each shoulder, he stepped lightly aside to avoid a puddle on the path.

It is curious; but till that moment I had never realized what it means to destroy a healthy, conscious man. When I saw the prisoner step aside to avoid the puddle, I saw the mystery, the unspeakable wrongness, of cutting a life short when it is in full tide. This man was not dying, he was alive just as we are alive. All the organs of his body were working — bowels digesting food, skin renewing itself, nails growing, tissues forming — all toiling away in solemn foolery. His nails would still be growing when he stood on the drop, when he was falling through the air with a tenth-of-a-second to live. His eyes saw the yellow gravel and the grey walls, and his brain still remembered, foresaw, reasoned — even about puddles. He and we were a party of men walking together, seeing, hearing, feeling, understanding the same world; and in two minutes, with a sudden snap, one of us would be gone — one mind less, one world less.

The gallows stood in a small yard, separate from the main

grounds of the prison, and overgrown with tall prickly weeds. It was a brick erection like three sides of a shed, with planking on top, and above that two beams and a crossbar with the rope dangling. The hangman, a greyhaired convict in the white uniform of the prison, was waiting beside his machine. He greeted us with a servile crouch as we entered. At a word from Francis the two warders, gripping the prisoner more closely than ever, half led, half pushed him to the gallows and helped him clumsily up the ladder. Then the hangman climbed up and fixed the rope round the prisoner's neck.

We stood waiting, five yards away. The warders had formed in a rough circle round the gallows. And then, when the noose was fixed, the prisoner began crying out to his god. It was a high, reiterated cry of "Ram! Ram! Ram! Ram!" not urgent and fearful like a prayer or cry for help, but steady, rhythmical, almost like the tolling of a bell. The dog answered the sound with a whine. The hangman, still standing on the gallows, produced a small cotton bag like a flour bag and drew it down over the prisoner's face. But the sound, muffled by the cloth, still persisted, over and over again: "Ram! Ram! Ram! Ram! Ram!" 12

The hangman climbed down and stood ready, holding the lever. Minutes seemed to pass. The steady, muffled crying from the prisoner went on and on, "Ram! Ram! Ram!" never faltering for an instant. The superintendent, his head on his chest, was slowly poking the ground with his stick; perhaps he was counting the cries, allowing the prisoner a fixed number — fifty, perhaps, or a hundred. Everyone had changed colour. The Indians had gone grey like bad coffee, and one or two of the bayonets were wavering. We looked at the lashed, hooded man on the drop, and listened to his cries — each cry another second of life; the same thought was in all our minds; oh, kill him quickly, get it over, stop that abominable noise! 13

Suddenly the superintendent made up his mind. Throwing up his head he made a swift motion with his stick. "Chalo!" he shouted almost fiercely. 14

There was a clanking noise, and then dead silence. The prisoner had vanished, and the rope was twisting on itself. I let go of the dog, and it galloped immediately to the back of the gallows; but when it got there it stopped short, barked, and then retreated into a corner of the yard, where it stood among the weeds, looking timor- 15 ously out at us. We went round the gallows to inspect the prisoner's body. He was dangling with his toes pointed straight downwards, very slowly revolving, as dead as a stone.

The superintendent reached out with his stick and poked the   16
bare brown body; it oscillated slightly. "He's all right," said the superintendent. He backed out from under the gallows, and blew out a deep breath. The moody look had gone out of his face quite suddenly. He glanced at his wrist-watch. "Eight minutes past eight. Well, that's all for this morning, thank God."

The warders unfixed bayonets and marched away. The dog,   17
sobered and conscious of having misbehaved itself, slipped after them. We walked out of the gallows yard, past the condemned cells with their waiting prisoners, into the big central yard of the prison. The convicts, under the command of warders armed with lathis, were already receiving their breakfast. They squatted in long rows, each man holding a tin pannikin, while two warders with buckets marched around ladling out rice; it seemed quite a homely, jolly scene, after the hanging. An enormous relief had come upon us now that the job was done. One felt an impulse to sing, to break into a run, to snigger. All at once everyone began chattering gaily.

The Eurasian boy walking beside me nodded towards the way   18
we had come, with a knowing smile: "Do you know, sir, our friend (he meant the dead man) when he heard his appeal had been dismissed, he pissed on the floor of his cell. From fright. Kindly take one of my cigarettes, sir. Do you not admire my new silver case, sir? From the boxwallah, two rupees eight annas. Classy European style."

Several people laughed — at what, nobody seemed certain.   19

Francis was walking by the superintendent, talking garrulous-   20
ly: "Well, sir, all has passed off with the utmost satisfactoriness. It was all finished — flick! Like that. It iss not always so — oah, no! I have known cases where the doctor wass obliged to go beneath the gallows and pull the prissoner's legs to ensure decease. Most disagreeable!"

"Wriggling about, eh? That's bad," said the superintendent.   21

"Arch, sir, it iss worse when they become refractory! One man,   22
I recall, clung to the bars of hiss cage when we went to take him out. You will scarcely credit, sir, that it took six warders to dislodge him, three pulling at each leg. We reasoned with him, 'My dear fellow,'

we said, 'think of all the pain and trouble you are causing to us!' But no, he would not listen! Ach, he wass very troublesome!"

I found that I was laughing quite loudly. Everyone was laughing. Even the superintendent grinned in a tolerant way. "You'd better all come out and have a drink," he said quite genially. "I've got a bottle of whisky in the car. We could do with it." 23

We went through the big double gates of the prison into the road. "Pulling at his legs!" exclaimed a Burmese magistrate suddenly, and burst into a loud chuckling. We all began laughing again. At that moment Francis' anecdote seemed extraordinarily funny. We all had a drink together, native and European alike, quite amicably. The dead man was a hundred yards away. 24

Meanings and Values

1. What was the real reason for the superintendent's impatience?
2. On first impression it may have seemed that the author gave undue attention to the dog's role in this narrative.
    a. Why was the episode such a "dreadful thing" (par. 6)?
    b. Why did the author think it worth noting that the dog was excited at "finding so many human beings together"?
    c. Of what significance was the dog's trying to lick the prisoner's face?
3. Explain how the prisoner's stepping around a puddle could have given the author a new insight into what was about to happen (par. 10).
4. Why was there so much talking and laughing after the hanging was finished?
5. What is the broadest meaning of Orwell's last sentence?

Expository Techniques

1. Cite examples of both objective and impressionistic description in the first paragraph.
2a. What is the primary time order used in this narrative?
  b. If there are any exceptions, state where.
3. Considering the relatively few words devoted to them, several of the characterizations in this essay are remarkably vivid — a result, obviously, of highly discriminating selection of details from the multitude of those that must have been available to the author. For

each of the following people, list the character traits that we can observe, and state whether these impressions come to us through details of description, action, and/or dialogue.

a.   The prisoner.

b.   The superintendent.

c.   Francis.

d.   The Eurasian boy.

4a. Why do you think the author included so many details of the preparation of the prisoner (par. 2)?

b.   Why did he include so many details about the dog and his actions?

c.   What is gained by the assortment of details in paragraph 10?

5.   The tone of a writing such as this can easily slip into sentimentality or even melodrama without the author's realizing what is happening. (See Guide to Terms: *Sentimentality*.) Select three places in this narrative where a less-skilled writer might have had such trouble, and note by what restraints Orwell prevented sentimentality.

Diction and Vocabulary

1.   A noteworthy element of Orwell's style is his occasional use of figurative language. Cite six metaphors and similes, and comment on their choice and effectiveness.

2.   Orwell was always concerned with the precise effects that words could give to meaning and style.

a.   Cite at least six nonfigurative words that seem to you particularly well chosen for their purpose.

b.   Show what their careful selection contributes to the description of atmosphere or to the subtle meanings of the author.

c.   How is this attention to diction a matter of style? (Guide: *Style/Tone*.)

Suggestions for Writing and Discussion

1.   Select *one* of the points of controversy over capital punishment and present both sides with equal objectivity.

2.   Consider the dilemma of a person whose "duty" seems to require one course of action and "conscience" just the opposite course. Use concrete illustrations to show how serious such dilemmas can be.

3.   Examine the moral right, or lack of it, of the people of one country to impose their laws on the people of another country.

4. Discuss one benefit of colonialism to the people colonized. Use specific illustrations.

5. Explain how, in your own experience, a seemingly minor incident led to much deeper insight into a matter not fully understood before.

(NOTE: Suggestions for topics requiring development by NARRATION are on page 311, at the end of this section.)

MAYA ANGELOU

MAYA ANGELOU, born Marguerita Johnson in 1928, in St. Louis, Missouri, spent the greater part of her childhood in rural Stamps, Arkansas, and later studied dance in San Francisco. She toured Europe and Africa for the State Department in *Porgy and Bess*, and taught dance in Rome and Tel Aviv. In collaboration with Godfrey Cambridge she produced, directed, and starred in *Cabaret for Freedom*, and also starred in Genet's *The Blacks*. At the request of Martin Luther King, Jr., Angelou became northern coordinator for the Southern Christian Leadership Conference. From this position she went to Africa to write for newspapers in Cairo and Ghana. She has written and produced a ten-part TV series on the positive traditions in American life. Angelou speaks French, Spanish, Italian, Arabic, and Fanti. Her autobiography thus far consists of four books: *I Know Why the Caged Bird Sings* (1970), *Gather Together in My Name* (1974), *Singin' and Swingin' and Gettin' Merry Like Christmas* (1976), and *The Heart of a Woman* (1981). She has also written several books of poetry: *Just Give Me a Cool Drink of Water . . . 'Fore I Die* (1971), *Oh Pray My Wings Are Gonna Fit Me Well* (1975), and *And Still I Rise* (1978).

Momma's Private Victory

"Momma's Private Victory" (editors' title) is the fifth chapter of Angelou's book *I Know Why the Caged Bird Sings*. Since their early childhood, she and her brother, who was a year older, had lived with their grandmother ("Momma" of the narrative), who operated a store in the front room of her home in the black section of their small Arkansas town.

"Thou shall not be dirty" and "Thou shall not be impudent" were the two commandments of Grandmother Henderson upon which hung our total salvation.

Each night in the bitterest winter we were forced to wash faces, 2
arms, necks, legs and feet before going to bed. She used to add, with
a smirk that unprofane people can't control when venturing into
profanity, "and wash as far as possible, then wash possible."

We would go to the well and wash in the ice-cold, clear water, 3
grease our legs with the equally cold stiff Vaseline, then tiptoe into
the house. We wiped the dust from our toes and settled down for
schoolwork, cornbread, clabbered milk, prayers and bed, always in
that order. Momma was famous for pulling the quilts off after we
had fallen asleep to examine our feet. If they weren't clean enough
for her, she took the switch (she kept one behind the bedroom door
for emergencies) and woke up the offender with a few aptly placed
burning reminders.

The area around the well at night was dark and slick, and boys 4
told about how snakes love water, so that anyone who had to draw
water at night and then stand there alone and wash knew that
moccasins and rattlers, puff adders and boa constrictors were winding their way to the well and would arrive just as the person
washing got soap in her eyes. But Momma convinced us that not
only was cleanliness next to Godliness, dirtiness was the inventor of
misery.

The impudent child was detested by God and a shame to its 5
parents and could bring destruction to its house and line. All adults
had to be addressed as Mister, Missus, Miss, Auntie, Cousin, Unk,
Uncle, Buhbah, Sister, Brother and a thousand other appellations
indicating familial relationship and the lowliness of the addressor.

Everyone I knew respected these customary laws, except for 6
the powhitetrash children.

Some families of powhitetrash lived on Momma's farm land 7
behind the school. Sometimes a gaggle of them came to the Store,
filling the whole room, chasing out the air and even changing the
well-known scents. The children crawled over the shelves and into
the potato and onion bins, twanging all the time in their sharp
voices like cigar-box guitars. They took liberties in my Store that I
would never dare. Since Momma told us that the less you say to
white-folks (or even powhitetrash) the better, Bailey and I would
stand, solemn, quiet, in the displaced air. But if one of the playful
apparitions got close to us, I pinched it. Partly out of angry frustration and partly because I didn't believe in its flesh reality.

They called my uncle by his first name and ordered him around 8 the Store. He, to my crying shame, obeyed them in his limping dip-straight-dip fashion.

My grandmother, too, followed their orders, except that she didn't seem to be servile because she anticipated their needs.

"Here's sugar, Miz Potter, and here's baking powder. You didn't buy soda last month, you'll probably be needing some."

Momma always directed her statements to the adults, but sometimes, Oh painful sometimes, the grimy, snotty-nosed girls would answer her.

"Naw, Annie . . ." — to Momma? Who owned the land they lived on? Who forgot more than they would ever learn? If there was any justice in the world, God should strike them dumb at once! — "Just give us some extra sody crackers, and some more mackerel."

At least they never looked in her face, or I never caught them doing so. Nobody with a smidgen of training, not even the worst roustabout, would look right in a grown person's face. It meant the person was trying to take the words out before they were formed. The dirty little children didn't do that, but they threw their orders around the Store like lashes from a cat-o'-nine-tails.

When I was around ten years old, those scruffy children caused me the most painful and confusing experience I had ever had with my grandmother.

One summer morning, after I had swept the dirt yard of leaves, spearmint-gum wrappers and Vienna-sausage labels, I raked the yellow-red dirt, and made half-moons carefully, so that the design stood out clearly and mask-like. I put the rake behind the Store and came through the back of the house to find Grandmother on the front porch in her big, wide white apron. The apron was so stiff by virtue of the starch that it could have stood alone. Momma was admiring the yard, so I joined her. It truly looked like a flat redhead that had been raked with a big-toothed comb. Momma didn't say anything but I knew she liked it. She looked over toward the school principal's house and to the right at Mr. McElroy's. She was hoping one of those community pillars would see the design before the day's business wiped it out. Then she looked upward to the school. My head had swung with hers, so at just about the same time we saw a troop of the powhitetrash kids marching over the hill and down by the side of the school.

I looked to Momma for direction. She did an excellent job of sagging from her waist down, but from the waist up she seemed to be pulling for the top of the oak tree across the road. Then she began to moan a hymn. Maybe not to moan, but the tune was so slow and the meter so strange that she could have been moaning. She didn't look at me again. When the children reached halfway down the hill, halfway to the Store, she said without turning, "Sister, go on inside."

I wanted to beg her, "Momma, don't wait for them. Come on inside with me. If they come in the Store, you go to the bedroom and let me wait on them. They only frighten me if you're around. Alone I know how to handle them." But of course I couldn't say anything, so I went in and stood behind the screen door.   17

Before the girls got to the porch I heard their laughter crackling and popping like pine logs in a cooking stove. I suppose my lifelong paranoia was born in those cold, molasses-slow minutes. They came finally to stand on the ground in front of Momma. At first they pretended seriousness. Then one of them wrapped her right arm in the crook of her left, pushed out her mouth and started to hum. I realized that she was aping my grandmother. Another said, "Naw, Helen, you ain't standing like her. This here's it." Then she lifted her chest, folded her arms and mocked that strange carriage that was Annie Henderson. Another laughed, "Naw, you can't do it. Your mouth ain't pooched out enough. It's like this."   18

I thought about the rifle behind the door, but I knew I'd never be able to hold it straight, and the .410, our sawed-off shotgun, which stayed loaded and was fired every New Year's night, was locked in the trunk and Uncle Willie had the key on his chain. Through the fly-specked screen-door, I could see that the arms of Momma's apron jiggled from the vibrations of her humming. But her knees seemed to have locked as if they would never bend again.   19

She sang on. No louder than before, but no softer either. No slower or faster.   20

The dirt of the girls' cotton dresses continued on their legs, feet, arms and faces to make them all of a piece. Their greasy uncolored hair hung down, uncombed, with a grim finality. I knelt to see them better, to remember them for all time. The tears that had slipped down my dress left unsurprising dark spots, and made the front yard blurry and even more unreal. The world had taken a deep breath and was having doubts about continuing to revolve.   21

The girls had tired of mocking Momma and turned to other means of agitation. One crossed her eyes, stuck her thumbs in both   22 sides of her mouth and said, "Look here, Annie." Grandmother hummed on and the apron strings trembled. I wanted to throw a handful of black pepper in their faces, to throw lye on them, to scream that they were dirty, scummy peckerwoods, but I knew I was as clearly imprisoned behind the scene as the actors outside were confined to their roles.

One of the smaller girls did a kind of puppet dance while her fellow clowns laughed at her. But the tall one, who was almost a woman, said something very quietly, which I couldn't hear. They all moved backward from the porch, still watching Momma. For an awful second I thought they were going to throw a rock at Momma, who seemed (except for the apron strings) to have turned into stone herself. But the big girl turned her back, bent down and put her hands flat on the ground — she didn't pick up anything. She simply shifted her weight and did a hand stand.

Her dirty bare feet and long legs went straight for the sky. Her dress fell down around her shoulders, and she had on no drawers, The slick pubic hair made a brown triangle where her legs came together. She hung in the vacuum of that lifeless morning for only a few seconds, then wavered and tumbled. The other girls clapped her on the back and slapped their hands.

Momma changed her song to "Bread of Heaven, bread of Heaven, feed me till I want no more."

I found that I was praying too. How long could Momma hold out? What new indignity would they think of to subject her to? Would I be able to stay out of it? What would Momma really like me to do?

Then they were moving out of the yard, on their way to town. They bobbed their heads and shook their slack behinds and turned, one at a time:

" 'Bye, Annie."

" 'Bye, Annie."

" 'Bye, Annie."

Momma never turned her head or unfolded her arms, but she stopped singing and said, " 'Bye, Miz Helen, 'bye, Miz Ruth, 'bye, Miz Eloise."

I burst. A firecracker July-the-Fourth burst. How could Momma call them Miz? The mean nasty things. Why couldn't she have come inside the sweet, cool store when we saw them breasting the hill?

What did she prove? And then if they were dirty, mean and impudent, why did Momma have to call them Miz?

She stood another whole song through and then opened the 33
screen door to look down on me crying in rage. She looked until I
looked up. Her face was a brown moon that shone on me. She was
beautiful. Something had happened out there, which I couldn't
completely understand, but I could see that she was happy. Then
she bent down and touched me as mothers of the church "lay hands
on the sick and afflicted" and I quieted.

"Go wash your face, Sister." And she went behind the candy 34
counter and hummed, "Glory, glory, hallelujah, when I lay my
burden down."

I threw the well water on my face and used the weekday 35
handkerchief to blow my nose. Whatever the contest had been out
front, I knew Momma had won.

I took the rake back to the front yard. The smudged footprints 36
were easy to erase. I worked for a long time on my new design and
laid the rake behind the wash pot. When I came back in the Store, I
took Momma's hand and we both walked outside to look at the
pattern.

It was a large heart with lots of hearts growing smaller inside, 37
and piercing from the outside rim to the smallest heart was an
arrow. Momma said, "Sister, that's right pretty." Then she turned
back to the Store and resumed, "Glory, glory, hallelujah, when I lay
my burden down."

Meanings and Values

1. Where would you place this narrative on an objective-to-subjective
continuum? Why? (See Guide to Terms: *Objective/Subjective*.)

2a. Is the point of view consistent throughout the narrative?

 b. Cite the limitations and the special advantages inherent in this point
of view.

3. Demonstrate how this narrative would have differed if written from
one of the other possible points of view.

4a. Explain how it was that these characters were all imprisoned in their
own roles (par 22).

 b. Show how it would have been an entirely different narration if one
of them had performed her role with any radical difference.

Expository Techniques

1. Explain carefully why the first paragraph is, or is not, an effective introduction for this *whole* narration.
2a. What is the structural function of paragraph 6?
  b. Of paragraph 14?
3a. Why do you think so many of Angelou's descriptive details have to do, one way or another, with dirtiness? (Another writer might have described the children once as "dirty," and let it go at that.)
  b. How different would the narrative have been if Momma had held different concepts of cleanliness and impudence?

Diction and Vocabulary

1. Demonstrate the significance of connotation by use of the apparently differing views of "dirtiness" held by the characters of this narrative. (Guide: *Connotation/Denotation.*)
2. Select several distinctive examples of Angelou's style — figurative and nonfigurative — and show what makes them distinctive. (Guide: *Style/Tone.*)

Suggestions for Writing and Discussion

1. Write a character study of Momma, using no narration and only the information you have available from this selection.
2. What *had* been the contest out front (par. 35)? Do you agree that Momma had won?

(NOTE: Suggestions for topics requiring development by NARRATION follow.)

Writing Suggestions for Section 9
Narration

Use narration as at least a partial pattern (e.g., in developed examples or in comparison) for one of the following expository themes or another suggested by them. Avoid the isolated personal account that has little broader significance. Remember, too, that development of the essay should itself make your point, without excessive moralizing.

1. People can still succeed without a college education.
2. The frontiers are not all gone.
3. When people succeed in communicating, they can learn to get along with each other.
4. Even with "careful" use of capital punishment, innocent people can be executed.
5. Homosexuals can't always be recognized by appearance and mannerisms.
6. True courage is different from boldness in time of sudden danger.
7. Conditioning to the realities of the job is as important to the police officer as professional training.
8. It is possible for employees themselves to determine when they have reached their highest level of competence.
9. Wartime massacres are not a new development.
10. Worn-out land can be restored without chemicals to its original productivity.
11. Back-to-the-earth, "family" style communes can be made to work.
12. Such communes (as in 11 above) are a good (or poor) place to raise children.
13. Both heredity and environment shape personality.
14. Physical and mental handicaps can be overcome in some ways, but they are still a burden.
15. Toxic wastes pose a problem for many communities.
16. Hunting is a worthwhile and challenging sport.

10

Reasoning by Use of *Induction* and *Deduction*

Induction and deduction, important as they are in argumentation, may also be useful methods of exposition. They are often used simply to explain a stand or conclusion, without any effort or need to win converts.

Induction is the process by which we accumulate evidence until, at some point, we can make the "inductive leap" and thus reach a useful *generalization*. The science laboratory employs this technique; hundreds of tests and experiments and analyses may be required before the scientist will generalize, for instance, that polio is caused by a certain virus. It is also the primary technique of the prosecuting attorney who presents pieces of inductive evidence, asking the jury to make the inductive leap and conclude that the accused did indeed kill the victim.

Even the commonplace "process of elimination" also may be considered a form of induction. If it can be shown, for instance, that "A" does not have the strength to swing the murder weapon, that "B" was in a drunken sleep at the time of the crime, and that "C" had recently become blind and could not have found her way to the boathouse, then we may be ready for the inductive leap, that the foul deed must have been committed by "X," the only other person on the island. (The use of this kind of induction, implies an added obligation, of course, to make certain that all the possibilities but *one* have been eliminated: if we fail to note that "Y," a visitor on a neighboring island, and his boat were unaccounted for that evening, then our conclusion is invalid.)

On a more personal level, of course, we all learned to use induction at a very early age. We may have disliked the taste of orange juice, winter squash, and carrots, and we were not too young to make a generalization: orange-colored food tastes bad.

Whereas induction is the method of reaching a potentially useful generalization (for example, Professor Melville always gives an "F" to students who cut his class three times), *deduction* is the method of *using* such a generality, now accepted as a fact (for example, if we cut this class again today, we will get an "F"). Working from a generalization already formulated — by ourselves, by someone else, or by tradition — we may deduce that a specific thing or circumstance that fits into the generality will act the same. Hence, if convinced that orange-colored food tastes bad, we will be reluctant to try pumpkin pie.

A personnel manager may have discovered over the years that electronics majors from Central College are invariably well trained in their field. His induction may have been based on the evidence of observations, records, and the opinions of fellow Rotary members; and, perhaps without realizing it, he has made the usable generalization about the training of Central College electronics majors. Later, when he has an application from Nancy Ortega, a graduate of Central College, his *de*ductive process will probably work as follows: Central College turns out well-trained electronics majors; Ortega was trained at Central; therefore, Ortega must be well trained. Here he has used a generalization to apply to a specific case.

Put in this simplified form (which, in writing, it seldom is),[1] the deductive process is also called a "syllogism" — with the beginning generality known as the "major premise" and the specific that fits into the generality known as the "minor premise." For example:

[1]Neither induction nor deduction is confined to a particular order of presentation. If we use specific evidence to *reach* a generalization, it is induction regardless of which part is stated first in a written or spoken account. (Very likely, both the prosecutor's opening remarks and Dr. Salk's written reports first presented their generalizations and then the inductive evidence by which they had been reached.) But if we use a generality in which to *place* a specific, it is still deduction, however stated. (Hence the reasoning of the personnel manager might be: "Ortega must be well trained because she was educated at C.C., and there's where they really know how to do it.")

Major premise — Orange-colored food is not fit to eat.
Minor premise — Pumpkin pie is orange-colored.
Conclusion — Pumpkin pie is not fit to eat.

Frequently, however, the validity of one or both of the premises may be questionable, and here is one of the functions of *in*duction: to give needed support — with evidence such as opinions of experts, statistics, and results of experiments or surveys — to the *de*ductive syllogism, whether stated or implied. Deductive reasoning, in whatever form presented, is only as sound as both its premises. The child's conviction that orange-colored food is not fit to eat was not necessarily true; therefore, the conclusion about pumpkin pie is not very trustworthy. The other conclusions, that we will automatically get an "F" by cutting Melville's class and that Ortega is well trained in electronics, can be only as reliable as the original generalizations that were used as deductive premises. If the generalizations themselves were based on flimsy or insufficient evidence, any future deduction using them is likely to be erroneous.

These two faults are common in induction: (1) the use of *flimsy* evidence — mere opinion, hearsay, or analogy, none of which can support a valid generalization — instead of verified facts or opinions of reliable authorities; and (2) the use of *too little* evidence, leading to a premature inductive leap.

The amount of evidence needed in any situation depends, of course, on purpose and audience. The success of two Central College graduates might be enough to convince some careless personnel director that all Central electronics graduates would be good employees, but two laboratory tests would not have convinced Dr. Salk, or any of his colleagues, that he had learned anything worthwhile about the polio virus. The authors of the Declaration of Independence, in justifying their argument for rebellion to a wide variety of readers and listeners, explained why they considered the king tyrannical, by listing twenty-eight despotic acts of his government, each of which was a verifiable fact, a matter of public record.

Induction and deduction are highly logical processes, and any trace of weakness can seriously undermine an exposition that depends on their reasonableness. (Such weakness can, of course, be even more disastrous in argument.) Although no induction or deduction ever reaches absolute, 100 percent, certainty, we should try to get from these methods as high a degree of *probability* as possible. (We can never positively prove, for instance, that the sun will rise in the east tomorrow, but thousands of years of inductive observation and theorizing make the fact extremely probable — and certainly sound enough for any working generalization.)

Students using induction and deduction in compositions, essay examinations, or term papers — showing that Stephen Crane was a naturalistic writer, or that our national policies are unfair to revolutionary movements — should always assume that they will have a skeptical audience that wants to know the logical basis for *all* generalizations and conclusions.

Sample Paragraph (Induction/Deduction)

The basic structure of the professor's article is *inductive*.

Each of these *inductive generalizations* helps explain the residents' satisfaction with life in the Valley.

(A full report needs to contain much more evidence, of course, in order to be convincing.)

Ever since Joseph Casey and his family built the first house in Ilona Valley, outsiders (and some residents, too) have wondered why people enjoy living here. Just last year, a professor from Bayport State College wrote an article for the Casey *Enquirer* explaining how people from the Valley feel about the area. Drawing on interviews with both new and longtime residents, he reported that most people like the physical beauty of the Valley and the many opportunities for hiking and fishing. Many of them admit that a big city like Bayport offers a lot more in the way of social and cultural activities, but they claim that performances of the Casey Community Symphony and the Riverton Chorus, plus the Valley Fair, dances sponsored by local groups, and the Summerfest give them plenty to do throughout the year. People with families praise the traditional values of Valley society, and just about everyone thinks the clean water and

The last inductive gener-
alization becomes the *major premise* for a *deductive
syllogism.*

air of the region make it a healthy
place to live. Most of all, residents like
the Valley because its relative isolation
has created a close-knit community
where people can depend on each
other. Ilona Valley's special qualities,
the professor concluded, depend upon
its isolation, and he warned that since

Minor premise.

this isolation would be destroyed by
the new four-lane highway the State is
once again proposing, Valley residents

Conclusion.

should continue to oppose the highway as effectively as they have in the
past.

(NOTE: This is formal
writing, with a logical
progression of ideas and
no use of such informali-
ties as first-person pro-
nouns, contractions, or
colloquial expressions.)

ELLEN GOODMAN

ELLEN GOODMAN was born in 1941, in Boston, where she now lives. She was graduated cum laude from Radcliffe College and then spent a year at Harvard on a Nieman Fellowship. Goodman has been with the Boston *Globe* as a reporter since 1967 and, since 1974, has been a full-time columnist. Her "At Large" columns are now published in over two hundred newspapers across the country, and her commentaries have been broadcast on both television and radio. Goodman's work has also appeared in *McCall's, The Village Voice, Family Circle, Harper's Bazaar*, and many other publications, and she has been the recipient of various journalistic honors and awards, including the 1980 Pulitzer Prize for distinguished commentary. Her columns have been collected in *Close to Home* (1979), *Turning Points* (1979), and *At Large* (1981).

Just Woman's Work?

"Just Woman's Work?" originally appeared as a newspaper column and was later reprinted in the collection *At Large* (1981). In this essay Goodman uses the inductive process to search for an explanation of a distressing phenomenon. The pattern of reasoning here is somewhat informal, making use of several partial explanations before it reaches an overall generalization, yet it provides a good example of one of the common uses of induction. Out of the inductive process also develops an informal deductive syllogism.

The young woman stood up before the college audience and talked earnestly about her new job and her new confusion.

A June graduate, she was now a teacher. She was lucky and she knew it. Yet each day she carried a sheaf of self-doubt to school along with the ditto papers and work sheets.

The women her age, you see, have been encouraged to become astronauts and senators, corporate vice-presidents and assorted firsts. Though she had elected to go through the more traditional door, somehow she couldn't shake the feeling that she was "just" a teacher. 3

As a parent seated with her on the podium, I felt a wave of concern. There is no outsider more important to our children's lives than their teachers, no job that we weigh more heavily in cost-accounting their futures. We want our children to be taught by the best, the brightest, the most lively and sensitive. To us, there is no such thing as "just" a teacher. 4

Yet, in her era of change, when the status and stroking of society has gone to the innovators, how many others have felt left behind: "just" a teacher, nurse, secretary, homemaker. And what effect does that have on the choices that young people are making? 5

I know it isn't popular to talk about this, even in an era when everyone is worrying about teacher "competency," but we are witnessing a young brain-drain from the old "women's jobs." 6

The young people planning to be teachers don't rank as high scholastically as they did. Dr. Timothy Weaver of Boston University studied this decline and it's a substantial one. In 1970, the high school students planning to be education majors tested in the top one-third of all students on their English boards. Six years later they were found in the bottom one-third. 7

On the graduate record exams taken by college seniors in the same time period, the scores of education majors dropped eighteen points in verbal aptitude. 8

There are other reasons for this decline. The teaching job market isn't what it used to be. Neither are the salaries. In 1972, teaching salaries were about 25 percent above the national average. Now, says Weaver, they are just about on a par. 9

But 70 percent of the teachers in this country are women. Their test scores were typically higher than those of men, their salaries relatively higher than those of other women. Now the opportunities for young women are greater and the decline in the test scores of women planning to teach is sharper. 10

Teaching isn't the only job or the best job for the ambitious and academically talented young woman today. As Weaver put it: 11

"Women do have more opportunities. They are encouraged to feel they have more opportunities in higher-paying professions and that is reflected in the data."

It isn't just teaching that's been affected. In nursing, where there are many jobs, the scores have also declined. And in clerical work, employers continually moan to each other that, "We just can't find the same kind of young secretaries anymore."

But this isn't just a case of Liberation Chic. It isn't just the lure of the new, and the prestige of the different. The fact is that a rise in status for women is associated, for better and for worse, with entry into the male world. That's where the prestige has always been.

We have simply done a better job at letting some women into "men's" jobs than at raising the status of "women's" jobs.

The care-takers — those who are helpers, nurturers, teachers, mothers — are still systematically devalued. We don't put our money where our mouths are.

Now the job market competes for the brightest women as well as the brightest men. If the projections are right and we have a teacher shortage, not a surplus by the mid-1980s, we'll have to do some fancy status shuffling.

Competency tests are nothing more than the last resort of despairing parents. There's no real secret to attracting and keeping the highest caliber applicants for any job. They need the rewards of independence, growth, initiative, respect, personal satisfaction and money. With these, no one is a "Just."

Meanings and Values

1a. At what kind of people do you think this essay was originally directed?

b. To what beliefs or attitudes of this audience does the author refer in the first several paragraphs of the essay?

c. What other attitudes discussed in the essay appear to be on a collision course with the attitudes identified in the first several paragraphs?

2a. What is the phenomenon Goodman is trying to explain? Describe it in your own words.

b. What does it mean to be " 'just' a teacher" (par. 3)?

3a. According to Goodman, who is to blame for the lack of highly qualified people going into teaching?

b.   What social forces are responsible?

c.   Are other professions facing (or likely to face) similar shortages? If so, are the causes the same?

4.   If you have read the Halsey essay in Section 6, explain to what extent, if at all, the attitudes she describes have contributed to the phenomenon examined in this selection.

5a. What are the solutions Goodman offers to the problem of attracting qualified people to teaching?

b.   What is "fancy status shuffling" (par. 16)?

6a. Where would you place this essay on an objective-to-subjective continuum? (See Guide to Terms: *Objective/Subjective*.)

b.   Is Goodman fair in the conclusions she draws? Are her explanations convincing? (Guide: *Evaluation*.)

Expository Techniques

1a. Who are the people referred to as "we" in paragraph 4?

b.   Why would Goodman shift to "we" in paragraph 4 after having used "I" in the preceding paragraphs?

c.   What is the author's point of view in this essay? (Consider: Are there two points of view, one corresponding to "I," the other to "we"?) (Guide: *Point of View*.)

2a. A number of generalities the author arrives at in the process of induction (pars. 6–15) can be considered partial explanations of the phenomenon described in paragraphs 1–5. What are these partial explanations?

b.   What generality does the author arrive at as a result of the entire inductive process?

c.   Does the author state the generality? If so, where?

d.   If not, how would you express it?

3.   Could the process of induction in this essay be viewed as a "process of elimination"? If so, in what way?

4a. Is the pattern of reasoning in the last two paragraphs inductive or deductive?

b.   Put in your own words a logical syllogism that sums up the meaning of the last two paragraphs.

5a. What standard opening techniques are used in this essay? (Guide: *Introductions*.)

b.   What standard closing techniques? (Guide: *Closings*.)

c.   Are the opening and closing of this essay effective? If so, why? (Guide: *Evaluation*.)

Diction and Vocabulary

1a. Is the last sentence in paragraph 15 a cliché, or is it a proverbial saying? (Guide: *Clichés.*)

  b. Why has the author chosen to use it here? Is it used effectively?

2a. What are the parallel structures in paragraph 4, and why are they used? (Guide: *Parallel Structure.*)

3a. What is a "sheaf of self-doubt" (par. 2)?

  b. What does this phrase add to the essay?

4. Trace the use of the word "just" in this essay, and show how Goodman uses it to emphasize her ideas. (Guide: *Emphasis.*)

5. What is the function of the rhetorical questions in paragraph 5? (Guide: *Rhetorical Questions.*)

Suggestions for Writing and Discussion

1. Take into account recent public controversy over the quality of American education and the quality of teaching, and discuss what you consider the reasons for the decline in the effectiveness of our schools. (If you think their effectiveness has not declined, argue in support of your position.)

2. Are the reforms Goodman suggests in paragraph 17 likely to bring about real change? Is there any chance they will be implemented?

3. Is Goodman's estimate of the importance of teachers correct? Don't other people and institutions — friends, churches, community groups, the media — have as great an effect on children as teachers? Explain and justify your answer.

4. Goodman seems to regard teaching as a woman's profession. Is this accurate in your experience? Will one of the positive (or negative) effects of raising the status of teaching and similar professions be that more men will be attracted to them? If so, will this be good or bad? Discuss.

(NOTE: Suggestions for topics requiring development by INDUCTION and DEDUCTION are on page 336, at the end of this section.)

LESTER C. THUROW

LESTER C. THUROW, born in 1938 in Montana, graduated from Williams College (magna cum laude), Balliol College, Oxford (where he earned an M.A.), and Harvard University (M.A. and Ph.D.). He has taught economics and done research at Harvard, the Kennedy School of Government, and the Institute of Politics, and is currently a professor at the Massachusetts Institute of Technology. He has been a TV commentator, has testified before Congress, and has served as consultant to government agencies and private corporations. He has written numerous books and articles for professional journals and popular magazines, including *Nation* and *Newsweek*.

Why Women Are Paid Less Than Men

"Why Women Are Paid Less Than Men," like the preceding selection, uses a form of induction to prepare for a logical syllogism. But there the similarity ends: the styles and the treatment methods are totally different, and this is to be expected because of the vast difference in purpose and subject matter. This selection was first published in *The New York Times*.

In the 40 years from 1939 to 1979 white women who work full time 1 have with monotonous regularity made slightly less than 60 percent as much as white men. Why?

Over the same time period, minorities have made substantial 2 progress in catching up with whites, with minority women making even more progress than minority men.

Black men now earn 72 percent as much as white men (up 16 3 percentage points since the mid-1950's) but black women earn 92 percent as much as white women. Hispanic men make 71 percent of what their white counterparts do, but Hispanic women make 82 percent as much as white women. As a result of their faster progress, fully employed black women make 75 percent as much as fully employed black men while Hispanic women earn 68 percent as much as Hispanic men.

This faster progress may, however, end when minority women   4
finally catch up with white women. In the bible of the New Right, George Gilder's "Wealth and Poverty," the 60 percent is just one of Mother Nature's constants like the speed of light or the force of gravity.

Men are programmed to provide for their families economically   5
while women are programmed to take care of their families emotionally and physically. As a result men put more effort into their jobs than women. The net result is a difference in work intensity that leads to that 40 percent gap in earnings. But there is no discrimination against women — only the biological facts of life.

The problem with this assertion is just that. It is an assertion   6
with no evidence for it other than the fact that white women have made 60 percent as much as men for a long period of time.

"Discrimination against women" is an easy answer but it also   7
has its problems as an adequate explanation. Why is discrimination against women not declining under the same social forces that are leading to a lessening of discrimination against minorities? In recent years women have made more use of the enforcement provisions of the Equal Employment Opportunities Commission and the courts than minorities. Why do the laws that prohibit discrimination against women and minorities work for minorities but not for women?

When men discriminate against women, they run into a prob-   8
lem. To discriminate against women is to discriminate against your own wife and to lower your own family income. To prevent women from working is to force men to work more.

When whites discriminate against blacks, they can at least think   9
that they are raising their own incomes. When men discriminate against women they have to know that they are lowering their own family income and increasing their own work effort.

While discrimination undoubtedly explains part of the male-female earnings differential, one has to believe that men are monumentally stupid or irrational to explain all of the earnings gap in terms of discrimination. There must be something else going on.

Back in 1939 it was possible to attribute the earnings gap to large differences in educational attainments. But the educational gap between men and women has been eliminated since World War II. It is no longer possible to use education as an explanation for the lower earnings of women. 11

Some observers have argued that women earn less money since they are less reliable workers who are more apt to leave the labor force. But it is difficult to maintain this position since women are less apt to quit one job to take another and as a result they tend to work as long, or longer, for any one employer. From any employer's perspective they are more reliable, not less reliable, than men. 12

Part of the answer is visible if you look at the lifetime earnings profile of men. Suppose that you were asked to predict which men in a group of 25-year-olds would become economically successful. At age 25 it is difficult to tell who will be economically successful and your predictions are apt to be highly inaccurate. 13

But suppose that you were asked to predict which men in a group of 35-year-olds would become economically successful. If you are successful at age 35, you are very likely to remain successful for the rest of your life. If you have not become economically successful by age 35, you are very unlikely to do so later. 14

The decade between 25 and 35 is when men either succeed or fail. It is the decade when lawyers become partners in the good firms, when business managers make it onto the "fast track," when academics get tenure at good universities, and when blue collar workers find the job opportunities that will lead to training opportunities and the skills that will generate high earnings. 15

If there is any one decade when it pays to work hard and to be consistently in the labor force, it is the decade between 25 and 35. For those who succeed, earnings will rise rapidly. For those who fail, earnings will remain flat for the rest of their lives. 16

But the decade between 25 and 35 is precisely the decade when women are most apt to leave the labor force or become part-time workers to have children. When they do, the current system of promotion and skill acquisition will extract an enormous lifetime price. 17

This leaves essentially two avenues for equalizing male and female earnings. 18

Families where women who wish to have successful careers, compete with men, and achieve the same earnings should alter their 19 family plans and have their children either before 25 or after 35. Or society can attempt to alter the existing promotion and skill acquisition system so that there is a longer time period in which both men and women can attempt to successfully enter the labor force.

Without some combination of these two factors, a substantial fraction of the male-female earnings differentials are apt to persist for the next 40 years, even if discrimination against women is eliminated.

Meanings and Values

1a. What is the author's point of view? (See Guide to Terms: *Point of View.*)

b. How could you best describe the tone of the selection? (Guide: *Style/Tone.*)

c. What, if anything, does the point of view have to do with the tone?

2. Is this selection best described as formal, informal, or familiar? Why? (Guide: *Essay.*)

3a. What is the central theme? (Guide: *Unity.*)

b. Do all parts of the selection flow into the theme, as tributaries into a river?

c. Does the essay have unity?

4. Does it seem to you that Thurow's reasoning is valid in paragraphs 8–9? Why, or why not?

5. Do you see any contradiction between the author's reasoning in paragraph 12 and his eventual conclusions in paragraphs 15–17? Explain.

Expository Techniques

1. How effectively do the first two paragraphs fulfill the three necessary functions of a good introduction? (Guide: *Introductions.*)

2. In which paragraph, or paragraphs, do we find the first minor use of the inductive process?

3a. Draw up a simple chart, showing the main inductive points and the paragraphs devoted to each point.

b. By what other term is this kind of induction sometimes known?

c. What appear to be the special limitations, if any, of this kind of induction?

4. A logical syllogism representing the author's reasoning in para-

graphs 15–17 would have as a major premise something like this: between the ages of twenty-five and thirty-five is the period when most people get into line for success, if they are to make it at all.

a.   What, then, would be his minor premise?

b.   From these two premises, what conclusion can logically be reached, completing the syllogism?

c.   Is this an inductive or a deductive process?

5.   Which other pattern of exposition already studied is apparent throughout this essay?

6a. Which of the standard techniques of closing are used in the last three paragraphs?

b.   How effectively are they used?

Diction and Vocabulary

1a. What are the distinctive characteristics, if any, of Thurow's style in diction or syntax? (Guide: *Style/Tone, Diction* and *Syntax.*)

b.   What justification can you see for this style?

2.   What reason, or reasons, can you see for the author's using a relatively simple vocabulary, with no "dictionary-type" words?

Suggestions for Writing and Discussion

1.   Discuss possible reasons why black and Hispanic women are doing better in relation to black and Hispanic men, respectively, than white women in relation to white men. Why does the same twenty-five to thirty-five explanation not apply to black and Hispanic women?

2.   Do you see any logic at all in the first two sentences of paragraph 5? If so, explain your view.

3.   Discuss — agreeing, disagreeing, or explaining — this statement from paragraph 14: "If you have not become economically successful by age 35, you are very unlikely to do so later."

4.   Would anything be gained by women having their families either before age twenty-five or after age thirty-five, as suggested in paragraph 19? Or do you think a several-year period away from their careers *any* time during their productive years would have the same effect? Explain.

5.   So, what *is* the answer to the pay discrepancy dilemma?

(NOTE: Suggestions for topics requiring development by INDUCTION and DEDUCTION are on page 336, at the end of this section.)

PETER FARB

PETER FARB (1929–1980) was born in New York and attended Vanderbilt University and Columbia University. Farb was a respected environmentalist and expert on the land and people of North and South America. His books include *Face of North America* (1963), *Man's Rise to Civilization as Shown by the Indians of North America* (1968), *Word Play: What Happens When People Talk* (1973), and (with George Armelagos) *Consuming Passions* (1980). Farb served as consultant to the Smithsonian Institution, as curator of American Indian Cultures at the Riverside Museum in New York City, and as visiting lecturer in English at Yale. He was a fellow of the American Association for the Advancement of Science and a member of numerous scientific societies.

In Other Words

This essay, a section of a chapter with the same title in *Word Play*, illustrates how inductive reasoning can lead to a generalization that in turn becomes the basis for a process of deduction. In the course of the essay Farb manages to cover a wide variety of topics — from "thinking" horses to elementary education — and to demonstrate their surprising but logical relationships.

Early in this century, a horse named Hans amazed the people of   1
Berlin by his extraordinary ability to perform rapid calculations in mathematics. After a problem was written on a blackboard placed in front of him, he promptly counted out the answer by tapping the low numbers with his right forefoot and multiples of ten with his left. Trickery was ruled out because Hans's owner, unlike owners of other performing animals, did not profit financially — and Hans even performed his feats whether or not the owner was present.

The psychologist O. Pfungst witnessed one of these performances and became convinced that there had to be a more logical explanation than the uncanny intelligence of a horse.

Because Hans performed only in the presence of an audience 2 that could see the blackboard and therefore knew the correct answer, Pfungst reasoned that the secret lay in observation of the audience rather than of the horse. He finally discovered that as soon as the problem was written on the blackboard, the audience bent forward very slightly in anticipation to watch Hans's forefeet. As slight as that movement was, Hans perceived it and took it as his signal to begin tapping. As his taps approached the correct number, the audience became tense with excitement and made almost imperceptible movements of the head — which signaled Hans to stop counting. The audience, simply by expecting Hans to stop when the correct number was reached, had actually told the animal when to stop. Pfungst clearly demonstrated that Hans's intelligence was nothing but a mechanical response to his audience, which unwittingly communicated the answer by its body language.

The "Clever Hans Phenomenon," as it has come to be known, 3 raises an interesting question. If a mere horse can detect unintentional and extraordinarily subtle body signals, might they not also be detected by human beings? Professional gamblers and con men have long been known for their skill in observing the body-language cues of their victims, but only recently has it been shown scientifically that all speakers constantly detect and interpret such cues also, even though they do not realize it.

An examination of television word games several years ago 4 revealed that contestants inadvertently gave their partners body-language signals that led to correct answers. In one such game, contestants had to elicit certain words from their partners, but they were permitted to give only brief verbal clues as to what the words might be. It turned out that sometimes the contestants also gave body signals that were much more informative than the verbal clues. In one case, a contestant was supposed to answer *sad* in response to his partner's verbal clue of *happy* — that is, the correct answer was a word opposite to the verbal clue. The partner giving the *happy* clue unconsciously used his body to indicate to his fellow contestant that an opposite word was needed. He did that by shifting his body and head very slightly to one side as he said *happy*, then to the other side in expectation of an opposite word.

Contestants on a television program are usually unsophisti-   5
cated about psychology and linguistics, but trained psychological
experimenters also unintentionally flash body signals which are
sometimes detected by the test subjects — and which may distort
the results of experiments. Hidden cameras have revealed that the
sex of the experimenter, for example, can influence the responses of
subjects. Even though the films showed that both male and female
experimenters carried out the experiments in the same way and
asked the same questions, the experimenters were very much aware
of their own sex in relation to the sex of the subjects. Male experimenters spent 16 per cent more time carrying out experiments
with female subjects than they did with male subjects; similarly,
female experimenters took 13 per cent longer to go through experiments with male subjects than they did with female subjects. The
cameras also revealed that chivalry is not dead in the psychological
experiment; male experimenters smiled about six times as often
with female subjects as they did with male subjects.

The important question, of course, is whether or not such   6
nonverbal communication influences the results of experiments.
The answer is that it often does. Psychologists who have watched
films made without the knowledge of either the experimenters or
the subjects could predict almost immediately which experimenters
would obtain results from their subjects that were in the direction of
the experimenters' own biases. Those experimenters who seemed
more dominant, personal, and relaxed during the first moments of
conversation with their subjects usually obtained the results that
they secretly hoped the experiments would yield. And they somehow communicated their secret hopes in a completely visual way,
regardless of what they said or their paralanguage when they
spoke. That was made clear when these films were shown to two
groups, one of which saw the films without hearing the sound track
while the other heard only the sound track without seeing the films.
The group that heard only the voices could not accurately predict
the experimenters' biases — but those who saw the films without
hearing the words immediately sensed whether or not the experimenters were communicating their biases.

A person who signals his expectations about a certain kind of   7
behavior is not aware that he is doing so — and usually he is
indignant when told that his experiment was biased — but the
subjects themselves confirm his bias by their performances. Such

bias in experiments has been shown to represent self-fulfilling prophecies. In other words, the experimenters' expectations about the results of the experiment actually result in those expectations coming true. That was demonstrated when each of twelve experimenters was given five rats bred from an identical strain of laboratory animals. Half of the experimenters were told that their rats could be expected to perform brilliantly because they had been bred especially for high intelligence and quickness in running through a maze. The others were told that their rats could be expected to perform very poorly because they had been bred for low intelligence. All the experimenters were then asked to teach their rats to run a maze.

Almost as soon as the rats were put into the maze it became 8 clear that those for which the experimenters had high expectations would prove to be the better performers. And the rats which were expected to perform badly did in fact perform very badly, even though they were bred from the identical strain as the excellent performers. Some of these poor performers did not even budge from their starting positions in the maze. The misleading prophecy about the behavior of the two groups of rats was fulfilled — simply because the two groups of experimenters unconsciously communicated their expectations to the animals. Those experimenters who anticipated high performance were friendlier to their animals than those who expected low performance; they handled their animals more, and they did so more gently. Clearly, the predictions of the experimenters were communicated to the rats in subtle and unintended ways — and the rats behaved accordingly.

Since animals such as laboratory rats and Clever Hans can 9 detect body-language cues, it is not surprising that human beings are just as perceptive in detecting visual signals about expectations for performance. It is a psychological truth that we are likely to speak to a person whom we expect to be unpleasant in such a way that we force him to act unpleasantly. But it has only recently become apparent that poor children — often black or Spanish-speaking — perform badly in school because that is what their teachers expect of them, and because the teachers manage to convey that expectation by both verbal and nonverbal channels. True to the teachers' prediction, the black and brown children probably will do poorly — not necessarily because children from minority groups are capable only of poor performance, but because poor performance has been expected of them. The first grade may be the place where teachers anticipate poor performances by children of certain racial, economic, and cultural backgrounds — and where the teachers actually teach these children how to fail.

Evidence of the way the "Clever Hans Phenomenon" works in many schools comes from a careful series of experiments by psychologist Robert Rosenthal and his co-workers at Harvard University. They received permission from a school south of San Francisco to give a series of tests to the children in the lower grades. The teachers were blatantly lied to. They were told that the test was a newly developed tool that could predict which children would be "spurters" and achieve high performance in the coming year. Actually, the experimenters administered a new kind of IQ test that the teachers were unlikely to have seen previously. After IQ scores were obtained, the experimenters selected the names of 20 percent of the children completely at random. Some of the selected children scored very high on the IQ test and others scored low, some were from middle-class families and others from lower-class. Then the teachers were lied to again. The experimenters said that the tests singled out this 20 per cent as the children who could be expected to make unusual intellectual gains in the coming year. The teachers were also cautioned not to discuss the test results with the pupils or their parents. Since the names of these children had been selected completely at random, any difference between them and the 80 per cent not designated as "spurters" was completely in the minds of the teachers.

All the children were given IQ tests again during that school year and once more the following year. The 20 per cent who had been called to the attention of their teachers did indeed turn in the high performances expected of them — in some cases dramatic increases of 25 points in IQ. The teachers' comments about these children also were revealing. The teachers considered them more happy, curious, and interesting than the other 80 per cent — and they predicted that they would be successes in life, a prophecy they had already started to fulfill. The experiment plainly showed that children who are expected to gain intellectually do gain and that their behavior improves as well.

The results of the experiment are clear — but the explanation for the results is not. It might be imagined that the teachers simply devoted more time to the children singled out for high expectations, but the study showed that was not so. Instead, the influence of the teachers upon these children apparently was much more subtle. What the teachers said to them, how and when it was said, the facial expressions, gestures, posture, perhaps even touch that accompanied their speech — some or all of these things must have communicated that the teachers expected improved performance from them. And when these children responded correctly, the teachers were quicker to praise them and also more lavish in their praise. Whatever the exact mechanism was, the effect upon the children who had been singled out was dramatic. They changed their ideas about themselves, their behavior, their motivation, and their learning capacities.

The lesson of the California experiment is that pupil performance does not depend so much upon a school's audio-visual equipment or new textbooks or enriching trips to museums as it does upon teachers whose body language communicates high expectations for the pupils — even if the teacher thinks she "knows" that a black, a Puerto Rican, a Mexican-American, or any other disadvantaged child is fated to do poorly in school. Apparently, remedial instruction in our schools is misdirected. It is needed more by the middle-class teachers than by the disadvantaged children. 13

Meanings and Values

1a. What generalizations does Farb arrive at in paragraph 3?

b. Can this be considered the central theme of the essay? (See Guide to Terms: *Unity*.)

c. If not, what is the central theme?

2. In your own words, define the "Clever Hans Phenomenon."

3. Where would you place this essay on an objective-to-subjective continuum? (Guide: *Objective/Subjective*.)

4. Are Farb's explanations of the behavior of TV contestants and of psychological experimenters convincing? Why, or why not?

5. Is the amount of evidence Farb supplies to support his conclusions appropriate for the subject and the purpose of the essay? If not, is more needed, or would even less have been satisfactory? Explain.

6. What does the example of the laboratory rats contribute to the reader's understanding of non-verbal behavior and its effects?

7. Is there something paradoxical about the behavior of the teachers as

reported in paragraph 9? If so, what is the paradox? (Guide: *Paradox.*)

8a.   The research on the effects of teachers' expectations on children's behavior involved lying to the subjects of the research. Do you think the lying makes the results of the research unreliable? Explain.

b.   In what ways does this research differ from that involving rats?

Expository Techniques

1a.   What process of reasoning is represented by Pfungst's study of Clever Hans?

b.   By paragraphs 1–3 of the essay?

c.   By paragraph 4? By paragraphs 5–6? 7–8? 9–13?

2a.   Are the discussions of each of the different topics in this essay clearly related to the central theme? (Guide: *Unity.*)

b.   If not, which sections of the essay damage its unity?

c.   What transitional devices does the author use to create coherence in the selection? (Guide: *Transitions* and *Coherence.*)

3a.   Why does Farb take up the topic of the effect of nonverbal behavior in the classroom *after* he discusses the other topics?

b.   Is there any logic behind the arrangement of the topics in this essay? Explain.

4.   At what points in the essay does the author take into account possible objections to his conclusions, and how does he answer them?

5.   How would this essay have to be changed to make it into an argument proposing changes in the way teachers deal with students? (Guide: *Argument.*)

Diction and Vocabulary

1a.   What is "body language" (par. 2)?

b.   What are "self-fulfilling prophecies" (par. 7)?

c.   If you do not know what "paralanguage" means, look up the prefix "para" in the dictionary and try to explain the use of the word in paragraph 6.

2a.   Identify some of the places in this essay where Farb makes use of qualifications and explain their functions. (Guide: *Qualification.*)

b.   What is the function of the rhetorical question in paragraph 3? (Guide: *Rhetorical Questions.*)

Suggestions for Writing and Discussion

1. If Farb is correct in his conclusions about the importance of teacher's expectations, what steps can we take to improve teaching? Be specific in your recommendations, and be ready to defend them.

2. In what situations other than those described in the essay can self-fulfilling prophecies affect us? Explain.

3. Does anything in your experience confirm what Farb has to say about either self-fulfilling prophecies or the importance of nonverbal communication? Describe your experiences in detail.

4. How much lying, if any, is justified in scientific experiments like those described in the essay? In medical experiments? Develop your answer into an essay.

5. Speculate on the long-term effects on the children whose elementary teachers are told, rightly or wrongly, that they are highly intelligent.

(NOTE: Suggestions for topics requiring development by INDUCTION and DEDUCTION follow.)

Writing Suggestions for Section 10
Induction and *Deduction*

Choose one of the following unformed topics and shape your central theme from it. This could express the view you prefer or an opposing view. Develop your composition primarily by use of induction, alone or in combination with deduction. Unless otherwise directed by your instructor, be completely objective and limit yourself to exposition, rather than engaging in argumentation.

1. Little League baseball (or the activities of 4-H clubs, Boy Scouts, Girl Scouts, etc.) as a molder of character.
2. Conformity as an expression of insecurity.
3. The display of *non*conformity as an expression of insecurity.
4. The status symbol as a motivator to success.
5. The liberal arts curriculum and its relevance to "real life."
6. Student opinion as the guide to better educational institutions.
7. College education as a prerequisite for worldly success.
8. The values of education, beyond dollars and cents.
9. Knowledge and its relation to wisdom.
10. The right of individuals to select the laws they obey.
11. Television commercials as a molder of morals.
12. The "other" side of one ecological problem.
13. The value of complete freedom from worry.
14. Decreased effectiveness of the home as an influence in adolescent development.
15. Raising mentally retarded children at home.

Using Patterns for *Argument*

Argument and exposition have many things in common. They both use the basic patterns of exposition; they share a concern for the audience; and they often deal with similar subjects, including social trends (expanding opportunities for women, the impact of video games); recent developments (the role of computers in business and school, medical treatment of the terminally ill); and issues of widespread concern (the quality of education, the effects of pollution). As a result, the study of argument is a logical companion to the study of exposition. Yet the two kinds of writing have very different purposes.

Expository writing shares information and ideas; it explores issues and explains problems. In exposition we select facts and ideas to give an accurate picture of a subject and arrange them as clearly as we can, emphasizing features likely to interest readers. To explain the importance of knowing how to use computers, for instance, an essay might provide examples of the rapidly expanding roles of computers in business, industry, education, and research; it might describe the uses of computers for personal budgeting, recordkeeping, and entertainment; and it might emphasize that more everyday tasks than we realize are already heavily dependent on computers.

Argumentative writing, however, has a different motivation. It asks readers to choose one side of an issue or take a particular action, whether it be to buy a product, vote for a candidate, or build a new highway. In argument we select facts and ideas that provide strong support for our point of view and arrange this evidence in the most logical and persuasive order, taking care to provide appropriate background information and to acknowledge and refute opposing points of view. The evidence we choose is determined to a great extent by the attitudes and needs of the people we are trying to convince. For example, suppose we want to argue successfully that a high school or college ought to give all students training in computer use. Our essay would need to provide examples of benefits to students that are great enough to justify the considerable expenses for equipment and staff. (Examples of greatly increased job opportunities and improved learning skills would make good evidence; discussions of how computers can be used for personal recordkeeping and managing household finances would not be likely to persuade school officials facing tight budgets.) And an effective essay would also answer possible objections to the proposal: Will only a limited number of students really benefit from computer training? Are computers developing so rapidly that only large businesses and specialized institutes can afford to provide up-to-date training?

At the heart of an argumentative essay is the opinion we want readers to share or the action we want them to take. In argument this central theme is called the *thesis* or *proposition* and is often expressed concisely in a *thesis statement* designed to alert readers to the point of the argument. Some writers like to arrive at a sharply focused thesis early in the process of composing and use it to guide the selection and arrangement of evidence. Others settle on a tentative ("working") thesis, which they revise as the essay takes shape. In either case, checking frequently to see that factual evidence and supporting ideas or arguments are clearly linked to the thesis is a good way for writers to make sure their finished essays are coherent, unified arguments.

The purpose of a simple argumentative essay often falls into one of three categories. Some essays ask readers to agree with a value judgment ("The present city government is corrupt and ineffective"). Others propose a specific action ("Money from the student activity fee at this college should be used to establish and staff a fitness program available to all students"). And still others advance an opinion quite different from that held by most people ("Contrary to what many people believe, investing in stocks and bonds is not just for the wealthy — it is for people who want to become wealthy, too"). In situations calling for more complex arguments, however, writers should feel free to combine these purposes as long as the relationship among them is made clear to the reader. In a complex argument, for instance, we might *first* show that the city government is inefficient and corrupt and *then* argue that it is better to change the city charter to eliminate the opportunities for the abuse of power than it is to try to vote a new party into office or to support a reform faction within the existing political "machine."

Another distinction is normally made between *logical argument* (usually called, simply, "argument") and *persuasive argument* (usually termed "persuasion".) Whereas logical argument appeals to reason, persuasive argument appeals to the emotions. The aim of both, however, is to convince, and they are nearly always blended into whatever mixture seems most likely to do the convincing. After all, reason and emotion are both important human elements — and we may have to persuade someone even to listen to our logic. The emphasis on one or the other, of course, should depend on the subject and the audience.

Some authorities make a slightly different distinction: they say we argue merely to get people to change their minds, and we use persuasion to get them to *do* something about it — for example, to vote a Republican ticket, not just agree with the party platform. But this view is not entirely inconsistent with the other. We can hardly expect to change a *mind* by emotional appeal, but we can hope to get someone to *act* because of it.

The choice of supporting evidence for an argument depends in part on the subject and in part on the audience and situation. There is a good deal of evidence to support the argument that industry should turn to labor-saving machines and new work arrangements to increase its competitiveness. Company executives looking for ways to increase profits are likely to find almost all of this evidence persuasive, but workers and union leaders worried about loss of jobs and cuts in wages will probably be harder to persuade. Writers addressing the second group would need to choose evidence to show that industrial robots and work rules calling for fewer people would lead to increased sales, not lower wages and fewer jobs. And if the changes might actually cause layoffs, writers would have to show that without the changes a company might be forced to shut down entirely, throwing everyone out of work.

Variety in evidence gives the writer a chance to present an argument fully and at the same time helps persuade readers. Examples, facts and figures, statements from authorities, personal experience or the experience of other people — all these can be valuable sources of support. The basic patterns of exposition, too, can be viewed as ways to support arguments. For instance, to persuade people to take sailing (hang-gliding, skin-diving) lessons, we might tell the story of the inexperienced sailor who almost drowned even though she was sailing in a "safe" boat on a small lake. Or we might combine this narrative with a discussion of how lack of knowledge causes sailing accidents, with a classification of the dangers facing beginning sailors, or with examples of things that can go wrong while sailing. Most writers choose to combine patterns on the grounds that variety helps convince readers, just as three pieces of evidence are more convincing than one — as long as all three point to the same conclusion.

All the expository patterns can also be used to arrange factual evidence and supporting ideas or arguments, though some patterns are more useful than others. Entire arguments structured as narratives are rare, except for stories designed to show what the world will be like if we do not change our present nuclear, military, or technological policies. But example, comparison and contrast, cause and effect, definition, and induction or deduction are frequently used to organize arguments. A series of *examples* can be an effective way of showing that a government social policy does not work and in fact hurts the people it is supposed to serve. *Cause and effect* can organize argument over who is to blame for a problem or over the possible consequences of a new program. *Comparison* and *Contrast* can guide choices among competing products, among ways of disposing of toxic waste, or among directions for national economic policy. *Definition* is helpful when a controversy hinges on the interpretation of a key term or when the meaning of an important word is itself the subject of disagreement. *Induction* and *deduction* are useful in argument because they provide the kind of careful, logical reasoning necessary to convince many readers, especially those who may at first have little sympathy for the writer's opinion.

An argument need not be restricted to a single pattern. The choice of a pattern or a combination of patterns depends on the subject, the specific purpose, and the kinds of evidence needed to convince the audience to which the essay is directed. Some arguments about complicated, significant issues make use of so many patterns that they can be called *complex arguments*.

In addition to using the patterns of exposition, most argumentative essays also arrange evidence according to its potential impact on the audience. Three of the most common arrangements are ascending order, refutation-proof, and con-pro. In *ascending order*, the strongest, most complex, or most emotionally moving evidence comes last, where it can build on the rest of the evidence in the essay and is likely to have the greatest impact on the reader. *Refutation-proof* acknowledges opposing points of view early in the essay and then goes on to show why the author's outlook is superior. *Con-pro* presents an opposing point of view and then refutes it, continuing until all opposition has been dealt with and all positive arguments voiced; this strategy is particularly useful when there is strong opposition to the writer's thesis. The strategies can be combined, of course, as in a refutation-proof essay that builds up to its strongest evidence.

Accuracy and fairness in argument are not only morally correct, they can also be a means of persuasion. Accuracy in the use of facts, figures, quotations, and references can encourage readers to trust what an author has to say. And writers who are able to acknowledge and refute opposing arguments fairly and without hostility add strength to their own arguments and may even win the respect of those who disagree with them.

But the most important elements of effective argument are careful choice of evidence and clear, logical reasoning. It is never possible to arrive at absolute proof — argument, after all, assumes that there are at least two sides to the matter under discussion — yet a carefully constructed case will convince many readers. At the same time, a flaw in logic can undermine an otherwise reasonable argument and destroy a reader's confidence in its conclusions. The introduction to Section 10, "Reasoning by Use of *Induction* and *Deduction*," discusses some important errors to avoid in reasoning or in choosing evidence. Here are some others:

— *Post hoc ergo propter hoc* ("After this therefore because of this") — Just because one thing happened *after* does not mean that the first event caused the second. In arguing without detailed supporting evidence that a recent drop in the crime rate is the result of a newly instituted anticrime policy, a writer might be committing this error because there are other equally plausible explanations: a drop in the unemployment rate, for example, or a reduction in the number of people in the fifteen to twenty-five age bracket, the segment of the population that is responsible for a high proportion of all crimes.

— *Begging the question* — A writer "begs the question" when he or she assumes the truth of something that is still to be proven. An argument that begins this way, "The recent, unjustified rise in utility rates should be reversed by the state legislature," assumes that the rise is "unjustified," though this important point needs to be proven.

— *Ignoring the question* — A writer may "ignore the question" by shifting attention away from the issue at hand to some loosely related or even irrelevant matter: for example, "Senator Jones's plan for encouraging new industries cannot be any good because in the past he has opposed tax cuts for corporations" (this approach shifts attention away from the merits of Senator Jones's proposal). A related problem is the *ad hominem* (toward the person) argument, which substitutes a personal attack for a discussion of the issue in question.

In composing argumentative essays, therefore, writers need to pay attention not only to what is necessary to convince an audience but also to the integrity of the evidence and arguments they advance in support of a thesis.

Sample Paragraph (Argument)

The issue stated briefly with a suggestion of the kind of arguments the state has advanced to justify the highway.

Once again the state is proposing to build a four-lane highway through Ilona Valley, from one end to the other, and on through the state forest to join up with I-5 beyond. The state claims this project will improve the quality of life in the valley. Valley residents argue that the State should not waste tax dollars on an uneconomical project that will adversely affect those who supplied the dollars in the first place. The Ilona Predisposition District

Thesis statement

has already marshalled most of the arguments against the project: (1) The road will cut a wide swath through some of the most productive farm land in the state. (2) One hundred fifty-nine residences and business places will be demolished. (3) The road will open up the valley to all the undesirable elements of the country at large, dooming its solid, law-abiding character. (4) Safety of children and old people will be continually threatened by increased traffic and speed. (5) The valley will be ruined aesthetically by litter and gas stations and junk-food drive-ins. (6) The road could be built further north with little community loss and far less expense (figures at hand). Valley residents hope the state will listen carefully to their arguments because they are worried about the kind of confrontation that might occur if the bulldozers turn up one day and start tearing up their land and homes.

Evidence and *supporting arguments*. (These six points will themselves need much more evidence, of course, in presenting the actual argument.)

Argument through Example

GEORGE F. WILL

> GEORGE F. WILL was born in 1941, in Champaign, Illinois. He was
> educated at Trinity College in Connecticut, Oxford University,
> and Princeton University. His syndicated column appears in over
> 350 newspapers, and he writes a biweekly column for *Newsweek*
> magazine. In 1977 he was awarded the Pulitzer Prize for distin-
> guished commentary. His columns have been collected in *The
> Pursuit of Happiness and Other Sobering Thoughts* (1979) and *The
> Pursuit of Virtue and Other Tory Notions* (1982). He has also pub-
> lished a book of political theory, *Statecraft as Soulcraft: What Gov-
> ernment Does* (1983).

No "Right" to Health

> This essay first appeared as a newspaper column in 1978 and was
> later reprinted in *The Pursuit of Virtue and Other Tory Notions*. Like
> many argumentative essays, it was written in response to a speci-
> fic situation: the public debate over national health insurance,
> which also prompted the statement from the Carter administra-
> tion cited in the essay. But the author also deals with a much
> broader question — the role of medical science in preserving
> health. In this selection Will uses examples as a primary means of
> developing his argument.

Human beings, unlike oysters, frequently reveal their emotions.
And they are prolific at discovering new "rights." Today they speak
often, and crossly, about their "right" to health. They are paying a
lot for medicine and are not getting all that they think they are
paying for, a guarantee to endless betterment. Their disappointment is rooted in mistaken inferences from a few spectacular medical achievements.

Twenty-five summers ago, many children were kept home   2
from theaters that were packed with peers watching Randolph Scott
cowboy movies. Many parents were afraid, and rightly so, of polio.
The Salk vaccine made summers safer, but that achievement has
given rise to unreasonable expectation based on the "polio paradigm." Many people assume that advances in public health have
generally resulted from a conquest of a disease by a new technology.
This is a misunderstanding of the social history of health.

When Shakespeare, Coke, Bacon and Drake were advancing   3
drama and poetry, jurisprudence, experimental science, navigation
and exploration, John Donne,[1] who was doing as much for poetry
and preaching, was being treated for fever by doctors who placed a
dead pigeon at his feet to draw "vapours" from his brain. Until this
century, medicine developed slowly, in a social setting in which
infant mortality was high, life expectancy was low even for those
who survived childhood, and diagnostic and therapeutic skills were
few. The sudden development of sophisticated medicine has coin-
cided, in fortunate societies, with sharp improvements in infant
survival and life expectancy, and undreamed-of freedom from
many diseases. As a result, medicine has been given undue credit
for mankind's betterment.

Many people believe that society's level of health depends   4
primarily on medical treatment of the sick. But the relationship
between increased investment in medicine and improvements in
health is tenuous. Behavior usually has more to do with how long
and healthily people live than does the soaring investment in medical treatments to restore health, or to slow its decline. Leon Kass of
the University of Chicago notes that other animals "instinctively eat
the right foods (when available) and act in such a way as to maintain
their naturally given state of health and vigor. Other animals do not
overeat, undersleep, knowingly ingest toxic substances, or permit
their bodies to fall into disuse through sloth, watching television
and riding in automobiles, transacting business or writing articles
about health." For humans, health must be nurtured by "taming
and moderating the admirable yet dangerous human desire to live
better than sows and squirrels." So in one way, it makes little more

---

[1]Major figures of the English Renaissance: William Shakespeare (1564–1616),
playwright; Edward Coke (1552–1634), judge and legal author; Francis Bacon (1561–
1626), politician, writer, and philosopher; Francis Drake (1540–1596), naval officer
and explorer; John Donne (1571–1631), poet and clergyman. — Eds.

sense to claim a right to health than to claim a right to wisdom or courage.

As Kass says, in an age that has cracked the genetic code, built kidney machines and performed organ transplants, the idea that prudence is the path to health seems banal. But there is much to be learned about the sociology of health, such as why some subgroups of the population are especially healthy. "If the incidence of each kind of cancer could be reduced to the level at which it occurs in the population in which its incidence is lowest, there would be 90 percent less cancer. Recent studies show that cancers of all sorts — not only cancers clearly correlated with smoking and drinking — occur less frequently among the clean-living Mormons and Seventh-Day Adventists."

Recent history illustrates the secondary importance of clinical medicine in improving public health. Eric Cassell of Cornell Medical College notes that in 1900 the death rate from tuberculosis was 200 per 100,000, and the rate declined to 20 per 100,000 by the 1950s, when the first effective anti-TB drugs became available. The decline was due primarily to better nutrition and less crowding. Typhoid became rare before effective drugs were available, thanks to chlorination of water and better sanitation and personal hygiene.

The decline of infant mortality occurred because of reduction of the diarrhea-pneumonia complex. This too was a result of social changes, not of preventive or therapeutic medications. Modern food packaging and distribution has done more than medicine against food-borne diseases. The swift decline of a soup company after reports of botulism demonstrated how much the mass media can do for public health. In the last five years, the death rate in the United States has undergone the sharpest decline since the advent of penicillin, primarily because of a reduction in heart diseases, owing to individual efforts at health maintenance.

A British writer, Robin Bates, contends that streptomycin may have accounted for only 3 percent of the reduction in tuberculosis deaths, and that medicine always concentrates on such a "3 percent solution." That is an understandable concentration for clinical medicine, but it is an unwise concentration for public policy, given the evidence that medical intervention has not been primarily responsible for the most substantial improvements in public health. But in an age when people are inventive and clamorous about "rights" and deny duties, they do not want to be told that health is primarily their duty, not medicine's or the government's responsibility.

Such an age is ripe for socialized medicine, which broadens 9 access to what Kass calls "hospital-centered, highly technological, disease-oriented, therapy-centered medical care." Recently a Carter Administration spokesman, advocating national health insurance, declared: "The highest priority must be to guarantee to all the American people a quality of health care and a standard of health that our worldwide lead in medicine currently guarantees only to an affluent minority . . ." Confused thinking promotes dubious policy: health is the product of medicine, so by controlling the distribution of medicine, government can "guarantee" a "standard of health" commensurate with the sophistication of medical technology.

But national health insurance might do harm by reinforcing 10 public acceptance of the "no-fault principle" that discounts personal responsibility for health. A better way to begin improving health insurance might be to institutionalize inducements to prudence. Payments for treatment of particular diseases could be reduced when patients discontinue behavior causatively linked to the diseases.

Human beings, unlike oysters, are organisms that make 11 choices. Today, much illness is willful, in the sense that it results from foolish living habits of people who have a duty to know better. And today, insurance plans spread the burden of paying for illness: the prudent and dutiful are paying heavily for the irresponsible. That is a wrong which should preoccupy people who are eager to establish "rights" where health is concerned.

Meanings and Values

1a. What widely held belief does Will argue against in this essay?

b. What belief does he want his readers to substitute for the one he argues against?

c. Is this new belief the same as the thesis of the essay? (see Guide to Terms: *Thesis.*)

d. If not, what is the thesis?

2a. What are the "Salk vaccine" and the "polio paradigm" (par. 2)? (Hint: You may wish to look them up in the dictionary under "poliomyelitis" and "Salk.")

b.   How could the "polio paradigm" have contributed to the "mis-understanding" (par. 2) Will discusses?

c.   If you can, name some other medical advances that may have contributed to the misunderstanding.

3a. When the author speaks of "mistaken inferences from a few spec-tacular medical achievements" (par. 1), to what kind of faulty logic is he referring? (See introduction to Section 10, "Reasoning by Use of *Induction* and *Deduction.*")

b.   In using the "polio paradigm" as a basis for their expectations, what form of reasoning are people using?

4.   What does the author mean when he says, "it makes little more sense to claim a right to health than to claim a right to wisdom or courage" (par. 4)?

5a. Does the author present enough evidence in the body of this essay to justify his objections to national health insurance (pars. 9–11)? Explain.

b.   Does he want his suggestions for a new approach to health insur-ance (par. 10) to be taken seriously?

c.   If so, are they practical? If not, why would he mention them?

6a. Do you find Will's argument persuasive? (Guide: *Evaluation.*)

b.   If so, why? (Was it because of the evidence presented or because your experience supports the author's argument?)

c.   If not, why? (Is it because his argument is flawed or because you know of strong contrary evidence that he does not take into account?)

Techniques of Argument

1a. What possible objections to the essay's thesis does the author ac-knowledge?

b.   What strategies are used to refute them? (Guide: *Refutation.*)

2.   How many different kinds of evidence does the author use? (Guide: *Argument.*)

3.   What purpose is served by the examples of major figures of the English Renaissance in paragraph 3?

4a. Is the thesis of this essay announced in a single thesis statement? If so, where is it? (Guide: *Thesis.*)

b.   If not, how is the thesis made plain to the reader?

5a. Is the evidence in this essay arranged in ascending order, as refuta-tion-proof, as con-pro, or in some combination of these patterns? Be specific.

b. Taking into account the subject of the essay and the author's purpose, explain why he might have chosen to arrange the essay as he did, and indicate whether you think the arrangement is successful. (Guide: *Evaluation.*)

6a. In how many paragraphs does the author use a topic sentence to emphasize an important stage in the argument? (Remember: The topic sentence is often, but not always, the first sentence in the paragraph.) (Guide: *Unity.*)

b. How many paragraphs consist simply of examples designed to support a generalization in a preceding paragraph?

Diction and Vocabulary

1. What different meanings does the word "right" have in the course of the essay, and how does the author use these changes in meaning to convey his theme?

2. What are the connotations of "Randolph Scott cowboy movies" (par. 2), and why would the author choose to indicate what kind of movies were playing in the theaters? (Guide: *Connotation/Denotation.*)

3a. What use is made of qualification in those passages where the author disagrees with people who see a strong link between medical science and the general health of society? (Guide: *Qualification.*)

b. What use does the author make of qualification in advancing his own arguments?

4a. How many sentences in the essay begin with the word "but," and what reason might the author have had for beginning them this way?

b. Are these sentences effective, or would some other strategy be more effective? Be specific.

5. If you are unfamiliar with any of the following words, consult your dictionary as necessary: paradigm (par. 2); jurisprudence, therapeutic (3); tenuous (4); banal (5); clinical (6); botulism (7); clamorous (8); commensurate (9); inducements (10).

Suggestions for Writing and Discussion

1. Medical costs have been rising rapidly in the last decade. Suggest ways of cutting medical costs without lowering the quality of health care and defend your proposals against possible objections.

2. If you believed before reading this essay that "advances in public health have generally resulted from a conquest of a disease by a new

technology" (par. 2), what experiences might have contributed to your belief?

3. Argue for or against a program of national health insurance or socialized medicine. Take what this essay says into account, but do not assume that the audience you are addressing knows the essay or the arguments it presents.

4. If health is part of our duty as individuals, what things can we do to improve our own health? To improve the health of others in our community?

(NOTE: Suggestions for topics requiring development by ARGUMENT are on page 406 at the end of this section.)

Argument through Cause and Effect

CARL T. ROWAN

CARL T. ROWAN was born in 1925 in Ravenscroft, Tennessee. He
received a B.A. from Oberlin College and an M.A. from the
University of Minnesota. He has been a reporter for the *Minneapolis Tribune*, an official in the State Department, U.S. ambassador to
Finland, director of the United States Information Agency, and
columnist for the *Chicago Sun-Times*. His syndicated column
appears in newspapers throughout the country, and he is a
regular panelist and commentator on national radio and television public affairs shows. His books include *South of Freedom*
(1952), *The Pitiful and the Proud* (1956), *Go South to Sorrow* (1957),
Wait Till Next Year: The Life Story of Jackie Robinson (1960), and *Just
Between Us Blacks* (1974).

The NCAA's Hypocrisy

"The NCAA's Hypocrisy," first published as a newspaper column, illustrates how useful the cause/effect pattern can be in an
essay dealing with a problem and a proposed solution. While
Rowan's opinion about the rules for athletic eligibility in college
may not convince everyone, his view is an important contribution
to a controversy that is likely to continue for some time.

The National Collegiate Athletic Association and the American   1
Council on Education have been rocked by a string of scandals
involving illegal recruiting and other irregularities in college sports.
The educators have been especially stung by charges that they use
athletes to fill stadiums, give the school national publicity, rake in
money and then throw the athletes out into the world with no
usable education. (The University of Georgia, of Herschel Walker

fame, has admitted many black athletes since 1971, but has graduated only six.)

Now the NCAA and ACE have come up with the pretense that they are preventing future scandals by laying tighter academic requirements on students seeking admission. The NCAA has approved "Proposition 48," which requires that any high school graduate wishing to compete in athletics in his freshman year of college must have a 2.0 average (on a 4.0 scale) while taking a "core curriculum" of three years of English, two of math, two of social studies and two of science. I approve. But the NCAA and ACE blunder in adding the requirement that, to be eligible for sports, the graduate must score at least 700 on the SAT (Scholastic Aptitude Test) or at least 15 on the ACT (American Collegiate Test). The advocates of this requirement surely knew they were effectively barring thousands of minority and poor white athletes from competition.

Aside from cultural biases and the reality that high school grades offer a far more accurate gauge of a black youngster's potential than do SAT and ACT exams, NCAA leaders surely know that kids from poor families score much lower on those tests than do the children of the affluent. The implication in Proposition 48 is that youngsters who don't score above 700 on the SAT or 15 on the ACT are virtually uneducable — or certainly will become an embarrassment to the university if allowed to participate in sports as freshmen. This is nonsense. More than half the students enrolling in predominantly black colleges score below 700 on the SAT and 15 on the ACT, but the great majority of them are learning, graduating and making significant contributions to society.

The scandalous results with regard to black athletes at the big Division I NCAA schools reflect the simple reality that in too many cases no real academic help was given. Too often, no one has given a damn whether the athlete learned anything. Proposition 48 will be a fraud until this changes.

The hypocrisy of Proposition 48 is manifest in the fact that the colleges want to mandate what high schools must teach athletes to make them eligible for freshman college competition, but the NCAA rejected Proposition 57, which would have required a specific grade point average for a student to *remain* eligible for athletic competition. The colleges chose to leave the eligibility standard at completion of a certain number of credit hours — which leaves the door open to all kinds of corner-cutting and fancy games with "nothing" courses to keep prize pieces of beef on the gridiron and basketball court. The scandals will continue.

Meanings and Values

1a. What is the problem Rowan identifies in paragraph 1?

  b. What do the actions of the NCAA and the ACE imply about the cause of the problem?

  c. What does Rowan believe is the real cause of the problem?

2a. To what extent does Rowan agree with the requirements set forth by the NCAA and ACE?

  b. What negative effects does he believe the recent actions of the NCAA and ACE will have?

  c. What alternative solution is implied in paragraph 5?

3. Does Rowan object to the actions of the NCAA and ACE primarily because they will affect blacks? If not, whom does he believe the actions will affect?

4. How would you describe the tone of this essay? (See Guide to Terms: *Style/Tone.*)

Techniques of Argument

1a. Is the thesis of this essay stated directly? If so, where? (Guide: *Thesis.*)

  b. If not, state the implied thesis in your own words.

2a. Does the author acknowledge opposing points of view? If so, where? (Guide: *Refutation.*)

  b. If not, does his failure to deal directly with the opposition weaken the argument? (Guide: *Evaluation.*)

3a. What evidence is presented in the essay to indicate that the problem it discusses is both real and serious?

  b. Is the evidence sufficient?

4a. Do the arguments and evidence in the essay appeal primarily to reason or to emotion? (Guide: *Argument.*)

  b. Would the essay have been more effective if the author had placed greater emphasis on emotion (or logic)? Explain.

Diction and Vocabulary

1. Rowan uses words like "pretense" (par. 2), "nonsense" (par. 3), and "hypocrisy" (par. 5) to refer to the position taken by the NCAA and ACE. Considering the purpose of the essay, is this diction appropriate? (Guide: *Diction, Evaluation.*)

2. To what extent does the diction of this essay contribute to the tone? Be specific. (Guide: *Style/Tone.*)

3. Why does the author refer to student athletes as "prize pieces of beef" (par. 5)?

Suggestions for Writing and Discussion

1. In your experience, are athletes held to the same academic standards as other students? If not, should they be? Explain and support your opinion.

2. In view of the tremendous popularity of college sports, are any actions of the NCAA or a similar organization likely to help prevent scandals? What actions might be taken to prevent future problems of the kind Rowan discusses in his essay?

3. Are SATs, ACTs, or similar tests fair measures of ability and achievement? Are other measures (such as grades) as good or better?

(NOTE: Suggestions for topics requiring development by ARGUMENT are on page 406 at the end of this section.)

Argument through Comparison and Contrast

CARL SAGAN

CARL SAGAN, born in New York City in 1934, is a noted astrono-
mer, educator, and author. He attended the University of Chicago, where he received a Ph.D. in 1960. He has taught and served
as visiting professor at various universities in this country and in
England, and has been on the faculty of Cornell University since
1968. Sagan also has been a member of various distinguished
advisory groups, such as NASA and the National Academy of
Sciences. He has served on the council for the Smithsonian Institution and been a lecturer for the Apollo flight crews. Sagan has
written several books, including *Other Worlds* (1975); *Dragons of
Eden* (1977), for which he won the Pulitzer Prize in 1978; *Broca's
Brain* (1979); and *Cosmos* (1980), a best-seller based on Sagan's
popular series on public television in 1979–1980.

In Defense of Robots

This essay, taken from *Broca's Brain*, shows how comparison and
contrast can provide evidence for an argument as well as an
overall organization. Although some of the innovations Sagan
predicts in this essay are hard to visualize, the rapid development
of technology may bring them about faster than we expect.

> Thou com'st in such a questionable shape
> That I will speak to thee . . .
>
> William Shakespeare,
> *Hamlet*, Act I, Scene 4

The word "robot," first introduced by the Czech writer Karel Čapek, 1
is derived from the Slavic root for "worker." But it signifies a
machine rather than a human worker. Robots, especially robots in
space, have often received derogatory notices in the press. We read
that a human being was necessary to make the terminal landing

adjustments on Apollo 11, without which the first manned lunar landing would have ended in disaster; that a mobile robot on the Martian surface could never be as clever as astronauts in selecting samples to be returned to Earth-bound geologists; and that machines could never have repaired, as men did, the Skylab sunshade, so vital for the continuance of the Skylab mission.

But all these comparisons turn out, naturally enough, to have been written by humans. I wonder if a small self-congratulatory element, a whiff of human chauvinism, has not crept into these judgments. Just as whites can sometimes detect racism and men can occasionally discern sexism, I wonder whether we cannot here glimpse some comparable affliction of the human spirit — a disease that as yet has no name. The word "anthropocentrism" does not mean quite the same thing. The word "humanism" has been preempted by other and more benign activities of our kind. From the analogy with sexism and racism I suppose the name for this malady is "speciesism" — the prejudice that there are no beings so fine, so capable, so reliable as human beings. 2

This is a prejudice because it is, at the very least, a prejudgment, a conclusion drawn before all the facts are in. Such comparisons of men and machines in space are comparisons of smart men and dumb machines. We have not asked what sorts of machines could have been built for the $30-or-so billion that the Apollo and Skylab missions cost. 3

Each human being is a superbly constructed, astonishingly compact, self-ambulatory computer — capable on occasion of independent decision making and real control of his or her environment. And, as the old joke goes, these computers can be constructed by unskilled labor. But there are serious limitations to employing human beings in certain environments. Without a great deal of protection, human beings would be inconvenienced on the ocean floor, the surface of Venus, the deep interior of Jupiter, or even on long space missions. Perhaps the only interesting results of Skylab that could not have been obtained by machines is that human beings in space for a period of months undergo a serious loss of bone calcium and phosphorus — which seems to imply that human beings may be incapacitated under 0 g for missions of six to nine months or longer. But the minimum interplanetary voyages have characteristic times of a year or two. Because we value human beings highly, we 4 are reluctant to send them on very risky missions. If we do send human beings to exotic environments, we must also send along their food, their air, their water, amenities for entertainment and waste recycling, and companions. By comparison, machines require no elaborate life-support systems, no entertainment, no companionship, and we do not yet feel any strong ethical prohibitions against sending machines on one-way, or suicide, missions.

Certainly, for simple missions, machines have proved themselves many times over. Unmanned vehicles have performed the first photography of the whole Earth and of the far side of the Moon; the first landings on the Moon, Mars and Venus; and the first thorough orbital reconnaissance of another planet, in the Mariner 9 and Viking missions to Mars. Here on Earth it is increasingly common for high-technology manufacturing — for example, chemical and pharmaceutical plants — to be performed largely or entirely under computer control. In all these activities machines are able, to some extent, to sense errors, to correct mistakes, to alert human controllers some great distance away about perceived problems.

The powerful abilities of computing machines to do arithmetic — hundreds of millions of times faster than unaided human beings — are legendary. But what about really difficult matters? Can machines in any sense think through a new problem? Can they make discussions of the branched-contingency tree variety which we think of as characteristically human? (That is, I ask Question 1; if the answer is A, I ask question 2; but if the answer is B, I ask Question 3; and so on.) Some decades ago the English mathematician A. M. Turing described what would be necessary for him to believe in machine intelligence. The condition was simply that he could be in teletype communication with a machine and be unable to tell that it was not a human being. Turing imagined a conversation between a man and a machine of the following quality:

INTERROGATOR: In the first line of your sonnet which reads "Shall I compare thee to a Summer's day,"[1] would not "a Spring day" do as well or better?

WITNESS: It wouldn't scan.

INTERROGATOR: How about "a Winter's day"? That would scan all right.

[1] The opening line of William Shakespeare's Sonnet 18. — EDS.

WITNESS: Yes, but nobody wants to be compared to a Winter's day.
INTERROGATOR: Would you say Mr. Pickwick[2] reminded you of Christmas?
WITNESS: In a way.
INTERROGATOR: Yet Christmas is a Winter's day, and I do not think Mr. Pickwick would mind the comparison.
WITNESS: I don't think you're serious. By a Winter's day one means a typical Winter's day, rather than a special one like Christmas.

No device of this sophistication has yet been built, although I am not sure how many humans would pass Turing's human test. But the amount of effort and money put into artificial intelligence has been quite limited, and there are only about a half-dozen major centers of such activity in the world. . . .

[One] sign of the intellectual accomplishments of machines is in games. Even exceptionally simple computers — those that can be wired by a bright ten-year-old — can be programmed to play perfect tic-tac-toe. Some computers can play world-class checkers. Chess is of course a much more complicated game than tic-tac-toe or checkers. Here programming a machine to win is more difficult, and novel strategies have been used, including several rather successful attempts to have a computer learn from its own experience in playing previous chess games. Computers can learn, for example, empirically the rule that it is better in the beginning game to control the center of the chessboard than the periphery. The ten best chess players in the world still have nothing to fear from any present computer. But the situation is changing. Recently a computer for the first time did well enough to enter the Minnesota State Chess Open. This may be the first time that a non-human has entered a major sporting event on the planet Earth (and I cannot help but wonder if robot golfers and designated hitters may be attempted sometime in the next decade, to say nothing of dolphins in free-style competition). The computer did not win the Chess Open, but this is the first time one has done well enough to enter such a competition. Chess-playing computers are improving extremely rapidly.

I have heard of machines demeaned (often with a just audible sigh of relief) for the fact that chess is an area where human beings are still superior. This reminds me very much of the old joke in

[2]The main character in Charles Dickens's novel *The Posthumous Papers of the Pickwick Club.* — EDS.

which a stranger remarks with wonder on the accomplishments of a checker-playing dog. The dog's owner replies, "Oh, it's not all that remarkable. He loses two games out of three." A machine that plays chess in the middle range of human expertise is a very capable machine; even if there are thousands of better human chess players, there are millions who are worse. To play chess requires strategy, foresight, analytical powers, and the ability to cross-correlate large numbers of variables and to learn from experience. These are excellent qualities in those whose job it is to discover and explore, as well as those who watch the baby and walk the dog.

With this as a more or less representative set of examples of the state of development of machine intelligence, I think it is clear that a major effort over the next decade could produce much more sophisticated examples. This is also the opinion of most of the workers in machine intelligence.

In thinking about this next generation of machine intelligence, it is important to distinguish between self-controlled and remotely controlled robots. A self-controlled robot has its intelligence within it; a remotely controlled robot has its intelligence at some other place, and its successful operation depends upon close communication between its central computer and itself. There are, of course, intermediate cases where the machine may be partly self-activated and partly remotely controlled. It is this mix of remote and *in situ* control that seems to offer the highest efficiency for the near future.

For example, we can imagine a machine designed for the mining of the ocean floor. There are enormous quantities of manganese nodules littering the abyssal depths. They were once thought to have been produced by meteorite infall on Earth, but are now believed to be formed occasionally in vast manganese fountains produced by the internal tectonic activity of the Earth. Many other scarce and industrially valuable minerals are likewise to be found on the deep ocean bottom. We have the capability today to design devices that systematically swim over or crawl upon the ocean floor; that are able to perform spectrometric and other chemical examinations of the surface material; that can automatically radio back to shop or land all findings; and that can mark the locales of especially valuable deposits — for example, by low-frequency radio-homing devices. The radio beacon will then direct great mining machines to the appropriate locales. The present state of the art in deep-sea submersibles and in spacecraft environmental sensors is clearly compatible with the development of such devices. Similar remarks can be made for off-shore oil drilling, for coal and other subterranean mineral mining, and so on. The likely economic returns from such devices would pay not only for their development, but for the entire space program many times over.

When the machines are faced with particularly difficult situations, they can be programmed to recognize that the situations are beyond their abilities and to inquire of human operators — working in safe and pleasant environments — what to do next. The examples just given are of devices that are largely self-controlled. The reverse also is possible, and a great deal of very preliminary work along these lines has been performed in the remote handling of highly radioactive materials in laboratories of the U.S. Department of Energy. Here I imagine a human being who is connected by radio link with a mobile machine. The operator is in Manila, say; the machine in the Mindanao Deep. The operator is attached to an array of electronic relays, which transmits and amplifies his movements to the machine and which can, conversely, carry what the machine finds back to his senses. So when the operator turns his head to the left, the television cameras on the machine turn left, and the operator sees on a great hemispherical television screen around him the scene the machine's searchlights and cameras have revealed. When the operator in Manila takes a few strides forward in his wired suit, the machine in the abyssal depths ambles a few feet forward. When the operator reaches out his hand, the mechanical arm of the machine likewise extends itself; and the precision of the man/ machine interaction is such that precise manipulation of material at the ocean bottom by the machine's fingers is possible. With such devices, human beings can enter environments otherwise closed to them forever.

In the exploration of Mars, unmanned vehicles have already soft-landed, and only a little further in the future they will roam about the surface of the Red Planet, as some now do on the Moon. We are not ready for a manned mission to Mars. Some of us are concerned about such missions because of the dangers of carrying terrestrial microbes to Mars, and Martian microbes, if they exist, to Earth, but also because of their enormous expense. The Viking landers deposited on Mars in the summer of 1976 have a very interesting array of sensors and scientific instruments, which are the extension of human senses to an alien environment.

The obvious post-Viking device for Martian exploration, one 16
which takes advantage of the Viking technology, is a Viking Rover
in which the equivalent of an entire Viking spacecraft, but with
considerably improved science, is put on wheels or tractor treads
and permitted to rove slowly over the Martian landscape. But now
we come to a new problem, one that is never encountered in
machine operation on the Earth's surface. Although Mars is the
second closest planet, it is so far from the Earth that the light travel
time becomes significant. At a typical relative position of Mars and
the Earth, the planet is 20 light-minutes away. Thus, if the
spacecraft were confronted with a steep incline, it might send a
message of inquiry back to Earth. Forty minutes later the response
would arrive saying something like "For heaven's sake, stand dead
still." But by then, of course, an unsophisticated machine would
have tumbled into the gully. Consequently, any Martian Rover
requires slope and roughness sensors. Fortunately, these are readily available and are even seen in some children's toys. When confronted with a precipitous slope or large boulder, the spacecraft
would either stop until receiving instructions from the Earth in
response to its query (and televised picture of the terrain), or back
off and start in another and safer direction.

Much more elaborate contingency decision networks can be 17
built into the onboard computers of spacecraft of the 1980s. For
more remote objectives, to be explored further in the future, we can
imagine human controllers in orbit around the target planet, or on
one of its moons. In the exploration of Jupiter, for example, I can
imagine the operators on a small moon outside the fierce Jovian
radiation belts, controlling with only a few seconds' delay the responses of a spacecraft floating in the dense Jovian clouds.

Human beings on Earth can also be in such an interaction loop, 18
if they are willing to spend some time on the enterprise. If every
decision in Martian exploration must be fed through a human con-
troller on Earth, the Rover can traverse only a few feet an hour. But
the lifetimes of such Rovers are so long that a few feet an hour
represents a perfectly respectable rate of progress. However, as we
imagine expeditions into the farthest reaches of the solar system —
and ultimately to the stars — it is clear that self-controlled machine
intelligence will assume heavier burdens of responsibility.

In the development of such machines we find a kind of conver- 19
gent evolution. Viking is, in a curious sense, like some great out-

sized, clumsily constructed insect. It is not yet ambulatory, and it is certainly incapable of self-reproduction. But it has an exoskeleton, it has a wide range of insectlike sensory organs, and it is about as intelligent as a dragonfly. But Viking has an advantage that insects do not: it can, on occasion, by inquiring of its controllers on Earth, assume the intelligence of a human being — the controllers are able to reprogram the Viking computer on the basis of decisions they make.

As the field of machine intelligence advances and as increasingly distant objects in the solar system become accessible to exploration, we will see the development of increasingly sophisticated onboard computers, slowly climbing the phylogenetic tree from insect intelligence to crocodile intelligence to squirrel intelligence and — in the not very remote future, I think — to dog intelligence. Any flight to the outer solar system must have a computer capable of determining whether it is working properly. There is no possibility of sending to the Earth for a repairman. The machine must be able to sense when it is sick and skillfully doctor its own illnesses. A computer is needed that is able either to fix or replace failed computer, sensor or structural components. Such a computer, which has been called STAR (self-testing and repairing computer), is on the threshold of development. It employs redundant components, as biology does — we have two lungs and two kidneys partly because each is protection against failure of the other. But a computer can be much more redundant than a human being, who has, for example, but one head and one heart.

Because of the weight premium on deep space exploratory ventures, there will be strong pressures for continued miniaturization of intelligent machines. It is clear that remarkable miniaturization has already occurred: vacuum tubes have been replaced by transistors, wired circuits by printed circuit boards, and entire computer systems by silicon-chip microcircuitry. Today a circuit that used to occupy much of a 1930 radio set can be printed on the tip of a pin. If intelligent machines for terrestrial mining and space exploratory applications are pursued, the time cannot be far off when household and other domestic robots will become commercially feasible. Unlike the classical anthropoid robots of science fiction, there is no reason for such machines to look any more human than a vacuum cleaner does. They will be specialized for their functions. But there are many common tasks, ranging from bartending to floor washing, that involve a very limited array of intellectual capabilities, albeit substantial stamina and patience. All-purpose ambulatory household robots, which perform domestic functions as well as a proper nineteenth-century English butler, are probably many decades off. But more specialized machines, each adapted to a specific household function, are probably already on the horizon.

It is possible to imagine many other civic tasks and essential functions of everyday life carried out by intelligent machines. By the early 1970s, garbage collectors in Anchorage, Alaska, and other cities won wage settlements guaranteeing them salaries of about $20,000 per annum. It is possible that the economic pressures alone may make a persuasive case for the development of automated garbage-collecting machines. For the development of domestic and civic robots to be a general civic good, the effective re-employment of those human beings displaced by the robots must, of course, be arranged; but over a human generation that should not be too difficult — particularly if there are enlightened educational reforms. Human beings enjoy learning.

We appear to be on the verge of developing a wide variety of intelligent machines capable of performing tasks too dangerous, too expensive, too onerous or too boring for human beings. The development of such machines is, in my mind, one of the few legitimate "spinoffs" of the space program. The efficient exploitation of energy in agriculture — upon which our survival as a species depends — may even be contingent on the development of such machines. The main obstacle seems to be a very human problem, the quiet feeling that comes stealthily and unbidden, and argues that there is something threatening or "inhuman" about machines performing certain tasks as well as or better than human beings; or a sense of loathing for creatures made of silicon and germanium rather than proteins and nucleic acids. But in many respects our survival as a species depends on our transcending such primitive chauvinisms. In part, our adjustment to intelligent machines is a matter of acclimatization. There are already cardiac pacemakers that can sense the beat of the human heart; only when there is the slightest hint of fibrillation does the pacemaker stimulate the heart. This is a mild but very useful sort of machine intelligence. I cannot imagine the wearer of this device resenting its intelligence. I think in a relatively short period of time there will be a very similar sort of acceptance for much more intelligent and sophisticated machines.

There is nothing inhuman about an intelligent machine; it is indeed an expression of those superb intellectual capabilities that only human beings, of all the creatures on our planet, now possess.

Meanings and Values

1a. In what ways does Sagan consider robots superior to human beings?

b. In what ways does he consider humans superior?

2. State the purpose of this essay in your own words. If you believe it has more than one purpose, indicate this in your statement. (See Guide to Terms: *Purpose.*)

3a. The title of this essay suggests a formal, legal "defense." Against what accusations is Sagan defending robots? Be specific.

b. What standard techniques of refutation does he use to deal with these accusations? (Guide: *Refutation.*)

4a. When the author says, "Each human being is a superbly constructed, astonishingly compact, self-ambulatory computer — capable on occasion of independent decision making and real control of his or her environment" (par. 4), is he being ironic? Is this statement a paradox? (Guide: *Irony* and *Paradox.*)

b. What is the purpose of this statement?

5a. At what points in the essay does the author use humor, and for what reasons does he use it?

b. Is the overall tone of the essay humorous or serious? (Guide: *Style/Tone.*)

6. Some paragraphs in this essay present so much information that they seem expository in aim. Identify several of these paragraphs and indicate what they contribute to the overall argumentative purpose of the essay. (Guide: *Unity.*)

7. If you have read the Jastrow essay in Section 3, compare his view of computer intelligence to Sagan's.

Techniques of Argument

1a. Does the opening of this essay make clear the controversy the author is addressing?

b. Does it announce his stand on the controversy? How?

c. Is the opening likely to get a general reader interested in the topic?

d. If not, how might the author go about gaining the attention and interest of a general audience? (Guide: *Introductions.*)

2a.   The basic pattern of this essay is a comparison of human beings and robots. Where and how does the author announce this strategy to the reader?

 b.   At what points in the course of the essay is the reader reminded of the strategy?

 c.   In which paragraphs of the essay is the comparison strategy explicit? Implicit? Be specific.

3a.   In the essay the author uses dialogue — a narrative technique — as evidence. What does the essay gain from this unusual kind of evidence?

 b.   Can this dialogue be considered a form of personification? Why, or why not? (Guide: *Figures of Speech.*)

4a.   What role is played by the definition at the end of paragraph 2?

 b.   What other definitions are presented in the essay, and what do they contribute to the argument?

5a.   Are the evidence and supporting arguments in this essay arranged in ascending order, as refutation-proof, as con-pro, or in some combination of these?

 b.   Make a rough outline of the essay in order to explain its arrangement.

6a.   Could some of the long paragraphs in this essay be omitted without destroying the logic of the argument? If so, which ones?

 b.   Would anything be lost by omitting these paragraphs?

7.   What expository patterns other than comparison and definition are used in this essay? Be specific.

8a.   Are paragraphs 19 and 20 designed to appeal to a reader's emotions or reason?

 b.   Is the humor in paragraphs 4, 9, 10, and 16 designed to appeal to reason or the emotions? (Note: The appeal in each paragraph may be different, and humor can be both logical and emotional at the same time.)

Diction and Vocabulary

1.   Identify and explain the function of the parallel structures in paragraphs 1, 4, 5, and 10. (Guide: *Parallel Structure.*)

2a.   Did you understand the allusions in paragraph 7 without having to read the footnote? If not, did the footnote help you understand the allusions? (Guide: *Figures of Speech.*)

 b.   Does Sagan assume that his readers will be able to understand the dialogue? (Remember, he says, "I am not sure how many humans would pass Turing's human test" — par. 8.)

c. If not, why did he bother to include it in the essay and risk irritating his readers by asking them to read something they might not understand?

3. Use the dictionary as needed to understand the meanings of the following words: derogatory (par. 1); chauvinism, anthropocentrism, benign (2); self-ambulatory, incapacitated, amenities (4); contingency, teletype (6); scan (7); demeaned (10); *in situ* (12); nodules, tectonic, spectrometric (13); abyssal (14); terrestrial (15); precipitous, query (16); exoskeleton (19); phylogenetic (20); anthropoid (21); onerous, fibrillation (23).

Suggestions for Writing and Discussion

1. Discuss any recent developments in computer or robot technology that seem to confirm Sagan's predictions. Discuss any that contradict his predictions.

2. Despite the optimism of people like Sagan, many other people fear that robots will eventually take over the world. If you believe this, either completely or in part, explain and defend your outlook. If you think such fears are groundless, explain and defend your position.

3. Write an essay describing how robots can help us by taking over some of the more meaningless tasks of our everyday lives.

4. If you believe there are some things that robots (and computers) will never be able to do, explain your reasoning.

(NOTE: Suggestions for topics requiring development by use of ARGUMENT are on page 406, at the end of this section.)

Argument through Definition

BARBARA LAWRENCE

BARBARA LAWRENCE was born in Hanover, New Hampshire. After receiving a B.A. in French literature from Connecticut College, she worked as an editor on *McCall's, Redbook, Harper's Bazaar,* and *The New Yorker*. During this period she also took an M.A. in philosophy from New York University. Currently an associate professor of humanities at the State University of New York's College at Old Westbury, Lawrence has published criticism, poetry, and fiction in *Choice, Commonweal, Columbia Poetry, The New York Times,* and *The New Yorker*.

Four-Letter Words Can Hurt You

"Four-Letter Words Can Hurt You" first appeared in *The New York Times* and was later published in *Redbook*. In arguing against the "earthy, gut-honest" language often preferred by her students, Lawrence also provides a thoughtful, even scholarly, extended definition of "obscenity" itself. To accomplish her purpose, the author makes use of several other patterns as well.

Why should any words be called obscene? Don't they all describe natural human functions? Am I trying to tell them, my students demand, that the "strong, earthy, gut-honest" — or, if they are fans of Norman Mailer, the "rich, liberating, existential" — language they use to describe sexual activity isn't preferable to "phony-sounding, middle-class words like 'intercourse' and 'copulate'?" "Cop You Late!" they say with fancy inflections and gagging grimaces. "Now, what is *that* supposed to mean?"

Well, what is it supposed to mean? And why indeed should one group of words describing human functions and human organs be acceptable in ordinary conversation and another, describing pre-

From *The New York Times*, October 27, 1973. © 1973 by The New York Times Company. Reprinted by permission.

sumably the same organs and functions, be tabooed — so much so, in fact, that some of these words still cannot appear in print in many parts of the English-speaking world?

The argument that these taboos exist only because of "sexual   3
hangups" (middle-class, middle-age, feminist), or even that they are a result of class oppression (the contempt of the Norman conquerors for the language of their Anglo-Saxon serfs), ignores a much more likely explanation, it seems to me, and that is the sources and functions of the words themselves.

The best known of the tabooed sexual verbs, for example,   4
comes from the German *ficken*, meaning "to strike"; combined according to Partridge's etymological dictionary *Origins*, with the Latin sexual verb *futuere:* associated in turn with the Latin *fustis*, "a staff or cudgel"; the Celtic *buc*, "a point, hence to pierce"; the Irish *bot*, "the male member"; the Latin *battuere*, "to beat"; the Gaelic *batair*, "a cudgeller"; the Early Irish *bualaim*, "I strike"; and so forth. It is one of what etymologists sometimes called "the sadistic group of words for the man's part in copulation."

The brutality of this word, then, and its equivalents ("screw,"   5
"bang," etc.), is not an illusion of the middle class or a crotchet of Women's Liberation. In their origins and imagery these words carry undeniably painful, if not sadistic, implications, the object of which is almost always female. Consider, for example, what a "screw" actually does to the wood it penetrates; what a painful, even mutilating, activity this kind of analogy suggests. "Screw" is particularly interesting in this context, since the noun, according to Partridge, comes from words meaning "groove," "nut," "ditch," "breeding sow," "scrofula" and "swelling," while the verb, besides its explicit imagery, has antecedent associations to "write on," "scratch," "scarify," and so forth — a revealing fusion of a mechanical or painful action with an obviously denigrated object.

Not all obscene words, of course, are as implicitly sadistic or   6
denigrating to women as these, but all that I know seem to serve a similar purpose: to reduce the human organism (especially the female organism) and human functions especially sexual and procreative) to their least organic, most mechanical dimension; to substitute a trivializing or deforming resemblance for the complex human reality of what is being described.

Tabooed male descriptives, when they are not openly denigrat-   7
ing to women, often serve to divorce a male organ or function from

any significant interaction with the female. Take the word "testes," for example, suggesting "witnesses" (from the Latin *testis*) to the sexual and procreative strengths of the male organ; and the obscene counterpart of this word, which suggests little more than a mechanical shape. Or compare almost any of the "rich," "liberating" sexual verbs, so fashionable today among male writers, with that much-derived Latin word "copulate" ("to bind or join together") or even that Anglo-Saxon phrase (which seems to have had no trouble surviving the Norman Conquest) "make love."

How arrogantly self-involved the tabooed words seem in comparison to either of the other terms, and how contemptuous of the female partner. Understandably so, of course, if she is only a "skirt," a "broad," a "chick," a "pussycat" or a "piece." If she is, in other words no more than her skirt, or what her skirt conceals; no more than a breeder, or the broadest part of her; no more than a piece of a human being or a "piece of tail."

The most severely tabooed of all the female descriptives, incidentally, are those like a "piece of tail," which suggests (either explicitly or through antecedents) that there is no significant difference between the female channel through which we are all conceived and born and the anal outlet common to both sexes — a distinction that pornographers have always enjoyed obscuring.

This effort to deny women their biological identity, their individuality, their humanness, is such an important aspect of obscene language that one can only marvel at how seldom, in an era preoccupied with definitions of obscenity, this fact is brought to our attention. One problem, of course, is that many of the people in the best position to do this (critics, teachers, writers) are so reluctant today to admit that they are angered or shocked by obscenity. Bored, maybe, unimpressed, aesthetically displeased, but — no matter how brutal or denigrating the material — never angered, never shocked.

And yet how eloquently angered, how piously shocked many of these same people become if denigrating language is used about any minority group other than women; if the obscenities are racial or ethnic, that is, rather than sexual. Words like "coon," "kike," "spic," "wop," after all, deform identity, deny individuality and humanness in almost exactly the same way that sexual vulgarisms and obscenities do.

No one that I know, least of all my students, would fail to question the values of a society whose literature and entertainment

rested heavily on racial or ethnic pejoratives. Are the values of a
society whose literature and entertainment rest as heavily as ours on
sexual pejoratives any less questionable?

Meanings and Values

1a. Explain the meaning of "irony" by use of at least one illustration
    from the latter part of this essay. (See Guide to Terms: *Irony.*)

 b. What kind of irony is it?

2a. Inasmuch as the selection itself includes many of the so-called
    "strong, earthy, gut-honest" words, could anyone logically call it
    obscene? Why, or why not?

 b. To what extent, if at all, does the author's point of view help
    determine your answer to question 2a? (Guide: *Point of View.*)

3a. Compose, in your own words, a compact statement of Lawrence's
    thesis. (Guide: *Thesis.*)

 b. Are all parts of the essay completely relevant to this thesis? Justify
    your answer.

 c. Does the writing have unity?

4. Evaluate this composition by use of our three-question system.
   (Guide: *Evaluation.*)

Techniques of Argument

1. What is the purpose of this essay? (Guide: *Purpose.*)

2a. What objection to her opinion does the author refute in paragraph 3,
    and how does she refute it? (Guide: *Refutation.*)

 b. Where else in the essay does she refute opposing arguments?

3a. Are the evidence and supporting arguments in this essay arranged
    in a refutation-proof pattern?

 b. If not, describe the arrangement of the essay?

4a. Which of the methods "peculiar to definition alone" (see the intro-
    duction to Section 7) does the author employ in developing this
    essay?

 b. Which of the regular patterns of exposition does she also use?

 c. Explain your reasons and cite examples to justify your answers to 4a
    and 4b.

5a. Which of the standard techniques of introduction are used? (Guide:
    Introductions.)

 b. Which methods are used to close the essay? (Guide: *Closing.*)

Diction and Vocabulary

1a. How, if at all, is this discussion of words related to "connotation"? (Guide: *Connotation/Denotation*.)

b. To what extent would connotations in this matter depend on the setting and circumstances in which the words are used? Cite illustrations to clarify your answer.

2. In view of the fact that the author uses frankly many of the "gut-honest" words, why do you suppose she plainly avoids others, such as in paragraphs 4 and 7?

3. The author says that a "kind of analogy" is suggested by some of the words discussed (par. 5). If you have studied Section 4 of this book, does her use of the term "analogy" seem in conflict with what you believed it to mean? Explain.

4. Study the author's uses of the following words, consulting the dictionary as needed: existential, grimaces (par. 1); etymological, cudgel (4); sadistic (4–6); crochet, scrofula, explicit, antecedent, scarify (5); denigrated (5–7, 10–11), aesthetically (10); pejoratives (12).

Suggestions for Writing and Discussion

1. Why is it the so-called middle class that is so often accused of having sexual hangups — and hence all sorts of sex-related taboos?

2. Probably most people using obscene language (obscene, at least, by Lawrence's definition) are not aware of the etymology of the words. Can they, therefore, be accused of denigrating women — or, unlike legal matters, is ignorance a suitable defense?

3. Does the author make a justifiable comparison between obscene words and ethnic pejoratives? Using illustrations for specificity, carry the comparison further to show why it is sound, or explain why you consider it a weak comparison.

(NOTE: Suggestions for topics requiring development by use of ARGUMENT are on page 406, at the end of this section.)

Argument through Induction and Deduction

LEWIS THOMAS

LEWIS THOMAS (born 1913), attended private schools in New York and then Princeton University and Harvard Medical School. As a United States naval officer he took part in the invasion of Okinawa during World War II. After the war he advanced steadily in medical research, teaching, and administration. A physician, he has also served in posts at the University of Minnesota and New York University Medical School and at Yale, Cornell, and Rockefeller universities. For several years Thomas has been president of Memorial Sloan-Kettering Cancer Center in New York. He remains active in committee work, frequently appears before congressional hearings in Washington, and also serves on the Harvard Board of Overseers. A lifelong interest in literature and writing led Thomas in 1970 to begin writing a monthly column for the *New England Journal of Medicine* — a practice that has evolved into his two collections of essays: *The Lives of a Cell: Notes of a Biology Watcher* (1974), which has become a steady best-seller, and *The Medusa and the Snail* (1979). *The Youngest Science: Notes of a Medicine-Watcher* (1983) is his personal account of how medicine has developed as a science and a profession during this century.

Nurses

In this essay, a chapter from *The Youngest Science*, Thomas uses an inductive pattern to guide his argument. This pattern seems a natural choice for him because it embodies the kind of reasoning he often uses in his medical research.

When my mother became a registered nurse at Roosevelt Hospital, in 1903, there was no question in anyone's mind about what nurses did as professionals. They did what the doctors ordered. The attending physician would arrive for his ward rounds in the early morning, and when he arrived at the ward office the head nurse would be waiting for him, ready to take his hat and coat, and his cane, and she would stand while he had his cup of tea before starting. Entering the ward, she would hold the door for him to go first, then his entourage of interns and medical students, then she followed. At each bedside, after he had conducted his examination and reviewed the patient's progress, he would tell the nurse what needed doing that day, and she would write it down on the part of the chart reserved for nursing notes. An hour or two later he would be gone from the ward, and the work of the rest of the day and the night to follow was the nurse's frenetic occupation. In addition to the stipulated orders, she had an endless list of routine things to do, all learned in her two years of nursing school: the beds had to be changed and made up with fresh sheets by an exact geometric design of folding and tucking impossible for anyone but a trained nurse; the patients had to be washed head to foot; bedpans had to be brought, used, emptied, and washed; temperatures had to be taken every four hours and meticulously recorded on the chart; enemas were to be given; urine and stool samples collected, labeled, and sent off to the laboratory; throughout the day and night, medications of all sorts, usually pills and various vegetable extracts and tinctures, had to be carried on trays from bed to bed. At most times of the year about half of the forty or so patients on the ward had typhoid fever, which meant that the nurse couldn't simply move from bed to bed in the performance of her duties; each typhoid case was screened from the other patients, and the nurse was required to put on a new gown and wash her hands in disinfectant before approaching the bedside. Patients with high fevers were sponged with cold alcohol at frequent intervals. The late-evening back rub was the rite of passage into sleep.

In addition to the routine, workaday schedule, the nurse was responsible for responding to all calls from the patients, and it was expected that she would do so on the run. Her rounds, scheduled as methodical progressions around the ward, were continually interrupted by these calls. It was up to her to evaluate each situation quickly: a sudden abdominal pain in a typhoid patient might signify intestinal perforation; the abrupt onset of weakness, thirst, and pallor meant intestinal hemorrhage; the coughing up of gross blood by a tuberculous patient was an emergency. Some of the calls came from neighboring patients on the way to recovery; patients on open wards always kept a close eye on each other: the man in the next bed might slip into coma or seem to be dying, or be indeed dead. For such emergencies the nurse had to get word immediately to the doctor on call, usually the intern assigned to the ward, who might be off in the outpatient department or working in the diagnostic laboratory (interns of that day did all the laboratory work themselves; technicians had not yet been invented) or in his room. Nurses were not allowed to give injections or to do such emergency procedures as spinal punctures or chest taps, but they were expected to know when such maneuvers were indicated and to be ready with appropriate trays of instruments when the intern arrived on the ward.

It was an exhausting business, but by my mother's accounts it 3 was the most satisfying and rewarding kind of work. As a nurse she was a low person in the professional hierarchy, always running from place to place on orders from the doctors, subject as well to strict discipline from her own administrative superiors on the nursing staff, but none of this came through in her recollections. What she remembered was her usefulness.

Whenever my father talked to me about nurses and their work, 4 he spoke with high regard for them as professionals. Although it was clear in his view that the task of the nurses was to do what the doctor told them to, it was also clear that he admired them for being able to do a lot of things he couldn't possibly do, had never been trained to do. On his own rounds later on, when he became an attending physician himself, he consulted the ward nurse for her opinion about problem cases and paid careful attention to her observations and chart notes. In his own days of intern training (perhaps partly under my mother's strong influence, I don't know) he developed a deep and lasting respect for the whole nursing profession.

I have spent all of my professional career in close association 5 with, and close dependency on, nurses, and like many of my faculty colleagues, I've done a lot of worrying about the relationship between medicine and nursing. During most of this century the nursing profession has been having a hard time of it. It has been largely, although not entirely, an occupation for women, and sensitive issues of professional status, complicated by the special issue of the changing role of women in modern society, have led to a stand-offish, often adversarial relationship between nurses and doctors. Already swamped by an increasing load of routine duties, nurses have been obliged to take on more and more purely administrative tasks: keeping the records in order; making sure the supplies are on hand for every sort of ward emergency; supervising the activities of the new paraprofessional group called LPNs (licensed practical nurses), who now perform much of the bedside work once done by RNs (registered nurses); overseeing ward maids, porters, and cleaners; seeing to it that patients scheduled for X rays are on their way to the X-ray department on time. Therefore, they have to spend more of their time at desks in the ward office and less time at the bedsides. Too late maybe, the nurses have begun to realize that they are gradually being excluded from the one duty which had previously been their most important reward but which had been so taken for granted that nobody mentioned it in listing the duties of a nurse: close personal contact with patients. Along with everything else nurses did in the long day's work, making up for all the tough and sometimes demeaning jobs assigned to them, they had the matchless opportunity to be useful friends to great numbers of human beings in trouble. They listened to their patients all day long and through the night, they gave comfort and reassurance to the patients and their families, they got to know them as friends, they were depended on. To contemplate the loss of this part of their work has been the deepest worry for nurses at large, and for the faculties responsible for the curricula of the nation's new and expanding nursing schools. The issue lies at the center of the running argument between medical school and nursing school administrators, but it is never clearly stated. Nursing education has been upgraded in recent years. Almost all the former hospital schools, which took in highschool graduates and provided an RN certificate after two or three years, have been replaced by schools attached to colleges and universities, with a four-year curriculum leading simultaneously to a bachelor's degree and an RN certificate.

The doctors worry that nurses are trying to move away from their historical responsibilities to medicine (meaning, really, to the doctors' orders). The nurses assert that they are their own profession, responsible for their own standards, coequal colleagues with physicians, and they do not wish to become mere ward administrators or technicians (although some of them, carrying the new and prestigious title of "nurse practitioner," are being trained within nursing schools to perform some of the most complex technological responsibilities in hospital emergency rooms and intensive care units). The doctors claim that what the nurses really want is to become substitute psychiatrists. The nurses reply that they have unavoidable responsibilities for the mental health and wellbeing of their patients, and that these are different from the doctors' tasks. Eventually the arguments will work themselves out, and some sort of agreement will be reached, but if it is to be settled intelligently, some way will have to be found to preserve and strengthen the traditional and highly personal nurse-patient relationship.

I have had a fair amount of firsthand experience with the issue, having been an apprehensive patient myself off and on over a three-year period on the wards of the hospital for which I work. I am one up on most of my physician friends because of this experience. I know some things they do not know about what nurses do.

One thing the nurses do is to hold the place together. It is an astonishment, which every patient feels from time to time, observing the affairs of a large, complex hospital from the vantage point of his bed, that the whole institution doesn't fly to pieces. A hospital operates by the constant interplay of powerful forces pulling away at each other in different directions, each force essential for getting necessary things done, but always at odds with each other. The intern staff is an almost irresistible force in itself, learning medicine by doing medicine, assuming all the responsibility within reach, pushing against an immovable attending and administrative staff, and frequently at odds with the nurses. The attending physicians are individual entrepreneurs trying to run small cottage industries at each bedside. The diagnostic laboratories are feudal fiefdoms, prospering from the insatiable demands for their services from the interns and residents. The medical students are all over the place, learning as best they can and complaining that they are not, as they believe they should be, at the epicenter of everyone's concern. Each individual worker in the place, from the chiefs of surgery to the dieticians to the ward maids, porters, and elevator operators, lives and works in the conviction that the whole apparatus would come to a standstill without his or her individual contribution, and in one sense or another each of them is right.

My discovery, as a patient first on the medical service and later 9 in surgery, is that the institution is held together, *glued* together, enabled to function as an organism, by the nurses and by nobody else.

The nurses, the good ones anyway (and all the ones on my floor 10 were good), make it their business to know everything that is going on. They spot errors before errors can be launched. They know everything written on the chart. Most important of all, they know their patients as unique human beings, and they soon get to know the close relatives and friends. Because of this knowledge, they are quick to sense apprehensions and act on them. The average sick person in a large hospital feels at risk of getting lost, with no identity left beyond a name and a string of numbers on a plastic wristband, in danger always of being whisked off on a litter to the wrong place to have the wrong procedure done, or worse still, *not* being whisked off at the right time. The attending physician or the house officer, on rounds and usually in a hurry, can murmur a few reassuring words on his way out the door, but it takes a confident, competent, and cheerful nurse, there all day long and in and out of the room on one chore or another through the night, to bolster one's confidence that the situation is indeed manageable and not about to get out of hand.

Knowing what I know, I am all for the nurses. If they are to 11 continue their professional feud with the doctors, if they want their professional status enhanced and their pay increased, if they infuriate the doctors by their claims to be equal professionals, if they ask for the moon, I am on their side.

Meanings and Values

1a. Summarize Thomas's description of the attitudes of doctors toward nurses.

 b. Summarize his view of the special skills and contributions of nurses.

 c. Does he consider nurses the equal of doctors? If not, what is his view?

2a. What is the thesis of this essay? (Guide: *Thesis.*)

 b. Does it contain a thesis statement?

3a. If Thomas supports changes in the role of nurses, why does he avoid making any specific proposals for altering the status or responsibilities of the profession or its relationship to the medical profession?

b.   If you think that changes are called for, what specific alterations would you suggest?

4a. Does the author acknowledge directly any objections to his view of the role nurses should play in medical treatment? If so, where?

b.   If not, how does he acknowledge and refute opposing points of view?

5.   If you have read George Will's essay, "No 'Right' to Health" earlier in this section, discuss how his view of the role of medical science in maintaining health might support Thomas's view of the importance of nurses.

Techniques of Argument

1a. Much of the evidence in this essay is personal. Does this add to or detract from its effectiveness? In what ways? (Guide: *Argument.*)

b.   Why is the evidence drawn from the author's own experience also a form of authoritative testimony?

2a. The author waits until well into the essay to explain the issue behind it fully and to make his point of view explicit. Is this approach consistent with the pattern of inductive reasoning used in the essay? How?

b.   What are the major stages of this argument? (Cite specific paragraphs in your answer.)

3.   What patterns other than induction are used in this essay, and where are they used?

4a. Are the evidence and supporting ideas in this essay arranged in ascending order, as refutation-proof, as con-pro, or in some combination of these?

b.   Make a rough outline representing the arrangement of the essay.

5a. What do the lists of nurse's duties in paragraphs 1 and 2 contribute to the argument? (Guide: *Unity.*)

b.   Are these lists of duties likely to make many readers lose interest in the selection? Why, or why not? (Guide: *Introductions.*)

c.   Is Thomas able to suggest in the opening paragraph something of the purpose and the thesis of the essay? How?

Diction and Vocabulary

1a. Identify the figures of speech in paragraphs 8 and 9 and tell why the author uses them. (Guide: *Figures of Speech.*)

b.   Why are there more figures of speech in these paragraphs than in other parts of the selection?

2a. What elements of syntax contribute to the emotional impact of paragraphs 9 and 10? (Guide: *Syntax*.)

b. In what ways is the vision of the hospital from a patient's perspective in paragraphs 7–10 a preparation for the judgment Thomas delivers in paragraph 11?

c. What do the parallel structures in paragraph 11 contribute to its impact? (Guide: *Parallel Structure*.)

3a. Does the last sentence in paragraph 3 contain anything that might be regarded as a paradox? What is it, and why is it paradoxical? (Guide: *Paradox*.)

b. How does his paradox aid the argument?

4. How does the diction in this essay help determine the tone, especially in those sections where Thomas speaks of nurses and their relationship to patients? (Guide: *Diction* and *Style/Tone*.)

5. Use your dictionary as necessary to become familiar with the following words: ward, rounds, entourage, frenetic, tinctures, typhoid fever (par. 1); taps (2); paraprofessional (5); feudal fiefdoms, epicenter (8).

Suggestions for Writing and Discussion

1. Some people might claim that recent conflicts between doctors and nurses are a result of the rising status of women during the past fifteen years. Do you agree or disagree? (You may wish to look at Ellen Goodman's essay, "Just Woman's Work?" in Section 10.)

2. To what extent can the ways women are raised in our society be seen as a preparation for the kind of work nurses do? Can men be expected to perform as well as women in such a profession? Be ready to defend your answer.

3. Prepare a written or oral composition from the point of view of a nursing director in a large hospital and argue that nurses should be given greater responsibility for running the hospital and caring for patients. Be as specific as you can in your proposals.

4. A recent report indicates that many female teachers choose not to seek higher-paying administrative jobs because they feel that administrative tasks will deprive them of the experiences of teaching and helping people for which they entered the profession. Comment on this dilemma as it applies to teaching, nursing, and similar professions. (Note: Many male teachers face the same dilemma.)

(NOTE: Suggestions for topics requiring development by ARGUMENT are on page 406, at the end of this section.)

THOMAS JEFFERSON

THOMAS JEFFERSON (1743–1826) was born in Virginia, where he spent his childhood and later attended William and Mary College. He became a lawyer, a member of the Virginia House of Burgesses and of the Continental Congress in 1775. His influence as a liberal democrat was always aided by his prolific and forceful writing. During the Revolutionary War he became governor of Virginia. After the war he served the new government in various capacities, including those of special minister to France, secretary of state under Washington, vice-president, and, for two terms, the country's third president. He died on July 4, the fiftieth anniversary of the signing of the Declaration of Independence.

The Declaration of Independence

The Declaration of Independence, written and revised by Jefferson, was later further revised by the Continental Congress, meeting then in Philadelphia. In this way, as Jefferson later remarked, it drew its authority from "the harmonizing sentiments of the day"; it was, when signed on July 4, 1776, "an expression of the American mind." However, the document still retained much of the form and style of Jefferson's writing, and as literature it has long been admired for its lean and forthright prose. We can find no clearer example of the practical combination of deductive and inductive argument.

When in the course of human events, it becomes necessary for one people to dissolve the political bands which have connected them with another, and to assume among the Powers of the earth, the separate and equal station to which the Laws of Nature and of Nature's God entitle them, a decent respect to the opinions of mankind requires that they should declare the causes which impel them to the separation.

We hold these truths to be self-evident, that all men are created 2 equal, that they are endowed by their Creator with certain unalienable Rights, that among these are Life, Liberty and the pursuit of Happiness. That to secure these rights, Governments are instituted among Men, deriving their just powers from the consent of the governed. That whenever any Form of Government becomes destructive of these ends, it is the Right of the People to alter or to abolish it, and to institute a new Government, laying its foundation on such principles and organizing its powers in such form, as to them shall seem most likely to effect their Safety and Happiness. Prudence, indeed, will dictate that Governments long established should not be changed for light and transient causes; and accordingly all experience hath shown that mankind are more disposed to suffer, while evils are sufferable, than to right themselves by abolishing the forms to which they are accustomed. But when a long train of abuses and usurpations pursuing invariably the same Object evinces a design to reduce them under absolute Despotism, it is their right, it is their duty, to throw off such government, and to provide new Guards for their future security. Such has been the patient sufferance of these Colonies; and such is now the necessity which constrains them to alter their former Systems of Government. The history of the present King of Great Britain is a history of repeated injuries and usurpations, all having in direct object the establishment of an absolute Tyranny over these States. To prove this, let Facts be submitted to a candid world.

He has refused his Assent to Laws, the most wholesome and 3 necessary for the public good.

He has forbidden his Governors to pass Laws of immediate and 4 pressing importance, unless suspended in their operation till his Assent should be obtained; and when so suspended, he has utterly neglected to attend to them.

He has refused to pass other Laws for the accommodation of 5 large districts of people, unless those people would relinquish the right of Representation in the Legislature, a right inestimable to them and formidable to tyrants only.

He has called together legislative bodies at places unusual, 6 uncomfortable, and distant from the depository of their Public Records, for the sole purpose of fatiguing them into compliance with his measures.

He has dissolved Representative Houses repeatedly, for op-   7
posing with manly firmness his invasions on the rights of the people.

He has refused for a long time, after such dissolutions, to cause   8
others to be elected; whereby the Legislative Powers, incapable of
Annihilation, have returned to the People at large for their exercise;
the State remaining in the mean time exposed to all the dangers of
invasion from without, and convulsions within.

He has endeavored to prevent the population of these States;   9
for that purpose obstructing the Laws of Naturalization of For-
eigners; refusing to pass others to encourage their migration hither,
and raising the conditions of new Appropriations of Lands.

He has obstructed the Administration of Justice, by refusing his   10
Assent to Laws for establishing Judiciary Powers.

He has made Judges dependent on his Will alone, for the tenure   11
of their offices, and the amount and payment of their salaries.

He has erected a multitude of New Offices, and sent hither   12
swarms of Officers to harass our People, and eat out their substance.

He has kept among us, in time of peace, Standing Armies   13
without the consent of our Legislature.

He has affected to render the Military independent of and   14
superior to the Civil Power.

He has combined with others to subject us to jurisdictions   15
foreign to our constitution, and unacknowledged by our laws; giving his Assent to their acts of pretended Legislation:

For quartering large bodies of armed troops among us: 16

For protecting them, by a mock Trial, from Punishment for any   17
Murders which they should commit on the Inhabitants of these
States:

For cutting off our Trade with all parts of the world: 1

For imposing Taxes on us without our Consent: 1

For depriving us in many cases, of the benefits of Trial by Jury: 2

For transporting us beyond Seas to be tried for pretended   2
offenses:

For abolishing the free System of English Laws in a Neighbour-   2
ing Province, establishing therein an Arbitrary government, and
enlarging its boundaries so as to render it at once an example and fit
instrument for introducing the same absolute rule into these Colonies:

For taking away our Charters, abolishing our most valuable 23
Laws, and altering fundamentally the Forms of our Governments:

For suspending our own Legislatures, and declaring them- 24
selves invested with Power to legislate for us in all cases whatsoever.

He has abdicated Government here, by declaring us out of his 25
Protection and waging War against us.

He has plundered our seas, ravaged our Coasts, burnt our 26
towns and destroyed the Lives of our people.

He is at this time transporting large Armies of foreign Merce- 27
naries to compleat the works of death, desolation and tyranny,
already begun with circumstances of Cruelty & perfidy scarcely
paralleled in the most barbarous ages, and totally unworthy the
Head of a civilized nation.

He has constrained our fellow Citizens taken Captive on the 28
high Seas to bear Arms against their Country, to become the execu-
tioners of their friends and Brethren, or to fall themselves by their
Hands.

He has excited domestic insurrections amongst us, and has 29
endeavored to bring on the inhabitants of our frontiers, the merci-
less Indian Savages, whose known rule of warfare, is an undistin-
guished destruction of all ages, sexes and conditions.

In every stage of these Oppressions We Have Petitioned for 30
Redress in the most humble terms: Our repeated petitions have
been answered only by repeated injury. A Prince, whose character
is thus marked by every act which may define a Tyrant, is unfit to be
the ruler of a free People.

Nor have We been wanting in attention to our British brethren. 31
We have warned them from time to time of attempts by their
legislature to extend an unwarrantable jurisdiction over us. We
have reminded them of the circumstances of our emigration and
settlement here. We have appealed to their native justice and magnanimity and we have conjured them by the ties of our common
kindred to disavow these usurpations, which would inevitably in-
terrupt our connections and correspondence. They too have been
deaf to the voice of justice and of consanguinity. We must, therefore, acquiesce in the necessity, which denounces our Separation,
and hold them, as we hold the rest of mankind, Enemies in War, in
Peace Friends.

We, therefore, the Representatives of the United States of America, in General Congress, Assembled, appealing to the Supreme Judge of the world for the rectitude of our intentions, do, in the Name, and by Authority of the good People of these Colonies, solemnly publish and declare, That these United Colonies are, and of Right ought to be, Free and Independent States; that they are Absolved from all Allegiance to the British Crown, and that all political connection between them and the State of Great Britain, is and ought to be totally dissolved; and that as Free and Independent States, they have full power to levy War, conclude Peace, contract Alliances, establish Commerce, and to do all other Acts and Things which Independent States may of right do. And for the support of this Declaration, with a firm reliance on the protection of Divine Providence, we mutually pledge to each other our lives, our Fortunes and our sacred Honor.

Meanings and Values

1. For what practical reasons (other than the "decent respect to the opinions of mankind" — (par. 1) did the Founding Fathers need to explain so carefully their reasons for declaring independence?

2a. By what justification can this selection be considered an argument?

  b. Why might it also be classified as exposition?

  c. Except for study purposes, is there any reason to categorize it at all? Explain.

3. Many American colonials opposed the break with England and remained loyal to the Crown throughout the struggle for independence. What do you suppose could inspire such loyalty to a king whom most of them had never seen and who had shown little concern for their welfare?

Techniques of Argument

1. The basis of the Declaration of Independence is deduction and can therefore be stated as a logical syllogism. The major premise, stated twice in the second paragraph, may be paraphrased as follows: when a government proves to be despotic, it is the people's right and duty to get rid of it. (See introduction to Section 10, "Reasoning by use of *Induction* and *Deduction.*")

  a. What, then, is the minor premise of the syllogism?

  b. Where is the syllogism's conclusion set forth? Restate it concisely in your own words.

c. Write this resulting syllogism in standard form.

2. Twenty-eight pieces of inductive evidence are offered as support for one of the deductive premises.

a. Which premise is thus supported?

b. Demonstrate the meaning of "inductive leap" by use of materials from this selection. (Remember that the order of presentation in inductive or deductive writing is merely an arrangement for *arguing*, not necessarily that of the original reasoning.)

3a. Why, according to the document itself, is the other premise not supported by any inductive reasoning?

b. Would everyone agree with this premise? If not, why do you suppose the Founding Fathers did not present inductive evidence to support it?

4. What benefits are gained in the Declaration by the extensive use of parallel structures? (Guide: *Parallel Structure.*)

5. Show as specifically as possible the effects that a "decent respect to the opinions of mankind" apparently had on the selection and use of materials in the Declaration of Independence.

Diction and Vocabulary

1. Select five words or phrases from the Declaration of Independence to demonstrate the value of an awareness of connotation. (Guide: *Connotation/Denotation.*)

2. If you are not already familiar with the following words as they are used in this selection, consult your dictionary for their meanings: impel (par. 1); transient, usurpations, evinces, sufferance, constrains (2); inestimable (5); depository (6); dissolutions (8); mercenaries, perfidy (27); redress (30); magnanimity, conjured, consanguinity, acquiesce (31); rectitude, absolved (32).

Suggestions for Writing and Discussion

1. George Santayana, an American writer and expatriate, called the Declaration of Independence "a salad of illusion." Develop this metaphor into a full-scale analogy to explain his meaning. Without arguing the matter, attempt to assess the truth of his allegation.

2. Select one important similarity or difference between the rebellion of the American colonials and that of some other country in recent history. Use comparison or contrast to develop a theme on this subject.

3. Compare or contrast any of the Declaration signers with one of the leaders of some other country that more recently severed ties with a colonial power.

4.   Give evidence from your knowledge of history to support, or to negate, the following statement by Patrick Henry, one of the signers of the Declaration: "It is impossible that a nation of infidels or idolators should be a nation of freemen. It is when a people forget God, that tyrants forge their chains. A vitiated state of morals, a corrupted public conscience, is incompatible with freedom."

(NOTE: Suggestions for topics requiring development by ARGUMENT are on page 406, at the end of this section.)

Complex Argument

MARTIN LUTHER KING, JR.

MARTIN LUTHER KING, JR. (1929–1968), was a Baptist minister, the president of the Southern Christian Leadership Conference, and a respected leader in the nationwide movement for equal rights for blacks. He was born in Atlanta, Georgia, and earned degrees from Morehouse College (A.B., 1948), Crozer Theological Seminary (B.D., 1951), Boston University (Ph.D., 1955), and Chicago Theological Seminary (D.D., 1957). He held honorary degrees from numerous other colleges and universities and was awarded the Nobel Peace Prize in 1964. Some of his books are *Why We Can't Wait* (1964), *Stride Toward Freedom* (1958), and *Strength to Love* (1963). King was assassinated April 4, 1968, in Memphis, Tennessee.

Letter from Birmingham Jail[1]

This letter, written to King's colleagues in the ministry, is a reasoned explanation for his actions during the civil rights protests in Birmingham. It is a good example of both persuasion and logical argument. Here the two are completely compatible, balancing each other in rather intricate but convincing and effective patterns.

[1]This response to a published statement by eight fellow clergymen from Alabama (Bishop C. C. J. Carpenter, Bishop Joseph A. Durick, Rabbi Hilton L. Grafman, Bishop Paul Hardin, Bishop Holan B. Harmon, the Reverend George M. Murray, the Reverend Edward V. Ramage and the Reverend Earl Stallings) was composed under somewhat constricting circumstances. Begun on the margins of the newspaper in which the statement appeared while I was in jail, the letter was continued on scraps of writing paper supplied by a friendly Negro trusty, and concluded on a pad my attorneys were eventually permitted to leave me. Although the text remains in substance unaltered, I have indulged in the author's prerogative of polishing it for publication. — King's note.

MY DEAR FELLOW CLERGYMEN:

While confined here in the Birmingham city jail, I came across your recent statement calling my present activities "unwise and untimely." Seldom do I pause to answer criticism of my work and ideas. If I sought to answer all the criticisms that cross my desk, my secretaries would have little time for anything other than such correspondence in the course of the day, and I would have no time for constructive work. But since I feel that you are men of genuine good will and that your criticisms are sincerely set forth, I want to try to answer your statement in what I hope will be patient and reasonable terms.

I think I should indicate why I am here in Birmingham, since you have been influenced by the view which argues against "outsiders coming in." I have the honor of serving as president of the Southern Christian Leadership Conference, an organization operating in every southern state, with headquarters in Atlanta, Georgia. We have some eighty-five affiliated organizations across the South, and one of them is the Alabama Christian Movement for Human Rights. Frequently we share staff, educational, and financial resources with our affiliates. Several months ago the affiliate here in Birmingham asked us to be on call to engage in a nonviolent direct-action program if such were deemed necessary. We readily consented, and when the hour came, we lived up to our promise. So I, along with several members of my staff, am here because I was invited here. I am here because I have organizational ties here.

But more basically, I am in Birmingham because injustice is here. Just as the prophets of the eighth century B.C. left their villages and carried their "thus saith the Lord" far beyond the boundaries of their home towns, and just as the Apostle Paul left his village of Tarsus and carried the gospel of Jesus Christ to the far corners of the Greco-Roman world, so am I compelled to carry the gospel of freedom beyond my own home town. Like Paul, I must constantly respond to the Macedonian call for aid.

Moreover, I am cognizant of the interrelatedness of all communities and states. I cannot sit idly by in Atlanta and not be concerned about what happens in Birmingham. Injustice anywhere is a threat to justice everywhere. We are caught in an inescapable network of mutuality, tied in a single garment of destiny. Whatever affects one directly, affects all indirectly. Never again can we afford to live with the narrow, provincial "outside agitator" idea. Anyone who lives inside the United States can never be considered an outsider anywhere within its bounds.

You deplore the demonstrations taking place in Birmingham. But your statement, I am sorry to say, fails to express a similar concern for the conditions that brought about the demonstrations. I am sure that none of you would want to rest content with the superficial kind of social analysis that deals merely with effects and does not grapple with underlying causes. It is unfortunate that demonstrations are taking place in Birmingham, but it is even more unfortunate that the city's white power structure left the Negro community with no alternative.

In any nonviolent campaign there are four basic steps: collection of the facts to determine whether injustices exist; negotiation; self-purification; and direct action. We have gone through all these steps in Birmingham. There can be no gainsaying the fact that racial injustice engulfs this community. Birmingham is probably the most thoroughly segregated city in the United States. Its ugly record of brutality is widely known. Negroes have experienced grossly unjust treatment in the courts. There have been more unsolved bombings of Negro homes and churches in Birmingham than in any other city in the nation. These are the hard, brutal facts of the case. On the basis of these conditions, Negro leaders sought to negotiate with the city fathers. But the latter consistently refused to engage in good-faith negotiation.

Then, last September, came the opportunity to talk with leaders of Birmingham's economic community. In the course of the negotiations, certain promises were made by the merchants — for example, to remove the stores' humiliating racial signs. On the basis of these promises, the Reverend Fred Shuttlesworth and the leaders of the Alabama Christian Movement for Human Rights agreed to a moratorium on all demonstrations. As the weeks and months went by, we realized that we were the victims of a broken promise. A few signs, briefly removed, returned; the others remained.

As in so many past experiences, our hopes had been blasted, and the shadow of deep disappointment settled upon us. We had no alternative except to prepare for direct action, whereby we would present our very bodies as a means of laying our case before the conscience of the local and the national community. Mindful of the difficulties involved, we decided to undertake a process of self-purification. We began a series of workshops on nonviolence, and we repeatedly asked ourselves: "Are you able to accept blows without retaliating?" "Are you able to endure the ordeal of jail?" We decided to schedule our direct-action program for the Easter season, realizing that except for Christmas, this is the main shopping period of the year. Knowing that a strong economic-withdrawal program would be the by product of direct action, we felt that this would be the best time to bring pressure to bear on the merchants for the needed change.

Then it occurred to us that Birmingham's mayoral election was coming up in March, and we speedily decided to postpone action until after election day. When we discovered that the Commissioner of Public Safety, Eugene "Bull" Connor, had piled up enough votes to be in the run-off, we decided again to postpone action until the day after the run-off so that the demonstrations could not be used to cloud the issues. Like many others, we waited to see Mr. Connor defeated, and to this end we endured postponement after postponement. Having aided in this community need, we felt that our direct-action program could be delayed no longer.

You may well ask, "Why direct action? Why sit-ins, marches, and so forth? Isn't negotiation a better path?" You are quite right in calling for negotiation. Indeed, this is the very purpose of direct action. Nonviolent direct action seeks to create such a crisis and foster such a tension that a community which has constantly refused to negotiate is forced to confront the issue. It seeks so to dramatize the issue that it can no longer be ignored. My citing the creation of tension as part of the work of the nonviolent-resister may sound rather shocking. But I must confess that I am not afraid of the word "tension." I have earnestly opposed violent tension, but there is a type of constructive, nonviolent tension which is necessary for growth. Just as Socrates felt that it was necessary to create a tension in the mind so that individuals could rise from the bondage of myths and half-truths to the unfettered realm of creative analysis and objective appraisal, so must we see the need for nonviolent gadflies to create the kind of tension in society that will help men rise from the dark depths of prejudice and racism to the majestic heights of understanding and brotherhood.

The purpose of our direct-action program is to create a situation so crisis-packed that it will inevitably open the door to negotiation. I therefore concur with you in your call for negotiation. Too long has our beloved Southland been bogged down in a tragic effort to live in monologue rather than dialogue.

One of the basic points in your statement is that the action that I 12 and my associates have taken in Birmingham is untimely. Some have asked: "Why didn't you give the new city administration time to act?" The only answer that I can give to this query is that the new Birmingham administration must be prodded about as much as the outgoing one, before it will act. We are sadly mistaken if we feel that the election of Albert Boutwell as mayor will bring the millennium to Birmingham. While Mr. Boutwell is a much more gentle person than Mr. Connor, they are both segregationists, dedicated to maintenance of the status quo. I have hoped that Mr. Boutwell will be reasonable enough to see the futility of massive resistance to desegregation. But he will not see this without pressure from devotees of civil rights. My friends, I must say to you that we have not made a single gain in civil rights without determined legal and nonviolent pressure. Lamentably, it is an historical fact that privileged groups seldom give up their privileges voluntarily. Individuals may see the moral light and voluntarily give up their unjust posture; but, as Reinhold Niebuhr has reminded us, groups tend to be more immoral than individuals.

We know through painful experience that freedom is never 13 voluntarily given by the oppressor; it must be demanded by the oppressed. Frankly, I have yet to engage in a direct-action campaign that was "well timed" in the view of those who have not suffered unduly from the disease of segregation. For years now I have heard the word "Wait!" It rings in the ear of every Negro with piercing familiarity. This "Wait" has almost always meant "Never." We must come to see, with one of our distinguished jurists, that "justice too long delayed is justice denied."

We have waited for more than 340 years for our constitutional 14 and God-given rights. The nations of Asia and Africa are moving with jetlike speed toward gaining political independence, but we still creep at horse-and-buggy pace toward gaining a cup of coffee at a lunch counter. Perhaps it is easy for those who have never felt the stinging darts of segregation to say, "Wait." But when you have seen vicious mobs lynch your mothers and fathers at will and drown your sisters and brothers at whim; when you have seen hate-filled policemen curse, kick, and even kill your black brothers and sisters; when you see the vast majority of your twenty million Negro brothers smothering in an airtight cage of poverty in the midst of an affluent society; when you suddenly find your tongue twisted and your speech stammering as you seek to explain to your six-year-old daughter why she can't go to the public amusement park that has just been advertised on television, and see tears welling up in her eyes when she is told that Funtown is closed to colored children, and see ominous clouds of inferiority beginning to form in her little mental sky, and see her beginning to distort her personality by developing an unconscious bitterness toward white people; when you have to concoct an answer for a five-year-old son who is asking, "Daddy, why do white people treat colored people so mean?"; when you take a cross-country drive and find it necessary to sleep night after night in the uncomfortable corners of your automobile because no motel will accept you; when you are humiliated day in and day out by nagging signs reading "white" and "colored"; when your first name becomes "nigger," your middle name becomes "boy" (however old you are) and your last name becomes "John," and your wife and mother are never given the respected title "Mrs."; when you are harried by day and haunted by night by the fact that you are a Negro, living constantly at tiptoe stance, never quite knowing what to expect next, and are plagued with inner fears and outer resentments; when you are forever fighting a degenerating sense of "nobodiness" — then you will understand why we find it difficult to wait. There comes a time when the cup of endurance runs over, and men are no longer willing to be plunged into the abyss of despair. I hope, sirs, you can understand our legitimate and unavoidable impatience.

You express a great deal of anxiety over our willingness to break laws. This is certainly a legitimate concern. Since we so diligently urge people to obey the Supreme Court's decision of 1954 outlawing segregation in the public schools, at first glance it may seem rather paradoxical for us consciously to break laws. One may well ask: "How can you advocate breaking some laws and obeying others?" The answer lies in the fact that there are two types of laws: just and unjust. I would be the first to advocate obeying just laws. One has not only a legal but a moral responsibility to obey just laws. Conversely, one has a moral responsibility to disobey unjust laws. I would agree with St. Augustine that "an unjust law is no law at all."

Now, what is the difference between the two? How does one

determine whether a law is just or unjust? A just law is a man-made code that squares with the moral law or the law of God. An unjust law is a code that is out of harmony with the moral law. To put it in the terms of St. Thomas Aquinas: An unjust law is a human law that is not rooted in eternal law and natural law. Any law that uplifts human personality is just. Any law that degrades human personality is unjust. All segregation statutes are unjust because segregation distorts the soul and damages the personality. It gives the segregator a false sense of superiority and the segregated a false sense of inferiority. Segregation, to use the terminology of the Jewish philosopher Martin Buber, substitutes an "I-it" relationship for an "I-thou" relationship and ends up relegating persons to the status of things. Hence segregation is not only politically, economically, and sociologically unsound, it is morally wrong and sinful. Paul Tillich has said that sin is separation. Is not segregation an existential expression of man's tragic separation, his awful estrangement, his terrible sinfulness? Thus it is that I can urge men to obey the 1954 decision of the Supreme Court, for it is morally right; and I can urge them to disobey segregation ordinances, for they are morally wrong.

Let us consider a more concrete example of just and unjust laws. An unjust law is a code that a numerical or power majority group compels a minority group to obey but does not make binding on itself. This is *difference* made legal. By the same token, a just law is a code that a majority compels a minority to follow and that it is willing to follow itself. This is *sameness* made legal.   17

Let me give another explanation. A law is unjust if it is inflicted on a minority that, as a result of being denied the right to vote, had no part in enacting or devising the law. Who can say that the legislature of Alabama which set up that state's segregation laws was democratically elected? Throughout Alabama all sorts of devious methods are used to prevent Negroes from becoming registered voters, and there are some counties in which, even though Negroes constitute a majority of the population, not a single Negro is registered. Can any law enacted under such circumstances be considered democratically structured?   18

Sometimes a law is just on its face and unjust in its application. For instance, I have been arrested on a charge of parading without a permit. Now, there is nothing wrong in having an ordinance which requires a permit for a parade. But such an ordinance becomes   19 unjust when it is used to maintain segregation and to deny citizens the First-Amendment privilege of peaceful assembly and protest.

I hope you are able to see the distinction I am trying to point   20
out. In no sense do I advocate evading or defying the law, as would the rabid segregationist. That would lead to anarchy. One who breaks an unjust law must do so openly, lovingly, and with a willingness to accept the penalty. I submit that an individual who breaks a law that conscience tells him is unjust, and who willingly accepts the penalty of imprisonment in order to arouse the conscience of the community over its injustice, is in reality expressing the highest respect for law.

Of course, there is nothing new about this kind of civil dis-   21
obedience. It was evidenced sublimely in the refusal of Shadrach, Meshach, and Abednego to obey the laws of Nebuchadnezzar, on the ground that a higher moral law was at stake. It was practiced superbly by the early Christians, who were willing to face hungry lions and the excruciating pain of chopping blocks rather than submit to certain unjust laws of the Roman Empire. To a degree, academic freedom is a reality today because Socrates practiced civil disobedience. In our own nation, the Boston Tea Party represented a massive act of civil disobedience.

We should never forget that everything Adolf Hitler did in   22
Germany was "legal" and everything the Hungarian freedom fighters did in Hungary was "illegal." It was "illegal" to aid and comfort a Jew in Hitler's Germany. Even so, I am sure that, had I lived in Germany at the time, I would have aided and comforted my Jewish brothers. If today I lived in a Communist country where certain principles dear to the Christian faith are suppressed, I would openly advocate disobeying that country's anti-religious laws.

I must make two honest confessions to you, my Christian and   23
Jewish brothers. First, I must confess that over the past few years I have been gravely disappointed with the white moderate. I have almost reached the regrettable conclusion that the Negro's great stumbling block in his stride toward freedom is not the White Citizen's Counciler or the Ku Klux Klanner, but the white moderate, who is more devoted to "order" than to justice; who prefers a negative peace which is the absence of tension to a positive peace which is the presence of justice; who constantly says, "I agree with you in the goal you seek, but I cannot agree with your methods of

direct action"; who paternalistically believes he can set the timetable for another man's freedom; who lives by a mythical concept of time and who constantly advises the Negro to wait for a "more convenient season." Shallow understanding from people of good will is more frustrating than absolute misunderstanding from people of ill will. Lukewarm acceptance is much more bewildering than outright rejection.

I had hoped that the white moderate would understand that 24 law and order exist for the purpose of establishing justice and that when they fail in this purpose they become the dangerously structured dams that block the flow of social progress. I had hoped that the white moderate would understand that the present tension in the South is a necessary phase of the transition from an obnoxious negative peace, in which the Negro passively accepted his unjust plight, to a substantive and positive peace, in which all men will respect the dignity and worth of human personality. Actually, we who engage in nonviolent direct action are not the creators of tension. We merely bring to the surface the hidden tension that is already alive. We bring it out in the open, where it can be seen and dealt with. Like a boil that can never be cured so long as it is covered up but must be opened with all its ugliness to the natural medicines of air and light, injustice must be exposed, with all the tension its exposure creates, to the light of human conscience and the air of national opinion, before it can be cured.

In your statement you assert that our actions, even though 25 peaceful, must be condemned because they precipitate violence. But is this a logical assertion? Isn't this like condemning a robbed man because his possession of money precipitated the evil act of robbery? Isn't this like condemning Socrates because his unswerving commitment to truth and his philosophical inquiries precipitated the act by the misguided populace in which they made him drink hemlock? Isn't this like condemning Jesus because his unique God-consciousness and never-ceasing devotion to God's will precipitated the evil act of crucifixion? We must come to see that, as the federal courts have consistently affirmed, it is wrong to urge an individual to cease his efforts to gain his basic constitutional rights because the quest may precipitate violence. Society must protect the robbed and punish the robber.

I had also hoped that the white moderate would reject the myth 26 concerning time in relation to the struggle for freedom. I have just received a letter from a white brother in Texas. He writes: "All Christians know that the colored people will receive equal rights eventually, but it is possible that you are in too great a religious hurry. It has taken Christianity almost two thousand years to accomplish what it has. The teachings of Christ take time to come to earth." Such an attitude stems from a tragic misconception of time, from the strangely irrational notion that there is something in the very flow of time that will inevitably cure all ills. Actually, time itself is neutral; it can be used either destructively or constructively. More and more I feel that the people of ill will have used time much more effectively than have the people of good will. We will have to repent in this generation not merely for the hateful words and actions of the bad people, but for the appalling silence of the good people. Human progress never rolls in on wheels of inevitability; it comes through the tireless efforts of men willing to be co-workers with God, and without this hard work, time itself becomes an ally of the forces of social stagnation. We must use time creatively, in the knowledge that the time is always ripe to do right. Now is the time to make real the promise of democracy and transform our pending national elegy into a creative psalm of brotherhood. Now is the time to lift our national policy from the quicksand of racial injustice to the solid rock of human dignity.

You speak of our activity in Birmingham as extreme. At first I was rather disappointed that fellow clergymen would see my non-violent efforts as those of an extremist. I began thinking about the fact that I stand in the middle of two opposing forces in the Negro community. One is a force of complacency, made up in part of Negroes who, as a result of long years of oppression, are so drained of self-respect and a sense of "somebodiness" that they have adjusted to segregation; and in part of a few middle-class Negroes who, because of a degree of academic and economic security and because in some ways they profit by segregation, have become insensitive to the problems of the masses. The other force is one of bitterness and hatred, and it comes perilously close to advocating violence. It is expressed in the various black nationalist groups that are springing up across the nation, the largest and best-known being Elijah Muhammad's Muslim movement. Nourished by the Negro's frustration over the continued existence of racial discrimination, this movement is made up of people who have lost faith in

America, who have absolutely repudiated Christianity, and who have concluded that the white man is an incorrigible "devil."

I have tried to stand between these two forces, saying that we   28
need emulate neither the "do-nothingism" of the complacent nor the hatred and despair of the black nationalist. For there is the more excellent way of love and nonviolent protest. I am grateful to God that, through the influence of the Negro church, the way of nonviolence became an integral part of our struggle.

If this philosophy had not emerged, by now many streets of the   29
South would, I am convinced, be flowing with blood. And I am further convinced that if our white brothers dismiss as "rabble-rousers" and "outside agitators" those of us who employ nonviolent direct action, and if they refuse to support our nonviolent efforts, millions of Negroes will, out of frustration and despair, seek solace and security in black-nationalist ideologies — a development that would inevitably lead to a frightening racial nightmare.

Oppressed people cannot remain oppressed forever. The   30
yearning for freedom eventually manifests itself, and that is what has happened to the American Negro. Something within has reminded him of his birthright of freedom, and something without has reminded him that it can be gained. Consciously or unconsciously, he has been caught up by the *Zeitgeist*, and with his black brothers of Africa and his brown and yellow brothers of Asia, South America, and the Caribbean, the United States Negro is moving with a sense of great urgency toward the promised land of racial justice. If one recognizes this vital urge that has engulfed the Negro community, one should readily understand why public demonstrations are taking place. The Negro has many pent-up resentments and latent frustrations, and he must release them. So let him march; let him make prayer pilgrimages to the city hall; let him go on freedom rides — and try to understand why he must do so. If his repressed emotions are not released in nonviolent ways, they will seek expression through violence; this is not a threat but a fact of history. So I have not said to my people, "Get rid of your discontent." Rather, I have tried to say that this normal and healthy discontent can be channeled into the creative outlet of nonviolent direct action. And now this approach is being termed extremist.

But though I was initially disappointed at being categorized as   31
an extremist, as I continued to think about the matter I gradually

gained a measure of satisfaction from the label. Was not Jesus an extremist for love: "Love your enemies, bless them that curse you, do good to them that hate you, and pray for them which despitefully use you, and persecute you." Was not Amos an extremist for justice: "Let justice roll down like waters and righteousness like an ever-flowing stream." Was not Paul an extremist for the Christian gospel: "I bear in my body the marks of the Lord Jesus." Was not Martin Luther an extremist: "Here I stand; I cannot do otherwise, so help me God." And John Bunyan: "I will stay in jail to the end of my days before I make a butchery of my conscience." And Abraham Lincoln: "This nation cannot survive half slave and half free." And Thomas Jefferson: "We hold these truths to be self-evident, that all men are created equal. . . ." So the question is not whether we will be extremists, but what kind of extremists we will be. Will we be extremists for hate or for love? Will we be extremists for the preservation of injustice or for the extension of justice? In that dramatic scene on Calvary's hill three men were crucified. We must never forget that all three were crucified for the same crime — the crime of extremism. Two were extremists for immorality, and thus fell below their environment. The other, Jesus Christ, was an extremist for love, truth, and goodness, and thereby rose above his environment. Perhaps the South, the nation, and the world are in dire need of creative extremists.

I had hoped that the white moderate would see this need. 32 Perhaps I was too optimistic; perhaps I expected too much. I suppose I should have realized that few members of the oppressor race can understand the deep groans and passionate yearnings of the oppressed race, and still fewer have the vision to see that injustice must be rooted out by strong, persistent, and determined action. I am thankful, however, that some of our white brothers in the South have grasped the meaning of this social revolution and committed themselves to it. They are still all too few in quantity, but they are big in quality. Some — such as Ralph McGill, Lillian Smith, Harry Golden, James McBride Dabbs, Anne Braden, and Sarah Patton Boyle — have written about our struggle in eloquent and prophetic terms. Others have marched with us down nameless streets of the South. They have languished in filthy, roach-infested jails, suffering the abuse and brutality of policemen who view them as "dirty nigger-lovers." Unlike so many of their moderate brothers and sisters, they have recognized the urgency of the moment and sensed the need for powerful "action" antidotes to combat the disease of segregation.

Let me take note of my other major disappointment. I have 33 been so greatly disappointed with the white church and its leadership. Of course, there are some notable exceptions. I am not unmindful of the fact that each of you has taken some significant stands on this issue. I commend you, Reverend Stallings, for your Christian stand on this past Sunday, in welcoming Negroes to your worship service on a nonsegregated basis. I commend the Catholic leaders of this state for integrating Spring Hill College several years ago.

But despite these notable exceptions, I must honestly reiterate 34 that I have been disappointed with the church. I do not say this as one of those negative critics who can always find something wrong with the church. I say this as a minister of the gospel, who loves the church; who was nurtured in its bosom; who has been sustained by its spiritual blessings and who will remain true to it as long as the cord of life shall lengthen.

When I was suddenly catapulted into the leadership of the bus 35 protest in Montgomery, Alabama, a few years ago, I felt we would be supported by the white church. I felt that the white ministers, priests, and rabbis of the South would be among our strongest allies. Instead, some have been outright opponents, refusing to understand the freedom movement and misrepresenting its leaders; all too many others have been more cautious than courageous and have remained silent behind the anesthetizing security of stained glass windows.

In spite of my shattered dreams, I came to Birmingham with the 36 hope that the white religious leadership of this community would see the justice of our cause and, with deep moral concern, would serve as the channel through which our just grievances could reach the power structure. I had hoped that each of you would understand. But again I have been disappointed.

I have heard numerous southern religious leaders admonish 37 their worshipers to comply with a desegregation decision because it is the law, but I have longed to hear white ministers declare: "Follow this decree because integration is morally right and because the Negro is your brother." In the midst of blatant injustices inflicted upon the Negro, I have watched white churchmen stand on the sideline and mouth pious irrelevancies and sanctimonious trivialities. In the midst of a mighty struggle to rid our nation of racial and economic injustice I have heard many ministers say: "Those are social issues, with which the gospel has no real concern." And I have watched many churches commit themselves to a completely otherworldly religion which makes a strange, un-Biblical distinction between body and soul, between the sacred and the secular.

I have traveled the length and breadth of Alabama, Mississippi, and all the other southern states. On sweltering summer days and crisp autumn mornings I have looked at the South's beautiful churches with their lofty spires pointing heavenward. I have beheld the impressive outlines of her massive religious-education buildings. Over and over I have found myself asking: "What kind of people worship here? Who is their God? Where were their voices when the lips of Governor Barnett dripped with words of interposition and nullification? Where were they when Governor Wallace gave a clarion call for defiance and hatred? Where were their voices of support when bruised and weary Negro men and women decided to rise from the dark dungeons of complacency to the bright hills of creative protest?"

Yes, these questions are still in my mind. In deep disappointment I have wept over the laxity of the church. But be assured that my tears have been tears of love. There can be no deep disappointment where there is not deep love. Yes, I love the church. How could I do otherwise? I am in the rather unique position of being the son, the grandson, and the great-grandson of preachers. Yes, I see the church as the body of Christ. But, oh! How we have blemished and scarred that body through social neglect and through fear of being nonconformists.

There was a time when the church was very powerful — in the time when the early Christians rejoiced at being deemed worthy to suffer for what they believed. In those days the church was not merely a thermometer that recorded the ideas and principles of popular opinion; it was a thermostat that transformed the mores of society. Whenever the early Christians entered a town, the people in power became disturbed and immediately sought to convict the Christians for being "disturbers of the peace" and "outside agitators." But the Christians pressed on, in the conviction that they were "a colony of heaven," called to obey God rather than man. Small in number, they were big in commitment. They were too God-intoxicated to be "astronomically intimidated." By their effort and example they brought an end to such ancient evils as infanticide and gladiatorial contests.

Things are different now. So often the contemporary church is a 41 weak, ineffectual voice with an uncertain sound. So often it is an archdefender of the status quo. Far from being disturbed by the presence of the church, the power structure of the average community is consoled by the church's silent — and often even vocal — sanction of things as they are.

But the judgment of God is upon the church as never before. If 42 today's church does not recapture the sacrificial spirit of the early church, it will lose its authenticity, forfeit the loyalty of millions, and be dismissed as an irrelevant social club with no meaning for the twentieth century. Every day I meet young people whose disappointment with the church has turned into outright disgust.

Perhaps I have once again been too optimistic. Is organized 43 religion too inextricably bound to the status quo to save our nation and the world? Perhaps I must turn my faith to the inner spiritual church, the church within the church, as the true *ekklesia*[2] and the hope of the world. But again I am thankful to God that some noble souls from the ranks of organized religion have broken loose from the paralyzing chains of conformity and joined us as active partners in the struggle for freedom. They have left their secure congregations and walked the streets of Albany, Georgia, with us. They have gone down the highways of the South on tortuous rides for freedom. Yes, they have gone to jail with us. Some have been dismissed from their churches, have lost the support of their bishops and fellow ministers. But they have acted in the faith that right defeated is stronger than evil triumphant. Their witness has been the spiritual salt that has preserved the true meaning of the gospel in these troubled times. They have carved a tunnel of hope through the dark mountain of disappointment.

I hope the church as a whole will meet the challenge of this 44 decisive hour. But even if the church does not come to the aid of justice, I have no despair about the future. I have no fear about the outcome of our struggle in Birmingham, even if our motives are at present misunderstood. We will reach the goal of freedom in Birmingham and all over the nation, because the goal of America is freedom. Abused and scorned though we may be, our destiny is

[2]The Greek New Testament word for the early Christian church. — EDS.

tied up with America's destiny. Before the pilgrims landed at Plymouth, we were here. Before the pen of Jefferson etched the majestic words of the Declaration of Independence across the pages of history, we were here. For more than two centuries our forebears labored in this country without wages; they made cotton king; they built the homes of their masters while suffering gross injustice and shameful humiliation — and yet out of a bottomless vitality they continued to thrive and develop. If the inexpressible cruelties of slavery could not stop us, the opposition we now face will surely fail. We will win our freedom because the sacred heritage of our nation and the eternal will of God are embodied in our echoing demands.

Before closing I feel impelled to mention one other point in your statement that has troubled me profoundly. You warmly commended the Birmingham police force for keeping "order" and "preventing violence." I doubt that you would have so warmly commended the police force if you had seen its dogs sinking their teeth into unarmed, nonviolent Negroes. I doubt that you would so quickly commend the policemen if you were to observe their ugly and inhumane treatment of Negroes here in the city jail; if you were to watch them push and curse old Negro women and young Negro girls; if you were to see them slap and kick old Negro men and young boys; if you were to observe them, as they did on two occasions, refuse to give us food because we wanted to sing our grace together. I cannot join you in your praise of the Birmingham police department.

It is true that the police have exercised a degree of discipline in handling the demonstrators. In this sense they have conducted themselves rather "nonviolently" in public. But for what purpose? To preserve the evil system of segregation. Over the past few years I have consistently preached that nonviolence demands that the means we use must be as pure as the ends we seek. I have tried to make clear that it is wrong to use immoral means to attain moral ends. But now I must affirm that it is just as wrong, or perhaps even more so, to use moral means to preserve immoral ends. Perhaps Mr. Connor and his policemen have been rather nonviolent in public, as was Chief Pritchett in Albany, Georgia, but they have used the moral means of nonviolence to maintain the immoral end of racial injustice. As T. S. Eliot has said, "The last temptation is the greatest treason: To do the right deed for the wrong reason."

I wish you had commended the Negro sit-inners and demon- 47
strators of Birmingham for their sublime courage, their willingness
to suffer, and their amazing discipline in the midst of great provocation. One day the South will recognize its real heroes. They will be
the James Merediths, with the noble sense of purpose that enables
them to face jeering and hostile mobs, and with the agonizing
loneliness that characterizes the life of the pioneer. They will be old,
oppressed, battered Negro women, symbolized in a seventy-two-
year-old woman in Montgomery, Alabama, who rose up with a
sense of dignity and with her people decided not to ride segregated
buses, and who responded with ungrammatical profundity to one
who inquired about her weariness: "My feets is tired, but my soul is
at rest." They will be the young high school and college students,
the young ministers of the gospel and a host of their elders,
courageously and nonviolently sitting in at lunch counters and
willingly going to jail for conscience' sake. One day the South will
know that when these disinherited children of God sat down at
lunch counters, they were in reality standing up for what is best in
the American dream and for the most sacred values in our Judaeo-
Christian heritage, thereby bringing our nation back to those great
wells of democracy which were dug deep by the founding fathers in
their formulation of the Constitution and the Declaration of Independence.

Never before have I written so long a letter. I'm afraid it is much 48
too long to take your precious time. I can assure you that it would
have been much shorter if I had been writing from a comfortable
desk, but what else can one do when he is alone in a narrow jail cell,
other than write long letters, think long thoughts, and pray long
prayers?

If I have said anything in this letter that overstates the truth and 49
indicates an unreasonable impatience, I beg you to forgive me. If I
have said anything that understates the truth and indicates my
having a patience that allows me to settle for anything less than
brotherhood, I beg God to forgive me.

I hope this letter finds you strong in the faith. I also hope that 50
circumstances will soon make it possible for me to meet each of you,
not as an integrationist or a civil-rights leader but as a fellow clergyman and a Christian brother. Let us all hope that the dark clouds of
racial prejudice will soon pass away and the deep fog of misunderstanding will be lifted from our fear-drenched communities, and in

some not too distant tomorrow the radiant stars of love and brotherhood will shine over our great nation with all their scintillating
beauty.

Yours for the cause of Peace and Brotherhood,
MARTIN LUTHER KING, JR.

Meanings and Values

1a.   Does King's purpose in this essay go beyond responding to the
       criticism of the white clergymen?

  b.   If so, what is his broader purpose?

2.   Reconstruct as many of the arguments in the clergymen's letter as
       you can by studying King's refutation of their accusations.

3.   What arguments are used in the essay to justify the demonstrations?

4.   Summarize the distinction King makes between just and unjust
       laws.

5a.   What kind of behavior did King expect from the white moderates?

  b.   Why was he disappointed?

6.   How does King defend himself and his followers against the accusa-
       tion that their actions lead to violence?

7.   What is the thesis of this essay?

8.   Like many other argumentative essays, this was written in response
       to a specific situation; yet it is widely regarded as a classic essay.
       What qualities give the essay its broad and lasting appeal?

Techniques of Argument

1.   How does King establish his reasonableness and fairness so that his
       audience will take the arguments in the essay seriously even if they
       are inclined at the start to reject his point of view?

2.   Identify as many of the expository patterns as you can in this essay
       and explain what each contributes to the argument. (Guide: *Unity*.)

3a.   What standard techniques of refutation are used in this essay to deal
       with the accusations made by the clergymen? (Guide: *Refutation*.)

  b.   Are any other strategies of refutation used in the essay?

4a.   State the argument in paragraph 6 as a syllogism. (See Section 10,
       "Reasoning by Use of *Induction* and *Deduction*.")

  b.   Do the same with the argument in paragraphs 15–22.

5.   Identify several examples of inductive argument in this essay.

6. At what points in the argument does King use several examples, where one would do, in order to strengthen the argument through variety in evidence?

Diction and Vocabulary

1. Locate an example of each of the following figures of speech in the essay and explain what it contributes to the argument. (Guide: *Figures of Speech.*)

    a. Metaphor.

    b. Allusion.

    c. Simile.

    d. Paradox.

2a. Discuss what resources of syntax King uses to construct a 37–line sentence in paragraph 14 — without confusing the reader. (Guide: *Syntax.*)

    b. Choose a paragraph that displays considerable variety in sentence length and structure and show how King uses variety in sentence style to convey his point. (Guide: *Style/Tone.*)

3. Choose two paragraphs, each with a different tone, and discuss how the diction of the passages differs and how the diction in each case contributes to the tone. (Guide: *Diction.*)

4. In many passages King uses the resources of diction and syntax to add emotional impact to logical argument. Choose such a passage and discuss how it mingles logic and emotion.

Suggestions for Writing and Discussion

1. Use some of King's arguments to construct a defense of a more recent act of protest or to encourage people to protest a policy you consider unjust. Or, if you wish, draw on his arguments to attack a recent protest on the grounds that it does not meet the high standards he sets.

2. Discuss the practical consequences of King's distinction between just and unjust laws.

3. To what extent does the racism against which King was protesting still exist in our society? Has it been replaced by other forms of discrimination?

(NOTE: Suggestions for topics requiring development by ARGUMENT follow.)

Writing Suggestions for Section 11
Argument

Choose one of the following topic areas, identify an issue (a conflict or problem) within it, and prepare an essay that tries to convince readers to share your opinion about the issue and to take any appropriate action. Use a variety of evidence in your essay, and choose any pattern of development you consider proper for the topic, for your thesis, and for the intended audience.

1. Gun control
2. The quality of education in American elementary and secondary schools
3. Treatment of critically ill newborn babies
4. Hunting
5. Euthanasia
6. Censorship in public schools and libraries
7. College athletics
8. The problem of acid rain or a similar environmental problem
9. The role of computers in education
10. The separation of church and state
11. Law on the drinking age or on drunk driving
12. Evolution vs. creationism
13. Arms control
14. Government spending on social programs
15. The quality of television programming
16. The impact of divorce
17. The effects of television viewing on children

Further Readings

JONATHAN SWIFT

JONATHAN SWIFT (1667–1745), an Anglican clergyman whose English family were longtime residents of Ireland, was Dean of Saint Patrick's in Dublin and also a poet and political pamphleteer. The greatest satirist of his period, Swift was noted for his clear, sharp prose and his effective indignation at social injustices of the day. His best-known works are *The Battle of the Books, Gulliver's Travels, The Tale of a Tub,* and *A Modest Proposal.* The last, written in 1729, remains one of the world's greatest satires[1] and is almost certainly the most vitriolic, grotesque in its details. It was aimed directly at his English compatriots for their oppression of the Irish people. Writing students should remember, however, that effective as satire can be as a rouser of emotions (i.e., as persuasion), it is not a reliable tool of logic (e.g., as in argument).

A Modest Proposal

FOR PREVENTING THE CHILDREN OF POOR PEOPLE IN IRELAND FROM BEING A BURDEN TO THEIR PARENTS OR COUNTRY, AND FOR MAKING THEM BENEFICIAL TO THE PUBLIC

It is a melancholy object to those who walk through this great town[2] or travel in the country, when they see the streets, the roads, and cabin doors, crowded with beggars of the female sex, followed by three, four, or six children, all in rags and importuning every passenger for an alms. These mothers, instead of being able to work for their honest livelihood, are forced to employ all their time in strolling to beg sustenance for their helpless infants, who, as they grow up, either turn thieves for want of work, or leave their dear native

[1]See Guide to Terms: *Satire.*
[2]Dublin.

408

country to fight for the Pretender in Spain, or sell themselves to the Barbadoes.[3]

2   I think it is agreed by all parties that this prodigious number of children in the arms, or on the backs, or at the heels of their mothers, and frequently of their fathers, is in the present deplorable state of the kingdom a very great additional grievance; and therefore whoever could find out a fair, cheap, and easy method of making these children sound, useful members of the commonwealth would deserve so well of the public as to have his statue set up for a preserver of the nation.

3   But my intention is very far from being confined to provide only for the children of professed beggars; it is of a much greater extent, and shall take in the whole number of infants at a certain age who are born of parents in effect as little able to support them as those who demand our charity in the streets.

4   As to my own part, having turned my thoughts for many years upon this important subject, and maturely weighed the several schemes of other projectors, I have always found them grossly mistaken in their computation. It is true, a child just dropped from its dam may be supported by her milk for a solar year, with little other nourishment; at most not above the value of two shillings, which the mother may certainly get, or the value in scraps, by her lawful occupation of begging; and it is exactly at one year old that I propose to provide for them in such a manner as instead of being a charge upon their parents or the parish, or wanting food and raiment for the rest of their lives, they shall on the contrary contribute to the feeding, and partly to the clothing, of many thousands.

5   There is likewise another great advantage in my scheme, that it will prevent those voluntary abortions, and that horrid practice of women murdering their bastard children, alas, too frequent among us, sacrificing the poor innocent babes, I doubt, more to avoid the expense than the shame, which would move tears and pity in the most savage and inhuman breast.

6   The number of souls in this kingdom being usually reckoned one million and a half, of these I calculate there may be about two hundred thousand couples whose wives are breeders; from which number I subtract thirty thousand couples who are able to maintain

---

[3]That is, bind themselves to work for a period of years, in order to pay for their transportation to a colony.

their own children, although I apprehend there cannot be so many under the present distress of the kingdom; but this being granted, there will remain an hundred and seventy thousand breeders. I again subtract fifty thousand for those women who miscarry, or whose children die by accident or disease within the year. There only remain an hundred and twenty thousand children of poor parents annually born. The question therefore is, how this number shall be reared and provided for, which, as I have already said, under the present situation of affairs, is utterly impossible by all the methods hitherto proposed. For we can neither employ them in handicraft nor agriculture; we neither build houses (I mean in the country) nor cultivate land. They can very seldom pick up a livelihood by stealing till they arrive at six years old, except where they are of towardly parts; although I confess they learn the rudiments much earlier, during which time they can however be looked upon only as probationers, as I have been informed by a principal gentleman in the country of Cavan, who protested to me that he never knew above one or two instances under the age of six, even in a part of the kingdom so renowned for the quickest proficiency in that art.

I am assured by our merchants that a boy or a girl before twelve 7 years old is no salable commodity; and even when they come to this age, they will not yield above three pounds, or three pounds and half a crown at most on the Exchange; which cannot turn to account either to the parents or the kingdom, the charge of nutriment and rags having been at least four times that value.

I shall now therefore humbly propose my own thoughts, which 8 I hope will not be liable to the least objection.

I have been assured by a very knowing American of my ac- 9 quaintance in London, that a young healthy child well nursed is at a year old a most delicious, nourishing, and wholesome food, whether stewed, roasted, baked, or boiled; and I make no doubt that it will equally serve in a fricassee or a ragout.

I do therefore humbly offer it to public consideration that of the 10 hundred and twenty thousand children, already computed, twenty thousand may be reserved for breed, whereof only one fourth part to be males, which is more than we allow to sheep, black cattle, or swine; and my reason is that these children are seldom the fruits of marriage, a circumstance not much regarded by our savages, therefore one male will be sufficient to serve four females. That the remaining hundred thousand may at a year old be offered in sale to the persons of quality and fortune through the kingdom, always advising the mother to let them suck plentifully in the last month, so as to render them plump and fat for a good table. A child will make two dishes at an entertainment for friends; and when the family dines alone, the fore or hind quarter will make a reasonable dish, and seasoned with a little pepper or salt will be very good boiled on the fourth day, especially in winter.

I have reckoned upon a medium that a child just born will weigh twelve pounds, and in a solar year if tolerably nursed increaseth to twenty-eight pounds. 11

I grant this food will be somewhat dear, and therefore very proper for landlords, who, as they have already devoured most of the parents, seem to have the best title to the children. 12

Infant's flesh will be in season throughout the year, but more plentiful in March, and a little before and after. For we are told by a grave author, an eminent French physician,[4] that fish being a prolific diet, there are more children born in Roman Catholic countries about nine months after Lent, than at any other season; therefore, reckoning a year after Lent, the markets will be more glutted than usual, because the number of popish infants is at least three to one in this kingdom; and therefore it will have one other collateral advantage, by lessening the number of Papists among us. 13

I have already computed the charge of nursing a beggar's child (in which list I reckon all cottagers, laborers, and four fifths of the farmers) to be about two shillings per annum, rags included; and I believe no gentleman would repine to give ten shillings for the carcass of a good fat child, which, as I have said, will make four dishes of excellent nutritive meat, when he hath only some particular friend or his own family to dine with him. Thus the squire will learn to be a good landlord, and grow popular among the tenants; the mother will have eight shillings net profit, and be fit for work till she produces another child. 14

Those who are more thrifty (as I must confess the times require) may flay the carcass; the skin of which artificially dressed will make admirable gloves for ladies, and summer boots for fine gentlemen. 15

As to our city of Dublin, shambles may be appointed for this purpose in the most convenient parts of it, and butchers we may be assured will not be wanting; although I rather recommend buying 16

[4]François Rabelais.

the children alive, and dressing them hot from the knife as we do roasting pigs.

A very worthy person, a true lover of his country, and whose virtues I highly esteem, was lately pleased in discoursing on this matter to offer a refinement upon my scheme. He said that many gentlemen of his kingdom, having of late destroyed their deer, he conceived that the want of venison might be well supplied by the bodies of young lads and maidens, not exceeding fourteen years of age nor under twelve, so great a number of both sexes in every county being now ready to starve for want of work and service; and these to be disposed of by their parents, if alive, or otherwise by their nearest relations. But with due deference to so excellent a friend and so deserving a patriot, I cannot be altogether in his sentiments; for as to the males, my American acquaintance assured me from frequent experience that their flesh was generally tough and lean, like that of our schoolboys, by continual exercise, and their taste disagreeable; and to fatten them would not answer the charge. Then as to the females, it would, I think with humble submission, be a loss to the public, because they soon would become breeders themselves; and besides, it is not improbable that some scrupulous people might be apt to censure such a practice (although indeed very unjustly) as a little bordering upon cruelty; which, I confess, hath always been with me the strongest objection against any project, how well soever intended.

But in order to justify my friend, he confessed that this expedient was put into his head by the famous Psalmanazar, a native of the island Formosa, who came from thence to London above twenty years ago, and in conversation told my friend that in his country when any young person happened to be put to death, the executioner sold the carcass to the persons of quality as a prime dainty; and that in his time the body of a plump girl of fifteen, who was crucified for an attempt to poison the emperor, was sold to his Imperial Majesty's prime minister of state, and other great mandarins of the court, in joints from the gibbet, at four hundred crowns. Neither indeed can I deny that if the same use were made of several plump young girls in this town, who without one single groat to their fortunes cannot stir abroad without a chair, and appear at the playhouse and assemblies in foreign fineries which they never will pay for, the kingdom would not be the worse.

Some persons of a desponding spirit are in great concern about that vast number of poor people who are aged, diseased, or maimed, and I have been desired to employ my thoughts what course may be taken to ease the nation of so grievous an encumbrance. But I am not in the least pain upon that matter, because it is very well known that they are every day dying and rotting by cold and famine, and filth and vermin, as fast as can be reasonably expected. And as to the younger laborers, they are now in almost as hopeful a condition. They cannot get work, and consequently pine away for want of nourishment to a degree that if any time they are accidentally hired to common labor, they have not strength to perform it; and thus the country and themselves are happily delivered from the evils to come.

I have too long digressed, and therefore shall return to my subject. I think the advantages by the proposal which I have made are obvious and many, as well as of the highest importance. 20

For first, as I have already observed, it would greatly lessen the number of Papists, with whom we are yearly overrun, being the principal breeders of the nation as well as our most dangerous enemies; and who stay at home on purpose to deliver the kingdom to the Pretender, hoping to take their advantage by the absence of so many good Protestants, who have chosen rather to leave their country than to stay at home and pay tithes against their conscience to an Episcopal curate. 21

Secondly, the poorer tenants will have something valuable of their own, which by law may be made liable to distress, and help to pay their landlord's rent, their corn and cattle being already seized and money a thing unknown. 22

Thirdly, whereas the maintenance of an hundred thousand children, from two years old and upwards, cannot be computed at less than ten shillings a piece per annum, the nation's stock will be thereby increased fifty thousand pounds per annum, besides the profit of a new dish introduced to the tables of all gentlemen of fortune in the kingdom who have any refinement in taste. And the money will circulate among ourselves, the goods being entirely of our own growth and manufacture. 23

Fourthly, the constant breeders, besides the gain of eight shillings sterling per annum by the sale of their children, will be rid of the charge for maintaining them after the first year. 24

Fifthly, this food would likewise bring great custom to taverns, where the vintners will certainly be so prudent as to procure the best 25 receipts for dressing it to perfection, and consequently have their houses frequented by all the fine gentlemen, who justly value themselves upon their knowledge in good eating; and a skillful cook, who understands how to oblige his guests, will contrive to make it as expensive as they please.

Sixthly, this would be a great inducement to marriage, which all wise nations have either encouraged by rewards or enforced by laws and penalties. It would increase the care and tenderness of mothers toward their children, when they were sure of a settlement for life to the poor babes, provided in some sort by the public, to their annual profit instead of expense. We should see an honest emulation among the married women, which of them could bring the fattest child to the market. Men would become as fond of their wives during the time of their pregnancy as they are now of their mares in foal, their cows in calf, or sows when they are ready to farrow; nor offer to beat or kick them (as is too frequent a practice) for fear of a miscarriage.

Many other advantages might be enumerated. For instance, the addition of some thousand carcasses in our exportation of barreled beef, the propagation of swine's flesh, and improvements in the art of making good bacon, so much wanted among us by the great destruction of pigs, too frequent at our tables, which are no way comparable in taste or magnificence to a well-grown, fat, yearling child, which roasted whole will make a considerable figure at a lord mayor's feast or any other public entertainment. But this and many others I omit, being studious of brevity.

Supposing that one thousand families in this city would be constant customers for infants' flesh, besides others who might have it at merry meetings, particularly weddings and christenings, I compute that Dublin would take off annually about twenty thousand carcasses, and the rest of the kingdom (where probably they will be sold somewhat cheaper) the remaining eighty thousand.

I can think of no one objection that will possibly be raised against this proposal, unless it should be urged that the number of people will be thereby much lessened in the kingdom. This I freely own, and it was indeed one principal design in offering it to the world. I desire the reader will observe, that I calculate my remedy for this one individual kingdom of Ireland and for no other that ever was, is, or I think ever can be upon earth. Therefore, let no man talk to me of other expedients: of taxing our absentees at five shillings a pound: of using neither clothes nor household furniture except what is of our own growth and manufacture: of utterly rejecting the materials and instruments that promote foreign luxury: of curing the expensiveness of pride, vanity, idleness, and gaming in our women: of introducing a vein of parsimony, prudence, and temperance: of learning to love our country, in the want of which we differ even from Laplanders and the inhabitants of Topinamboo[5]: of quitting our animosities and factions, nor acting any longer like the Jews, who were murdering one another at the very moment their city was taken: of being a little cautious not to sell our country and conscience for nothing: of teaching landlords to have at least one degree of mercy toward their tenants: lastly, of putting a spirit of honesty, industry, and skill into our shopkeepers; who, if a resolution could now be taken to buy only our native goods, would immediately unite to cheat and exact upon us in the price, the measure, and the goodness, nor could ever yet be brought to make one fair proposal of just dealing, though often and earnestly invited to it.[6]

Therefore, I repeat, let no man talk to me of these and the like 30 expedients, till he hath at least some glimpse of hope that there will ever be some hearty and sincere attempt to put them in practice.

But as to myself, having been wearied out for many years with 31 offering vain, idle, visionary thoughts, and at length utterly despairing of success, I fortunately fell upon this proposal, which, as it is wholly new, so it hath something solid and real, of no expense and little trouble, full in our own power, and whereby we can incur no danger in disobliging England. For this kind of commodity will not bear exportation, the flesh being of too tender a consistence to admit a long continuance in salt, although perhaps I could name a country which would be glad to eat up our whole nation without it.

After all, I am not so violently bent upon my own opinion as to 32 reject any offer proposed by wise men, which shall be found equally innocent, cheap, easy, and effectual. But before something of that kind shall be advanced in contradiction to my scheme, and offering a better, I desire the author or authors will be pleased maturely to consider two points. First, as things now stand, how they will be

[5]A district in Brazil.
[6]Swift himself had made these various proposals in previous works.

able to find food and raiment for an hundred thousand useless mouths and backs. And secondly, there being a round million of creatures in human figure throughout this kingdom, whose sole subsistence put into a common stock would leave them in debt two millions of pounds sterling, adding those who are beggars by profession to the bulk of farmers, cottagers, and laborers, with their wives and children who are beggars in effect; I desire those politicians who dislike my overture, and may perhaps be so bold to attempt an answer, that they will first ask the parents of these mortals whether they would not at this day think it a great happiness to have been sold for food at a year old in this manner I prescribe, and thereby have avoided such a perpetual scene of misfortunes as they have since gone through by the oppression of landlords, the impossibility of paying rent without money or trade, the want of common sustenance, with neither house nor clothes to cover them from the inclemencies of the weather, and the most inevitable prospect of entailing the like or greater miseries upon their breed forever.

I profess, in the sincerity of my heart, that I have not the least   33
personal interest in endeavoring to promote this necessary work, having no other motive than the public good of my country, by advancing our trade, providing for infants, relieving the poor, and giving some pleasure to the rich. I have no children by which I can propose to get a single penny; the youngest being nine years old, and my wife past childbearing.

HENRY DAVID THOREAU

HENRY DAVID THOREAU (1817–1862), lived all but one year of his life in Concord, Massachusetts, where he was known as a non-conformist, an eccentric. He did some teaching and lecturing, and gained a sound reputation as a naturalist, and, of course, as an author, contributing both verse and prose to magazines and newspapers of the day. In *Walden,* his book of essays, Thoreau leaves us an account of his "experiment in living" (alone in the woods at Walden Pond), but he also gives us a careful study of nature, a critical view of then-modern society, and a work of much artistic merit. But probably none of his work has had such far-reaching effects as the essay "Civil Disobedience." It has been read, pondered, and acted upon in various parts of the world — for example, by Mahatma Gandhi in his long and nonviolent struggle for a free India. The following is a portion of that essay.

from "Civil Disobedience"

I heartily accept the motto, — "That government is best which   1
governs least"; and I should like to see it acted up to more rapidly and systematically. Carried out, it finally amounts to this, which also I believe, — "That government is best which governs not at all"; and when men are prepared for it, that will be the kind of government which they will have. Government is at best but an expedient; but most governments are usually, and all governments are sometimes, inexpedient. The objections which have been brought against a standing army, and they are many and weighty, and deserve to prevail, may also at last be brought against a stand-ing government. The standing army is only an arm of the standing government. The government itself, which is only the mode which the people have chosen to execute their will, is equally liable to be abused and perverted before the people can act through it. Witness the present Mexican war, the work of comparatively a few indi-

viduals using the standing government as their tool; for, in the outset, the people would not have consented to this measure.

This American government, — what is it but a tradition, though a recent one, endeavoring to transmit itself unimpaired to posterity, but each instant losing some of its integrity? It has not the vitality and force of a single living man; for a single man can bend it to his will. It is a sort of wooden gun to the people themselves. But it is not the less necessary for this; for the people must have some complicated machinery or other, and hear its din, to satisfy that idea of government which they have. Governments show thus how successfully men can be imposed on, even impose on themselves, for their own advantage. It is excellent, we must all allow. Yet this government never of itself furthered any enterprise, but by the alacrity with which it got out of its way. *It* does not keep the country free. *It* does not settle the West. *It* does not educate. The character inherent in the American people has done all that has been accomplished; and it would have done somewhat more, if the government had not sometimes got in its way. For government is an expedient by which men would fain succeed in letting one another alone; and, as has been said, when it is most expedient, the governed are most let alone by it. Trade and commerce, if they were not made of India-rubber, would never manage to bounce over the obstacles which legislators are continually putting in their way; and, if one were to judge these men wholly by the effects of their actions and not partly by their intentions, they would deserve to be classed and punished with those mischievous persons who put obstructions on the railroads.

But, to speak practically and as a citizen, unlike those who call themselves no-government men, I ask for, not at once no government, but *at once* a better government. Let every man make known what kind of government would command his respect, and that will be one step toward obtaining it.

After all, the practical reason why, when the power is once in the hands of the people, a majority are permitted, and for a long period continue, to rule is not because they are most likely to be in the right, nor because this seems fairest to the minority, but because they are physically the strongest. But a government in which the majority rule in all cases cannot be based on justice, even as far as men understand it. Can there not be a government in which majorities do not virtually decide right and wrong, but conscience? — in which majorities decide only those questions to which the rule of expediency is applicable? Must the citizen ever for a moment, or in the least degree, resign his conscience to the legislator? Why has every man a conscience, then? I think that we should be men first, and subjects afterward. It is not desirable to cultivate a respect for the law, so much as for the right. The only obligation which I have a right to assume is to do at any time what I think right. It is truly enough said, that a corporation has no conscience; but a corporation of conscientious men is a corporation *with* a conscience. Law never made men a whit more just; and, by means of their respect for it, even the well-disposed are daily made the agents of injustice. A common and natural result of an undue respect for law is, that you may see a file of soldiers, colonel, captain, corporal, privates, powder-monkeys, and all, marching in admirable order over hill and dale to the wars, against their wills, ay, against their common sense and consciences, which makes it very steep marching indeed, and produces a palpitation of the heart. They have no doubt that it is a damnable business in which they are concerned; they are all peaceably inclined. Now, what are they? Men at all? Or small movable forts and magazines, at the service of some unscrupulous man in power? Visit the Navy-Yard, and behold a marine, such a man as an American government can make, or such as it can make a man with its black arts, — a mere shadow and reminiscence of humanity, a man laid out alive and standing, and already, as one may say, buried under arms with funeral accompaniments, though it may be, —

Not a drum was heard, not a funeral note,
    As his corse to the rampart we hurried;
Not a soldier discharged his farewell shot
    O'er the grave where our hero we buried.

    The mass of men serve the state thus, not as men mainly, but as machines, with their bodies. They are the standing army, and the militia, jailors, constables, posse comitatus, etc. In most cases there is no free exercise whatever of the judgment or of the moral sense; but they put themselves on a level with wood and earth and stones; and wooden men can perhaps be manufactured that will serve the purpose as well. Such command no more respect than men of straw or a lump of dirt. They have the same sort of worth only as horses and dogs. Yet such as these even are commonly esteemed good

    5

citizens. Others — as most legislators, politicians, lawyers, ministers, and office-holders — serve the state chiefly with their heads; and, as they rarely make any moral distinctions, they are as likely to serve the Devil, without *intending* it, as God. A very few, as heroes, patriots, martyrs, reformers in the great sense, and *men*, serve the state with their consciences also, and so necessarily resist it for the most part; and they are commonly treated as enemies by it. A wise man will only be useful as a man, and will not submit to be "clay," and "stop a hole to keep the wind away," but leave that office to his dust at least:

I am too high-born to be propertied,
To be a secondary at control,
Or useful serving-man and instrument
To any sovereign state throughout the world.

He who gives himself entirely to his fellow-men appears to   6
them useless and selfish; but he who gives himself partially to them
is pronounced a benefactor and philanthropist.

How does it become a man to behave toward this American   7
government to-day? I answer, that he cannot without disgrace be
associated with it. I cannot for an instant recognize that political
organization as *my* government which is the *slave's* government
also.

All men recognize the right of revolution; that is, the right to   8
refuse allegiance to, and to resist, the government, when its tyranny
or its inefficiency are great and unendurable. But almost all say that
such is not the case now. But such was the case, they think, in the
Revolution of '75. If one were to tell me that this was a bad government
because it taxed certain foreign commodities brought to its
ports, it is most probable that I should not make an ado about it, for I
can do without them. All machines have their friction; and possibly
this does enough good to counterbalance the evil. At any rate, it is a
great evil to make a stir about it. But when the friction comes to have
its machine, and oppression and robbery are organized, I say, let us
not have such a machine any longer. In other words, when a sixth of
the population of a nation which has undertaken to be the refuge of
liberty are slaves, and a whole country is unjustly overrun and
conquered by a foreign army, and subjected to military law, I think
that it is not too soon for honest men to rebel and revolutionize.

What makes this duty the more urgent is the fact that the country so overrun is not our own, but ours is the invading army. . . .

Practically speaking, the opponents to a reform in Massachusetts are not a hundred thousand politicians at the South, but a hundred thousand merchants and farmers here, who are more interested in commerce and agriculture than they are in humanity, and are not prepared to do justice to the slave and to Mexico, *cost what it may.* I quarrel not with far-off foes, but with those who, near at home, coöperate with, and do the bidding of, those far away, and without whom the latter would be harmless. We are accustomed to say, that the mass of men are unprepared, but improvement is slow, because the few are not materially wiser or better than the many. It is not so important that many should be as good as you, as that there be some absolute goodness somewhere; for that will leaven the whole lump. There are thousands who are *in opinion* opposed to slavery and to the war, who yet in effect do nothing to put an end to them; who, esteeming themselves children of Washington and Franklin, sit down with their hands in their pockets, and say that they know not what to do, and do nothing; who even postpone the question of freedom to the question of free-trade, and quietly read the prices-current along with the latest advices from Mexico, after dinner, and, it may be, fall asleep over them both. What is the price-current of an honest man and patriot to-day? They hesitate, and they regret, and sometimes they petition; but they do nothing in earnest and with effect. They will wait, well disposed, for others to remedy the evil, that they may no longer have it to regret. At most, they give only a cheap vote, and a feeble countenance and Godspeed, to the right, as it goes by them. There are nine hundred and ninety-nine patrons of virtue to one virtuous man. But it is easier to deal with the real possessor of a thing than with the temporary guardian of it.

All voting is a sort of gaming, like checkers or backgammon, with a slight moral tinge to it, a playing with right and wrong, with moral questions; and betting naturally accompanies it. The character of the voters is not staked. I cast my vote, perchance, as I think right; but I am not vitally concerned that that right should prevail. I am willing to leave it to the majority. Its obligation, therefore, never exceeds that of expediency. Even voting *for the right* is *doing* nothing for it. Is it only expressing to men feebly your desire that it should prevail. A wise man will not leave the right to the mercy of chance, nor wish it to prevail through the power of the majority. There is but little virtue in the action of masses of men. When the majority shall at length vote for the abolition of slavery, it will be because they are indifferent to slavery, or because there is but little slavery left to be abolished by their vote. *They* will then be the only slaves. Only *his* vote can hasten the abolition of slavery who asserts his own freedom by his vote.

I hear of a convention to be held at Baltimore, or elsewhere, for   11
the selection of a candidate for the Presidency, made up chiefly of editors, and men who are politicians by profession; but I think, what is it to any independent, intelligent, and respectable man what decision they may come to? Shall we not have the advantage of his wisdom and honesty, nevertheless? Can we not count upon some independent votes? Are there not many individuals in the country who do not attend conventions? But no: I find that the respectable man, so called, has immediately drifted from his position, and despairs of his country, when his country has more reason to despair of him. He forthwith adopts one of the candidates thus selected as the only *available* one, thus proving that he is himself *available* for any purposes of the demagogue. His vote is of no more worth than that of any unprincipled foreigner or hireling native, who may have been bought. O for a man who is a *man*, and, as my neighbor says, has a bone in his back which you cannot pass your hand through! Our statistics are at fault: The population has been returned too large. How many *men* are there to a square thousand miles in this country? Hardly one. Does not America offer any inducement for men to settle here? The American has dwindled into an Odd Fellow, — one who may be known by the development of his organ of gregariousness, and a manifest lack of intellect and cheerful self-reliance; whose first and chief concern, on coming into the world, is to see that the Alms-houses are in good repair; and, before yet he has lawfully donned the virile garb, to collect a fund for the support of the widows and orphans that may be; who, in sort, ventures to live only by the aid of the Mutual Insurance company, which has promised to bury him decently.

It is not a man's duty, as a matter of course, to devote himself to   12
the eradication of any, even the most enormous wrong; he may still properly have other concerns to engage him; but it is his duty, at least, to wash his hands of it, and, if he gives it no thought longer,

not to give it practically his support. If I devote myself to other pursuits and contemplations, I must first see, at least, that I do not pursue them sitting upon another man's shoulders. I must get off him first, that he may pursue his contemplations too. See what gross inconsistency is tolerated. I have heard some of my townsmen say, "I should like to have them order me out to help put down an insurrection of the slaves, or to march to Mexico; — see if I would go"; and yet these very men have each, directly by their allegiance, and so indirectly, at least, by their money, furnished a substitute. The soldier is applauded who refuses to serve in an unjust war by those who do not refuse to sustain the unjust government which makes the war; is applauded by those whose own act and authority he disregards and sets at naught; as if the state were penitent and to that degree that it hired one to scourge it while it sinned, but not to that degree that it left off sinning for a moment. Thus, under the name of Order and Civil Government, we are all made at last to pay homage to and support our own meanness. After the first blush of sin comes its indifference, and from immoral it becomes, as it were, *un*moral, and not quite unnecessary to that life which we have made.

The broadest and most prevalent error requires the most disin- 13
terested virtue to sustain it. The slight reproach to which the virtue of patriotism is commonly liable, the noble are most likely to incur. Those who, while they disapprove of the character and measures of a government, yield to it their allegiance and support are undoubtedly its most conscientious supporters, and so frequently the most serious obstacles to reform. Some are petitioning the state to dissolve the Union, to disregard the requisitions of the President. Why do they not dissolve it themselves, — the union between themselves and the state, — and refuse to pay their quota into its treasury? Do not they stand in the same relation to the state that the state does to the Union? And have not the same reasons prevented the state from resisting the Union which have prevented them from resisting the state?

How can a man be satisfied to entertain an opinion merely, and 14
enjoy *it?* Is there any enjoyment in it, if his opinion is that he is aggrieved? If you are cheated out of a single dollar by your neighbor, you do not rest satisfied with knowing that you are cheated, or with saying that you are cheated, or even with petitioning him to pay you your due; but you take effectual steps at once to obtain the full

amount, and see that you are never cheated again. Action from principle, the perception and the performance of right, changes things and relations; it is essentially revolutionary, and does not consist wholly with anything which was. It not only divides states and churches, it divides families; ay, it divides the *individual*, separating the diabolical in him from the divine.

Unjust laws exist: shall we be content to obey them, or shall we   15
endeavor to amend them, and obey them until we have succeeded, or shall we transgress them at once? Men generally, under such a government as this, think that they ought to wait until they have persuaded the majority to alter them. They think that, if they should resist, the remedy would be worse than the evil. But it is the fault of the government itself that the remedy *is* worse than the evil. *It* makes it worse. Why is it not more apt to anticipate and provide for reform? Why does it not cherish its wise minority? Why does it cry and resist before it is hurt? Why does it not encourage its citizens to be on the alert to point out its faults and *do* better than it would have them? Why does it always crucify Christ, and excommunicate Copernicus and Luther, and pronounce Washington and Franklin rebels? . . .

I meet this American government, or its representative, the   16
state government, directly, and face to face, once a year — no more — in the person of its tax-gatherer; this is the only mode in which a man situated as I am necessarily meets it; and it then says distinctly, Recognize me; and the simplest, most effectual, and, in the present posture of affairs, the indispensablest mode of treating with it on this head, of expressing your little satisfaction with and love for it, is to deny it then. My civil neighbor, the tax-gatherer, is the very man I have to deal with, — for it is, after all, with men and not with parchment that I quarrel, — and he has voluntarily chosen to be an agent of the government. How shall he ever know well what he is and does as an officer of the government, or as a man, until he is obliged to consider whether he shall treat me, his neighbor, for whom he has respect, as a neighbor and well-disposed man, or as a maniac and disturber of the peace, and see if he can get over this obstruction to his neighborliness without a ruder and more impetuous thought or speech corresponding with his action. I know this well, that if one thousand, if one hundred, if ten men whom I could name, — if ten *honest* men only, — ay, if *one* HONEST man, in this State of Massachusetts, *ceasing to hold slaves*, were actually to

withdraw from this co-partnership, and be locked up in the county jail therefor, it would be the abolition of slavery in America. For it matters not how small the beginning may seem to be: what is once well done is done forever. But we love better to talk about it: that we say is our mission. Reform keeps many scores of newspapers in its service, but not one man. If my esteemed neighbor, the State's ambassador, who will devote his days to the settlement of the question of human rights in the Council Chamber, instead of being threatened with the prisons of Carolina, were to sit down the prisoner of Massachusetts, that State which is so anxious to foist the sin of slavery upon her sister, — though at present she can discover only an act of inhospitality to be the ground of a quarrel with her, — the Legislature would not wholly waive the subject the following winter.

Under a government which imprisons any unjustly, the true 17 place for a just man is also a prison. The proper place to-day, the only place which Massachusetts has provided for her freer and less desponding spirits, is in her prisons, to be put out and locked out of the State by her own act, as they have already put themselves out by their principles. It is there that the fugitive slave, and the Mexican prisoner on parole, and the Indian come to plead the wrongs of his race should find them; on that separate, but more free and honorable ground, where the State places those who are not *with* her, but *against* her, — the only house in a slave State in which a free man can abide with honor. If any think that their influence would be lost there, and their voices no longer afflict the ear of the State, that they would not be as an enemy within its walls, they do not know by how much truth is stronger than error, nor how much more eloquently and effectively he can combat injustice who has experienced a little in his own person. Cast your whole vote, not a strip of paper merely, but your whole influence. A minority is powerless while it conforms to the majority; it is not even a minority then; but it is irresistible when it clogs by its whole weight. If the alternative is to keep all just men in prison, or give up war and slavery, the State will not hesitate which to choose. If a thousand men were not to pay their tax bills this year, that would not be a violent and bloody measure, as it would be to pay them, and enable the State to commit violence and shed innocent blood. This is, in fact, the definition of a peaceable revolution, if any such is possible. If the tax-gatherer, or any other public officer, asks me, as one has done, "But what shall I do?" my answer is, "If you really wish to do anything, resign your office." When the subject has refused allegiance, and the officer has resigned his office, then the revolution is accomplished. But even suppose blood should flow. Is there not a sort of blood shed when the conscience is wounded? Through this wound a man's real manhood and immortality flow out, and he bleeds to an everlasting death. I see this blood flowing now. . . .

I have paid no poll-tax for six years. I was put into a jail once on this account, for one night; and, as I stood considering the walls of solid stone, two or three feet thick, the door of wood and iron, a foot thick, and the iron grating which strained the light, I could not help being struck with the foolishness of that institution which treated me as if I were mere flesh and blood and bones, to be locked up. I wondered that it should have concluded at length that this was the best use it could put me to, and had never thought to avail itself of my services in some way. I saw that, if there was a wall of stone between me and my townsmen, there was a still more difficult one to climb or break through before they could get to be as free as I was. I did not for a moment feel confined, and the walls seemed a great waste of stone and mortar. I felt as if I alone of all my townsmen had paid my tax. They plainly did not know how to treat me, but behaved like persons who are underbred. In every threat and in every compliment there was a blunder; for they thought that my chief desire was to stand the other side of that stone wall. I could not but smile to see how industriously they locked the door on my meditations, which followed them out again without let or hindrance, and *they* were really all that was dangerous. As they could not reach me, they had resolved to punish my body; just as boys, if they cannot come at some person against whom they have a spite, will abuse his dog. I saw that the State was half-witted, that it was timid as a lone woman with her silver spoons, and that it did not know its friends from its foes, and I lost all my remaining respect for it, and pitied it.

Thus the State never intentionally confronts a man's sense, intellectual or moral, but only his body, his senses. It is not armed with superior wit or honesty, but with superior physical strength. I was not born to be forced. I will breathe after my own fashion. Let us see who is the strongest. What force has a multitude? They only can force me who obey a higher law than I. They force me to become like themselves. I do not hear of *men* being *forced* to live this way or that by masses of men. What sort of life were that to live? When I meet a government which says to me, "Your money or your life," why should I be in haste to give it my money? It may be in a great strait, and not know what to do: I cannot help that. It must help itself: do as I do. It is not worth the while to snivel about it. I am not responsible for the successful working of the machinery of society. I am not the son of the engineer. I perceive that when an acorn and a chestnut fall side by side, the one does not remain inert to make way for the other, but both obey their own laws, and spring and grow and flourish as best they can, till one, perchance, overshadows and destroys the other. If a plant cannot live according to its nature, it dies; and so a man.

GEORGE ORWELL

GEORGE ORWELL published "Politics and the English Language" in 1945. It became one of his most famous essays. (A biographical sketch of Orwell appears on page 296 in Section 9.)

Politics and the English Language

Most people who bother with the matter at all would admit that the English language is in a bad way, but it is generally assumed that we cannot by conscious action do anything about it. Our civilization is decadent and our language — so the argument runs — must inevitably share in the general collapse. It follows that any struggle against the abuse of language is a sentimental archaism, like preferring candles to electric light or hansom cabs to aeroplanes. Underneath this lies the half-conscious belief that language is a natural growth and not an instrument which we shape for our own purpose.

Now, it is clear that the decline of a language must ultimately have political and economic causes: it is not due simply to the bad influence of this or that individual writer. But an effect can become a cause, reinforcing the original cause and producing the same effect in an intensified form, and so on indefinitely. A man may take to drink because he feels himself to be a failure, and then fail all the more completely because he drinks. It is rather the same thing that is happening to the English language. It becomes ugly and inaccurate because our thoughts are foolish, but the slovenliness of our language makes it easier for us to have foolish thoughts. The point is that the process is reversible. Modern English, especially written

English, is full of bad habits which spread by imitation and which can be avoided if one is willing to take the necessary trouble. If one gets rid of these habits one can think more clearly, and to think clearly is a necessary first step towards political regeneration: so that the fight against bad English is not frivolous and is not the exclusive concern of professional writers. I will come back to this presently, and I hope that by that time the meaning of what I have said here will have become clearer. Meanwhile, here are five specimens of the English language as it is now habitually written.

These five passages have not been picked out because they are 3 especially bad — I could have quoted far worse if I had chosen — but because they illustrate various of the mental vices from which we now suffer. They are a little below the average, but are fairly representative samples. I number them so that I can refer back to them when necessary:

(1) I am not, indeed, sure whether it is not true to say that the Milton who once seemed not unlike a seventeenth-century Shelley had not become, out of an experience ever more bitter in each year, more alien [*sic*] to the founder of that Jesuit sect which nothing could induce him to tolerate.

Professor Harold Laski (Essay in *Freedom of Expression*)

(2) Above all, we cannot play ducks and drakes with a native battery of idioms which prescribes such egregious collocations of vocables as the Basic *put up with* for *tolerate* or *put at a loss* for *bewilder*.

Professor Lancelot Hogben (*Interglossa*).

(3) On the one side we have the free personality: by definition it is not neurotic, for it has neither conflict nor dream. Its desires, such as they are, are transparent, for they are just what institutional approval keeps in the forefront of consciousness; another institutional pattern would alter their number and intensity; there is little in them that is natural, irreducible, or culturally dangerous. But *on the other side,* the social bond itself is nothing but the mutual reflection of these self-secure integrities. Recall the definition of love. Is not this the very picture of a small academic? Where is there a place in this hall of mirrors for either personality or fraternity?

Essay on psychology in *Politics* (New York)

(4) All the "best people" from the gentlemen's clubs, and all the frantic fascist captains, united in common hatred of Socialism and bestial horror of the rising tide of the mass revolutionary movement, have turned to acts of provocation, to foul incendiarism, to medieval legends of poisoned wells, to

legalize their own destruction of proletarian organizations, and rouse the agitated petty-bourgeoisie to chauvinistic fervor on behalf of the fight against the revolutionary way out of the crisis.

Communist pamphlet

(5) If a new spirit *is* to be infused into this old country, there is one thorny and contentious reform which must be tackled, and that is the humanization and galvanization of the B.B.C. Timidity here will bespeak cancer and atrophy of the soul. The heart of Britain may be sound and of strong beat, for instance, but the British lion's roar at present is like that of Bottom in Shakespeare's *Midsummer Night's Dream* — as gentle as any sucking dove. A virile new Britain cannot continue indefinitely to be traduced in the eyes or rather ears, of the world by the effete languors of Langham Place, brazenly masquerading as "standard English." When the Voice of Britain is heard at nine o'clock, better far and infinitely less ludicrous to hear aitches honestly dropped than the present priggish, inflated, inhibited, school-ma'amish arch braying of blameless bashful mewing maidens!

Letter in *Tribune*

Each of these passages has faults of its own, but, quite apart from avoidable ugliness, two qualities are common to all of them. The first is staleness of imagery; the other is lack of precision. The writer either has a meaning and cannot express it, or he inadvertently says something else, or he is almost indifferent as to whether his words mean anything or not. The mixture of vagueness and sheer incompetence is the most marked characteristic of modern English prose, and especially of any kind of political writing. As soon as certain topics are raised, the concrete melts into the abstract and no one seems to think of turns of speech that are not hackneyed: prose consists less and less of *words* chosen for the sake of their meaning, and more and more of *phrases* tacked together like the sections of a prefabricated henhouse. I list below, with notes and examples, various of the tricks by means of which the work of prose-construction is habitually dodged:

DYING METAPHORS

A newly invented metaphor assists thought by evoking a visual image, while on the other hand a metaphor which is technically "dead" (e.g., *iron resolution*) has in effect reverted to being an ordinary word and can generally be used without loss of vividness. But in between these two classes there is a huge dump of worn-out metaphors which have lost all evocative power and are merely used because they save people the trouble of inventing phrases for themselves. Examples are: *ring the changes on, take up the cudgels for, toe the line, ride roughshod over, stand shoulder to shoulder with, play into the hands of, no axe to grind, grist to the mill, fishing in troubled waters, on the order of the day, Achilles' heel, swan song, hotbed.* Many of these are used without knowledge of their meaning (what is a "rift", for instance?), and incompatible metaphors are frequently mixed, a sure sign that the writer is not interested in what he is saying. Some metaphors now current have been twisted out of their original meaning without those who use them even being aware of the fact. For example, *toe the line* is sometimes written *tow the line.* Another example is *the hammer and the anvil,* now always used with the implication that the anvil gets the worst of it. In real life it is always the anvil that breaks the hammer, never the other way about: a writer who stopped to think what he was saying would be aware of this, and would avoid perverting the original phrase.

OPERATORS OR VERBAL FALSE LIMBS

These save the trouble of picking out appropriate verbs and nouns, and at the same time pad each sentence with extra syllables which give it an appearance of symmetry. Characteristic phrases are: *render inoperative, militate against, make contact with, be subjected to, give rise to, give grounds for, have the effect of, play a leading part (role) in, make itself felt, take effect, exhibit a tendency to, serve the purpose of,* etc., etc. The keynote is the elimination of simple verbs. Instead of being a single word, such as *break, stop, spoil, mend, kill,* a verb becomes a *phrase,* made up of a noun or adjective tacked on to some general-purpose verb such as *prove, serve, form, play, render.* In addition, the passive voice is wherever possible used in preference to the active, and noun constructions are used instead of gerunds (*by examination of* instead of *by examining*). The range of verbs is further cut down by means of the *-ize* and *de-* formation, and the banal statements are given an appearance of profundity by means of the *not un-* formation. Simple conjunctions and prepositions are replaced by such phrases as *with respect to, having regard to, the fact that, by dint of, in view of, in the interests of, on the hypothesis that;* and the ends of sentences are saved from anticlimax by such resounding common places as *greatly to be desired, cannot be left out of account, a development to be expected in the near future, deserving of serious consideration, brought to a satisfactory conclusion,* and so on and so forth.

PRETENTIOUS DICTION

Words like *phenomenon, element, individual* (as noun), *objective, cate-* 7
gorical, effective, virtual, basic, primary, promote, constitute, exhibit, exploit, utilize, eliminate, liquidate, are used to dress up simple statements and give an air of scientific impartiality to biased judgments. Adjectives like *epoch-making, epic, historic, unforgettable, triumphant, age-old, inevitable, inexorable, veritable,* are used to dignify the sordid processes of international politics, while writing that aims at glorifying war usually takes on an archaic color, its characteristic words being: *realm, throne, chariot, mailed fist, trident, sword, shield, buckler, banner, jackboot, clarion.* Foreign words and expressions such as *cul de sac, ancien régime, deus ex machina, mutatis mutandis, status quo, gleichshaltung, weltanschauung,* are used to give an air of culture and elegance. Except for the useful abbreviations *i.e., e.g.,* and *etc.,* there is no real need for any of the hundreds of foreign phrases now current in English. Bad writers, and especially scientific, political and sociological writers, are nearly always haunted by the notion that Latin or Greek words are grander than Saxon ones, and unnecessary words like *expedite, ameliorate, predict, extraneous, deracinated, clandestine, subaqueous* and hundreds of others constantly gain ground from their Anglo-Saxon opposite numbers.[1] The jargon peculiar to Marxist writing (*hyena, hangman, cannibal, petty bourgeois, these gentry, lacquey, flunkey, mad dog, White Guard,* etc.) consists largely of words and phrases translated from Russian, German, or French; but the normal way of coining a new word is to use a Latin or Greek root with the appropriate affix and, where necessary, the *-ize* formation. It is often easier to make up words of this kind (*deregionalize, impermissible, extramarital, nonfragmentatory* and so forth) than to think up the English words that will cover one's meaning. The result, in general, is an increase in slovenliness and vagueness.

---

[1] An interesting illustration of this is the way in which the English flower names which were in use till very recently are being ousted by Greek ones, *snapdragon* becoming *antirrhinum, forget-me-not* becoming *myosotis,* etc. It is hard to see any practical reason for this change of fashion: it is probably due to an instinctive turning-away from the more homely word and a vague feeling that the Greek word is scientific.

MEANINGLESS WORDS

In certain kinds of writing, particularly in art criticism and literary criticism, it is normal to come across long passages which are almost completely lacking in meaning.[2] Words like *romantic, plastic, values, human, dead, sentimental, natural, vitality,* as used in art criticism, are strictly meaningless in the sense that they not only do not point to any discoverable object, but are hardly ever expected to do so by the reader. When one critic writes, "The outstanding feature of Mr. X's work is its living quality," while another writes, "The immediately striking thing about Mr. X's work is its peculiar deadness," the reader accepts this as a simple difference of opinion. If words like *black* and *white* were involved, instead of the jargon words *dead* and *living,* he would see at once that language was being used in an improper way. Many political words are similarly abused. The word *Fascism* has now no meaning except in so far as it signifies "something not desirable." The words *democracy, socialism, freedom, patriotic, realistic, justice,* have each of them several different meanings which cannot be reconciled with one another. In the case of a word like *democracy,* not only is there no agreed definition, but the attempt to make one is resisted from all sides. It is almost universally felt that when we call a country democratic we are praising it: consequently the defenders of every kind of régime claim that it is a democracy, and fear that they might have to stop using the word if it were tied down to any one meaning. Words of this kind are often used in a consciously dishonest way. That is, the person who uses them has his own private definition, but allows his hearer to think he means something quite different. Statements like *Marshal Pétain was a true patriot, The Soviet Press is the freest in the world, The Catholic Church is opposed to persecution,* are almost always made with intent to deceive. Other words used in variable meanings, in most cases more or less dishonestly, are: *class, totalitarian, science, progressive, reactionary, bourgeois, equality.*

[2]Example: "Comfort's catholicity of perception and image, strangely Whitmanesque in range, almost the exact opposite in aesthetic compulsion, continues to evoke that trembling atmospheric accumulative hinting at a cruel, an inexorably serene timelessness . . . Wrey Gardiner scores by aiming at simple bull's-eyes with precision. Only they are not so simple, and through this contented sadness runs more than the surface bitter-sweet of resignation." (*Poetry Quarterly.*)

8

Now that I have made this catalogue of swindles and perver-   s
sions, let me give another example of the kind of writing that they
lead to. This time it must of its nature be an imaginary one. I am
going to translate a passage of good English into modern English of
the worst sort. Here is a well-known verse from *Ecclesiastes:*

> I returned and saw under the sun, that the race is not to the swift, nor
> the battle to the strong, neither yet bread to the wise, nor yet riches to men
> of understanding, nor yet favour to men of skill; but time and chance
> happeneth to them all.

Here it is in modern English:

> Objective consideration of contemporary phenomena compels the con-
> clusion that success or failure in competitive activities exhibits no tendency
> to be commensurate with innate capacity, but that a considerable element of
> the unpredictable must invariably be taken into account.

This is a parody, but not a very gross one. Exhibit (3), above, for   ▮
instance, contains several patches of the same kind of English. It will
be seen that I have not made a full translation. The beginning and
ending of the sentence follow the original meaning fairly closely,
but in the middle the concrete illustrations — race, battle, bread —
dissolve into the vague phrase "success or failure in competitive
activities." This had to be so, because no modern writer of the kind I
am discussing — no one capable of using phrases like "objective
consideration of contemporary phenomena" — would ever tabu-
late his thoughts in that precise and detailed way. The whole
tendency of modern prose is away from concreteness. Now analyze
these two sentences a little more closely. The first contains forty-
nine words but only sixty syllables, and all its words are those of
everyday life. The second contains thirty-eight words of ninety
syllables: eighteen of its words are from Latin roots, and one from
Greek. The first sentence contains six vivid images, and only one
phrase ("time and chance") that could be called vague. The second
contains not a single fresh, arresting phrase, and in spite of its
ninety syllables it gives only a shortened version of the meaning
contained in the first. Yet without a doubt it is the second kind of
sentence that is gaining ground in modern English. I do not want to
exaggerate. This kind of writing is not yet universal, and outcrops of
simplicity will occur here and there in the worst-written page. Still,
if you or I were told to write a few lines on the uncertainty of human

fortunes, we should probably come much nearer to my imaginary sentence than to the one from *Ecclesiastes.*

As I have tried to show, modern writing at its worst does not consist in picking out words for the sake of their meaning and inventing images in order to make the meaning clearer. It consists in gumming together long strips of words which have already been set in order by someone else, and making the results presentable by sheer humbug. The attraction of this way of writing is that it is easy. It is easier — even quicker once you have the habit — to say *In my opinion it is a not unjustifiable assumption that* than to say *I think*. If you use ready-made phrases, you not only don't have to hunt about for words; you also don't have to bother with the rhythms of your sentences, since these phrases are generally so arranged as to be more or less euphonious. When you are composing in a hurry — when you are dictating to a stenographer, for instance, or making a public speech — it is natural to fall into a pretentious, Latinized style. Tags like *a consideration which we should do well to bear in mind* or *a conclusion to which all of us would readily assent* will save many a sentence from coming down with a bump. By using stale metaphors, similes and idioms, you save much mental effort, at the cost of leaving your meaning vague, not only for your reader but for yourself. This is the significance of mixed metaphors. The sole aim of a metaphor is to call up a visual image. When these images clash — as in *The Fascist octopus has sung its swan song, the jackboot is thrown into the melting pot* — it can be taken as certain that the writer is not seeing a mental image of the objects he is naming; in other words he is not really thinking. Look again at the examples I gave at the beginning of this essay. Professor Laski (1) uses five negatives in fifty-three words. One of these is superfluous, making nonsense of the whole passage, and in addition there is the slip *alien* for *akin*, making further nonsense, and several avoidable pieces of clumsiness which increase the general vagueness. Professor Hogben (2) plays ducks and drakes with a battery which is able to write prescriptions, and, while disapproving of the everyday phrase *put up with*, is unwilling to look *egregious* up in the dictionary and see what it means. (3), if one takes an uncharitable attitude towards it, is simply meaningless: probably one could work out its intended meaning by reading the whole of the article in which it occurs. In (4), the writer knows more or less what he wants to say, but an accumulation of stale phrases chokes him like tea leaves blocking a sink.

In (5), words and meaning have almost parted company. People who write in this manner usually have a general emotional meaning — they dislike one thing and want to express solidarity with another — but they are not interested in the detail of what they are saying. A scrupulous writer, in every sentence that he writes, will ask himself at least four questions, thus: What am I trying to say? What words will express it? What image or idiom will make it clearer? Is this image fresh enough to have an effect? And he will probably ask himself two more: Could I put it more shortly? Have I said anything that is avoidably ugly? But you are not obliged to go to all this trouble. You can shirk it by simply throwing your mind open and letting the ready-made phrases come crowding in. They will construct your sentences for you — even think your thoughts for you, to a certain extent — and at need they will perform the important service of partially concealing your meaning even from yourself. It is at this point that the special connection between politics and the debasement of language becomes clear.

In our times it is broadly true that political writing is bad writing. Where it is not true, it will generally be found that the writer is some kind of rebel, expressing his private opinions and not a "party line." Orthodoxy, of whatever color, seems to demand a lifeless, imitative style. The political dialects to be found in pamphlets, leading articles, manifestos, White Papers and the speeches of under-secretaries do, of course, vary from party to party, but they are all alike in that one almost never finds in them a fresh, vivid, home-made turn of speech. When one watches some tired hack on the platform mechanically repeating the familiar phrases — *bestial atrocities, iron heel, bloodstained tyranny, free peoples of the world, stand shoulder to shoulder* — one often has a curious feeling that one is not watching a live human being but some kind of dummy, a feeling which suddenly becomes stronger at moments when the light catches the speaker's spectacles and turns them into blank discs which seem to have no eyes behind them. And this is not altogether fanciful. A speaker who uses that kind of phraseology has gone some distance towards turning himself into a machine. The appropriate noises are coming out of his larynx, but his brain is not involved as it would be if he were choosing his words from himself. If the speech he is making is one that he is accustomed to make over and over again, he may be almost unconscious of what he is saying, as one is when one utters the responses in church. And this reduced state of consciousness, if not indispensable, is at any rate favorable to political conformity.

In our time, political speech and writing are largely the defense   13
of the indefensible. Things like the continuance of British rule in India, the Russian purges and deportations, the dropping of the atom bombs on Japan, can indeed be defended, but only by arguments which are too brutal for most people to face, and which do not square with the professed aims of political parties. Thus political language has to consist largely of euphemism, question-begging and sheer cloudy vagueness. Defenseless villages are bombarded from the air, the inhabitants driven out into the countryside, the cattle machine-gunned, the huts set on fire with incendiary bullets: this is called *pacification*. Millions of peasants are robbed of their farms and sent trudging along the roads with no more than they can carry: this is called *transfer of population* or *rectification of frontiers*. People are imprisoned for years without trial, or shot in the back of the neck or sent to die of scurvy in Arctic lumber camps: this is called *elimination of unreliable elements*. Such phraseology is needed if one wants to name things without calling up mental pictures of them. Consider for instance some comfortable English professor defending Russian totalitarianism. He cannot say outright, "I believe in killing off your opponents when you can get good results by doing so." Probably, therefore, he will say something like this:

"While freely conceding that the Soviet régime exhibits certain   14
features which the humanitarian may be inclined to deplore, we must, I think, agree that a certain curtailment of the right to political opposition is an unavoidable concomitant of transitional periods, and that the rigors which the Russian people have been called upon to undergo have been amply justified in the sphere of concrete achievement."

The inflated style is itself a kind of euphemism. A mass of Latin   15
words falls upon the facts like soft snow, blurring the outlines and covering up all the details. The great enemy of clear language is insincerity. When there is a gap between one's real and one's declared aims, one turns as it were instinctively to long words and exhausted idioms, like a cuttlefish squirting out ink. In our age there is no such thing as "keeping out of politics." All issues are political issues, and politics itself is a mass of lies, evasions, folly, hatred and schizophrenia. When the general atmosphere is bad, language must suffer. I should expect to find — this is a guess which I have not

sufficient knowledge to verify — that the German, Russian and Italian languages have all deteriorated in the last ten or fifteen years, as a result of dictatorship.

But if thought corrupts language, language can also corrupt thought. A bad usage can spread by tradition and imitation, even among people who should and do know better. The debased language that I have been discussing is in some ways very convenient. Phrases like *a not unjustifiable assumption, leaves much to be desired, would serve no good purpose, a consideration which we should do well to bear in mind,* are a continuous temptation, a packet of aspirins always at one's elbow. Look back through this essay, and for certain you will find that I have again and again committed the very faults I am protesting against. By this morning's post I have received a pamphlet dealing with conditions in Germany. The author tells me that he "felt impelled" to write it. I open it at random, and here is almost the first sentence that I see: "(The Allies) have an opportunity not only of achieving a radical transformation of Germany's social and political structure in such a way as to avoid a nationalistic reaction in Germany itself, but at the same time of laying the foundations of a co-operative and unified Europe." You see, he "feels impelled" to write — feels, presumably, that he has something new to say — and yet his words, like cavalry horses answering the bugle, group themselves automatically into the familiar dreary pattern. This invasion of one's mind by ready-made phrases (*lay the foundations, achieve a radical transformation*) can only be prevented if one is constantly on guard against them, and every such phrase anaesthetizes a portion of one's brain.

I said earlier that the decadence of our language is probably curable. Those who deny this would argue, if they produced an argument at all, that language merely reflects existing social conditions, and that we cannot influence its development by any direct tinkering with words and constructions. So far as the general tone or spirit of a language goes, this may be true, but it is not true in detail. Silly words and expressions have often disappeared, not through any evolutionary process but owing to the conscious action of a minority. Two recent examples were *explore every avenue* and *leave no stone unturned,* which were killed by the jeers of a few journalists. There is a long list of flyblown metaphors which could similarly be got rid of if enough people would interest themselves in the job; and it should also be possible to laugh the *not un-* formation out of existence,[3] to reduce the amount of Latin and Greek in the average sentence, to drive out foreign phrases and strayed scientific words, and, in general, to make pretentiousness unfashionable. But all these are minor points. The defense of the English language implies more than this, and perhaps it is best to start by saying what it does *not* imply.

To begin with it has nothing to do with archaism, with the salvaging of obsolete words and turns of speech, or with the setting up of a "standard English" which must never be departed from. On the contrary, it is especially concerned with the scrapping of every word or idiom which has outworn its usefulness. It has nothing to do with correct grammar and syntax, which are of no importance so long as one makes one's meaning clear, or with the avoidance of Americanisms, or with having what is called a "good prose style." On the other hand, it is not concerned with fake simplicity and the attempt to make written English colloquial. Nor does it even imply in every case preferring the Saxon word to the Latin one, though it does imply using the fewest and shortest words that will cover one's meaning. What is above all needed is to let the meaning choose the word, and not the other way about. In prose, the worst thing one can do with words is to surrender to them. When you think of a concrete object, you think wordlessly, and then, if you want to describe the thing you have been visualizing you probably hunt about till you find the exact words that seem to fit. When you think of something abstract, you are more inclined to use words from the start, and unless you make a conscious effort to prevent it, the existing dialect will come rushing in and do the job for you, at the expense of blurring or even changing your meaning. Probably it is better to put off using words as long as possible and get one's meaning as clear as one can through pictures or sensations. Afterwards one can choose — not simply *accept* — the phrases that will best cover the meaning, and then switch round and decide what impression one's words are likely to make on another person. This last effort of the mind cuts out all stale or mixed images, all prefabricated phrases, needless repetitions, and humbug and vagueness

18

[3]One can cure oneself of the *not un-* formation by memorizing this sentence: *A not unblack dog was chasing a not unsmall rabbit across a not ungreen field.*

generally. But one can often be in doubt about the effect of a word or a phrase, and one needs rules that one can rely on when instinct fails. I think the following rules will cover most cases:

(i) Never use a metaphor, simile or other figure of speech which you are used to seeing in print.

(ii) Never use a long word where a short one will do.

(iii) If it is possible to cut a word out, always cut it out.

(iv) Never use the passive where you can use the active.

(v) Never use a foreign phrase, a scientific word or jargon word if you can think of an everyday English equivalent.

(vi) Break any of these rules sooner than say anything outright barbarous.

These rules sound elementary, and so they are, but they demand a deep change in attitude in anyone who has grown used to writing in the style now fashionable. One could keep all of them and still write bad English, but one could not write the kind of stuff that I quoted in those five specimens at the beginning of this article.

I have not here been considering the literary use of language, but merely language as an instrument for expressing and not for concealing or preventing thought. Stuart Chase and others have come near to claiming that all abstract words are meaningless, and have used this as a pretext for advocating a kind of political quietism. Since you don't know what Fascism is, how can you struggle against Fascism? One need not swallow such absurdities as this, but one ought to recognize that the present political chaos is connected with the decay of language, and that one can probably bring about some improvement by starting at the verbal end. If you simplify your English, you are freed from the worst follies of orthodoxy. You cannot speak any of the necessary dialects, and when you make a stupid remark, its stupidity will be obvious, even to yourself. Political language — and with variations this is true of all political parties, from Conservatives to Anarchists — is designed to make lies sound truthful and murder respectable, and to give an appearance of solidity to pure wind. One cannot change this all in a moment, but one can at least change one's own habits, and from time to time one can even, if one jeers loudly enough, send some worn-out and useless phrase — some *jackboot, Achilles' heel, hotbed, melting pot, acid test, veritable inferno* or other lump of verbal refuse —into the dustbin where it belongs.

A Guide to Terms

Abstract (See *Concrete/Abstract.*)

Allusion (See *Figures of Speech.*)

Analogy (See Section 4.)

Argument is writing that uses factual evidence and supporting ideas to convince readers to share the author's opinion on an issue or to take some action the writer considers appropriate or necessary. Like exposition, argument conveys information, but it does so not to explain but to induce readers to favor one side in a conflict or to choose a particular course of action.

Some arguments appeal primarily to reason, other's primarily to emotion. Most, however, mix reason and emotion in whatever way is appropriate for the issue and the audience. (See Section 11.)

Support for an argument can take a number of forms:

1. *Examples* — Real-life examples, or hypothetical examples (used sparingly) can be convincing evidence if they are typical and if the author provides enough of them to illustrate all the major points in the argument or combines them with other kinds of evidence. (See Will, Sagan.)

2. *Facts and figures* — Detailed information about a subject, particularly if presented in statistical form, can help convince readers by showing that the author's perspective on an issue is consistent with what is known about the subject. But facts whose accuracy is questionable or statistics that are confusing can undermine an argument.

3. *Authority* — Supporting an argument with the ideas or the actual words of someone who is recognized as an expert can

be an effective strategy as long as the author can show that the expert is a reliable witness and can combine the expert's opinion with other kinds of evidence that point in the same direction. (See Will.)

4. *Personal experience* — Examples drawn from personal experience or the experience of friends can be more detailed and vivid (and hence more convincing) than other kinds of evidence, but a writer should use this kind of evidence sparingly because readers may sometimes suspect that it represents no more than one person's way of looking at events. When combined with other kinds of evidence, however, examples drawn from personal experience can be an effective technique for persuasion. (See Thomas.)

In addition, all the basic expository patterns can be used to support an argument. (See Section 11.)

Cause (See Section 6.)

Central theme (See *Unity.*)

Classification (See Section 2.)

Clichés are tired expressions, perhaps once fresh and colorful, that have been overused until they have lost most of their effectiveness and become trite or hackneyed. The term is also applied, less commonly, to trite ideas or attitudes.

We may need to use clichés in conversation, of course, where the quick and economical phrase is an important and useful tool of expression — and where no one expects us to be constantly original. We are fortunate, in a way, to have a large accumulation of clichés from which to draw. To describe someone, without straining our originality very much, we can always declare that he is *as innocent as a lamb, as thin as a rail,* or *as fat as a pig;* that he is *as dumb as an ox, as sly as a fox,* or *as wise as an owl;* that he is *financially embarrassed* or *has a fly in the ointment* or *his ship has come in;* or that, *last but not least, in this day and age,* the *Grim Reaper* has taken him to *his eternal reward.* There is indeed *a large stockpile* from which we can draw for ordinary conversation.

But the trite expression, written down on paper, is a permanent reminder that the writer is either lazy or not aware of the dullness of stereotypes — or, even more damaging, it is a clue that the ideas themselves may be threadbare, and therefore can be adequately expressed in threadbare language.

Occasionally, of course, a writer can use obvious clichés deliberately (see Roiphe, par. 4; Sheehy, par. 12; B. Lawrence, par. 1). But usually to be fully effective writing must be fresh, and should seem to have been written specifically for the occasion. Clichés, however fresh and appropriate at one time, have lost these qualities.

Closings are almost as much of a problem as introductions, and they are equally important. The function of a closing is simply "to close," of course, but this implies somehow tying the entire writing into a neat package, giving the final sense of unity to the whole endeavor, and thus leaving the reader with a sense of satisfaction instead of an uneasy feeling that there ought to be another page. There is no standard length for closings. A short composition may be effectively completed with one sentence — or even without any real closing at all, if the last point discussed is a strong or climactic one. A longer piece of writing, however, may end more slowly, perhaps through several paragraphs.

A few types of weak endings are so common that warnings are in order here. Careful writers will avoid these faults: (1) giving the effect of having suddenly become tired and quit; (2) ending on a minor detail or an apparent afterthought; (3) bringing up a new point in the closing; (4) using any new qualifying remark in the closing (if they want their opinions to seem less dogmatic or generalized, they should go back to do their qualifying where the damage was done); (5) ending with an apology of any kind (authors who are not interested enough to become at least minor experts in their subject should not be wasting the reader's time).

Of the several acceptable ways of giving the sense of finality to a paper, the easiest is the *summary*, but it is also the least desirable for most short papers. Readers who have read and understood something only a page or two before probably do not need to have it reviewed for them. Such a review is apt to seem merely repetitious. Longer writings, of course, such as research or term papers, may require thorough summaries.

Several other closing techniques are available to writers. The following, which do not represent all the possibilities, are useful in many situations, and they can frequently be employed in combination:

1. *Using word signals* — e.g., *finally, at last, thus, and so, in conclusion,* as well as more original devices suggested by the subject itself. (See Thurber, Halsey, Simpson.)

2. *Changing the tempo* — usually a matter of sentence length or pace. This is a very subtle indication of finality, and it is difficult to achieve. (For examples of modified use, see Greene, Simpson.)

3. *Restating the central idea* of the writing — sometimes a "statement" so fully developed that it practically becomes a summary itself. (See Catton, Will.)

4. *Using climax* — a natural culmination of preceding points or, in some cases, the last major point itself. This is suitable, however, only if the materials have been so arranged that the last point is outstanding. (See Catton, Rettie, B. Lawrence, Korda.)

5. *Making suggestions,* perhaps mentioning a possible solution to the problem being discussed — a useful technique for exposition as well as for argument, and a natural signal of the end. (See Thurow.)

6. *Showing the topic's significance,* its effects, or the universality of its meaning — a commonly used technique that, if carefully handled, is an excellent indication of closing. (See Buckley, Rettie, Halsey, B. Lawrence, Thurow, Hoffman, Sagan.)

7. *Echoing the introduction* — a technique that has the virtue of improving the effect of unity by bringing the development around full circle, so to speak. The echo may be a reference to a problem posed or a significant expression, quotation, analogy, or symbol used in the introduction or elsewhere early in the composition. (See Thurber, Goodman.)

8. *Using some rhetorical device* — a sort of catchall category, but a good supply source that includes several very effective techniques: pertinent quotations, anecdotes and brief dialogues, metaphors, allusions, ironic comments, and various kinds of witty or memorable remarks. All, however, run the risk of seeming forced and hence amateurish; but properly handled, they make for an effective closing. (See White, Rettie, Sheehy, Halsey, B. Lawrence, Simpson, Greene, King, Douglas.)

Coherence is the quality of good writing that results from the presentation of all parts in logical and clear relations.

    Coherence and unity are usually studied together and, indeed, are almost inseparable. But whereas unity refers to the relation of parts to the central theme (see *Unity*), coherence refers to their relations with each other. In a coherent piece of writing, each sentence, each paragraph, each major division seems to grow out of those preceding it.

    Several transitional devices (see *Transition*) help to make these relations clear, but far more fundamental to coherence is the sound organization of materials. From the first moment of visualizing the subject materials in pattern, the writer's goal must be clear and logical development. If it is, coherence is almost ensured.

Colloquial Expressions are characteristic of conversation and informal writing, and they are normally perfectly appropriate in those contexts. However, most writing done for college, business, or professional purposes is considered "formal" writing; and for such usage, colloquialisms are too informal, too *folksy* (itself a word most dictionaries would label "colloq.").

    Some of the expressions appropriate only for informal usage are *kid* (for child), *boss* (for employer), *flunk, buddy, snooze, gym, a lot of, phone, skin flicks, porn*. In addition, contractions such as *can't* and *I'd* are usually regarded as colloquialisms and are never permissible in, for instance, a research or term paper.

    Slang is defined as a low level of colloquialism, but it is sometimes placed "below" colloquialism in respectability; even standard dictionaries differ as to just what the distinction is. (Some of the examples in the preceding paragraph, if included in dictionaries at all, are identified both ways.) At any rate, slang generally comprises words either coined or given novel meanings in an attempt at colorful or humorous expression. Slang soon becomes limp with overuse, however, losing whatever vigor it first had. In time, slang expressions either disappear completely or graduate to more acceptable colloquial status and thence, possibly, into standard usage. (That is one way in which our language is constantly changing.) But until their "graduations," slang and colloquialism have an appropriate place in formal writing only if used sparingly and for special effect. Because dictionaries frequently differ in matters of usage, the student should be sure to use a standard edition approved by the instructor. (For further examples, see Roiphe; Wolfe; Sheehy; Simpson, pars. 8, 16, 17.)

Comparison (See Section 3.)

Conclusions (See *Closings.*)

Concrete and **Abstract** words are both indispensable to the language, but a good rule in most writing is to use the concrete whenever possible. This policy also applies, of course, to sentences that express only abstract ideas, which concrete examples can often make clearer and more effective. Many expository and argumentative paragraphs are constructed with an abstract topic sentence and its concrete support. (See *Unity.*)

A concrete word names something that exists as an entity in itself, something that can be perceived by the human senses. We can see, touch, hear, and smell a horse — hence *horse* is a concrete word. But a horse's *strength* is not. We have no reason to doubt that strength exists, but it does not have an independent existence: something else must *be* strong or there is no strength. Hence *strength* is an abstract word.

Purely abstract reading is difficult for average readers; with no concrete images provided, they are constantly forced to make their own. Concrete writing helps readers to visualize and is therefore easier and faster to read.

(See *Specific/General* for further discussion.)

Connotation and **Denotation** both refer to the meanings of words. Denotation is the direct, literal meaning as it would be found in a dictionary, whereas connotation refers to the response a word *really* arouses in the reader or listener. (See Wolfe, par. 14; B. Lawrence.)

There are two types of connotation: personal and general. Personal connotations vary widely, depending on the experiences and moods that an individual associates with the word. (This corresponds with personal symbolism; see *Symbol.*) *Waterfall* is not apt to have the same meaning for the happy young honeymooners at Yosemite as it has for the grieving mother whose child has just drowned in a waterfall. General connotations are those shared by many people. *Fireside,* far beyond its obvious dictionary definition, generally connotes warmth and security and good companionship. *Mother,* which denotatively means simply "female parent," means much more connotatively.

A word or phrase considered less distasteful or offensive than a more direct expression is called a *euphemism,* and this is also a matter of connotation. (See Mitford.) The various expressions used instead of the more direct "four-letter words" referring to daily bathroom events are examples of euphemisms. (See Wolfe's "mounting" or D. H. Lawrence's "dirt.") *Remains* is often used instead of *corpse,* and a few newspapers still have people *passing away* and being *laid to rest,* rather than *dying* and being *buried.*

But a serious respect for the importance of connotations goes far beyond euphemistic practices. Young writers can hardly expect to know all the different meanings of words for all their potential readers, but they can at least be aware that words do *have* different meanings. Of course, this is most important in persuasive writing — in political speeches, in advertising copywriting, and in any endeavor where some sort of public image is being created. When President Franklin Roosevelt began his series of informal radio talks, he called them "fireside chats," thus putting connotation to work. An advertising copywriter trying to evoke the feeling of love and tenderness associated with motherhood is not seriously tempted to use *female parent* instead of *mother.*

In exposition, where the primary purpose is to explain, the writer ordinarily tries to avoid words that may have emotional overtones, unless these can somehow be used to increase understanding. In argument, however, a writer may on occasion wish to appeal to the emotions.

Contrast (See Section 3.)

Deduction (See Section 10.)

Denotation (See *Connotation/Denotation.*)

Description (See Section 8.)

Diction refers simply to "choice of words," but, not so simply, it involves many problems of usage, some of which are explained under several other headings in this guide, e.g., *Clichés, Colloquial Expressions, Connotation/Denotation, Concrete/Abstract —*

anything, in fact, that pertains primarily to word choices. But the characteristics of good diction may be more generally classified as follows:

1. *Accuracy* — the choice of words that mean exactly what the author intends.

2. *Economy* — the choice of the simplest and fewest words that will convey the exact meaning intended.

3. *Emphasis* — the choice of fresh, strong words, avoiding clichés and unnecessarily vague or general terms.

4. *Appropriateness* — the choice of words that suit the subject matter, the prospective reader-audience, and the purpose of the writing.

(For contrasts of diction see Sagan, Thurber, Dillard, King, Thomas, Greene.)

Division (See Section 2.)

Effect (See Section 6.)

Emphasis is almost certain to fall *somewhere,* and the author should be the one to decide where. A major point, not some minor detail, should be emphasized.

Following are the most common ways of achieving emphasis. Most of them apply to the sentence, the paragraph, or the overall writing — all of which can be seriously weakened by emphasis in the wrong places.

1. By *position* — the most emphatic position is usually at the end, the second most emphatic at the beginning. (There are a few exceptions, including news stories and certain kinds of scientific reports.) The middle, therefore, should be used for materials that do not deserve special emphasis. (See Buckley, for saving the most significant example until last; Catton, par. 16; and Rettie, for the long withheld revelation of the real central theme.)

A sentence in which the main point is held until the last is called a *periodic sentence,* e.g., "After a long night of suspense and horror, the cavalry arrived." In a *loose sentence,* the main point is disposed of earlier and followed by dependencies, e.g., "The cavalry arrived after a long night of suspense and horror." (See Thomas, par. 11, second sentence, for an effective periodic sentence that concludes an essay.)

2. By *proportion* — Ordinarily, but not necessarily, important elements are given the most attention and thus auto-

matically achieve a certain emphasis. (See Rettie for a unique kind of *reverse* application of this method.)

3. By *repetition* — Words and ideas may sometimes be given emphasis by reuse, usually in a different manner. If not cautiously handled, however, this method can seem merely repetitious, not emphatic. (See Thurber, D. H. Lawrence.)

4. By *flat statement* — Although an obvious way to achieve emphasis is simply to *tell* the reader what is most important, it is often least effective, at least when used as the only method. Readers have a way of ignoring such pointers as "most important" and "especially true." (See Catton, par. 16; Korda, the last part.)

5. By *mechanical devices* — Emphasis can be achieved by using italics (underlining), capital letters, or exclamation points. But too often these devices are used, however unintentionally, to cover deficiencies of content or style. Their employment can quickly be overdone and their impact lost. (For very limited and therefore especially emphatic use of italics and capitalization, see D. H. Lawrence and the "Inner Wonderfulness" of Halsey. Notice that Mitford, with a more emphatic style than most, uses none of these devices.)

6. By *distinctiveness of style* — The author can emphasize subtly with fresh and concrete words or figures of speech, crisp or unusual structures, and careful control of paragraph or sentence lengths. (These methods are used in many essays in this book: see Thurber; Buckley; Twain, who changes style radically for the second half of his essay; Catton; Rettie, par. 19; Wolfe; Thomas, pars. 9–10; Curtin, pars. 7–15.) *Verbal irony* (see *Irony)*, including *sarcasm* (see Buckley) and the rather specialized form known as *understatement*, if handled judiciously, is another valuable means of achieving distinctiveness of style and increasing emphasis. (See Wolfe, Mitford, D. H. Lawrence.)

Essay refers to a brief prose composition on a single topic, usually, but not always, communicating the author's personal ideas and impressions. Beyond this, because of the wide and loose application of the term, no really satisfactory definition has been universally accepted.

Classifications of essay types have also been widely varied and sometimes not very meaningful. One basic and useful distinction, however, is between *formal* and *informal* essays, although many defy classification even in such broad categories as these. It is best to regard the two types as opposite ends of a continuum, along which most essays may be placed.

The formal essay usually develops an important theme through a logical progression of ideas, with full attention to unity and coherence, and in a serious tone. Although the style is seldom completely impersonal, it is literary rather than colloquial. (For examples of essays that are somewhere near the "formal" end of the continuum, see Buckley, Will, Catton, Winn, B. Lawrence, Jastrow, Thurow. Note that the Declaration of Independence, a completely formal document, is not classifiable as an "essay" at all.)

The informal, or personal, essay is less elaborately organized and more chatty in style. First-person pronouns, contractions, and other colloquial or even slang expressions are often freely used. Informal essays are less serious in apparent purpose than formal essays. Although most do contain a worthwhile message or observation of some kind, an important purpose of many is to entertain. (See Thurber, Wolfe.)

The more personal and intimate informal essays may be classifiable as *familiar* essays, although, again, there is no well-established boundary. Familiar essays pertain to the author's own experience, ideas, or prejudices, frequently in a light and humorous style. (See Roiphe, Curtin, White, Angelou.)

Evaluation of a literary piece, as for any other creative endeavor, is meaningful only when based somehow on the answers to three questions: (1) What was the author's purpose? (2) How successfully was it fulfilled? (3) How worthwhile was it?

An architect could hardly be blamed for designing a poor gymnasium if the commission had been to design a library. Similarly, an author who is trying to explain for us why women are paid less than men, as is Thurow, cannot be faulted for failing to make the reader laugh. An author whose purpose is simply to amuse (a worthy goal) should not be condemned for teaching little about trichobothria (as did Petrunkevitch). (Nothing prevents the author from trying to explain pornography through the use of humor, or trying to amuse by comparing two Civil War generals, but in these situations the purpose has changed — and grown almost unbearably harder to achieve.)

An architect who was commissioned to design a gymnasium, and who, in fact, designed one, however, could be justifiably criticized on whether the building is successful and attractive *as a gymnasium.* If an author is trying to show why the "me" generation is headed in the opposite direction from happiness (as is Halsey), the reader has a right to expect sound reasoning and clear expository prose; and varied, detailed support ought to be expected in an essay that defends the intelligence and usefulness of robots (Sagan).

Many things are written and published that succeed very well in carrying out the author's intent — but simply are not worthwhile. Although this is certainly justifiable grounds for unfavorable criticism, readers should first make full allowance for their own limitations and perhaps their narrow range of interests, evaluating the work as nearly as possible from the standpoint of the average reader for whom the writing was intended.

Figures of Speech are short, vivid comparisons, either stated or implied; but they are not literal comparisons (e.g., "Your car is like my car," which is presumably a plain statement of fact). Figures of speech are more imaginative. They imply analogy but, unlike analogy, are used less to inform than to make quick and forceful impressions. All figurative language is a comparison of unlikes, but the unlikes do have some interesting point of likeness, perhaps one never noticed before.

A *metaphor* merely suggests the comparison and is worded as if the two unlikes are the same thing — e.g., "the language of the river" and "was turned to blood" (Twain, par. 1) and "a great chapter in American life" (Catton, par. 1). (For some of the many other examples in this book, see Roiphe, Thomas, Halsey, Greene, King.)

A *simile* (which is sometimes classified as a special kind of metaphor) expresses a similarity directly, usually with the word *like* or *as* (Rettie, par. 6; Halsey, par. 9; Angelou, par. 33.)

A *personification,* which is actually a special type of either metaphor or simile, is usually classified as a "figure" in its own right. In personification, inanimate things are treated as if they had the qualities or powers of a person. Some people would also label as personification any characterization of inanimate objects as animals, or of animals as humans — as in the descriptions and "love displays" of the Thurber piece.

An *allusion* is literally any casual reference, any alluding, to something, but rhetorically it is limited to a figurative reference to a famous or literary person, event, or quotation, and it should be distinguished from the casual reference that has a literal function in the subject matter. Hence casual mention of Judas Iscariot's betrayal of Jesus is merely a reference, but calling a modern traitor a "Judas" is an allusion. A rooster might be referred to as "the Hitler of the barnyard," or a lover as a "Romeo." Many allusions refer to mythological or biblical persons or places. (See Buckley, par. 11; Rettie, title; Wolfe, title and par. 1; Petrunkevitch, par. 9; Simpson, par. 2.)

Irony and paradox (both discussed under their own headings) and analogy (see Section 4) are also frequently classed as figures of speech, and there are several other less common types that are really subclassifications of those already discussed.

General (See *Specific/General.*)

Illustration (See Section 1.)

Impressionistic Description (See Section 8.)

Induction (See Section 10.)

Introductions give readers their first impressions, which often turn out to be the lasting ones. In fact, unless an introduction succeeds in somehow attracting a reader's interest, he probably will go no further. The importance of the introduction is one reason that writing it is nearly always difficult.

When the writer remains at a loss to know how to begin, it may be a good idea to forget about the introduction for a while and go ahead with the main body of the writing. Later the writer may find that a suitable introduction has suggested itself or even that the way the piece begins is actually introduction enough.

Introductions may vary in length from one sentence in a short composition to several paragraphs or even several pages in longer and more complex expositions and arguments, such as research papers and reports of various kinds.

Good introductions in expository writing have at least three and sometimes four functions:

1. *To identify the subject and set its limitations,* thus building a solid foundation for unity. This function usually includes some indication of the central theme, letting the reader know what point is to be made about the subject. Unlike the other forms of prose, which can often benefit by some degree of mystery, exposition has the primary purpose of explaining, so the reader has a right to know from the beginning just *what* is being explained.

2. *To interest the readers,* and thus ensure their attention. To be sure of doing this, writers must analyze their prospective readers and the readers' interest in their subject. The account of a new X-ray technique would need an entirely different kind of introduction if written for doctors than if written for the campus newspaper.

3. *To set the tone* of the rest of the writing. (See *Style/Tone.*) Tone varies greatly in writing, just as the tone of a person's voice varies with the person's mood. One function of the introduction is to let the reader know the author's attitude since it may have a subtle but important bearing on the communication.

4. *Frequently,* but not always, *to indicate the plan of organization.* Although seldom important in short, relatively simple compositions and essay examinations, this function of introductions can be especially valuable in more complex papers.

These are the necessary functions of an introduction. For best results, keep these guidelines in mind: (1) Avoid referring to the title, or even assuming that the reader has seen it. Make the introduction do all the introducing. (2) Avoid crude and uninteresting beginnings, such as "This paper is about. . . . " (3) Avoid going too abruptly into the main body — smooth transition is at least as important here as anywhere else. (4) Avoid overdoing the introduction, either in length or in extremes of style.

Fortunately, there are many good ways to introduce expository writing (and argumentative writing), and several of the most useful are illustrated by the selections in this book. Many writings, of course, combine two or more of the following techniques for interesting introductions.

1. *Stating the central theme,* which is sometimes fully enough explained in the introduction to become almost a pre-

view-summary of the exposition or argument to come. (See Thurber, D. Morris, Petrunkevitch.)

2. *Showing the significance of the subject,* or stressing its importance. (See Catton, Wolfe, Simpson, Hoffman.)

3. *Giving the background of the subject,* usually in brief form, in order to bring the reader up to date as early as possible for a better understanding of the matter at hand. (See Lurie, Halsey, Schoenbrun, Sagan.)

4. *"Focusing down" to one aspect of the subject,* a technique similar to that used in some movies, showing first a broad scope (of subject area, as of landscape) and then progressively narrowing views until the focus is on one specific thing (perhaps the name "O'Grady O'Connor" on a mailbox by a gate — or the silent sufferers on Buckley's train). (See also Rooney, Rettie.)

5. *Using a pertinent rhetorical device* that will attract interest as it leads into the main exposition — e.g., an anecdote, analogy, allusion, quotation, or paradox. (See Sheehy, Halsey, Simpson.)

6. *Using a short but vivid comparison or contrast* to emphasize the central idea. (See Thurber, Petrunkevitch, Halsey, Murray.)

7. *Posing a challenging question,* the answering of which the reader will assume to be the purpose of the writing. (See Douglas, B. Lawrence, Thurow.)

8. *Referring to the writer's experience with the subject,* perhaps even giving a detailed account of that experience. Some writings are simply continuations of experience so introduced, perhaps with the expository purpose of making the telling entirely evident only at the end or slowly unfolding it as the account progresses. (See Roiphe, White.)

9. *Presenting a startling statistic or other fact* that will indicate the nature of the subject to be discussed. (See Thurber, Thurow.)

10. *Making an unusual statement* that can intrigue as well as introduce. (See Thurber, Roiphe, Berne, Wolfe, Sheehy, Gansberg, Greene.)

11. *Making a commonplace remark* that can draw interest because of its very commonness in sound or meaning. (See Berne.)

Irony, in its verbal form sometimes classed as a figure of speech, consists of saying one thing on the surface but meaning exactly (or nearly) the opposite — e.g., "this beautiful neighborhood of ours" may mean that it is a dump. (For other illustrations, see Thurber, Wolfe, Mitford.)

Verbal irony has a wide range of tones, from the gentle, gay, or affectionate to the sharpness of outright *sarcasm* (see Buckley), which is always intended to cut. It may consist of only a word or phrase (see Halsey's "Inner Wonderfulness"), it may be a simple *understatement* (see Mitford), or it may be sustained as one of the major components of satire.

Irony can be an effective tool of exposition if its tone is consistent with the overall tone and if the writer is sure that the audience is bright enough to recognize it. In speech, a person usually indicates by voice or eye-expression that he is not to be taken literally; in writing, the words on the page have to speak for themselves.

In addition to verbal irony, there is also an *irony of situation,* in which there is a sharp contradiction between what is logically expected to happen and what does happen — e.g., a man sets a trap for an obnoxious neighbor and then gets caught in it himself. Or the ironic situation may simply be some discrepancy that an outsider can see while those involved cannot. (See Thurber; Thomas; Sheehy, par. 9; B. Lawrence, pars. 11–12.)

Logical Argument (See Section 11.)
Loose Sentences (See *Emphasis.*)
Metaphor (See *Figures of Speech.*)
Narration (See Section 9.)
Objective writing and **Subjective** writing are distinguishable by the extent to which they reflect the author's personal attitudes or emotions. The difference is usually one of degree, as few writing endeavors can be completely objective or subjective.

Objective writing, seldom used in its pure form except in business or scientific reports, is impersonal and concerned almost entirely with straight narration, with logical analysis, or with the description of external appearances. (For somewhat objective writing, see Berne, Simpson, Thurow, Jastrow.)

Subjective writing (in description called "impressionistic" — see Section 8) is more personalized, more expressive of the beliefs, ideals, or impressions of the author. Whereas in objective writing the emphasis is on the object being written about, in subjective writing the emphasis is on the way the author sees and interprets the object. (For some of the many examples in this book, see Thurber, Twain, Wolfe, Mitford, Halsey, B. Lawrence, D. H. Lawrence, Greene, Dillard, Angelou.)

Paradox is a statement or remark that, although seeming to be contradictory or absurd, actually contains some truth. Many paradoxical statements are also ironic. ("The leader follows, though a step ahead," from Korda's paragraph 9, is a paradox.)

Paragraph Unity (See *Unity.*)

Parallel Structure refers in principle to the same kind of "parallelism" that is studied in grammar: the principle that coordinate elements should have coordinate presentation, as in a pair of a series of verbs, prepositional phrases, gerunds. It is often as much a matter of "balance" as it is of parallelism.

But the principle of parallel structure, far from being just a negative "don't mix" set of rules, is also a positive rhetorical device. Many writers use it as an effective means of stressing variety or profusion in a group of nouns or modifiers, or of emphasizing parallel ideas in sentence parts, in two or more sentences, or even in two or more paragraphs. At times it can also be useful stylistically, to give a subtle poetic quality to the prose.

(For illustrations of parallel parts within a sentence, see Berne, par. 5; Murray, pars. 21, 26; Wolfe, pars. 1, 4; of parallel sentences themselves, see Berne, par. 4; Catton, par. 14; Jefferson; of both parallel parts and parallel sentences, see Twain; of parallel paragraphs, see the beginnings of Rettie's paragraphs 6–14; Jefferson.)

Periodic Sentence (See *Emphasis.*)

Personification (See *Figures of Speech.*)

Point of view in *argument* means the author's opinion on an issue or the thesis being advanced in an essay. In *exposition,* however, point of view is simply the position of the author in relation to the subject matter. Rhetorical point of view in exposition has little in common with the grammatical sort and differs somewhat from point of view in fiction.

A ranch in a mountain valley is seen differently by the ranchhand working at the corral, by the gardener deciding where to plant the petunias, by the artist or poet viewing the ranch from the mountainside, and by the geographer in a plane above, map-sketching the valley in relation to the entire range. It is the same ranch, but the positions and attitudes of the viewers are different.

So it is with expository prose. The position and attitude of the author are the important lens through which the reader sees the subject. Consistency is important, because if the lens is changed without sufficient cause and explanation, the reader will become disconcerted, if not annoyed.

Obviously, since the point of view is partially a matter of attitude, the tone and often the style of writing are closely linked to it. (See *Style/Tone.*)

The expository selections in this book provide examples of numerous points of view. Douglas's, Veninga and Spradley's, and Twain's are those of authority in their own fields of experience; Mitford's is as the debunking prober. In each of these (and the list could be extended to include all the selections in the book), the subject would seem vastly different if seen from some other point of view.

Process Analysis (See Section 5.)

Purpose that is clearly understood by the author before beginning to write is essential to both unity and coherence. A worthwhile practice, certainly in the training stages, is to write down the controlling purpose before even beginning to outline. Some instructors require both a statement of purpose and a statement of central theme or thesis. (See *Unity, Thesis.*)

The most basic element of a statement of purpose is the commitment to "explain" or, in some assignments, to "convince" (argument). But the statement of purpose, whether written down or only decided upon, goes further — e.g., "to argue that 'dirty words' are logically offensive because of the sources and connotations of the words themselves" (B. Lawrence).

Qualification is the tempering of broad statements to make them more valid and acceptable, the authors themselves admitting the probability of exceptions. This qualifying can be done inconspicuously, to whatever degree needed, by the use of *possibly, nearly always* or *most often, usually* or *frequently, sometimes* or *occasionally.* Instead of saying, "Chemistry is the most valuable field of study," it would probably be more accurate and defensible to say that it is for *some* people, or that it *can* be the most valuable.

Refutation of opposing arguments is an important element in most argumentative essays, especially where the opposition is strong enough or reasonable enough to provide a real alternative to the author's opinion. A refutation consists of a brief summary of the opposing point of view along with a discussion of its inadequacies, a discussion which often helps support the author's own thesis.

Here are three commonly used strategies for refutation:

1. *Pointing out weaknesses in evidence* — If an opposing argument is based on inaccurate, incomplete, or misleading evidence, or if the argument does not take into account some new evidence that contradicts it, then the refutation should point out these weaknesses.

2. *Pointing out errors in logic* — If an opposing argument is loosely reasoned or contains major flaws in logic, then the refutation should point these problems out to the reader.

3. *Questioning the relevance of an argument* — If an opposing argument does not directly address the issue under consideration, then the refutation should point out that even though the argument may well be correct, it is not worth considering because it is not relevant.

Refutations should always be moderate in tone and accurate in representing opposing arguments; otherwise, readers may feel that the writer has treated the opposition unfairly and as a result judge the author's own argument more harshly.

Rhetorical Questions are posed with no expectation of receiving an answer; they are merely structural devices for launching or furthering a discussion or for achieving emphasis. (See Berne's title; Roiphe, pars. 4, 6; Rettie's last sentence; Sheehy; B. Lawrence; D. H. Lawrence.)

Sarcasm (See *Irony.*)

Satire, sometimes called "extended irony," is a literary form that brings wit and humor to the serious task of pointing out frailties or evils of human institutions. It has thrived in Western literature since the time of the ancient Greeks, and English literature of the eighteenth century was particularly noteworthy for the extent and quality of its satire. Broadly, two types are recognized: *Horatian satire*, which is gentle, smiling, and aims to correct by invoking laughter and sympathy; and *Juvenalian satire*, which is sharper and which points with anger, contempt, and/or moral indignation to corruption and evil. (Swift's "A Modest Proposal" belongs in this category.)

Sentimentality, also called *sentimentalism*, is an exaggerated show of emotion, whether intentional or caused by lack of restraint. An author can sentimentalize almost any situation, but the trap is most dangerous when writing of timeworn emotional symbols or scenes — e.g., a broken heart, mother love, a lonely death, the conversion of a sinner. However sincere the author may be, if readers are not fully oriented to the worth and uniqueness of the situation described, they may be either resentful or amused at any attempt to play on their emotions. Sentimentality is, of course, one of the chief characteristics of melodrama. (For examples of writing that, less adeptly handled, could easily have slipped into sentimentality, see Twain, Catton, Thomas, Douglas, Curtin, Simpson, Gansberg.)

Simile (See *Figures of Speech.*)

Slang (See *Colloquial Expressions.*)

Specific and **General** terms, and the distinctions between the two, are similar to concrete and abstract terms (as discussed under their own heading), and for our purpose there is no real need to keep the two sets of categories separated. Whether *corporation* is thought of as "abstract" and *Ajax Motor Company* as "concrete," or whether they are assigned to "general" and "specific" categories, the principle is the same: in most writing, *Ajax Motor Company* is better.

But "specific" and "general" are relative terms. For instance, the word *apple* is more specific than *fruit* but less so than *Winesap*. And *fruit*, as general as it certainly is in one respect, is still more specific than *food*. Such relationships are shown more clearly in a series, progressing from general to specific: *food, fruit, apple, Winesap;* or *vehicle, automobile, Ford, Mustang.* Modifiers and verbs can also have degrees of specificity: *bright, red, scarlet;* or *moved, sped, careened.* It is not difficult to see the advantages to the reader — and, of course, to the writer who needs to communicate an idea clearly — in "the scarlet Mustang careened through the pass," instead of "the bright-colored vehicle moved through the pass."

Obviously, however, there are times when the general or the abstract term or statement is essential — e.g., "A balanced diet includes some fruit," or "There was no vehicle in sight." But the use of specific language whenever possible is one of the best ways to improve diction and thus clarity and forcefulness in writing.

(Another important way of strengthening general, abstract writing is, of course, to use examples or other illustrations. See Section 1.)

Style and **Tone** are so closely linked and so often even elements of each other that it is best to consider them together.

But there is a difference. Think of two young men, each with his girl friend on separate moonlight dates, whispering in nearly identical tender and loving tones of voice. One young man says, "Your eyes, dearest, reflect a thousand sparkling candles of heaven," and the other says, "Them eyes of yours — in this light — they sure do turn me on." Their *tones* were the same; their *styles* considerably different.

The same distinction exists in writing. But, naturally, with more complex subjects than the effect of moonlight on a lover's eyes, there are more complications in separating the two qualities, even for the purpose of study.

The tone is determined by the *attitude* of the writer toward his subject and toward his audience. He, too, may be tender and loving, but he may be indignant, solemn, playful, enthusiastic, belligerent, contemptuous — the list could be as long as a list of the many "tones of voice." (In fact, wide ranges of tone may be illustrated by essays of this book. Compare, for example, those of the two parts of Twain; Dillard; and Mitford; B. Lawrence and Greene; Will and Thomas.)

Style, on the other hand, expresses the author's individuality through choices of words (see *Diction*), sentence patterns (see *Syntax*), and selection and arrangement of details and basic materials. (All these elements of style are illustrated in the contrasting statements of the moonstruck lads.) These matters of style are partially prescribed, of course, by the adopted tone, but they are still bound to reflect the writer's personality and mood, education and general background.

(Some of the more distinctive styles — partially affected by and affecting tone — represented by selections in this book are those of Thurber, Rettie, Wolfe, Buckley, Dillard, White, D. H. Lawrence, Lurie.)

Subjective Writing (See *Objective/Subjective.)*

Symbol refers to anything that although real itself also suggests something broader or more significant — not just in greater numbers, however, as a person would not symbolize a group or even humankind itself, although a person might be typical or representative in one or more abstract qualities. On the most elementary level, even words are symbols — e.g., *bear* brings to mind the furry beast itself. But more important is that things, persons, or even acts may also be symbolic, if they invoke abstract concepts, values, or qualities apart from themselves or their own kind. Such symbols, in everyday life as well as in literature and the other arts, are generally classifiable according to three types, which, although terminology differs, we may label *natural, personal,* and *conventional.*

In a natural symbol, the symbolic meaning is inherent in the thing itself. The sunrise naturally suggests new beginnings to most people, an island is almost synonymous with isolation, a cannon automatically suggests war; hence these are natural symbols. It does not matter that some things, by their nature, can suggest more than one concept. Although a valley may symbolize security to one person and captivity to another, both meanings, contradictory as they might seem, are inherent, and in both respects the valley is a natural symbol.

The personal symbol, depending as it does on private experience or perception, is meaningless to others unless they are told about it or allowed to see its significance in context (as in literature). Although the color green may symbolize the outdoor life to the farm boy trapped in the gray city (in this respect perhaps a natural symbol), it can also symbolize romance to the young woman proposed to while wearing her green blouse, or dismal poverty to the woman who grew up in a weathered green shanty; neither of these meanings is suggested by something *inherent* in the color green, so they are personal symbols. Anything at all could take on private symbolic meaning, even the odor of marigolds or the sound of a lawnmower. The sunrise itself could mean utter despair, instead of fresh opportunities, to the man who has long despised his daily job and cannot find another.

Conventional symbols usually started as personal symbols, but continued usage in life or art permits them to be generally recognized for their broader meanings, which depend on custom rather than any inherent quality — e.g., the olive branch for peace, the flag for love of country, the cross for Christianity, the raised fist for black power.

Symbols are used less in expository and argumentative writing than in fiction and poetry, but a few authors represented in this book have either referred to the subtle symbolism of others or made use of it in developing their own ideas. Morris mentions "symbolic battle" and says that the human animal "cocks its leg symbolically all over his home base," and symbolism is the basis of Lurie's discussion of hats.

Syntax is a very broad term — too broad, perhaps, to be very useful — referring to the arrangement of words in a sentence. Good syntax implies the use not only of correct grammar but also of effective patterns. These patterns depend on sentences with good unity, coherence, and emphasis, on the use of subordination and parallel construction as appropriate, on economy, and on a consistent and interesting point of view. A pleasing variety of sentence patterns is also important in achieving effective syntax.

Theme (See *Unity.*)

Thesis In an argumentative essay, the central theme is often referred to as the *thesis*, and to make sure that readers recognize it, the thesis is often summed up briefly in a *thesis statement*. In a very important sense, the thesis is the center of an argument because the whole essay is designed to make the reader agree with it and, hence, with the author's opinion. (See *Unity.*)

Tone (See *Style/Tone.*)

Transition is the relating of one topic to the next, and smooth transition is an important aid to the coherence of a sentence, a paragraph, or an entire piece of writing. (See *Coherence.*)

The most effective coherence, of course, comes about naturally with sound development of ideas, one growing logically into the next — and that depends on sound organization. But sometimes beneficial even in this situation, particularly in going from one paragraph to the next, is the use of appropriate transitional devices.

Readers are apt to be sensitive creatures, easy to lose. (And, of course, the writers are the real losers since they are the ones who presumably have something they want to communicate.) If the readers get into a new paragraph and the territory seems familiar, chances are that they will continue. But if there are no identifying landmarks, they will often begin to feel uneasy and will either start worrying about their slow comprehension or take a dislike to the author and the subject matter. Either way, a communication block arises, and very likely the author will soon have fewer readers.

A good policy, then, unless the progression of ideas is exceptionally smooth and obvious, is to provide some kind of familiar identification early in the new paragraph, to keep the reader feeling at ease with the different ideas. The effect is subtle but important. These familiar landmarks or transitional devices are sometimes applied deliberately but more often come naturally, especially when the prospective reader is kept constantly in mind at the time of writing.

An equally important reason for using some kinds of transitional devices, however, is a logical one: while functioning as bridges between ideas, they also assist the basic organization by pointing out the *relationship* of the ideas — and thus contributing still further to readability.

Transitional devices useful for bridging paragraph changes (and, some of them, to improve transitional flow within paragraphs) may be roughly classified as follows:

1. *Providing an "echo"* from the preceding paragraph. This may be the repetition of a key phrase or word, or a pronoun referring back to such a word, or a casual reference to an idea. (See Thurber; Wolfe, especially from 1 to 2 and 4 to 5; Mitford; Halsey, 1 to 2 and 8 to 9.) Such an echo cannot be superimposed on new ideas, but must, by careful planning, be made an organic part of them.

2. *Devising a whole sentence or paragraph* to bridge other important paragraphs or major divisions. (See Halsey, par. 3).

3. *Using parallel structure* in an important sentence of one paragraph and the first sentence of the next. This is a subtle means of making the reader feel at ease in the new surroundings, but it is seldom used because it is much more limited in its potential than the other methods of transition. (See B. Lawrence, pars. 1 to 2.)

4. *Using standard transitional expressions,* most of which have the additional advantage of indicating relationship of ideas. Only a few of those available are classified below, but nearly all the selections in this book amply illustrate such transitional expressions:

Time — soon, immediately, afterward, later, meanwhile, after a while.

Place — nearby, here, beyond, opposite.

Result — as a result, therefore, thus, consequently, hence.

Comparison — likewise, similarly, in such a manner.

Contrast — however, nevertheless, still, but, yet, on the other hand, after all, otherwise.

Addition — also, too, and, and then, furthermore, moreover, finally, first, second, third.

Miscellaneous — for example, for instance, in fact, indeed, on the whole, in other words.

Trite (See *Clichés.*)

Unity in writing is the same as unity in anything else — in a picture, a musical arrangement, a campus organization — and that is a *one*ness, in which all parts contribute to an overall effect.

Many elements of good writing contribute in varying degrees to the effect of unity. Some of these are properly designed introductions and closings; consistency of point of view, tone, and style; sometimes the recurring use of analogy or thread of symbolism; occasionally the natural time boundaries of an experience or event, as in the selections of Rettie, Angelou, Mitford, Simpson, Greene, Gansberg, and Orwell ("A Hanging").

But in most expository and argumentative writing the only dependable unifying force is the *central theme,* which every sentence, every word, must somehow help to support. (The central theme is also called the *central idea* or the *thesis* when pertaining to the entire writing and is almost always called the *thesis* in argument. In an expository or argumentative paragraph it is the same as the *topic sentence,* which may be implied or, if stated, may be located anywhere in the paragraph, but is usually placed first.) As soon as anything appears that is not related to the central idea, there are *two* units instead of one. Hence unity is basic to all other virtues of good writing, even to coherence and emphasis, the other two organic essentials. (See *Coherence, Emphasis.*)

An example of unity may be found in a single river system (for a practical use of analogy), with all its tributaries, big or little, meandering or straight, flowing into the main stream and making it bigger — or at least flowing into another tributary that finds its way to the main stream. This is *one* river system, an example of unity. Now picture another stream nearby that does not empty into the river but goes off in some other direction. There are now two systems, not one, and there is no longer unity.

It is the same way with writing. The central theme is the main river, flowing along from the first capital letter to the last period. Every drop of information or evidence must find its way into this theme-river, or it is not a part of the system. It matters not even slightly if the water is good, the idea-stream perhaps deeper and finer than any of the others: if it is not a tributary, it has no business pretending to be relevant to *this* theme of writing.

And that is why most students are required to state their central idea or thesis, usually in solid sentence form, before even starting to organize their ideas. If the writer can use only tributaries, it is very important to know from the start just what the river is.

To the Student:

Part of our job as educational publishers is to try to improve the textbooks we publish. Thus, when revising, we take into account the experience of both instructors and students with the previous edition. At some time your instructor will be asked to comment extensively on *Patterns of Exposition 9*, but right now we want to hear from you. After all, though your instructor assigned this book, you are the one who paid for it.

Please help us by completing this questionnaire and returning it to College English, Little, Brown and Company, 34 Beacon Street, Boston, Massachusetts 02106.

School _____ Course title _____

Instructor's name _____

Other books assigned _____

	Liked best			Liked least	Didn't read
Schoenbrun, A Traffic Light Is a Brainless Machine	5	4	3	2	1 _____
Rooney, In and of Ourselves We Trust	5	4	3	2	1 _____
Thurber, Courtship Through the Ages	5	4	3	2	1 _____
Buckley, Why Don't We Complain?	5	4	3	2	1 _____
Douglas, The Butterfly Connection	5	4	3	2	1 _____
Berne, Can People Be Judged By Their Appearance?	5	4	3	2	1 _____
Barber, Four Types of President	5	4	3	2	1 _____
Lurie, Hats	5	4	3	2	1 _____
Morris, Territorial Behaviour	5	4	3	2	1 _____
Twain, Two Ways of Seeing a River	5	4	3	2	1 _____
Catton, Grant and Lee: A Study in Contrasts	5	4	3	2	1 _____
Roiphe, Confessions of a Female Chauvinist Sow	5	4	3	2	1 _____
Jastrow, Brains and Computers	5	4	3	2	1 _____
Shames, Champs	5	4	3	2	1 _____
Rettie, "But a Watch in the Night": A Scientific Fable	5	4	3	2	1 _____
Wolfe, O Rotten Gotham — Sliding Down into the Behavioral Sink	5	4	3	2	1 _____
Dillard, Sojourner	5	4	3	2	1 _____
Murray, The Maker's Eye: Revising Your Own Manuscripts	5	4	3	2	1 _____
Petrunkevitch, The Spider and the Wasp	5	4	3	2	1 _____
Veninga and Spradley, The Stress Response	5	4	3	2	1 _____
Mitford, To Dispel Fears of Live Burial	5	4	3	2	1 _____
Tavris, Seeing Red	5	4	3	2	1 _____
Sheehy, $70,000 a Year, Tax Free	5	4	3	2	1 _____

Halsey, What's Wrong with "Me, Me, Me"?	5	4	3	2	1	_____
Christopher, The Fruits of Industry	5	4	3	2	1	_____
Winn, Television Addiction	5	4	3	2	1	_____
Caras, What's a Koala?	5	4	3	2	1	_____
Lawrence, Pornography	5	4	3	2	1	_____
Korda, What It Takes to Be a Leader	5	4	3	2	1	_____
Curtin, Aging in the Land of the Young	5	4	3	2	1	_____
White, Once More to the Lake	5	4	3	2	1	_____
Hoffman, The Gay Bar	5	4	3	2	1	_____
Simpson, The War Room at Bellevue	5	4	3	2	1	_____
Gansberg, 38 Who Saw Murder Didn't Call the Police	5	4	3	2	1	_____
Greene, That's Entertainment	5	4	3	2	1	_____
Orwell, A Hanging	5	4	3	2	1	_____
Angelou, Momma's Private Victory	5	4	3	2	1	_____
Goodman, Just Woman's Work?	5	4	3	2	1	_____
Thurow, Why Women Are Paid Less Than Men	5	4	3	2	1	_____
Farb, In Other Words	5	4	3	2	1	_____
Will, No "Right" to Health	5	4	3	2	1	_____
Rowan, The NCAA's Hypocrisy	5	4	3	2	1	_____
Sagan, In Defense of Robots	5	4	3	2	1	_____
Lawrence, Four-Letter Words Can Hurt You	5	4	3	2	1	_____
Thomas, Nurses	5	4	3	2	1	_____
Jefferson, The Declaration of Independence	5	4	3	2	1	_____
King, Letter from Birmingham Jail	5	4	3	2	1	_____
Swift, A Modest Proposal	5	4	3	2	1	_____
Thoreau, from "Civil Disobedience"	5	4	3	2	1	_____
Orwell, Politics and the English Language	5	4	3	2	1	_____

1. Are there any authors not included whom you would like to see represented? _____

2. Were the biographical sketches and introductions useful? _____ How might they be improved? _____

3. Will you keep this book for your library? _____

4. Please add any comments or suggestions. _____

_____

_____

5. May we quote you in our promotional efforts for this book? _____ yes _____ no

date _____ signature _____

mailing address _____